GW01376944

CHRISTIAN ASTROLOGY
MODESTLY
Treated of in three Books.

The *first* containing the use of an EPHEMERIS, the erecting of a Scheam of Heaven; nature of the twelve Signs of the Zodiack, of the Planets; with a most easie Introduction to the whole Art of ASTROLOGY.

The *second*, by a most Methodicall way, Instructeth the Student how to Judge or Resolve all manner of Questions contingent unto Man, *viz.* of Health, Sicknesse, Riches, Marriage, Preferment, Journies, &c. Severall Questions inserted and Judged.

The *third*, containes an exact Method, whereby to Judge upon Nativities; severall wayes how to rectifie them; How to judge the generall fate of the Native by the twelve Houses of Heaven, according to the naturall influence of the STARS; How his particular and Annuall Accidents, by the Art of Direction, and its exact measure of Time by Profections, Revolutions, Transits. A Nativity Judged by the Method preceding.

By WILLIAM LILLY Student in Astrology.

Omne meum, nil meum :   *Nihil dictum, quod non dictum prius.*

✠✠✠✠✠✠✠✠✠✠✠✠✠

LONDON:
Printed by *Tho. Brudenell* for *John Partridge* and *Humph. Blunden*, in *Black-friers* at the Gate going into *Carter-lane*, and in *Cornbil*, 1647.

Part 1

GULIELMUS LILLIUS Astrologus *Natus Comitat: Leicest:*
1° *May* 1602.

Guliel: Marshall sculpsit.

To his moſt learned and vertuous friend
BOLSTROD WHITLOCK, Eſq..
one of the Members of the honorable
Houſe of COMMONS in this
preſent PARLIAMENT.

Much honored Sir:

I Hope this Dedicatory Epiſtle of mine publiſhed without your knowledge, ſhall beget no ſuch ſiniſter conſtruction in you, but that the fault ſhall be admitted as a veniall tranſgreſſion; and this my preſumption finde eaſie remiſſion at your moſt gentle hands. I am now ſo well acquainted with your pleaſing native Diſpoſition, that in things of this nature where you are not in queſtion, I dare a little offend; for its a fixed naturall Maxime ingraffed in you, to love your friends ſincerely, and rarely to take offence upon ſlight failings.

Pardon this boldneſſe; verily, ſo many, ſo numberleſſe are my engagements unto you, that I could doe no leſſe, having no other meanes remaining whereby to ex-

The Epistle Dedicatory.

presse a gratefull heart, or to acquaint the present and future times, of your ardent and continuall promoting me and my poore labours, since first Divine Providence made me knowne unto you; so that I doe freely acknowledge, next unto Almighty God, your selfe have been the Instrumentall meanes of inabling me to performe, not onely what is already publique, but also this ensuing Treatise, which now I humbly offer unto your Patronage, as a thankfull testimony of my sincere respects due unto you: for had not you persevered all along a firme and an assured *Mæcenas* unto me, my carkasse and Conceptions had beene buried in eternall silence; so that the Students in this Art must acknowledge the Restauration of *Astrologie* unto your goodnesse. For, S I R, you have countenanced me your self; you have commended me to your Friends; you have never omitted to doe me, or my friends for my sake, any civill courtesies: And this I shall adde to your honour, that I no sooner at any time importuned your favour, but I was instantly sensible of your actuall and reall performance of the thing I required.

Should I enumerate your vertues or curtesies in this kinde performed unto many besides my selfe, the day would faile me of time, and my hand grow weary of writing: but as in private you assist your friends, so have you most faithfully for almost seven yeeres served your Countrey in this present Parliament, even to the manifest decay of your health, to my owne knowledge, and consumption of many thousand pounds of your Estate: you have refused no paines to benefit this *Commonwealth*; and being ever delegated an honourable *Commissioner* upon all Treaties for Peace betwixt the King and Parliament, you have demeaned your selfe with

such

The Epistle Dedicatory.

such candour, judgement and integrity in all of them, that the whole Kingdome are satisfied therewith, and we of the Commonalty stand indebted unto you.

Brevity best pleaseth you, few words may become me; yet I cannot rest in quiet untill I deliver those excellent expressions of yours, which my owne eares heard from your mouth in 1 6 4 4. at what time this present Parliament was loe, and your selfe tampered withall to become Turncoat and renounce this Parliament ; *N O, I'le not remove from this present Parliament now sitting at* Westminster, *for unto this place was I called, and hither sent by my Countrey for their service, and if God have so decreed, that his Majesty shall overcome us, yet am I resolved to abide here, and to dye within the wals of that very House; and I will take the same portion which God hath assigned to those honourable Members that shall continue firme in this cause.* These words you have made good even unto this day, to your eternall honour ; nor can the blacke mouthes of the most accursed snarling Curs detract a graine from your worth.

I have now a large Field to walke in, and should I further proceed, I am assured I should move that sweet disposed temper of yours, which is not easily offended ; I am silent ; onely ;

Faveas (precor) primitiis crescentis Indolis, quæ si sub tuo sole adoleverit, & justam tandem maturitatem consequuta fuerit, non indignos fructus retributarum confido.

SIR, I hope you shall have no dishonour to Patronize the Ensuing Worke, wherein I lay downe the whol

natu-

The Epistle Dedicatory.

naturall grounds of the Art, in a fit Method: that thereby I may undeceive those, who misled by some Pedling Divines, have upon no better credit then their bare words, conceived Astrology to consist upon Diabolicall Principles: a most scandalous untruth, foysted into both the Nobility and Gentries apprehensions, to deter them from this Study, and to reserve it intyre unto their owne selves.

Wishing to you and your honourable Consort all happinesse, I conclude in these last words, that I am with all my heart,

Your most humble Servant,

Strand 16.
Aug. 1647.

WILLIAM LILLY.

To the READER.

I *Have oft in my former Works hinted the many feares I had of that danger I was naturally like to be in in the yeer* 1647. *as any may read, either in my Epistle before the Conjunction of* Saturne *and* Jupiter, *printed* 1644. *or in page thereof* 108. *or in the Epistle of* Anglicus 1645. *where you shall find these words :* I have run over more dayes then fifteen thousand five hundred fifty and nine, before I am sixteen thousand four hundred twenty two dayes old, I shall be in great hazard of my life, but that yeer which afflicts me will stagger a Monarch and Kingdome, &c. *What concernes my selfe, hath almost in full measure proved true, in* 1647. *having in this untoward yeer been molested with palpitation of the Heart, with Hypocondry melancholy, a disaffected Spleen, the Scurvy, &c. and now at this present, viz.* August 1647. *when I had almost concluded this Treatise, I am shut up of the Plague, having the fourth of* August *buried one Servant thereof, and on the* 28. *of the same moneth another, my selfe and remainder of my Family enforced to leave my proper seat, and betake my selfe to change of ayre ; so that if either my present Epistles, or the latter part of the Book it selfe be any thing defective, as well they may, being written when my Family and selfe were in such abundant sorrow and perplexity ; I desire the Reader to be so civill, as to passe over those slight imperfections (if any be) with a candid censure.*

I thank almighty God, who hath prolonged my life to this present, and

(a) *hath*

To the READER.

hath been so gracious unto me, as to spare me so long, whereby I have been enabled now at length to perfect that Introduction so oft by me promised, so earnestly desired by many wel-wishers unto this learning.

The latter part of my prediction concerning Monarchy, is now upon the stage and eyes the of millions attending what shall become of it: let us leave the event hereof unto God, who is hastening to require a strict accompt of some people entrusted in the Kingdomes affaires; fiat Justitia; vivat Rex; floreat Parliamentum.

The Citizens of London make small reckoning of Astrology; there are in one of those Epistles of mine, words significant, and of which time will make them sensible (that they were not wrote in vaine) but now too late, actum est. To the work in hand, viz. the Book ensuing, which is divided into three Treatises; the first whereof doth with much facility, and after a new method, instruct the Student how to begin his work, viz. it teacheth him the use of an Ephemeris, of the Table of Houses, &c. it acquaints him how to erect a figure of heaven, how therein to place the Planets, how to rectifie their motions to the hour of his Figure; it unfolds the nature of the Houses, of the Planets, of the Signes of the Zodiack, their division, and subdivision, their severall properties, terms of Art, and whatever else is fit for the Learner to know before he enter upon judgment: unto whom and every one that will be studious this way, I give these cautions.

Use of the first Book.

First, that he be very exact in knowing the use of his Ephemeris, and in setting a Scheame of Heaven for all the hours of the day or night, and in reducing the motions of the Planets to the hour thereof when need requireth, and to know their characters distinctly and readily.

Cautions for young Students.

Secondly, I would have the Student very perfect in knowing the nature of the Houses, that he may the better discover from what house to require judgment upon the question propounded, lest for want of true understanding he mistake one thing for another.

Thirdly, I would have him ready in, and well to understand the Debilities and Fortitudes of every Planet, both Essentiall and Accidentall.

Fourthly, he must be well versed in discovering the Nature of the Significator, what he signifies naturally, what accidentally, and how to vary his signification, as necessity shall require.

Fiftly, let him well understand the nature of the Signes, their properties

To the READER.

ties and qualities, and what forme, shape and conditions they give of themselves naturally, and what by the personall existence of a Planet in any of them.

Sixtly, that he be ready in the shape and description which every Planet designes, and how to vary their shape as they are posited in Signe and house, or affected of the Moon or any other Planet.

Seventhly, he must oft read the termes of Art, and have them fresh in his memory, and especially the twentieth and one and twentieth Chapters of the first Book.

If God almighty shall preserve my life, I may hereafter adde many things, and much light unto this Art, and therefore I desire the Students herein, that if they meet with any extraordinary casualty in their practice, they would communicate it unto me.

I have with all uprightnesse and sincerity of heart, plainly and honestly delivered the Art, and have omitted nothing willingly, which I esteemed convenient or fit, or what might any thing assist the yong Students herein; I have refused the Methods of all former Authors, and framed this De Novo, which I have ever found so easie and succesfull, that as yet I never undertook the instruction of any, whom I have not abundantly satisfied, and made very capable of the Art, in lesse time then any could expect; for although I am not yet six and forty yeers of age compleat, and have studied this Science but since 1632. and have lived six yeers since that time in the Country, yet I know I have made more Schollers in this Profession, then all that professe this Art in England. It remaines, that I give every Author his due, and deale plainly, unto which of them I am engaged for such matter as they have assisted me with in the Introductory part: verily the Method is my owne, it's no translation; yet have I conferred my owne notes with Dariot, Bonatus, Ptolomey, Haly, Etzler, Dietericus, Naibod, Hasfurtus, Zael, Tanstetter, Agrippa, Ferriers, Duret, Maginus, Origanus, Argol.

The second part of this Treatise judging of horary *Questions,* is very large, and farre beyond my first intentions, hath exceeded its just proportion: In building this Work I advised with Bonatus, Haly, Dariot, Leupoldus, Pontanus, Avenezra, Zael: I examined the Manuscripts

The second Book.

To the READER.

Manuscrips of *Ancient* and *Reverend* Professors *in this* Art, *who lived more remote from these corrupt Times, (for unto the vulgar* Professors *now residing in this City, am I no wayes engaged;) and though it was no small trouble unto me, to see the discrepancy of judgment amongst them and the more ancient printed Authors, yet I have with some trouble reconciled their disagreements, and reformed and corrected what might have led the* Reader *into an errour: for indeed the Writings of our Fore-fathers in the Language they did deliver their minds in, was sound and solid, but the simplicity of such as undertook their translations was much and did beget mistakes, whilest they endeavouring to translate the Authors into Latin, or any other Language they thought fit, did not understand the Art or the Termes thereof; so that of those their Labours, they rendred an ill accompt unto Posterity, as any may see in the translation of that we call the* Judicium in Novem Judiciis, &c. *and in other pieces of* Alkindus, *one whereof lately a learned Gentleman gave me, guilty of the same deficiency in the translation.*

In this second Book I have omitted nothing which I could devise to be helpfull, and if my owne way of judicature please any, it being somewhat different from that of the Ancients, *he may in many Chapters make use of it. I have illustrated every house with one or more Figures, and therein shewed the method of judgment, which I held very convenient for Learners, it being my whole intention to advance this* Art, *and make even a slender wit capable hereof.*

The third Book.

You may in the third Book behold the entire Art of Nativities, *I have made it plaine and significant: part of the Method, and much of the matter I had from* Leovitius, *who was the first that methodized the Art of* Nativities, *before his time extreemly defective in that point; where he was not copious, I supplyed my selfe, or enlarged from* Origanus, Junctine, Pezelius, Naibod, Cardan, Garceus, Schonerus, Albubater, Montulmo, Judeus, Ptolomey, Lindholt: *Perhaps some will accuse me for dissenting from* Ptolomey; *I confesse I have done so, and that I am not the first, or shall I that have done so, be the last; for I am more led by reason and experience, then by the single authority of any one man, &c. I have inserted many judgements*

To the READER.

ments of my owne, I could have added many more : but who am I? being all errour, that should contradict the sayings of so many wise men, whose learnings and paines I so much esteem and reverence.

Little did I think this Work of Nativities *would have swolen to so great a bulk; I assure you it exceeds my first intentions : the paines however hath been mine, and notwithstanding the importunities of some, and they not a few, who desired I should not deliver the* Art *in so plaine and easie a method; yet I professe, their words rather invited me to discover all I knew, then to conceale one sillable materiall.*

Had I respected my owne private lucre, I need not have wrote at all; who could have compelled me? my owne fortune is competent : but this thing we call the publick good, was ever, and shall be my maxime to guide me in such like actions : how shall I my selfe expect truth in any Author, if I my selfe, being an Author, play the knave in the same kind : Quod non vis tibi, ne facias alteri.

This Art of Astrology hath many more parts in it then at this present time I have handled, or indeed as yet have leisure to doe; yet I know it will be expected I should have wrote of Elections, *of the Effects of the greater and lesser Conjunctions of the Planets, of* Eclipses, Comets, *prodigious* Apparitions, *the variation and inclination of the* Weather, De generalibus Accidentibus Mundi, *and by the ingresse of the* Sunne *into* Aries, *of every yeers particular* Fate, *of* Monethly Observations, *&c. Verily such things as these may justly be required at my hands ; for, unto God be the glory, they are all in a large measure knowne unto me, and I can performe them all, blessed be his name therefore : But as for* Elections, *me thinks he can be no ingenious* Astrologian, *that having studied or well entred into this my Book shall not be able* (ad libitum) *to frame his owne Figure of* Elections, *let the quere be what it will.*

He that shall read my Discourse upon the Conjunction of ♄ *and* ♃, *may make himselfe capable to write of the Major and Minor Conjunctions ; I had no president for that, but wrought it out of the fire, at what time I had great leasure. I doe write Annually of* Eclipses, *as they happen in the yeer, of prodigious Appearances twice I have Astrologically wrote, both time to good purpose, so did never any before that I read of.*

Of Commets *I have had no occasion as yet, but somewhat I began in*

B 3 *that*

To the READER.

that *Tract* of the ☌ of ♄ and ♃, *wherein I a little treated of the Commet in* 1618. *Posterity may know by twat little, what Method I hold fittest to be followed, in that kinde of judgement. Of Weather, the knowledge thereof is so vulgar, yet withall the true Key so difficult, it requires a long time of experience; and besides,* Master *Booker hath promised to undertake that burthen; and indeed, he is onely able of all the* English *Nation I know to performe it: I have great hopes of* Master Vincent Wing, *but he is yet more* Mathematicall *then* Astrologicall; *there may be many private men of great judgement therein, but its my unhappinesse I know them not.*

Annuall and Monthly judgements I have not yet digested into a Method, I hope to live and performe it; I am the first of men that ever adventured upon Monetbly Observations in such plaine language, yet is it my harty desire to communicate hereafter what ever I know unto Posterity. Having been of late traduced by some halfe-witted fooles, I deliver my selfe to Posterity who I am, and of what profession; I was borne at Diseworth *in* Leicestershire *May* 1602. *in an obscure Village, and bred a Grammer Scholler at* Ashby, *and intended for* Cambridge, &c. 1618. *and* 1619. *my Father decayed his Estate so much, that he was not capable of sending me thither; those two yeers I lived in some penury and discontent; in* 1620. *an* Atturney *sent me up unto* London *to wait on a Gentleman, one* Gilbert Wright, *who lived aud dyed in the House I now live in; he never was of any Profession, but had sometimes attended the Lord Chancellour* Egerton, *and then lived privately.* 1624. *his wife dyed of a Cancer in her left brest.* 1625. *I lived in* London *where I now doe, during all that great Sicknesse, God be praised I had it not.* February 1626. *my Master married againe; he dyed* May 22. 1627. *having before setled twenty pounds per annum of me during my life, which to this day I thanke God I enjoy; nor did I ever live so freely as when I was his servant. Ere the yeer* 1627. *was quite run out my Mistris was pleased to accept of me for her husband. During some yeers of her life I passed my time privately and with much obscurity, yet we lived exceeding lovingly together; but in* 1632 *I was strangely affected to* Astrology, *and desirous to study it, onely to see if there were any verity in it, there being at that time some Impostors, that set out Bils publiquely what they could doe. I met with a Master I confesse, but such a one, as of all*

was

To the READER.

was the veriest Knave: This gave me small encouragement; after six weekes I cast him off, nor to this day doe we converse together. I was then forced to study hard, for rather then to intangle my selfe with another coxcombe, I was resolved to lay all aside; but by diligence and hard study, and many times conference with some as ignorant as my selfe, I at last became capable of knowing truth from falshood, and perceived the *vulgar* Astrologer *that meerly lived of the Art, was a Knave.*

In September 1633 *my wife dyed, not knowing any one in the world that had affinity unto her; she left me a competent fortune; and this I shall acquaint Posterity with, that having some Lands to dispose of, rather then she would suffer me to be at twenty* Nobles *charges to convey it unto me, she gave me the whole money, and sold it for* 200 l.

In November 1634. *I married againe. In* 1635. *I was oppressed with the Hypocondryack Melancholly so sorely, that I was enforced to leave* London, *and removed into* Surrey 1636. *where untill* September 1641. *I lived amongst such whom I may name the most rurall of all men living. I then came for* London, *staggering in my judgement in point of Church-government; and knowing that it is necessary, I ever loved Monarchy, but still thought without a Parliament preserved in their just rights, it would vanish to nothing. I was nothing knowne then, or taken notice of by any; time produced me acquaintance, and amongst these a good Lady in* 1643. *about* February, *desired I would give judgement upon a most noble Gentlemans Urine a Councellor at Law, who then was not well; I consented, the Urine was brought, my judgement returned; I visited him, whom I no sooner beheld, but I knew there was aboundance of gallantry in the man; for indeed he is all Gentleman and a friend in very great earnest; my visit of him was the happiest day I ever saw in my whole life; for by his alone generosity and countenance, I am what I am, and* Astrology *is in despight of her enemies restored, and must call him her Restaurator.*

Being by his goodnesse admitted to visit him, I presented him with a small Manuscript of my Astrologicall Judgment *of the yeer* 1644. *wherein I was free in delivering my opinion modestly of that yeers affaires: it pleased him to communicate it. Copies were obtained and dispersed; so that by his alone commendation of that poore Manuscript unto his private frriends, this noble Art at first had respect amongst our*
Worthies

To the READER.

Worthies in the Parliament; since which time, the Judicious of the whole Kingdome had it in a better esteem; therefore let his name live unto Posterity in an honourable esteem, that upon so slender acquaintance with the Author, with the Art, hath been so advantagious unto both.

The Errataes perhaps are many, I desire the Student to correct them before he enter upon the Discourse; I wish they were lesse: but in a work of this nature, it's impossible.

All the Curtesies which either the Authors precedent to this Age, or at present living, have afforded me, I verily beleeve I have mentioned: I am heartily sorry if I have committed any errours, or omitted any corrections.

Corner house over against
Strand-bridge, August
21. 1647.

WILLIAM LILLY.

To his honored Friend the AUTHOR.

WHat! *Perſian, Caldee, Arabick*, the *Greeke,*
Latin Aſtrologers, all taught to ſpeake
In Engliſh! *Triſmegiſtus, Hercules,*
Pythagoras, Thales, Archimedes,
Great *Ptolomy*, and *Julius Firmicus,*
Albumazar, and *Albategnius,*
Hali, Bonatus, our owne *Eſchuidus,*
And *John de Regiomonte, Ganivetus,*
Riſſe, Leovitius, Michael Noſtradame,
Cardan, and *Nabod, Ticho*, men of fame;
All theſe, and more, are dead, all learned Men;
Were they alive, they might come learn again.
But are they dead? Behold Aſtrologie,
Now *Phœnix* like, reviv'd againe in thee!
Queſtions reſolv'd, Nativities, Directions,
Tranſites, with Revolutions and Profections.
Saturne muſt lay his ſullen prankes aſide,
And *Mars* his madneſſe, leſt he be deſcride;
Venus her luſts; his thefts muſt *Mercury*;
Sol his ambition; *Jove* his jollity:
Luna her fickle and unconſtant motion,
Is now notorious to each vulgar notion.
Aske what you will, Would you reſolved be?
Obſerve your time, learne your Nativitie:
Were *Picus, Chambers, Perkins, Melton, Geree,*
Vicars, to write againe, all men would jeer yee.
You durſt not let us know when you were borne,
Your ignorance is brought to publick ſcorn:
Our Latin *Lilly* is for Boyes are young;
Our Engliſh *Lilly* is for Men more ſtrong.
The *Sybils* Books were burnt, they are all gone;
I will preſerve my choyce, This is that one:
Be you for or againſt, or will ye, nill ye;
I'm for the Art, and th' Author *William Lilly.*

JOHN BOOKER.

Upon the learned Worke of the AUTHOR.

BEhold *Urania* with a *Lilly* deckt,
Presents her selfe to *Englands* gracious view.
Let Envies square, or opposite aspect
Not dare at her a frowning looke to shew;
  Lest it be said, for such ungratefull scornes,
  A *Lilly* late hath sprung among the thornes.

WILL. ROE.

To the Reader of CHRISTIAN ASTROLOGY.

W onder you may! the volumes of the Skye
I n our owne Characters you here descry.
L *una* and *Hermes*, *Venus* and the great
L ight of the World, and *Mars* in *English* treat;
I *ove* and old *Saturne*; they their influence send:
A nd their Conjunctions in our Tongue are penn'd.
M ay not *Apollo* then, the sacred Bayes
L et fall upon his head, who casts their Rayes
I nto the language of our *Albion* quill?
L oe! he hath taught great *Ptolom's* secret skill.
L earning, that once in brazen piles did stand,
Y ou now may see is Printed in our Land.

R. L. *in Med. Studens &*

Philo-Mathemat.

On this unparalelled peece of Art.

Not to commend the Author, 'tis the least
   Of all my thoughts, this Work will doe it best;
Nor yet to vex the prying Readers sence
   with bumbast words instead of Eloquence,
Doe I crowd in these rude unpolisht lines:
   But rather to informe the giddy times
How much they are his Debtors; what they owe
   To him, whose Labours freely doth bestow
On them his Art, his paines, his piercing sight,
   His lampe of life, to give their darknesse light.
Tis now a crime, and quite grown out of fashion,
   T'incourage Art amongst the *English* Nation.
Tell them of it, or Natures mysteries,
   Tush, cry they: Ignorance they idolize.
The glorious Stars, they think God doth not use them
   To doe his will: Lord! how doe men abuse them?
Nor will allow the Planets to fulfill
   (As instruments) Gods high decree or will.
Nay, some there are, though letter wise, they can
   Not yet beleeve that all was made for Man.
Barke black mouth'd Envie; carpe at what's well done,
   This Book shall be my choyce companion.

                        W. W.

                                    Anagram

Upon this WORKE.

THe Author's God, Compoſer and the Setter
   Of all his works, and therin every letter.
Heaven is his Book; the Stars both great & ſmal
   Are letters Nonperill and Capitall
Diſperſt throughout; therin our learnings dull,
   In this thy Work it is compleat and full :
Could man compoſe or ſet Heavens letters right
   he would, like Printing, bring to publick ſight
All what was done, nay what was thought upõ;
   For by this way, I ſee it may be done.

I. P.

The Contents of the three Books.

The first Book.

THE *number of Planets, Signes, Aspects, with their severall names and characters.* Page 25

Of the use of the Ephemeris. p. 27

The right hand page of the Ephemeris unfolded, 30

How to erect a figure of Heaven by the Ephemeris and Table of Houses aforesaid, 33

Of the daily motion of the Planets, and how to reduce their motion to any hour of the day, and to the Meridian of London, 42

How to finde the quantity of the hourly motion of any Planet by the Table following, 44

Of the twelve houses of Heaven, and some names or termes of Astrologie, 47

Of the twelve houses of heaven their nature and signification, 50

Of the Planet Saturn, and his significations, 57

Of the Planet Jupiter, and his significations, 61

Of the Planet Mars, and his severall significations, 65

Of the Sun, his generall and particular significations, 69

Of the Planet Venus, and her severall significations and nature, 72

Of Mercury, his significations, nature and property, 76

Of the Moon, her properties and significations, 80

Another brief description of the shapes and formes of the Planets, 84

Of the twelve Signes of the Zodiack and their manifold divisions, 86

The Nature, Place, Countries, generall description and Diseases signified by the twelve houses, 93

Teaching what use may be made of the former discourse of the twelve Signes, 100

Of the Essentiall Dignities of the Planets, 101

A Table of the Essentiall Dignities of the Planets, 104

Of severall Termes, Aspects, words of Art, Accidents belonging to the Planets, with other necessary rules, 105

A Table of the aspects of the Signes amongst one another, 108

A ready Table whereby to examine the Fortitudes and Debilities of the Planets, 115

A Table shewing the masculine and feminine degrees of every Sign, 116

A Table shewing what members in mans body every Planet signifieth in any of the twelve Signes, 119

Considerations before judgment, 121

What Significator, Querent and Quesited are: An Introduction to judgment, 123

To know whether a thing demanded will come to passe yea or not, 124

(b 3) The

The Contents.

The Contents of the second Book, containing the resolution of Questions.

Questions concerning the first House.

If the Querent is likely to live long yea or not, page 129
Signes of health or long life, idem.
The time when any accident shall happen, 130
To what part of heaven it's best the Querent direct his affaires, 132
What part of his life is like to be best 134
An Astrologicall figure judging the former Demands, 135
Of the Part of Fortune, and how to take it either by day or night, 143
How to examine its fortitudes, 145
If one shall find the party at home one would speak with, 147
Of a thing suddenly happening, whether it signifie good or ill, 148
What marke, mole or scar the Querent hath, idem.
Whether one absent be dead or alive, 151
An Astrologicall figure explaining the aforesaid demands, 152
A Woman whether her Sonne were with his Master or not, 153
Of a Ship at Sea, her safety or destruction, 157
Example of a Ship at Sea upon a figure judged, 162
Example of another Ship, 165
The time of receiving any Question, 166

Judgments concerning the second house, viz. of Riches.

Whether the Querent shall be rich, 167
By what means attain Riches, 168
The reason or cause why the Querent may not attain a Fortune, 172
If the Querent shall obtain the Substance he hath lent, 173
If one shall acquire his wages or Stipend owing him, 174
Of the time when the accindents treated of may happen, 175
A figure resolving the doubts and demands aforesaid, 177
Of that Planet or Planets impediting the effecting or performance of what is demanded in every Question, 184
If the Querent shall continue rich, 186

Of the third house, viz. of Brethren, Sisters, Kinred, short Journeys.

If the Querent and his Brother, Neighbour or Sister shall agree, 188
Of a Brother that is absent, 189
Of Reports, Intelligence or Feares, if true or false, or signifie good or evil, 192
If Rumours be true or false, 193
Of councell or advice, whether good or evill, 194

Whether

The Contents.

Whether the Querent have Brethren or Sisters, 195
Of a short Journey, if good to goe; which way, 195
An Astrologicall figure of an absent Brother, 196
If Cambridge was taken yea or no, 200

Of the fourth house, viz. of Parents, Lands, Tenements, Cities, Townes.

To find a thing hid or mislaid, 202
What part of the house or ground, 203
Of buying and selling Lands, Houses, Farmes, &c. 204
Of the goodnesse or badnesse of the Land or house, 205
Quality of the ground, 206
Tenants good or ill, idem.
If Wood on the ground, idem.
If good to hire or take the Farme or house desired, 208
If the Querent shall enjoy the Estate of his Father, 210
If good to remove from one house to another, 212
Of turning the course of Rivers, &c 214
Of Treasure hid in the ground, 215
If the Querent shall obtaine it, 217
If the Author should purchase some Houses, an Astrologicall Figure thereof, 219

Of the fift house, and its questions.

If one shall have children, 222
If a Woman ask whether she may conceive, 223
Whether the Querent shall have children, be he man or woman that asketh, 224
If a man shall have Children by his Wife yea or no, or of any other Woman whom he nominates, 225
Whether she is with child or not, 226
If the man ask unknowne to the Woman, 228

Other Judgments.

Whether a Woman be with child or not, 229
If a Woman doe conceive with child of more then one, 230
If male or female, idem.
How long the Woman hath been conceived, 231
Of the time when the Birth will be, 231
Whether the birth shall be by day or night, 232
Whether unity is like to be between the Infant and Parent, 234
Of Embassadours and Messengers, 235
Of a Messenger sent forth upon any errand, 236
If the Querent should ever have children, a figure judged thereof, 238
If one were with child of a male female; what time she should be delivered, a figure thereupon judged, 240

The Contents.

Of the sixt House, and its questions, *viz.* of Sickness, Servants, small Cattle.

Judgment of sickneße by Astrologie, 243
What part of the body is afflicted, 243
From what cause the sickness is, 244
Diseases signified by the Houses, 245
Diseases signified by the Signes, 245
Diseases of the Planets, 246
Whether the disease will be long or short, 247
Signes of a long or short sickness, 248
Testimonies that the Querent shall live and not dye of the Infirmity now afflicting, 253
Arguments of death, 255
Dariot abridged, 258
If the party be sick of whom the question is demanded, 259
Cause of the Disease, inward or outward, 259
Of the quality and nature of the Disease, 261
Whether the Disease be in the right or left side, 263
Whether the Disease be in the body, minde, or both, 264
Of the Crysis, or dayes criticall, 266
How long ere the sick recover, 267
Hermes Trismegistus upon the Decumbiture of the sick, 268
Of the Signes and conjectures of the Disease, and of life and death by the good or ill disposition of the ☽ at the time of the Patients first lying down, pag. 273 to 281
Astrologicall Aphorismes judging of Sickness, 282
A figure of a sick Doctor, if curable, 286
A figure set to know whether the sick would live or dye, 289
Of the Crysis in Diseases, 290
A Table shewing how to set a figure in sickness of sixteen sides, 294
If a Servant shall get free from his Master, 296

Significations of the seventh House, *viz.* of Marriage, Enemies, Law-suits, Contracts, Wars, Fugitives, Thefts.

Aphorismes considerable before judgment, 298
Of Marriage, 302
More Aphorismes of Marriage by Alkindus, 303
Of Marriage whether it shall take effect or not, idem.
Of Marriage, 304
What shall be the occasion of hindring the Marriage, 305
Which love or desire it most, idem.
Whether a man shall Marry, 307
The time of Marriage, idem.
How many Husbands a Woman shall have, idem.
From what part one shall Marry, 308
What manner of person he or she is, idem.
Whether a man or woman be more noble, idem.
Who shall be master of the two, idem.
Whether

The Contents.

Whether she be rich or not, 309
Whether the Marriage be legitimate, idem.
How they shall agree after Marriage, idem.
Disagree. idem.
Who shall be cause of their strife, 310
That the Marriage shall be broken, and the cause thereof, idem.
Whether a man or his Wife shall dye first, 311
Which of the two shall live longest, idem.
Whether she be a Maid, or chaste, 312
Whether a Damosell be a Maid or not, idem.
Whether a woman be honest to her Husband or not, 313
Of a woman whether she hath a Lover besides her Husband, idem.
Whether a Woman is honest, 314
Whether a woman trades with any but her husband, idem.
If ones Sweet-heart have a Lover besides himself, 316
Hath she a Lover, idem.
If a Marriage shall be perfected or not, 317
Whether the child conceived is the son of the reputed Father, 318
Whether a woman living from her husband, shall be received into favour, or live with him again, 318
Of Servants fled, Beasts strayed, and things lost, 319
The place where the thing is that is lost, 320
How the Goods were lost, 321
Whether the Cattle be stolne or not, id.
Whether the thing missing fled of it self, idem.

Of Beasts strayed, or Fugitives, 323
Of Beasts or strayes, 324
That the Beasts are lost, 325
Dead or alive, idem.
In Pound or not, idem.
The Cattle shall be found again, id.
How far off a thing lost is from the Owner, 326
Beasts stolne or strayed, in what place which way, idem.
In what ground, 327
The Cattle shall to Pound and be long in Pound, idem.
Escape the Pound, 328
Whether the Fugitive shall be taken, idem.
Of ☽ in questions of fugitives, idem.
Whether he shall be taken, 329
If a Fugitive shall be found or come again, idem.
Distance of the Fugitive, 330
A Woman flying from her Husband, idem.
Of a Thief and Theft, idem.
Of the Significator of the Thief, 331
The Significator of the thing stolne, idem.
Approved judgments of Theft, 332
Whether it be stolne or no, 334
The Goods are stolne, 335
Not stolne, idem.
It will be, or is intended to be stolne, idem.
It's lost or stolne, idem.
Age of the Thief, 336
Of the same, 337
Whether the Thief be man or woman 338
If one Thief or more, 339
Of the Cloaths of the Thief, idem:

(c) Names

The Contents.

Names of Theeves or men according to Astrologie, 340
Whether the Thief be of the house or not, 342
Stranger or familiar, idem.
Rules by the Lord of the seventh house, 343
Whether the Thief be in the Town or not, 344
Distance betwixt the Owner and the Thief. 345
Where the Thief is, idem.
Towards what part the Thief is gone, 346
Of the house of the Thief, and marks thereof, 347
Door of the house, idem.
Tokens of the Thiefes house, 348
The Goods in the Owners hands, 349
Whether the Goods be in the custody of the Thief, idem.
If he carried all with him, 350
Distance of the thing from the Owner, idem.
Place where the Goods stolen are, 351
Where the Goods are, 352
Lost or stolne, in what part of the house, 453
The form or likeness of the entring of the house, idem.
What is stolne by the Lord of the second or tenth house, 354
The quality of the Goods stolen, id.
Sign of recovery, 355
If it shall be recovered, idem.
In what time it shal be recovered, 356
Aphorisms concerning Recovery, id.
The discovery of the Thief, and recovery of the Goods, 358
Of Theft, 359

Whether the Thief shall be known or not, 366
Whether the Thief be suspected of the Owner or not, idem.
Who did the deed or fact, idem.
Whether it be the first fact the Thief did, 360
Lillie's experimented Rules of Theft, idem.
Of Battle, War, or other contentions, 361
If one shall return safe from War or a dangerous Voyage, 367
What will ensue of the War, 368
Who shall do best in a Law-suit, 369
Of Partnership betwixt two, if it shall be, and who shall do best, 369
Of familiarity betwixt Neighbour and Neighbour, 370
Of removing from place to place, id.
If good to remove or stay in any Town or City, 371
Of Hunting, idem.
Of a Law-suit or controversie betwixt two, who should do best, 372
Of buying and selling Commodities, 376
Of Partnership, 377
Whether a City, Town or Castle besieged shall be taken, 379
Of Commanders in Armies, their abilities, fidelity, &c. 380
If two Armies shall fight, 383
If the Querent have open enemies, id:
A figure to know if a Lady should marry the party desired, 385
A second figure if the woman should marry the man beloved, 389
A figure for a fugitive Servant, 390
A figure for a Dog missing, 392

Money

The Contents.

Money lost, who stole it, a figure thereupon, 395
Fish stolne, a figure for it, 397
A figure to know if Sir William Waller and Sir Ralph Hopton were engaged, 399
A figure to know if the Earle of Essex should take Reading. 401

Of the eighth House, viz. of Death, Dowry, &c.

If the absent party be alive or dead, 404
Whether one absent will return or not, and when, 406
The time when he will return, 407
Of the death of the Querent, or space of his own life, 408
When or about what time the Querent may dye, 409
Whether the Man or Wife shall dye first, 411
What manner of death the Querent shall dye, 412
Whether the Portion of the wife will be great, or easily obtained, or if the woman will be rich, idem.
If one be afraid of a thing, whether he shall be in danger thereof or not, 414
A figure to know whether man or woman should dye first, 415
A figure of a womans to know if her husband at Sea were alive or dead, 417
A figure to know what manner of death Canterbury should dye, 419
A figure to know if the Querent should have the Portion promised, 421

Of the ninth House, viz. long Journeys, Religion, Dreames.

Of a Voyage by Sea, and successe thereof, 422
What wind he will have, 423
Of him that taketh a Journey, idem.
Of the short or slow return of him that taketh a journey, 424
When he shall return that is gone a long Journey, 425
The cause of a Journey, and successe thereof, 428
Successe and length thereof, 428
If one shall profit by his knowledge, &c. in Chymistry or Chyrurgery, 429
Of ones Science or wisdom whether it be true, 431
Of many persons travelling, in what condition they are, idem.
To what part of Heaven the Traveller had best direct his Journey, 432
If a Parson shall obtain a good Benefice, 432
Of Dreames whether they signifie any thing or not. 434
A figure adjudged concerning Dreames, 436
A figure to know if one should obtain a Parsonage, 437
A figure erected to know if Presbytery shall stand, 439
A figure to know if the Querent should obtain the Phylosophers stone, 442

Of the tenth House, viz. of Government, Dignity, Office, Command.

If the Querent shall obtain the Office desired or not, 444
If one shall continue in the Command or Office he is in, 447
Whether a King expulsed his Kingdom, or an Officer removed from his Office, shall return to his Kingdom or Office, or not, 448

(c 2) Of

The Contents.

Of the Profession or Trade any one is capable of, 450
If Prince Rupert should get honour by our wars, a figure thereof, 452
If he should worst the E. of Essex, 453
What should become of him, 454
If his Majesty should procure Forces out of Ireland to harm the Parliament, a Figure thereupon, and judgment delivered, 445
If the Queen then in the North, would advance with her Army; if she would prosper; when she and his Majesty would meet, idem.
If attain the Preferment desired, 456

Eleventh House, viz. House of Friends, Hope, Substance of Kings.

Of good or ill in questions concerning this house, 457
If a Man shall have the Thing hoped for, 458
Of the agreeing of Friends, 459
Of love betwixt two, idem.

Of the twelfth House, viz. Imprisonment, Great Cattle, Witchery, private Enemies, Labour, banished Men.

Of secret enemies not named, 460
To know who a secret enemy is, id.
Whether any man committed to prison shall soon be delivered, 461
Of the Imprisoned, 462
If a question be asked for a Captive or Prisoner, 463
Of a Captive or Slave, 463
If one be bewitched or not, 464
Naturall Remedies against witchcraft, 465
A figure for a Horse lost, 467
A figure to know if one were Bewitched, 468
A figure of a Prisoner escaped out of Prison. 470
A Lady of her husband in prison, a figure of it, 471
A figure upon the Earle of Essex his last going into the west, 473
A Table of the Planetary hour, 474
To finde out what Planet ruleth any hour of the day or night, 482

The Contents of the third Book.

A Table converting hours and min. of time into degr. and min. of the Æquator, 489
A Table of right ascentions, 492
A Table of oblique ascentions for the latitude of 34. degrees, 494
A Table of oblique ascentions for the latitude of 49. degrees, 496
A Table of oblique ascentions for the latitude of 53. degrees, 498
Divers wayes of rectifying Nativities, 500
Correction of an estimate figure by Trutine of Hermes, 502
Rectification of a Nativity by Animodar, 505
Rectification by Accidents, the way to frame an Astrologicall Speculum, 507
A Speculum of a Nativity, 509
Characters of the new aspects, the number of the degrees of the aspect, 512
Erection of a Scheam by Regiomontanus, 519

Things

The Contents.

Things considerable before judgment given upon a Nativity, 524
Of the space of life, whether the Native shall live long or not, 525
Of Hylech or Aphæta, and the interficient Planet, 527
Of the Lord of the Geniture, 531
Of the Complexion, temperament of the body, quality of Planets and Signes, 532
Manners of the Native, 534
Quality of manners discernable from the Planets, 539
Of the understanding of the Native, 543
Of the stature, shape and form of body, 446
Nature of the Signes, colour of the Face and Hair, 547
Of the grossenesse or leannesse of Bodies, 549
Of the generall fortune or misery of the Native, 551

Of the second House, viz. of Riches, or the goods of Fortune.

Whether the Native shall be rich, 553
By what meanes the Native shall attain Wealth, 554
If the Native shall attain his Estate by just or indirect dealing, 561
If the Estate of the Native shall be durable, 562

Judgments upon the third House.

Of Kinred, Brethren, Sisters, 564
If have Brethren or Sisters, idem.
Fortune & condition of Brethren, 566
Of the unity or concord betwixt the Native and his Brethren, 567
Number of Brethren 568

Judgments upon the fourth House, concerning Parents, &c.

Of the Father, 569
Of the Mother, 570
If the Mother had difficult labour at the Native's Birth, 572
If the Native shall enjoy the Estate of his Father, idem.
Of the mutuall agreement of Parents, 573
Of the Parents mutuall love to the Native, 574
Significations of great fortune out of Mines, 575

Of the fixt House, viz. of Infirmities.

Of the Infirmities of Bodies, 576
Aphorismes useful for this house, 577
Kinds and qualities of Diseases, how discoverable from the Planets and Signes, 578
Of weaknesse in the Sight, or casualties portended to the Eyes, 581
Defects in the Eares, 582
Impediments in the Tongue, idem.
Of the Tooth-ach, 583
Of the falling Sicknesse, idem.
Of the Stone, 584
Of the Gout, 585
Of violent Falls, idem.
Whether the Diseases of the Native are curable or not. idem.
Of Servants and small Cattle, 586

Of the seventh House.

Of mens Marriages, 586
Whether

The Contents.

Whether the Native shall marry or not, idem.
Signes of Marriage, 588
Whether the Native shall obtain his wife with ease or much difficulty, 589
The time of Marriage, idem.
Of the number of wives, 590
From whence, or what quarter the Native shall marry, 592
What manner of wife or wives the Native shall have, 593
Aphorismes concerning the positure of ♀, 595
Of the mutual love and concord betwixt man and wife, 597
Whether the Native or his wife shall dye first, 599
Of the Marriage of women, 600
If the woman shall marry, idem.
If with difficulty; when; from whence; what manner of man, 601
If rich: If agree, 602

The fift House.

Of Children, idem.
Aphorisms concerning this house, 603
How many Children the Native may have, 604
Whether male or female, 605
Aphorisms of Albubater, idem.

Judgments upon the ninth House, of Journeys and Religion.

Whether the Native shall travell or not, 606
To what part of the World the Native shall travell, 607
Whether travel by land or water, 608
The cause of travell, 609
Haly his Aphorismes, idem.
Of successe in travell, 610
What Region or Country will be best to travell into, 611
The Religion of the Native, idem.
Aphorisms belonging thereunto, 612
Of Dreames, 913

Of the tenth House.

Of the Honour or Dignity of the Native, 615
Whether the Native shall have Preferment or not, idem.
Rules from the two Luminaries, 617
Aphorismes from the ☉, 618
Concerning the ☽, 619
Of the Mid-heaven, idem.
Of the Ascendant, 620
Of the fixed Stars, idem.
What manner of Preferment, its quality; 621
If the Dignity or Honour shall continue, 622
Speciall Aphorismes concerning that judgment, 623
Of the Profession of the Native, 624
Experimented Aphorismes concerning the Natives Profession, 626
Of ☿ when Lord of the Profession, 627
When joyned with others, idem.
Of ♀ when alone signifies the Profession, 628
When mixed with others, idem.
Of ♂ when Significator of the Profession, 629
When mixed with others, idem.
Of ☿ and ♀ when commixed. 630
Of ☿ with ♂, idem.
Of ♂ and ♀ when Significators of Art, 631
With

The Contents.

With what successe the Native shall handle it, idem,

Judgments belonging to the eleventh House.

Of Friends, 634
Speciall rules concerning that house, 635
Quality of Friends, 636
Constancy of Friends, idem.

Of enemies, 639
What manner of enemies, their quality, 640
If the Native shall overcome his enemies, 641
Whose friendship the Native shall most avoid, 642
Of Captivity or Imprisonment, id.

Quality of the Profession, 633

Whether there may be unity or concord betwixt two, 637
Whether of the Friends is more sincere, 639

Of the twelfth House.

Of death, arguments of a violent death, 644
The kinds of a violent death, 645
From the Sign, from the House the quality of a violent death, 646
From ♄ and ♂, 647
From the Lord of the Ascendant and fixed Stars. 648

The effects of Directions.

Directions wherefore, 651
Effects of Directions, 652
What places of Heaven, what Planets Directed, and for what, 653
How long the effects of a Direction last, 654
The Ascendant its signification, when directed to the body, term or aspect of ♄, 656
The Ascendant directed to the Terms, body or aspect of ♃, 657
To the body, Terms or other aspect of ♂, 659
To the body or other aspect of ☉, 660
To the body, Term or aspect of ♀, 661
To the body, Term or any aspect of ☿, 662
To the ☌ ✶ △ □ or ☍ of ☽, 663
To the ☊ ☋, or to ⊕, or cusp of the second, third or fourth house, 665
To severall fixed Stars, 666, 667

Mid-heaven directed to Promittors, and the reason why directed, 668
To the body of ♄, or his Term, aspect, 669
To the body, Term or rayes of ♃, idem.
To the body, Term or severall aspects of ♂, 671
To the aspects or ☌ of ☉, 672
To the body, Term, &c. of ♀, 673
To the severall aspects or Terms of ☿, 674
To the body of ☽ or her aspects, 675
M.C. to the 11 or 12 house, 676
M.C. to severall fixed Stars, id.
The ☉ directed to Promittors, and wherefore, 679
To the Body or aspects of ♄, 680
To the aspects or body of ♃, 681
To the body or aspect of ♂, 682
To the body or aspect of ♀, 683

To

The Contents.

To the like of ☿,   685
To the like of ☽,   686
To ☊ or ☋, or ⊗, or cusp of any of the houses   687, 688
The ☉ directed to principall fixed stars   689
The ☽ directed to Promittors, viz. to ♄ his body or aspect,   691
To the body, terme or aspect of ♃,   694
To the aspet, terme or body of ♂,   695
To the body or aspect of ☉,   696
To the body, terme or aspect of ♀,   697
To the body or aspect of ☿,   698
To the ☊, ☋, ⊗, and to the twelve houses,   700
To the fixed Stars,   701
⊗ wherefore directed, its effects when directed to ♄ or his aspects,   703
To the aspect of ♃ ♂ and ☉,   704
To the aspects of ♀ and ☿,   705
To ☽ and her aspects, to ☊ and ☋. 706
To the cusps of the twelve houses, 707
Of the measure of time in Directions,   708
The first and second way of measuring time,   709
The third measure of time, according to Naibod,   713
Of annuall Profections, mensurnall and diurnall,   715, 716

A Table of Profections exactly made,   717
The use of Profections and their effects   718
Lord of the yeer, what Planet,   720
A Table converting degrees into dayes and hours, &c.   721
A table of the dayes of the yeer, teaching what moneth and day of the moneth when the Profectionall Significator or other, and the Promittor meet; severall examples,   722
How to judge a figure of Profections,   726
Judgments upon the Profections of the ascendant & ☽, their signification. 729
What the mid-heaven and ☉ signifie,   731
Signification of ⊗,   732
Of Revolutions,   734
The Returne of the Planets to their owne places, and of other Planets in a Revolution,   738
The transit of the Planets,   741
Astrologicall judgments by way of example upon the twelve houses, and upon Directions, Profections, Revolutions and transits, upon a Merchants Nativity,   742

AN

To the Student in ASTROLOGY.

MY Friend, whoever thou art, that with so much ease shalt receive the benefit of my hard *Studies*, and dost intend to proceed in this heavenly knowledge of the Stars, wherein the great and admirable works of the invisible and alglorious God are so manifestly apparent. In the first place, consider and admire thy *Creator*, and be thankful unto him, be thou humble, and let no natural knowledge, how profound and transcendent soever it be, elate thy minde to neglect that *divine Providence*, by whose all-seeing order and appointment, all things heavenly and earthly, have their constant motion; but the more thy knowledge is enlarged, the more do thou magnifie the power and wisdom of *Almighty God*, and strive to preserve thy self in his faveur; being confident, the more holy thou art, and more neer to God, the purer *Judgment* thou shalt give. Beware of pride and self-conceit, and remember how that long ago, no irrational *Creature* durst offend Man, the *Microcosm*; but did faithfully serve and obey him, so long as he was Mr. of his own Reason and Passions, or until he subjected his Will to the unreasonable part. But alas! when iniquity abounded, and man gave the reins to his own *affection*, and deserted reason, then every *Beast*, *Creature* and outward harmful thing, became rebellious and unserviceable to his command. Stand fast, oh man! to thy *God*, and assured *principles*, then consider thy own nobleness, how all created things, both present and to come, were for thy sake created; nay, for thy sake *God* became *Man* : thou art that *Creature*, who being conversant with *Christ*, livest and raignest above the heavens, and sits above all power and authority. How many *pre-eminences*, *priviledges*, *advantages* hath God bestowed on thee? thou rangest above the heavens by *contemplation*, conceivest the *motion* and *magnitude* of the *stars*; thou talkest with *Angels*, yea with *God* himself; thou hast all *Creatures* within thy *dominion*, and keepest the *Devils* in subjection: Do not then for shame deface thy *nature*, or make thy self unworthy of such *gifts*, or deprive thy self of that great *power*, glory and *blessedness* God hath alotted thee, by casting from thee his fear, for possession of a few imperfect *pleasures*. Having considered thy God, and what thy self art, during thy being Gods servant; now receive instruction how in thy practice I would have thee carry thy self. As thou daily conversest with the heavens, so instruct and form thy minde according to the image of *Divinity* ; learn all the ornaments of *vertue*, be sufficiently instructed therein; be humane, curteous, familiar to all, easie of access, afflict not the *miserable* with terror of a harsh *judgment*; in such cases, let them know their hard fate by degrees; direct them to call on *God* to divert his *judgments* impending over them : be modest, conversant with the *learned, civil, sober man*, covet not an *estate*; give freely to the *poor*, both *money* and *judgment* : let no wordly wealth procure an *erroneous judgment* from thee, or such as may dishonour the *Art*, or this divine Science : Love good men, cherish those honest men that cordially Study this *Art:* Be sparing in delivering Judgment against the *Common-wealth* thou livest in. Give not judgment of the death of thy Prince; yet I know experimentally, that *Reges subjacent legibus Stellarum·* marry a *wife* of thy own, rejoyce in the number of thy friends, avoid law and controversie : in thy Study, be *totus in illis* that thou maist be *singulus in arte*; be not extravagant or desirous to learn every *Science*, be not *aliquid in omnibus*; be faithful, tenacious, betray no ones secrets, no, no I charge thee never divulge either friend or enemies trust committed to thy faith. Instruct all men to Live well, be a good example thy self, avoid the fashion of the times, love thy own Native *Country* : exprobrate no man, no not an enemy : be not dismaid, if ill spoken of, *Conscientia mille testes*; God suffers no sin unpunished, no lye unrevenged.

B *WILLIAM LILLY.*

JANUARY hath xxxi. dayes.

The daily Motion of the Planets and ☊.

		M	D	M	D	M	A			M	D	M	D				
		♄		♃		♂		☉		♀		☿		☽		☊	
		♈		♊		♑		♑		♓		♒		♏		♌	
1	a	27	48	28 R	12	10	5	21	34	5	7	5	29	21	23	12	34
2	b	27	50	28	6	10	51	22	35	6	17	7	8	3 ♐	17	12	45
3	c	27	52	27	59	11	37	23	36	7	26	8	44	15	8	12	42
4	D	27	54	27	53	12	23	24	37	8	35	10	18	26	59	12	24
5	e	27	56	27	46	13	9	25	38	9	44	11	49	8 ♑	54	11	52
6	f	27	58	27	40	13	55	26	39	10	53	13	18	20	54	11	10
7	g	28	0	27	34	14	41	27	41	12	2	14	45	3 ♒	1	10	24
8	a	28	2	27	28	15	27	28	42	13	10	16	10	15	17	9	24
9	b	28	4	27	22	16	17	29	43	14	18	17	33	27	44	9	9
10	c	28	6	27	17	17	0	0 ♒	44	15	26	18	50	10 ♓	23	8	50
11	D	28	9	27	11	17	46	1	46	16	34	20	2	23	14	8	49
12	e	28	11	27	6	18	32	2	47	17	42	21	7	6 ♈	18	9	6
13	f	28	14	27	1	19	19	3	48	18	50	22	6	19	38	9	36
14	g	28	17	26	56	20	5	4	49	19	57	23	0	3 ♉	15	10	17
15	a	28	20	26	51	20	51	5	50	21	4	23	47	17	9	10	59
16	b	28	23	26	46	21	37	6	51	22	11	24	25	1 ♊	22	11	34
17	c	28	26	26	42	22	2	7	52	23	17	24	47	15	52	11	55
18	D	28	29	26	37	23	10	8	53	24	23	24	57	2 ♋	34	11	54
19	e	28	32	26	33	23	56	9	54	25	29	25	0	15	23	11	29
20	f	28	36	26	29	24	43	10	55	26	35	24 R	53	0 ♌	11	10	44
21	g	28	39	26	24	25	29	11	56	27	41	24	33	14	50	9	49
22	a	28	43	26	21	26	15	12	57	28	47	23	53	29	12	8	58
23	b	28	46	26	17	27	2	13	58	29	52	23	9	13 ♍	18	8	22
24	c	28	50	26	13	27	48	14	58	0 ♈	57	22	21	26	59	8	5
25	D	28	54	26	10	28	35	15	59	2	2	21	29	10 ♎	15	8	8
26	e	28	58	26	7	29	21	16	59	3	6	20	33	23	9	8	27
27	f	29	2	26	4	0 ♒	8	18	0	4	10	19	33	5 ♏	36	8	58
28	g	29	6	26	2	0	54	19	1	5	14	18	26	17	49	9	33
29	a	29	11	25	59	1	41	20	2	6	18	17	14	29	48	10	9
30	b	29	15	25	57	2	28	21	3	7	21	15	58	11 ♐	39	10	38
31	c	29	20	25	55	3	4	22	4	8	24	14	50	23	27	11	1
lat	1	2	31	0	5	0	47			1	13	1	45				
of	10	2	29	0	4	0	51			0	39	0	26				
pla	20	2	26	0	2	0	55			0 S	9	2 S	10				

JANUARY 1646.

		The Lunar Aspects.						The Planets Mutuall Aspects.
		♄	♃	♂	☉	♀	☿	
		Occid.	Occid.	Orient.		Occid.	Occid.	
1	a				✶ 0			
2	b					□ 6	△ 9	
3	c							✶ ♄ ♃ 21
4	D	△ 2	☍ 2					☽ Apog.
5	e			☌ 9		✶ 2		[Eclip. ☉
6	f	□ 14			☌ 11:48			Vc ☉ ♃ SS ♂ ☿
7	g							□ ☉ ♄ 8 ☽ ☋
8	a		△ 23				☌ 2	
9	b	✶ 0						
10	c			✶ 14		☌ 11		
11	D		□ 7		✶ 17			
12	e			□ 23				☿ in Elong.Max
13	f	☌ 15	✶ 13				✶ 5	
14	g				□ 25			✶ ♂ ♀ 9
15	a			△ 6		✶ 7	□ 12	
16	b				△ 10			
17	c	✶ 20	☌ 17			□ 13	△ 15	
18	D							SS ♀ ☿ ☽ Perig
19	e	□ 21		☍ 14		△ 18		□ ♃ ♀ 22
20	f				☍ 18			
21	g	△ 23	✶ 19				☍ 15	SS ♄ ♀ ☽ ☊ E-
22	a							Vc ♃ ♂ [clip.totall
23	b		□ 23					
24	c			△ 1		☍ 8		
25	D				△ 11		△ 19	□ ♄ ♂ 11Q ☉ ♄
26	e	☍ 11	△ 6	□ 13				
27	f						Orient.	☌ ☉ ☿ 17
28	g				□ 3.15		□ 1	
29	a			✶ 4		△ 13		
30	b				✶ 20		✶ 8	
31	c	△ 12	☍ 5					

A Table of Houses for the Latitude of 52. degrees.

☉ in ♈ time from Noon.	10 House	11 House	12 House	1 House.	2 House.	3 House.
Ho. Min.	deg. min. ♈	deg. min. ♉	deg. min. ♊	deg. min. ♋	deg. min. ♌	deg. min. ♍
0 0	0 0	12 51	28 55	27 2	16 7	4 31
0 4	1 0	14 1	29 46	27 42	16 47	5 17
0 7	2 0	15 11	0 ♋ 36	28 22	17 28	6 3
0 11	3 0	16 21	1 26	29 1	18 8	6 50
0 15	4 0	17 29	2 15	29 41	18 48	7 36
0 18	5 0	18 37	3 4	0 ♌ 21	19 28	8 23
0 22	6 0	19 44	3 53	1 0	20 8	9 9
0 26	7 0	20 51	4 42	1 39	20 48	9 56
0 29	8 0	21 59	5 29	2 18	21 27	10 42
0 33	9 0	23 6	6 18	2 58	22 8	11 30
0 37	10 0	24 12	7 6	3 38	22 48	12 17
0 40	11 0	25 16	7 53	4 17	23 27	13 3
0 44	12 0	26 22	8 40	4 56	24 8	13 51
0 48	13 0	27 26	9 27	5 35	24 48	14 37
0 52	14 0	28 30	10 12	6 14	25 28	15 24
0 55	15 0	29 34	10 59	6 54	26 9	16 11
0 59	16 0	0 ♊ 37	11 45	7 32	26 50	16 59
1 3	17 0	1 38	12 30	8 12	27 30	17 46
1 6	18 0	2 41	13 16	8 52	28 11	18 33
1 10	19 0	3 43	14 1	9 31	28 52	19 21
1 14	20 0	4 45	14 47	10 10	29 33	20 9
1 18	21 0	5 45	15 32	10 49	0 ♍ 14	20 57
1 21	22 0	6 46	16 17	11 29	0 55	21 45
1 25	23 0	7 46	17 2	12 8	1 36	22 32
1 29	24 0	8 46	17 46	12 47	2 17	23 20
1 33	25 0	9 46	18 31	13 27	2 58	24 9
1 36	26 0	10 46	19 16	14 7	3 40	24 58
1 40	27 0	11 45	20 1	14 46	4 22	25 46
1 44	28 0	12 45	20 45	15 26	5 3	26 35
1 48	29 0	13 44	21 29	16 5	5 45	27 23
1 52	30 0	14 41	22 13	16 45	6 26	28 12

A Table of Houses for the Latitude of 52. degrees.

☉ in ♉	10 House	11 House	12 House	1 House	2 House	3 House
Time frō Noon.	deg. min.	deg. min.	deg. min.	deg. min.	deg. min.	deg. min.
Ho. Min.	♉	Ⅱ	♋	♌	♍	♍
1 52	0 0	14 41	22 13	16 45	6 26	28 12
1 55	1 0	15 38	22 57	17 25	7 8	29 1
1 59	2 0	16 36	23 42	18 5	7 50	29 50
2 3	3 0	17 33	24 27	18 45	8 33	0 ♎ 40
2 7	4 0	18 29	25 10	19 25	9 14	1 29
2 11	5 0	19 26	25 55	20 5	9 57	2 19
2 15	6 0	20 23	26 38	20 45	10 39	3 8
2 19	7 0	21 20	27 23	21 26	11 23	3 58
2 22	8 0	22 17	28 7	22 7	12 6	4 48
2 26	9 0	23 13	28 51	22 47	12 48	5 38
2 30	10 0	24 9	29 35	23 27	13 31	6 28
2 34	11 0	25 5	0 ♌ 19	24 8	14 14	7 19
2 38	12 0	26 1	1 4	24 49	14 58	8 9
2 42	13 0	26 56	1 47	25 30	15 41	8 59
2 46	14 0	27 51	2 32	26 12	16 25	9 50
2 50	15 0	28 46	3 16	26 53	17 8	10 40
2 54	16 0	29 41	4 1	27 34	17 52	11 32
2 58	17 0	0 ♋ 38	4 46	28 17	18 36	12 24
3 2	18 0	1 33	5 30	28 58	19 21	13 14
3 6	19 0	2 27	6 15	29 40	20 5	14 6
3 10	20 0	3 22	7 0	0 ♍ 23	20 50	14 57
3 14	21 0	4 17	7 45	1 5	21 34	15 49
3 18	22 0	5 11	8 30	1 47	22 19	16 40
3 22	23 0	6 5	9 15	2 29	23 4	17 32
3 26	24 0	6 59	10 0	3 12	23 49	18 24
3 30	25 0	7 53	10 44	3 54	24 35	19 16
3 35	26 0	8 48	11 30	4 37	25 20	20 8
3 39	27 0	9 43	12 15	5 20	26 6	21 1
3 43	28 0	10 36	13 1	6 3	26 51	21 53
3 47	29 0	11 30	13 46	6 46	27 31	22 46
3 51	30 0	12 24	14 31	7 29	28 23	23 38

A Table of Houses for the Latitude of 52. degrees.

☉ in ♊ time from Noon. Ho.Min.	10 House deg. min. ♊	11 House deg. min. ♋	12 House deg. min. ♌	1 House deg. min ♍	2 House deg. min ♍	3 House deg. min ♎
3 51	0 0	12 24	14 31	7 29	28 23	23 38
3 55	1 0	13 19	15 17	8 13	29 9	24 31
4 0	2 0	14 14	16 3	8 57	29 55	25 24
4 4	3 0	15 8	16 49	9 41	0 ♎ 42	26 17
4 8	4 0	16 2	17 35	10 25	1 28	27 0
4 12	5 0	16 56	18 21	11 9	2 15	28 2
4 16	6 0	17 50	19 7	11 53	3 1	28 56
4 21	7 0	18 44	19 53	12 37	3 48	29 49
4 25	8 0	19 38	20 40	13 22	4 35	0 ♏ 43
4 29	9 0	20 31	21 25	14 6	5 21	1 36
4 33	10 0	21 25	22 11	14 51	6 9	2 29
4 38	11 0	22 19	22 58	15 35	6 56	3 23
4 42	12 0	23 14	23 45	16 21	7 44	4 17
4 46	13 0	24 8	24 31	17 5	8 31	5 11
4 50	14 0	25 2	25 18	17 50	9 18	6 5
4 55	15 0	25 57	26 5	18 35	10 6	6 59
4 59	16 0	26 51	26 53	19 21	10 54	7 53
5 3	17 0	27 44	27 39	20 6	11 41	8 47
5 8	18 0	28 38	28 27	20 51	12 28	9 40
5 12	19 0	29 32	29 14	21 37	13 16	10 34
5 16	20 0	0 ♌ 27	0 ♍ 2	22 22	14 3	11 28
5 21	21 0	1 21	0 50	23 8	14 51	12 22
5 25	22 0	2 15	1 37	23 53	15 39	13 17
5 29	23 0	3 9	2 24	24 39	16 20	14 11
5 34	24 0	4 4	3 12	25 25	17 14	15 6
5 38	25 0	4 57	4 0	26 10	18 2	15 59
5 42	26 0	5 52	4 47	26 56	18 50	16 53
5 47	27 0	6 47	5 35	27 42	19 38	17 47
5 51	28 0	7 41	6 23	28 28	20 25	18 42
5 56	29 0	8 35	7 10	29 13	21 13	19 36
6 0	30 0	9 29	7 58	0 ♎ 0	22 1	20 30

A Table of Houses for the Latitude of 52. degrees.

☉ in ♋ time from Noon. Ho. Min.	10 House deg. min. ♋	11 House deg. min. ♌	12 House deg. min. ♍	1 House. deg. min. ♎	2 House. deg. min. ♎	3 House. deg. min. ♏
6 0	0 0	9 29	7 58	0 0	22 1	20 30
6 4	1 0	10 24	8 47	0 46	22 50	21 25
6 9	2 0	11 18	9 34	1 32	23 37	22 19
6 13	3 0	12 12	10 22	2 17	24 24	23 12
6 18	4 0	13 7	11 10	3 4	25 12	24 7
6 22	5 0	14 1	11 58	3 49	26 0	25 2
6 26	6 0	14 54	12 45	4 35	26 47	25 56
6 31	7 0	15 49	13 33	5 21	27 35	26 51
6 35	8 0	16 43	14 21	6 7	28 23	27 45
6 39	9 0	17 37	15 9	6 52	29 10	28 39
6 44	10 0	18 32	15 56	7 37	29 58	29 33
6 48	11 0	19 26	15 44	8 23	0 ♏ 45	0 ♐ 27
6 52	12 0	20 20	17 31	9 8	1 33	1 22
6 57	13 0	21 13	18 19	9 54	2 20	2 16
7 1	14 0	22 7	19 6	10 39	3 7	3 9
7 5	15 0	23 1	19 54	11 24	3 55	4 3
7 10	16 0	23 55	20 42	12 10	4 42	4 57
7 14	17 0	24 49	21 28	12 54	5 28	5 51
7 18	18 0	25 42	22 15	13 39	6 15	6 46
7 22	19 0	26 37	23 4	14 24	7 2	7 40
7 27	20 0	27 30	23 51	15 9	7 48	8 35
7 31	21 0	28 24	24 38	15 54	8 35	9 29
7 35	22 0	29 17	25 25	16 37	9 20	10 22
7 39	23 0	0 ♍ 11	26 12	17 22	10 6	11 16
7 44	24 0	1 4	26 58	18 7	10 53	12 10
7 48	25 0	1 57	27 45	18 51	11 39	13 3
7 52	26 0	2 51	28 21	19 35	12 25	13 57
7 56	27 0	3 43	29 18	20 19	13 11	14 51
8 0	28 0	4 36	0 ♎ 4	21 3	13 59	15 46
8 5	29 0	5 29	0 51	21 47	14 43	16 41
8 9	30 0	6 22	1 37	22 31	15 29	17 31

A Table of Houses for the Latitude of 52. degrees.

☉ in ♌ time from Noon.	10 House	11 House	12 House	1 House.	2 House.	3 House.
Ho. Min.	deg. min. ♌	deg. min. ♍	deg. min. ♎	deg. min. ♎	deg. min. ♏	deg. min. ♐
8 9	0 0	6 22	1 37	22 31	15 29	17 35
8 13	1 0	7 14	2 23	23 14	16 14	18 29
8 17	2 0	8 7	3 9	23 57	16 59	19 23
8 21	3 0	8 59	3 54	24 40	17 44	20 17
8 25	4 0	9 51	4 39	25 23	18 30	21 12
8 30	5 0	10 44	5 25	26 6	19 15	22 7
8 34	6 0	11 36	6 10	26 48	20 0	23 1
8 38	7 0	12 28	6 55	27 31	20 44	23 55
8 42	8 0	13 19	7 41	28 13	21 29	24 49
8 46	9 0	14 11	8 25	28 55	22 15	25 43
8 50	10 0	15 2	9 10	29 37	23 0	26 37
8 54	11 0	15 54	9 55	0 ♏ 19	23 45	27 33
8 58	12 0	16 45	10 39	1 1	24 29	28 27
9 2	13 0	17 36	11 23	1 43	25 14	29 22
9 6	14 0	18 28	12 8	2 25	25 59	0 ♑ 18
9 10	15 0	19 20	12 52	3 7	26 44	1 14
9 14	16 0	20 10	13 35	3 48	27 28	2 8
9 18	17 0	21 1	14 19	4 29	28 12	3 4
9 22	18 0	21 51	15 2	5 10	28 56	3 59
9 26	19 0	22 41	15 45	5 51	29 40	4 54
9 30	20 0	23 32	16 28	6 32	0 ♐ 25	5 50
9 34	21 0	24 22	17 12	7 13	1 9	6 46
9 38	22 0	25 12	17 54	7 53	1 52	7 42
9 41	23 0	26 2	18 37	8 34	2 37	8 40
9 45	24 0	26 51	19 20	9 15	3 22	9 37
9 49	25 0	27 41	20 3	9 55	4 5	10 33
9 53	26 0	28 31	20 45	10 35	4 49	11 30
9 57	27 0	29 20	21 27	11 14	5 33	12 26
10 1	28 0	0 ♎ 9	22 9	11 55	6 18	13 24
10 5	29 0	0 59	22 52	12 35	7 2	14 22
10 8	30 0	1 48	23 33	13 14	7 47	15 19

A Table of Houses for the Latitude of 52. degrees.

☉ in ♍ time from Noon. Ho. Min.	10 House deg. min. ♍	11 House deg. min. ♎	12 House deg. min. ♎	1 House. deg. min. ♏	2 House. deg. min. ♐	3 House. deg. min. ♑
10 8	0 0	1 48	23 33	13 14	7 47	15 9
10 12	1 0	2 37	24 15	13 54	8 31	16 16
10 16	2 0	3 25	24 56	14 34	9 15	17 15
10 20	3 0	4 13	25 38	15 14	9 59	18 14
10 24	4 0	5 2	26 20	15 53	10 44	19 14
10 27	5 0	5 50	27 1	16 33	11 28	20 14
10 31	6 0	6 39	27 42	17 12	12 13	21 14
10 35	7 0	7 27	28 23	17 51	12 57	22 14
10 39	8 0	8 15	29 4	18 31	13 42	23 14
10 42	9 0	9 3	29 46	19 10	14 28	24 15
10 46	10 0	9 51	0 ♏ 27	19 49	15 13	25 15
10 50	11 0	10 38	1 8	20 29	15 58	26 17
10 54	12 0	11 26	1 49	21 8	16 44	27 19
10 57	13 0	12 14	2 30	21 48	17 29	28 21
11 1	14 0	13 1	3 10	22 27	18 15	29 23
11 5	15 0	13 49	3 51	23 6	19 1	0 ♒ 26
11 8	16 0	14 36	4 32	23 46	19 47	1 30
11 12	17 0	15 23	5 12	24 25	20 33	2 33
11 16	18 0	16 9	5 52	25 3	21 19	3 37
11 20	19 0	16 57	6 32	25 43	22 7	4 43
11 23	20 0	17 43	7 12	26 22	22 54	5 48
11 27	21 0	18 30	7 52	27 1	23 42	6 54
11 31	22 0	19 18	8 32	27 41	24 30	8 1
11 34	23 0	20 4	9 12	28 21	25 18	9 8
11 38	24 0	20 51	9 52	29 0	26 7	10 16
11 42	25 0	21 37	10 32	29 39	26 56	11 23
11 45	26 0	22 24	11 12	0 ♐ 19	27 45	12 31
11 49	27 0	23 10	11 52	0 58	28 34	13 39
11 53	28 0	23 57	12 32	1 38	29 23	14 48
11 56	29 0	24 42	13 12	2 18	0 ♑ 14	15 59
12 0	30 0	25 29	13 53	2 58	1 5	17 9

C

A Table of Houses for the Latitude of 52. degrees.

☉ in ♎ time from Noon.	10 House	11 House	12 House	1 House.	2 House.	3 House.
Ho. Min.	deg. min. ♎	deg. min. ♎	deg. min. ♏	deg. min. ♐	deg. min. ♑	deg. min. ♒
12 0	0 0	25 29	13 53	2 58	1 5	17 9
12 4	1 0	26 15	14 33	3 37	1 56	18 21
12 7	2 0	27 1	15 13	4 17	2 48	19 32
12 11	3 0	27 47	15 53	4 58	3 40	20 45
12 15	4 0	28 34	16 33	5 38	4 33	21 57
12 18	5 0	29 20	17 13	6 10	5 26	23 11
12 22	6 0	0 ♏ 6	17 53	7 1	6 20	24 24
12 26	7 0	0 52	18 33	7 41	7 15	25 38
12 29	8 0	1 38	19 14	8 22	8 10	26 53
12 33	9 0	2 25	19 55	9 4	9 6	28 11
12 37	10 0	3 12	20 35	9 46	10 2	29 26
12 40	11 0	3 57	21 15	10 27	10 59	0 ♓ 43
12 44	12 0	4 44	21 57	11 10	11 58	2 1
12 48	13 0	5 30	22 38	11 51	12 57	3 19
12 52	14 0	6 17	23 18	12 34	13 56	4 37
12 55	15 0	7 3	24 0	13 17	14 57	5 57
12 59	16 0	7 50	24 41	14 1	15 58	7 17
13 3	17 0	8 36	25 22	14 44	16 59	8 37
13 6	18 0	9 22	26 4	15 27	18 2	9 58
13 10	19 0	10 8	26 45	16 12	19 7	11 19
13 14	20 0	10 55	27 27	16 55	20 13	12 42
13 18	21 0	11 42	28 9	17 41	21 20	14 4
13 21	22 0	12 29	28 51	18 27	22 29	15 29
13 25	23 0	13 16	29 33	19 12	23 37	16 52
13 29	24 0	14 2	0 ♐ 15	19 57	24 45	18 16
13 33	25 0	14 50	0 58	20 44	25 56	19 40
13 36	26 0	15 37	1 40	21 32	27 9	21 6
13 40	27 0	16 24	2 23	22 19	28 23	22 31
13 44	28 0	17 11	3 7	23 7	29 33	23 57
13 48	29 0	17 58	3 49	23 56	0 ♒ 55	25 22
13 52	30 0	18 46	4 32	24 44	2 12	26 49

A Table of Houses for the Latitude of 52. degrees.

☉ in ♏	10 House	11 House	12 House	1 House	2 House	3 House
Time frō Noon.	deg. min.	deg. min.	deg. min.	deg. min.	deg. min.	deg. min.
Ho. Min.	♏	♏	♐	♐	♒	♓
13 52	0 0	18 46	4 32	24 44	2 12	26 49
13 55	1 0	19 33	5 16	25 34	3 32	28 15
13 59	2 0	20 21	6 1	26 25	4 54	29 43
14 3	3 0	21 9	6 45	27 16	6 19	1 ♈ 11
14 7	4 0	21 57	7 29	28 7	7 42	2 37
14 11	5 0	22 44	8 14	28 59	9 7	4 6
14 15	6 0	23 32	8 59	29 52	10 35	5 33
14 19	7 0	24 22	9 45	0 ♑ 46	12 6	7 1
14 22	8 0	25 11	10 31	1 41	13 38	8 30
14 26	9 0	25 59	11 16	2 36	15 10	9 57
14 30	10 0	26 48	12 3	3 32	16 45	11 25
14 34	11 0	27 38	12 49	4 29	18 23	12 52
14 38	12 0	28 27	13 37	5 26	20 3	14 20
14 42	13 0	29 16	14 24	6 25	21 45	15 48
14 46	14 0	0 ♐ 6	15 12	7 25	23 30	17 16
14 50	15 0	0 55	16 0	8 26	25 14	18 44
14 54	16 9	1 45	16 48	9 28	27 3	20 10
14 58	17 0	2 36	17 38	10 33	28 54	21 38
15 2	18 0	3 26	18 28	11 38	0 ♓ 45	23 6
15 6	19 0	4 16	19 17	12 43	2 37	24 31
15 10	20 0	5 7	20 8	13 51	4 33	25 58
15 14	21 0	5 58	20 59	15 0	6 31	27 24
15 18	22 0	6 50	21 51	16 10	8 31	28 50
15 22	23 0	7 41	22 43	17 21	10 32	0 ♉ 15
15 26	24 0	8 33	23 35	18 33	12 35	1 39
15 30	25 0	9 24	24 29	19 48	14 39	3 4
15 35	26 0	10 17	25 23	21 5	16 47	4 28
15 39	27 0	11 9	26 17	22 23	18 56	5 52
15 43	28 0	12 2	27 12	23 43	21 4	7 15
15 47	29 0	12 54	28 8	25 5	23 12	8 36
15 51	30 0	13 47	29 3	26 30	25 21	9 59

C 2

| A Table of Houses for the Latitude of 52. degrees. |

☉ in ♐ | 10 House | 11 House | 12 House | 1 House. | 2 House. | 3 House.

Time frō Noon.

Ho. Min.	deg. min. ♐	deg. min. ♐	deg. min. ♐	deg. min. ♑	deg. min. ♓	deg. min. ♉
15 51	0 0	13 47	29 3	26 30	25 21	9 59
15 55	1 0	14 41	0 ♑ 1	27 57	27 33	11 21
16 0	2 0	15 35	0 59	29 26	29 49	12 43
16 4	3 0	16 30	1 58	0 ♒ 57	2 ♈ 2	14 4
16 8	4 0	17 25	2 57	2 31	4 14	15 24
16 12	5 0	18 20	3 57	4 8	6 26	16 43
16 16	6 0	19 15	4 58	5 46	8 35	18 1
16 21	7 0	20 10	6 1	7 29	10 47	19 19
16 25	8 0	21 7	7 4	9 13	13 0	20 38
16 29	9 0	22 2	8 7	11 0	15 10	21 55
16 33	10 0	22 59	9 11	12 51	17 21	23 12
16 38	11 0	23 56	10 16	14 42	19 30	24 28
16 42	12 0	24 53	11 24	16 41	21 39	25 45
16 46	13 0	25 50	12 32	18 41	23 44	27 0
16 50	14 0	26 47	13 41	20 44	25 48	28 14
16 55	15 0	27 46	14 51	22 52	27 52	29 28
16 59	16 0	28 45	16 2	25 0	29 57	0 ♊ 41
17 3	17 0	29 44	17 13	27 12	1 ♉ 49	1 53
17 8	18 0	0 ♑ 44	18 28	29 28	3 47	3 5
17 12	19 0	1 44	19 43	1 ♓ 49	5 44	4 17
17 16	20 0	2 44	21 1	4 11	7 28	5 28
17 21	21 0	3 45	22 19	6 35	9 31	6 34
17 25	22 0	4 46	23 38	9 2	11 22	7 47
17 29	23 0	5 47	24 57	11 32	13 10	8 57
17 34	24 0	6 50	26 20	14 7	14 57	10 6
17 38	25 0	7 53	27 44	16 42	16 38	11 14
17 42	26 0	8 56	29 11	19 21	18 21	12 23
17 47	27 0	10 0	0 ♒ 37	21 57	20 1	13 30
17 51	28 0	11 4	2 5	24 37	21 38	14 36
17 56	29 0	12 8	3 36	27 17	23 13	15 41
18 0	30 0	13 13	5 10	0 ♈ 0	24 50	16 47

A Table of Houses for the Latitude of 52. degrees.

☉ in ♑ time from Noon.	10 House	11 House	12 House	1 House.	2 House.	3 House.
Ho. Min	deg. min. ♑	deg. min. ♑	deg. min. ♒	deg. min. ♈	deg. min. ♉	deg. min. ♊
18 0	0 0	13 13	5 10	0 0	24 50	16 47
18 4	1 0	14 19	6 47	2 42	26 24	17 52
18 9	2 0	15 24	8 22	5 22	27 54	18 56
18 13	3 0	16 29	9 58	8 2	29 23	20 0
18 18	4 0	17 38	11 40	10 40	0 ♊ 51	21 4
18 22	5 0	18 45	13 21	13 17	2 16	22 7
18 26	6 0	19 54	15 3	15 52	3 39	23 9
18 31	7 0	21 3	16 50	18 28	5 2	24 12
18 35	8 0	22 13	18 38	20 58	6 21	25 14
18 39	9 0	23 22	20 29	23 24	7 40	26 15
18 44	10 0	24 32	22 22	25 49	8 59	27 16
18 48	11 0	25 42	24 16	28 11	10 16	28 16
18 52	12 0	26 54	26 13	0 ♉ 32	11 32	29 16
18 57	13 0	28 7	28 11	2 47	12 46	0 ♋ 16
19 1	14 0	29 19	0 ♓ 7	5 0	13 58	1 14
19 5	15 0	0 ♒ 31	2 8	7 8	15 9	2 13
19 10	16 9	1 46	4 11	9 15	16 19	3 12
19 14	17 0	3 0	6 15	11 19	17 28	4 10
19 18	18 0	4 15	8 21	13 19	18 36	5 7
19 22	19 0	5 32	10 30	15 17	19 43	6 4
19 27	20 0	6 48	12 39	17 9	20 49	7 1
19 31	21 0	8 5	14 49	19 0	21 53	7 50
19 35	22 0	9 22	17 0	20 47	22 56	8 53
19 39	23 0	10 40	19 12	22 31	23 59	9 50
19 44	24 0	11 59	21 25	24 14	25 2	10 45
19 48	25 0	13 17	23 34	25 52	26 3	11 40
19 52	26 0	14 36	25 45	27 28	27 3	12 35
19 56	27 0	15 16	27 58	29 3	28 2	13 29
20 0	28 0	17 17	0 ♈ 13	0 ♊ 34	29 1	14 24
20 5	29 0	18 39	2 27	2 3	29 59	15 19
20 9	30 0	20 1	4 39	3 30	0 ♋ 56	16 13

A Table of Houses for the Latitude of 52. degrees.

☉ in ♒ time from Noon. Ho. Min.	10 House deg. min. ♒	11 House deg. min. ♒	12 House deg. min. ♈	1 House. deg. min. ♊	2 House. deg. min. ♋	3 House. deg. min. ♋
20 9	0 0	20 1	4 39	3 20	0 56	16 13
20 13	1 0	21 23	6 48	4 54	1 52	17 6
20 17	2 0	22 45	8 56	6 17	2 47	17 58
20 21	3 0	24 8	11 4	7 37	3 43	18 51
20 25	4 0	25 31	13 12	8 55	4 37	19 43
20 30	5 0	26 56	15 21	10 12	5 31	20 35
20 34	6 0	28 20	17 25	11 26	6 24	21 27
20 38	7 0	29 45	19 28	12 39	7 17	22 18
20 42	8 0	1 ♓ 1	21 29	13 49	8 9	23 10
20 46	9 0	2 36	23 29	15 0	9 1	24 2
20 50	10 0	4 1	25 27	16 9	9 52	24 53
20 54	11 0	5 28	27 23	17 16	10 42	25 44
20 58	12 0	6 54	29 15	18 22	11 32	26 34
21 2	13 0	8 21	1 ♉ 5	19 27	12 21	27 24
21 6	14 0	9 50	2 56	20 31	13 11	28 15
21 10	15 0	11 16	4 45	21 34	14 0	29 5
21 14	16 0	12 43	6 30	22 34	14 48	29 54
21 18	17 0	14 12	8 14	23 35	15 36	0 ♌ 44
21 22	18 0	15 39	9 56	24 33	16 23	1 33
21 26	19 0	17 7	11 37	25 31	17 10	2 22
21 30	20 0	18 35	13 14	26 27	17 56	3 12
21 34	21 0	20 3	14 50	27 23	18 43	4 1
21 38	22 0	21 30	16 21	28 19	19 29	4 48
21 41	23 0	22 58	17 54	29 14	20 15	5 38
21 45	24 0	34 27	19 24	0 ♋ 8	21 1	6 27
21 49	25 0	25 54	20 52	1 1	21 45	7 15
21 53	26 0	27 22	22 17	1 53	22 30	8 3
21 57	27 0	28 49	23 41	2 44	23 14	8 51
22 1	28 0	0 ♈ 16	25 6	3 35	23 59	9 31
22 5	29 0	1 44	26 28	4 26	24 44	10 27
22 8	30 0	3 11	27 47	5 15	25 27	11 14

A Table of Houses for the Latitude of 52. degrees.

☉ in ♓ time from Noon. Ho.Min.	10 House deg. min. ♓	11 House deg. min. ♈	12 House deg. min. ♉	1 House. deg. min. ♋	2 House. deg. min. ♋	3 House. deg. min. ♌
22 8	0 0	3 11	27 47	5 15	25 27	11 14
22 12	1 0	4 37	29 5	6 4	26 10	12 1
22 16	2 0	6 3	0 ♉ 21	6 52	26 53	12 48
22 20	3 0	7 28	1 36	7 40	27 36	13 36
22 24	4 0	8 54	2 51	8 28	28 19	14 23
22 27	5 0	10 19	4 4	9 15	29 2	15 10
22 31	6 0	11 44	5 15	10 2	29 45	15 57
22 35	7 0	13 7	6 23	10 48	0 ♌ 27	16 44
22 39	8 0	14 31	7 30	11 33	1 9	17 31
22 42	9 0	15 55	8 39	12 19	1 51	18 18
22 46	10 0	17 18	9 47	13 4	2 33	19 5
22 50	11 0	18 41	10 53	13 47	3 15	19 52
22 54	12 0	20 1	11 58	14 31	3 56	20 38
22 57	13 0	21 23	13 1	15 16	4 38	21 24
23 1	14 0	22 42	14 2	15 59	5 18	22 10
23 5	15 0	24 3	15 3	16 43	6 0	22 57
23 8	16 0	25 23	16 4	17 26	6 41	23 43
23 12	17 0	26 40	17 3	18 8	7 22	24 29
23 16	18 0	27 58	18 2	18 50	8 3	25 16
23 20	19 0	29 17	19 1	19 32	8 44	26 2
23 23	20 0	0 ♉ 33	19 50	20 14	9 25	26 48
23 27	21 0	1 49	20 54	20 55	10 5	27 35
23 31	22 0	3 7	21 50	21 37	10 46	28 22
23 34	23 0	4 22	22 44	22 18	11 26	29 7
23 38	24 0	5 36	23 39	22 59	12 6	29 54
23 42	25 0	6 49	24 33	23 40	12 47	0 ♍ 40
23 45	26 0	8 2	25 27	24 21	13 27	1 26
23 49	27 0	9 15	26 20	25 2	14 7	2 13
23 53	28 0	10 27	27 12	25 42	14 47	2 59
23 56	29 0	11 39	28 4	26 22	15 27	3 45
24 0	30 0	12 51	28 55	27 2	16 7	4 21

AN
INTRODUCTION
TO ASTROLOGY.

CHAP. I.

The number of Planets, Signes, Aspects, with their severall Names and Characters.

IN the first place you must know that there are seven Planets, so called and charactered.

Saturne ♄, Jupiter ♃, Mars ♂, Sol ☉, Venus ♀, Mercury ☿, Luna ☽: there is also the *Head of the Dragon*, thus noted ☊; and the *Tayle* ☋. ☊ and ☋ are not Planets but Nodes.

There be also twelve Signes: *Aries* ♈, *Taurus* ♉, *Gemini* ♊, *Cancer* ♋, *Leo* ♌, *Virgo* ♍, *Libra* ♎, *Scorpio* ♏, *Sagittarius* ♐, *Capricornus* ♑, *Aquarius* ♒, *Pisces* ♓: Through these twelve Signes the Planets continually move, and are ever in one or other degree of them. It's necessary you can perfectly distinguish the character of every Planet and Signe, before you proceed to any part of this study; and also the characters of these Aspects that follow, *viz.* ✶ □ △ ☍ ☌.

D   You

You must know, every Signe containes in longitude thirty degrees, and every degree sixty minutes, &c. the beginning is from ♈, and so in order one Signe after another: so the whole Zodiack containes 360. degrees, the second degree of ♉ is the the two and thirtieth degree of the Zodiack, the tenth of ♉ is the fortieth, and so in order all throughout the twelve Signes; yet you must ever account the Aspects from that degree of the Zodiack wherein the Planet is, as if ♄ be in ten degrees of ♊, and I would know to what degree of the Ecliptick he casteth his sinister Sextil Aspect; rekoning from ♈ to the tenth degree of ♊, I find ♄ to be in the seventieth degree of the Zodiack, according to his longitude; if I adde fixty degrees more to seventy, they make one hundred and thirty, which answers to the tenth degree of the Signe ♌, to which ♄ casteth his ✶ Aspect, or to any Planet in that degree.

When two Planets are equally distant one from each other, sixty degrees, we say they are in a *Sextill* Aspect, and note it with this character ✶.

When two Planets are ninety degrees distant one from another, wee call that Aspect a *Quartill* Aspect, and write it thus, ☐.

When Planets are one hundred and twenty degrees distant, we say they are in a *Trine* Aspect, and we write it thus △.

When two Planets are one hundred and eighty degrees distant, we call that Aspect an *Opposition*, and character the Aspect thus ☍.

When two Planets are in one and the same degree and minute of any Signe, we say they are in *Conjunction*, and write it thus ☌.

So then if you find ♄ in the first degree of ♈, and ☽ or any other Planet in the first degree of ♊, you shall say they are in a *Sextill* Aspect, for they are distant one from another sixty degrees, and this Aspect is indifferent good.

If ♄ or any other Planet be in the first degree of ♈, and another Planet in the first degree of ♋, you must say they are in a ☐ Aspect, because there is ninety degrees of the Zodiack betwixt them: this Aspect is of emnity and not good.

If ♄ be in the first degree of ♈, and any Planet in the first

degree

An Introduction to Astrologie.

degree of ♌, there being now the distance of an hundred and twenty degrees, they behold each other with a *Trine* Aspect; and this doth denote Unity, Concord and Friendship.

If you find ♄ in the first degree of ♈, and any Planet in the first degree of ♎, they being now an hundred and eighty degrees each from other, are said to be in *Opposition* : A bad Aspect : and you must be mindfull to know what Signes are opposite each to other, for without it you cannot erect the Figure.

When ♄ is in the first degree of ♈, and any Planet is in the same degree, they are then said to to be in *Conjunction* : And this Aspect is good or ill, according to the nature of the question demanded.

Signes Opposite to one an another are

♈ ♉ ♊ ♋ ♌ ♍
♎ ♏ ♐ ♑ ♒ ♓

That is ♈ is opposite to ♎, and ♎ to ♈; ♉ to ♏, ♏ to ♉: and so in order as they stand.

I would have all men well and readily apprehend what precedes, and then they will most easily understand the Ephemeris; which is no other thing, then a Book containing the true places of the Planets, in degrees and minutes, in every of the twelve Signes both in longitude and latitude, every day of the yeer at noon, and every hour of the day, by correction and equation. *Ephemeris what, and it use.*

I have inserted an Ephemeris of the moneth of *January* 1646 and after it a Table of Houses for the latitude of 52. degrees, which will serve in a manner, all the Kingdome of *England* on this side *Newark* upon *Trent*, without sensible errour ; and this I have done of purpose to teach by them, the use of an Ephemeris, and the manner and meanes of erecting a Figure of Heaven, without which nothing can be knowne or made use of in Astrology.

Chap. II.
Of the use of the Ephemeris.

THe first line on the left-hand page, tels you, *January* hath 31. dayes.

In the second line you find, The daily motions of the Planets and the Dragons head.

In the third line and over the character of ♄ you have M. D. M. signifying *Meridionall*, D. *Descending*; that is, ♄ hath Meridionall latitude, and is Descending.

In the next column you find M. D. and underneath ♃; that is, *Jupiter* hath South or Meridionall latitude, and is descending.

In the third column you find M. A. and under those letters ♂; that is, ♂ hath Meridionall latitude, and is ascending.

The ☉ hath never any latitude.

In the next column to the ☉ you find ♀ and then ☿, with the title of their latitude: Now if over any of the Planets you find S. A. or D. it tels you that Planet hath *Septentrionall* or North latitude, and is either ascending or descending, as the letters A. or D. do manifest.

In the fourth line you see ♄ ♃ ♂ ☉ ♀ ☿ ☽ ☊; now you must observe ever, the ☋ is in the opposite Signe and degree to the ☊, though he is never placed in the Ephemeris.

In the fifth line you have ♈ ♊ ♑ ♑ ♓ ♒ ♏ ♌: Over ♈ you have ♄, that is to acquaint you, that ♄ is in the Signe of ♈: Over ♊ you have ♃, *viz.* ♃ is in the Signe of ♊: And so over ♑ stands ♂: And so of all the rest one after another.

In the sixt line you have the figure 1. telling of you it's the first day of *January*, and so underneath it to the lower end, you have the day of the moneth.

Next to the Figure *one*, you have the letter A, which is the letter of the day of the week; and if you run downe under that column, you see the great letter to be D, which is the Sunday or Dominicall letter of the yeer 1646.

Over against the first day of *January* under the character of ♄ you find 27. 48. over those figures you see ♈; the meaning is, ♄ is the first day of *January* in 27. degrees and 48. minutes of ♈: now you must observe, sixty minutes make one degree, and that when any Planet hath passed thirty degrees in a Signe, he goeth orderly into the next; as out of ♈ into ♉, out of ♉ into ♊, &c.

In

An Introduction to Astrologie. 29

In the fourth column, over against the first of the moneth, you find 28 R 12, over them ♊, and over it ♃; that is, ♃ the first of *January* is in 28 degrees of ♊ and 12 minutes: The letter R. tels you that he is Retrograde; had you found Di. or D. it had told you he was then come to be Direct in motion. Of all these termes hereafter by themselves.

In the fifth column you find 10 5, over those figures ♑ ♂, viz. ♂ is the first of *January* in the tenth degree and five minutes of ♑.

And so by this order you find the ☉ to be in 21 degrees, and 34 minutes of ♑; and ♀ in 5 degr. 7 min. of ♓; ☿ in 5 degr. and 29 min. of ♒; the ☽ in 21 23 of ♏; ☊ in 12 deg. and 34 min. of ♌.

So that you see on the left-hand page, there are ten severall columns; the first containing the day of the moneth; the second, the week-day letter; the third, the degree and minutes of ♄; the fourth containes the degrees and minutes ♃ is in; and so every column the like for the rest of the Planets.

Over against the tenth of *January*, under the column of the ☉, you find 0 ♒ 14 minutes, which onely sheweth you the ☉ to be that day at Noon, in 0 degrees and 14 minsutes of ♒, &c.

In the lower end of the left-side page, after the 31 of *January* you find Lat. of Pla. that is, the Latitude of the Planets.

Under the letter C you find 1 10 20.

Under the column of ♄ over against 1, you find 2 3 1; then continuing your eye, you have under ♃ 0 5; under ♂ 0 47; under ♀ 1 13; under ☿ 1 45. The meaning hereof is, that the first day of *January* ♄ hath 2 degr: and 31 min: of latitude; ♃ 0 degr: 5 min: ♂ 0 degr: 47 min: ♀ 1 degr: 13 min: ☿ 1 degr: 45 min: of latitude: To know whether it is North or South, cast your eye to the upper column, and you may see over the character of ♄ stands M. D. that is, Meridionall Descending, or South latitude; where you find S. it tels you the latitune is North; if you find A. the Planet is Ascending in his latitude; if D. then Descending.

D 3 CHAP.

Chap. III.
The right-hand page of the Ephemeris unfolded.

THere are eight columns: the first contains the dayes of the moneth; the fix next containes the manner, quality and name of those Aspects the ☽ hath to the Planets; as also, the hour of the day or night when they perfectly meet in Aspect; the eighth column hath onely those Aspects which ♄ ♃ ♂ ☉ ♀ ☿ make to each other, and the time of the day or night when.

In the fourth line under ♄ you find *Occid.* that is, ♄ is *Occidentall* of the ☉, or sets after him; and so of ♃, or where you find *Occid.* it noteth as much.

Under ♂ you find *Orient.* that is, ♂ is *Orientall*, or riseth before the ☉. And so at any time.

For better understanding the true time when the ☽ comes to the Aspect of any Planet, you are to observe, that all those that write *Ephemerides*, compute the motion of the Planets for the noon time, or just at twelve: And you must know, we and they ever begin our day at Noon, and so reckon 24 hours from the noon of one day to the noon of the next, and after this manner you must reckon in the Aspects. As for example:

Over against the first of *January* 1646. which is Thursday, and under the column appropriate to the ☉, you find ✶ 0. The meaning whereof is, that the ☽ is in ✶ aspect with the ☉ that first day of *January* at noon, or no hours P. M. or *Post Meridiem*.

Over against Friday the second of *Ianuary*, you find under the column of ♀ □ 6. and on the right hand over against the same day, under ☿ ✶ 9. which is no more then this, *viz.* the second of *Ianuary* at six a clock after noon, the ☽ comes to the □ or Quartill aspect of ♀; and at nine of clock she meets with the ✶ of ☿.

Over against the fixt day of *Ianuary*, being Tuesday, under ♄ you find □ 14. that is, fourteen hours after noon of that day, the ☽ comes to the □ of ♄: now you may easily find, that the fourteenth

An Introduction to Astrologie. 31

teenth hour after noon of Tuesday, is two of clock in the morning on Wednesday.

Againe, under the column of the ☉ you find ☌ 11 48. which is no more but this, the ☽ comes to ☌ with the ☉ at 48 minutes after eleven of clock at night: now you must know the ☽ her ☌ with the ☉ is her change, her next ☐ after ☌ with the ☉ is the first quarter, her ☍ with the ☉ is full ☽, her ☐ after ☍ is her last quarter.

If you nuderstand but this, that thirteen hours is one of clock the day subsequent, fourteen hours two of clock, fifteen hours three of clock in the morning, sixteen is four of clock, seventeen hours is five in the morning, eighteen is six of clock, nineteen hours is seven of clock, twenty hours is eight in the morning, twenty one hours is nine of clock, twenty two hours after noon is ten of clock the next day, twenty three hours is eleven of clock, &c. Now we never say twenty four hours after noon, for then it's just noon, and if we say 00. 00. after noon that is just at noon, or then it's full twelve of clock: Understand this and you cannot erre.

In that column under the Planets mutuall Aspects, over against the third of *January* being Saturday, you find ✶ ♄ ♃ 21 that is ♄ and ♃ are in ✶ aspect 21 hours after noon of the Saturday; and that is, at nine of clock on the Sunday morning following.

Over against the fourth day you find ☽ *Apogæum*, that is, she is then neerest to the earth: over against the eighteenth day in the outmost column you find ☽ *Perigæon*, that is, the ☽ is then most remote from the earth.

Over against the twelfth day, in the same outmost column, you find ☿ *in Elong. Max.* it should be ☿ *in Maxima Elongatione*; or that day ☿ is in his greatest elongation or distance from the ☉.

Over against the sixt of *January*, you find in the outside columne Vc ☉ ♃ SS ♂ ☿; that is, the ☉ and ♃ are in a *Quincunx* aspect that day; now that aspect consisteth of five Signes. or 150 degrees.

SS is a *Semisextil*, and tels you, that day ♂ and ☿ are in *Semisextil* to each other: this aspect consisteth of 30 degrees.

Over

Over against the 25 of *Ianuary*, you find in the outmost column ☐ ♄ ♂ 11, and Q ☉ ♄: The meaning is, that at eleven of clock after noon, ♄ and ♂ are in a Quartill aspect; and Q ☉ ♄ tels you, the ☉ and ♄ have a Quintill aspect to each other that day: A Quintill consists of two Signes twelve degrees, or when Planets are distant 72 degrees from each other: we seldome use more aspects then the ☌ ✶ ☐ △ ☍ : to these of late one KEPLER, a learned man, hath added some new ones, as follow, *viz.*

A Semisextill, charactered SS, consisting of thirty degrees.
A Quintil Q consisting of seventy two degrees.
A Tredecile Td consisting of 108 degrees.
A Biquintill Bq consisting of 144 degrees.
A Quincunx Vc consisting of 150 degrees.

I only acquaint you with these, that finding them any where you may apprehend their meaning.

After those two sides of an Ephemeris, followeth in order, A Table of Houses; for without a present Ephemeris and Table of Houses, it's impossible to instruct you to set a Figure, without which we can give no judgment, or perform any thing in this Art.

The use of the Table of houses.

As there are twelve Signes in the Zodiack, through which the ☉ and all the Planets make their daily motion, so are there as you may see twelve severall great pages; and as ♈ is the first Signe of the Zodiack, so in the first line of the first great page doe you find ☉ in ♈; in the second grand page and first line you find ☉ in ♉; in the third page and first line ☉ in ♊; and so in order according to the succession of Signes one after another through the twelve pages: By help of these Tables we frame a Figure, as I shall now acquaint you.

CHAP

Chap. IV.

How to erect a Figure of Heaven by the Ephemeris and Table of Houses, aforesaid.

IN the first place you are to draw the Figure thus; and to know that those twelve empty spaces are by us called the twelve Houses of Heaven, that square in the middle is to write the day, yeer, and hour of the day when we set a figure: the first house begins ever upon that line where you see the figure 1 placed, the second house where you see the figure of 2 stand, the third house where you see the figure 3, the fourth house begins where you find the figure of 4, the fifth house where you see the figure 5, the sixth house where you see the figure 6, the seventh house where you find the figure 7, the eighth house where you find the figure 8, the ninth house where you find the figure 9, the 10h house where you find the figure 10, the eleventh where you find the figure 11, the twelfth house where you find the figure 12 : what space is contained between the figure one to the figure two, is of the first house, or what Planet you shall find to be in that space, you shall say he is in the first house; yet if he be within five degrees of the Cusp of any house, his vertue shal be assigned to that house to whose Cusp he is neerest, &c. but of this hereafter. The Cusp or very entrance of any house, or first beginning, is upon the line where you see the figures placed ; upon which line you must ever place the Signe and degree of the Zodiack, as you find it in the Table of Houses, as if you

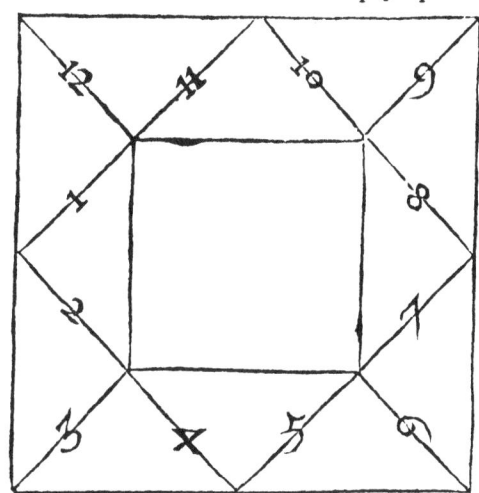

E find

find 10 degrees of ♈ for the tenth houſe, you muſt place the number 10 and Signe of ♈ upon the line of the tenth houſe, and that ſame tenth degree is the Cuſp or beginning of that houſe, and ſo in the reſt.

In erecting or ſetting your Figure, whether of a Queſtion or Nativity, you are to conſider theſe three things.

Firſt, the yeer, moneth, day of the week, houre or part of the houre of that day.

Secondly, to obſerve in the Ephemeris of that yeer and day the true place of the ☉ in Signe, degree and minute at noon.

Thirdly, what hours and minutes in the Table of Houſes doe anſwer or ſtand on the left hand againſt the degree of that Signe the ☉ is in the day of the Queſtion; for by adding the hour of the day, and hours and minutes anſwering to the place of the ☉, your Figure is made, and this Signe where the ☉ is you muſt alwayes look for in that great column under the title of the tenth houſe, where you find the ☉ and that Signe together; as if upon any day of the yeer when I ſet my Figure, the ☉ is in ♈, then the firſt great page or ſide ſerveth, for there you find ☉ in ♈; if the ☉ be in ♉, then the ſecond page ſerveth, and ſo in order: and as in the uppermoſt line you find ☉ in ♈ ♉ ♊, &c. ſo underneath thoſe characters, and under the tenth houſe, you ſee 0 1 2 3 4 5 6, and ſo all along to 30 degrees; ſo that let the ☉ be in what degree he will, you have it exactly to degrees in the ſecond leſſe column, under the title of the tenth houſe; if any minutes adhere to the place of the ☉ as alwayes there doth, if thoſe minutes exceeds thirty, take the hours and minutes adhering to the next greater degree the ☉ is in; if leſſe minutes then thirty belong to the ☉, take the ſame you find him with, for you muſt know it breeds no error in an Horary Queſtion.

Example by one Figure following. I would erect a Figure of Heaven the ſixt of *January*, being Tueſday, 1646. one hour thirty minutes afternoon, or *P. M.* that is, *Poſt Meridiem*: Firſt, I look in the Ephemeris over againſt the ſixth of *January*, for the true place of the ☉ and I find it to be 26 39 ♑; then I look in the Table of Houſes untill I find ☉ in ♑, which I doe in the tenth great page, and under the number 10, which ſignifieth the tenth houſe, I find

♑ 1

♑; I enter with the degree of the ☉ which being 26 39 I look for 27, and on the left hand against it, I find 19 h 56 m; in the head of the Table over them H. M. signifying Houres and Minutes: These hours and minutes *viz.* 19,56, I adde to the time of day in my Question, *viz.* 1, 30 (and so I

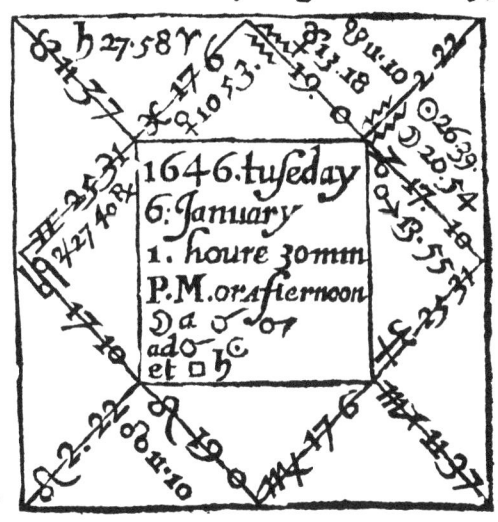

figure: astrological chart dated 1646, tuesday 6: January, 1. houre 30 mm P.M. or Afternoon

must alwayes in every Question adde both numbers together, and if they make more then 24 hours, I must cast away 24 hours, and enter the Table of Houses, under the title of time from noon, seeking for the remainder, or the neerest number to it, and on the right hand over against it, under the severall columns, you shall have the Cusps of the tenth, eleventh, twelfth, first, second, third, fourth houses: but to my former purpose: I add 19,56 to 1,30 and they produce 21 hours, 26 minutes; which number I seek for in that column, entituled *Time from noon*, or Hours, minutes, and which number I find precisely in the eleventh great page, under the ☉ in ♒; and over against 21,26 on the right hand under the column of the tenth house, I find 19, *Tenth house.* and over its head upward, the Signe of ♒, so then I put the 19 degree of ♒ upon the Cusp of the tenth house.

In the third column, over against 21,26 I find 17,6, over it *Eleventh* the Signe of ♓, above ♓ the number 11, which appoints you *house.* 17 degrees, and 6 minutes of ♓ for the Cuspe of the eleventh house.

In the 4th column you find over against the former number *Twelft* 11,37, over that the character ♉, at the upper end 12, which tels *house.* you, that 11,37 degrees of ♉ must be placed on the Cusp of the twelfth house.   E 2   In

First house.   In the fifth column over against the former number, you have 25 31, over it ♊, over ♊ 1 House, and directs you to place the 25 degrees and 31 minutes of ♊ upon the line or Cusp of the first house.

Second house.   In the sixth column you find 17 10, over that ♋, 2 House, which tels you 17 10 degrees of the Signe ♋ must be placed on the Cusp or line of the second house.

Third house.   In the seventh little column over against the former number you have 2 22, over it the Signe ♌, and in the upper line 3 House ; so you are directed to put the 2 deg.and 22 minutes of ♌ upon the Cusp of the third house.

Having now perfected the tenth, eleventh, twelfth, first, second and third House, I must direct you how to performe the rest.

You must for understanding hereof know, that the first six Signes of the Zodiack are opposite to the six last, as formerly I told you.

       ♈   ♉   ♊   ♋   ♌   ♍
       ♎   ♏   ♐   ♑   ♒   ♓

Viz. ♈ is opposite to ♎, and ♎ to ♈ ; ♉ to ♏, and ♏ to ♉, and so all the rest in order.

The twelve Houses also are opposite each to other : as thus

     10   11   12   1   2   3
     4   5   6   7   8   9

So that the tenth house is opposite to the fourth, the fourth to the tenth ; the eleventh to the fifth, the fifth to the eleventh, and so all the rest as you find placed : The use you are to make of it is this, That if on the Cusp of the tenth house you find the Signe ♈, then must you place on the Cusp of the fourth the Signe ♎ ; and look what degree and minute possesseth the Signe of the tenth house, the same degree and minute of the opposite Signe must be placed on the Cusp of the fourth house, and so of all the other Signes and Cusps of houses ; and this is generall, and ever holdeth true ; without which rule observed, you cannot erect the Figure aright.

In our former Figure you see 19 ♒ on the Cusp of the tenth house,

An Introduction to Astrologie. 37

house, ♌ is opposite to ♒, and the fourth house to the tenth; so then I place the 19 degree of ♌ upon the Cuspe of that house.

Upon the line or Cusp of the eleventh house you see ♓ 17 6 ♍ is the Signe opposite to ♓, and the fifth house to the eleventh; so that I place the 17 degree and 6 minutes of ♍ upon the Cusp of the fifth house.

The Cusp of the twelfth house is the 11 37 of ♉, I see ♏ is opposite to ♉, and the sixth house to the twelfth; I therefore put the 11 degree and 37 minutes of ♏ on the Cusp of the sixth house.

I doe so in the rest of the houses, and by this meanes I have framed the twelve houses, and placed the severall Signes of the Zodiack upon the Cusps as they ought to be.

Having finished your twelve Houses by the Method preceding, you must now learne to place the Planets therein; which you must doe by observing in the Ephemeris, the exact place of the Planet in Signe and Degree at noone the day of the Figure, and in what House you shall finde the Sign wherein the Planet is, in that House must you place the Planet, within the House if the Planet be in more Degrees then the Cuspe of the House; without the House, if his Degrees be lesse then those of the Cusp of the Houses.

Over against the sixt day of *January* aforesaid, I finde ♄ to be in 27. 58. of ♈: I look for ♈ in the Figure, but find it not; I find ♓ on the Cuspe of the eleventh, and ♉ on the Cuspe of the twelfth House; so I conclude that the Signe ♈ is intercepted; for so we say when a Signe is not upon any of the Cuspes of Houses, but is included betwixt one House and another: I therefore place ♄ in the 11 House, as you may see.

In the next place I finde the place of ♃ to be 27.45 ♊. I find 25.31. ♊ to be on the Cuspe of the first House, because the Degrees adhering to ♃ are greater then the Cuspe, I place ♃ within the House. And because he is noted Retrograde I place the letter R, the better to informe my judgement.

In the fifth column of the Ephemeris I find ♂ the sixth of *January* to be in the 13. 55. ♑; which Signe in the Figure is the Cusp of the eighth House: I therefore place ♂ as neer the Cusp

E 3

as I can, but his Degrees in the Signe being leſſe then the Cuſpe of the Houſe, I place him without the Houſe.

I finde the ☉ the ſixth day of *Ianuary* to be in 26.39. ♑ whom I place beyond the Cuſpe of the eighth Houſe, becauſe the Degrees of the ☉ in ♑ are more then the Cuſpe of the Houſe.

In the ſame line, and over againſt the ſixt of *Ianuary*, I finde ♀ to be in 10. Degrees, and 53 minuts of ♓.

I finde the Signe of ♓ on the Cuſpe of the eleventh Houſe, and there I put ♀ in the tenth Houſe, neer the Cuſpe of the eleventh Houſe, but not in the Houſe, becauſe the Degrees of the Signe ſhe is in are not equivalent to the Degrees of the Cuſpe of the eleventh Houſe, but are ſhort of them.

In the eight Column I finde under the Caracter of ☿ 13.18. above it ♒. I therefore place ☿ neer the Cuſpe of the tenth Houſe, but not in the Houſe; for you may ſee he is neerer in Degrees to the Cuſpe of the tenth Houſe then the ninth; for by how much neerer he is in Degrees to the Cuſpe of any Houſe, having the ſame Signe, by ſo much the neerer he ought to be placed to the Cuſpe of that Houſe.

In the ninth Column, under the Column of the ☽ I finde over againſt the ſixth of *Ianuary* 20. 54. and over the Figures ♑: ſo then I place the ☽ very neer the ☉ in the eighth Houſe, and betwixt the Cuſpe of the Houſe and the ☉; for you may ſee the ☽ hath not ſo many Degrees as may put her beyond the ☉; nor hath ſhe ſo few to be without the eighth Houſe. How to reduce the motion of the ☽ and other Planets to any houre of the day, you ſhall be inſtructed hereafter.

In the tenth column I find over againſt my ſaid day, 11. 10. over againſt it ♌ and ☊: ſo you ſee the ☊ is in 11. deg. 10. min. of ♌; which I place in the middle of the third houſe, becauſe ten degrees are very neare as nigh the Cuſp of the third houſe as fourth; the ☋ being alwayes in the oppoſite Signe and degree to the ☊, I place in the ninth houſe, *viz.* in 11 degrees 10 minutes of ♒; This being done, I muſt obſerve how the ☽ ſeperates and applies the ſame day; I find the ſixt of *Ianuary* on the right-hand page of the Book, that the ☽ did laſt ſeperate from a ☌ of ♂ and now is applying to a ☌ of ☉ at 11 48, that is, at eleven of clock and 48 minutes after at night, then to a □

of

An Introduction to Astrologie. 39

of ♄ at fourteen hours after noon, or at two of clock the next morning.

Thus have you one Figure of Heaven erected, and the Planets therein placed, though not rectified to the hour of the day, for now to reduce their motion to any hour I shall shew hereafter: But because I have by experience found, that many Learners have been much stumbled for want of sufficient directions in former Introductions to set a Scheame of Heaven, I shall be a little more copious, and shew an example or two more.

I would erect a Figure on Saturday the 17 of *Ianuary* 1646. for eleven of clock and twenty after noon: the ☉ that day at noon is in 7 degrees and 52 of ♒: in the eleventh page of the Table of Houses I find ☉ in ♒; under the column of the tenth house I look for the eighth degree of ♒, because 52 minutes want but little of a degree; over against the eighth degree on the left hand, under the title of *Time from noon*, I find 20 42, *viz.* 20 hours 42 minutes; so then I work thus,

         Time of the day is 11 20
                20 42

hours and minutes answering to the eighth degree of ♒, there being 62 min. *viz.* two min. more then one hour, I take that hour and adde both numbers toge- hou. min. ther,   and they make 32 02
From 32 hours and 2 min. I subduct 24 hours, as I must ever doe, if there be more then 24 hours, and then there remaines as you see, 8 hours and   32 02
2 min. which I find not   24 *Subducted.*
precisely in the Table of
Houses, but I find 8 0,   8 2 *Remaines.*
which is neer my number, and which serves very well; over against 8 h and 0 m I find 28 0, and in the upper part I find ♋, and over it the tenth house, so then I have 28 degrees, 0 min. of ♋ for the Cusp of my tenth house: in the same line, on the right hand to this 28 degr. of ♋, you shall find 4 36, over it ♍, in the upper part the eleventh house: so then 4 degr. 36 min. of ♍ are the Cusp of the eleventh house; then have you over against the said number of 8 hours 0 min. in the fourth

column

column, 0 ♎ 4, over its head the twelfth houſe, this tels you the Cuſp of the twelfth houſe is 0 degr. 4 min. of ♎: in the fifth column over againſt the ſaid former number, you have 21 3, over them figures at the top of the page, ♎, and then the firſt houſe; which ſignifies, that you muſt place the 21 deg. and 3 min. of ♎ on the Cuſp of the firſt houſe: adjoyning to the 21 degr. and 3 min. of ♎ in the ſixth column, I find 13 57, over it the Signe ♏, in the upper part the ſecond houſe, by which I know, that 13 degr. and 57 min. of ♏ muſt be placed on the Cuſp of the ſecond houſe. In the ſeventh and utmoſt column over againſt my foreſaid number of 8 hours and 0 min. I find 15 46, over them the Signe ♐, in the upper column over their head the third houſe, pointing out 15 degr. 46 min. of ♐ for the Cuſp of the third houſe; ſo then your Cuſps of houſes ſtand thus:

        Tenth houſe 28 ♋.
        Eleventh houſe 4 36 ♍.
        Twelfth houſe 0 4 ♎.
        Firſt houſe 21 3 ♎.
        Second houſe 13 57 ♏.
        Third houſe 15 46 ♐.

  The Cuſps of the other houſes are found out by the oppoſite Signes and houſes, as I formerly directed, *viz.* the fourth houſe being oppoſite ever to the tenth, and the Signe ♑ to ♋, I place the 28 degr. of ♑ on the Cuſp of the fourth houſe: the fifth is oppoſite to the eleventh, and ♓ is the oppoſite Signe to ♍, I therefore place the 4 degr. 36 min. of ♓ for the Cuſp of the fifth: the twelfth houſe is oppoſite to the ſixth, ſo is ♈ oppoſite to ♎, therefore I place 0 degr. 4 min. of ♈ on the Cuſp of the ſixth houſe: the ſeventh houſe is oppoſite to the firſt houſe, and ♈ to ♎, I therefore place the 21 degr. and 3 min. of ♈, the oppoſite Signe to ♎, on the Cuſp of the ſeventh houſe: the eighth houſe is oppoſite to the ſecond, and ♉ to ♏, I therefore place the 13 degr. and 57 min. of ♉ on the Cuſp of the eighth houſe: the ninth houſe is oppoſite to the third, and ♊ to ♐, I therefore make the 15 degr. and 46 of ♊ the Cuſp of the ninth houſe: The Planets are to be placed in the Figure

An Introduction to Astrologie. 41

gure as formerly directed ; nor let it trouble you, if you find sometimes two Signes in one house, or almost three, or sometimes one Signe to be on the Cusps of three houses, ever place your Planets orderly as neer the degree of the house, as the number of degrees your Planet is in will permit.

You must ever remember that if your hour of the day be in the morning, or as we say *Ante Meridiem*, or before noon, you must reckon the time, as from the noon of the day preceding : As for example.

I would erect a Figure the 26. day of *Ianuary* 1646. being Munday, for 9. of the clock and 45 min. before noon.

My time stands thus : 9 ^{ho}. 45 ^{min}.

To this I adde 12. houres, because it is properly in our account, the 21. houre and 45 minuts after noon of the Sunday preceding : so then you may say thus ; the Figure is set for 9. hours and 45. minutes *ante meridiem*, or before noon of the Monday.

Or else 25. of *January*, being Sunday, 21 hours and 45 min. *post meridiem*, or after noon, which is all one with the former time.

I find the ☉ at noon the same 26 day, to be in 16 degr. and 59 min. of ♒; I look in the Table of Houses what hours and min. correspond to the 17 degrees of ♒ in the tenth house ; in the eleventh page I find the Signe ♒, and along in the column of the tenth 17 degr. 0 min. on the left hand I find over against them, 21 hours 18 min. to these I add the hours and min. of the day, *viz.* 21 45 ; added together, they make   43^h 03^m from which in regard they are more then 24 hours, I substract 24.

                                   43   03
                                   24
                 Rests   19   03

With my 19 hours and 3 min. I enter the Table of Houses, and under the title of hours and minutes, or Time from noon, I seek my number, In the tenth page I find 19 hours and 1 min. which is the next number unto my desire, over against it I see 14 0, and in the upper part ♑ and tenth house, signifying the 14 degr. of the Signe ♑ is to be placed on the Cusp of the tenth house, the rest of the houses are found out in order as they stand in the Table of Houses over against my number of 19 hours and 1 min. I hope these examples will be sufficient for all young Learners; but that they may presently consider whether they have set their Figure right yea or no, let them take this general rule, that if the Figure be erected from noon to Sun set, the ☉ will be in the ninth, eighth or seventh house; if it be erected from Sun set till midnight, he shall find the ☉ in the sixt, fift or fourth house; if it be set from midnight till ☉ rise, he shall find the ☉ in the third, second or first house; if the Figure be set from ☉ rise till noon, then he shall find the ☉ in the twelfth, elenth or tenth house, &c.

Chap. V.

Of the daily motion of the Planets, and how to reduce their motion to any houre of the day, and to the Meridian of London.

WE have seldome occasion to erect a Scheame of Heaven just at noon, to which time the motions of the Planets are exactly calculated, and need not any rectification; but usually all Questions are made either some hours before, or after noon; therfore it is needfull you know how to take their diurnall or daily motion, or how many degrees or min. they move in 24 hours, that thereby you may have a proportion to adde to the place of your Planets according to the hour of the day or night when you set your Figure: And although in horary Questions, it occasioneth no error (except in the motion of the ☽) yet I thought fit to instruct the Learner herewith, that so he may know how to doe his work handsomely. *Example.*

You must set downe the place of your Planet in Signe, degree and minute as you find him at noon; and if your Planet be direct, you must substract him in degree and minute from the place he is in the day subsequent: but when a Planet is retrograd, you must doe the contrary, *viz.* substract the motion of your Planet the day subsequent from the day going before.

Example:

An Introduction to Astrologie. 43
Example:

January 7. at noon, ♄ is 28 0 ♈   *Daily motion is 2. min.*
January 6. at noon, ♄ is 27 58

Here you see the daily motion of ♄ is onely two minutes.

Jan. 6. ♃ R 27 40 ♊   *Daily motion is 6. min.*
Jan. 7. ♃   27 34

Ian. 7. ♂ is in 14 41 ♑
Ian. 6. ♂ is in 13 55
              46

So the diurnall motion of ♂ is 46. min.

Ian. 7. ☉ is in 27 40 ♑
Ian. 6. ☉ is in 26 39
           1 01

The daily motion of the ☉ is one derg. and one min.

Ian. 7. ♀ is in 12 2 ♓
Ian. 6. ♀ is in 10 53
           1 9

The daily motion of ♀ is 1. degr. and 9. min.

Jan. 7. ☿ is in 14 45 ♒
Jan. 6. ☿ is in 13 18
           1 27

So the diurnall motion of ☿ is 1. degr. 27. min.

Jan. 7. ☽ is in 3 1 ♒
Jan. 6. ☽ is in 20 54 ♑

Substract 20. degr. 54. min of ♑ from 30. degr. the complement of a Signe, and there rest 9. degr. 6. min. which added to 3. degr. 1. min. of ♒, make the diurnall motion of the ☽ to be 12 degr. and 7. min. The work had been easier, but that the ☽ was removed into another Signe before the day subsequent at noon.

F 2   *Jan.*

Ian. 6. ☊ is in 11 10 ♌
Ian. 7. ☊ is in 10 24
───────
46

The motion of the ☊ is 46. min. whom you must carefully observe, for he sometimes moves forward in the Signe, sometimes backward, which you may easily perceive by the Ephemeris, without further instruction.

How to find the quantity of the hourly motion of any Planet by the Table following.

IN every Figure you set, the place of the Planets ought to be rectified to the hour of the setting the Figure, especially the place of the ☽, because of her swift motion; in the Planets you need not be scrupulous, but take whole degrees without sensible error, or indeed any at all: this I meane in Questions; but in Nativities, you are to have the places of them exactly to degrees and minutes; and above all, the motion of the Sun to minutes and seconds, because by his motion we set the yeerly revolutions of Nativities.

I shall onely deliver the practice of two or three Examples, and leave the rest to the diligence of every Learner. The Table followeth.

Deg.

An Introduction to Astrologie. 45

de.	mi	sec	th.
mi	sec	th.	4ʰ
1	0	2	30
2	0	5	0
3	0	7	30
4	0	10	0
5	0	12	30
6	0	15	0
7	0	17	30
8	0	20	0
9	0	22	30
10	0	25	0
11	0	27	30
12	0	30	0
13	0	32	30
14	0	35	0
15	0	37	30
16	0	40	0
17	0	42	30
18	0	45	0
19	0	47	30
20	0	50	0
21	0	52	30

de.	mi	sec	th.
mi	sec	th.	4ʰ
22	0	55	0
23	0	57	30
24	1	0	0
25	1	2	30
26	1	5	0
27	1	7	30
28	1	10	0
29	1	12	30
30	1	15	0
31	1	17	30
32	1	20	0
33	1	22	30
34	1	25	0
35	1	27	30
36	1	30	0
37	1	32	30
38	1	35	0
39	1	37	30
40	1	40	0
41	1	42	30
42	1	45	0

de.	mi	sec	th.
mi	sec	th.	4ʰ
43	1	47	30
44	1	50	0
45	1	52	30
46	1	55	0
47	1	57	30
48	2	0	0
49	2	2	30
50	2	5	0
51	2	7	30
52	2	10	0
53	2	12	30
54	2	15	0
55	2	17	30
56	2	20	0
57	2	22	30
58	2	25	0
59	2	27	30
60	2	30	0
61	2	32	30

In the preceding Scheam of the sixt of *Ian.* you find the diurnall motion of the Sun to be 61 min. or one deg. one min. in the very last line of this Table I find 61, over the head of it *deg. min.* but over against 61 to the right hand, I find 2 32 30, which tels you, that the hourly motion of the Sun is, 2 min. 32 seconds, and thirty thirds, as you may see in the upper part of the column over the heads of the figures.

The daily motion of ♂ is 46 min. in the Figure abovenamed:

F 3

I enter downe the firſt column, and find 46, againſt it I find 1 min. 55 ſeconds to be one hours motion of ♂, when in 24 hours he moves 46 min.

You muſt note, if you enter with minutes, you muſt have minutes, if with ſeconds, ſeconds; and ſo in the reſt: This in the motion of ♄ ♃ ♂ ☉ ♀ ☿; with the ☽ otherwayes.

If the motion of your Planet be above 61 min. *viz.* 70 or 75 or 80 min. then enter the Table twice: as for example.

The motion of ☿ is, as you perceive, 1 degr. and 27 min. I would know what his hourly motion is, I enter firſt with 60 min. againſt which I find 2 30, *viz.* 2 min. 30 ſeconds, then I enter with 27, againſt which I find 1 7 30, *viz.* 1 min. 7 ſeconds, thirty thirds, which I caſt away, and adde the two former ſummes together thus,   2   30
   1   7
  ―――――
   3   37

added together they make 3 min. 37 ſeconds, and ſo much is the hourly motion of ☿, when his diurnall motion is 87 minutes.

The daily motion of the ☽ you ſee is 12 degr. and 7 min.

I enter downe the firſt column with 12, againſt it I find 0 30 0, *viz.* 0 degr. 30 min. 0 ſeconds.

I enter with 7, over againſt it I find   0 17 30
I adde the number to it   30   0   0

they produce 30 min. 17 ſeconds, and 30 thirds for the hourly motion of the ☽ in our figure: you may in her operation reject the ſeconds and thirds.

By this rule I would know where the true place of the ☉ is at that hour when we erected the Figure.

The hour of the day is 1 30, the time admitted by *Eichſtadius* for reducing his Ephemeris to the *Meridian of London*, is 50 min. of an hour in motion, for they being more Eaſt then we, the ☉ comes ſooner to them at their noon, then to us that are more Weſt-ward, by ſo much time: I adde 50 min. to my former time, *viz.* 1 30, the whole is then 2 hours 20 min. now if the motion of the ☉ in one hour be   2 min. 32 ſeconds,
then in two hours it will be   ―2 min. 32 ſeconds more:
         added together they are   5 min. 4 ſeconds:
                                                                              Which

An Introduction to Astrologie. 47

Which being added to the place of the ☉ at noon, make the true place of the ☉ at time of erection of the Figure, 26 deg 44 min. and 4 sec. of ♑; there is 20 min. of one hour more but because they produce nothing of consequence, I omit further trouble herein.

The place of the ☽ the same day at noon is 20 54 ♑; if you adde her motion in two hours, you shall see it will be twice 30 min. viz. one whole degr. and then her true place will be 21 54 ♑.

We that set many Figures, never care for this exactnesse, but use this generall rule; In the motion of the ☉ ♀ and ☿, if the Figure be set six or seven hours after noon, we adde about 15 min. to their places at noon, and so allowing for every six hours 15 min. motion.

Because the ☽ goeth 12, 13 or 14 degr. in on day, we constantly adde to her place at noon 3 degr. for every six hours, and some min. over; doe so with the other Planets according to their diurne motion: He that would doe them more exact, may work them by multiplication and division, or procure some old Ephemeris, wherein there is usually large proportionall Tables concerning this businesse.

Now as I have acquainted you, that in motion of the Planets you must in a Nativity or Question, if you please, allow the Planets so much to be added unto their place at noon as can be got in 50 min. of an hour, so you must obseve the contrary in the Aspects: As for example: The sixt of *Ianuary* you find ☽ in □ ♄ 14 P.M. viz. the ☽ comes to the □ aspect of ♄ at 14 hours after the noon of the sixt day of *Ianuary*, or at two of the clock the next morning on the seventh day: now you must subduct 50 min. of an hour from 14 hours, and then the true time of the ☽ her perfect □ to ♄ with us at *London*, is at 13 hours and 10 min. after noon: doe so in all the Aspects &c.

CHAP. VI.
Of the twelve Houses of Heaven, and some Names or Termes of Astrologie.

THe whole Spheare of Heaven is divided into four equall parts by the *Meridian* and *Horizon*, and againe into four
Quadrants,

Quadrants, and every Quadrant againe into three parts, according to other Circles drawne by points of Sections of the aforesaid Meridian and Horizon; so the whole Heaven is divided into twelve equall parts, which the Astrologers call Houses or Mansions, taking their beginning from the East.

The first Quadrant is described from the East to the Midheaven, or from the line of the first house to the line of the tenth house, and contains the twelfth, eleventh and tenth houses, it's called the *Orientall, Vernall, Masculine, Sanguine, Infant quarter.*

The second Quadrant is from the Cusp of the Mid-heaven to the Cusp of the seventh house, containg the ninth, eighth and seventh houses, and is called the *Meridian, Estivall, Feminine, Youthfull, Cholerick quarter.*

The third Quadrant is from the Cusp of the seventh house to the Cusp of the fourth house, and containes the sixth, fifth and fourth houses, is called *Occidentall, Autumnall, Masculine, Melancholique, Manhood, cold and dry.*

The fourth Quadrant is from the Cusp of the fourth to the Cusp of the first house, and containes the third, second and first house, is *Northerne, Feminine Old age, of the nature of Winter, Phlegmatique.*

The first, tenth, seventh and fourth houses hereof are called *Angles*, the eleventh, second, eight and fift are called *Succedants*, the third, twelfth, ninth and sixth, are tearmed *Cadents*: the Angles are most powerfull, the Succedants are next in vertue, the Cadents poore, and of little efficacy: the Succedant houses follow the Angles, the Cadents come next the Succedants; in force and vertue they stand so in order:

1 10 7 4 11 5 9 3 2 8 6 12

The meaning whereof is this, that two Planets equally dignified, the one in the Ascendant, the other in the tenth house, you shall judge the Planet in the Ascendant somewhat of more power to effect what he is Significator of, then he that is in the tenth: doe so in the rest as they stand in order, remembring that Planets in Angles doe more forcibly shew their effects.

When we name the Lord of the Ascendant, or Significator of

An Introduction to Astrologie.

of the Querent, or thing quesited ; we meane no other thing then that Planet who is Lord of that Signe which afcends, or Lord of that Signe from which houfe the thing demanded is required ; as if from the feventh houfe, the Lord of that Signe defcending on the Cufp is Significator, and fo in the reft : but of this in the enfuing Judgments.

Cofignificator is when you find another Planet in afpect or conjunction with that Planet who is the principall Significator ; this faid Planet fhall have fignification more or leffe, and either affift or not in effecting the thing defired, and fo hath fomething to doe in the Judgment, and ought to be confidered : if a friendly Planet, he notes good ; if an infortune the contrary, *viz.* either the deftruction of the thing, or difturbance in it.

Almuten, of any houfe is that Planet who hath moft dignities in the Signe afcending or defcending upon the Cufp of any houfe, whereon or from whence you require your judgment.

Almuten of a Figure, is that Planet who in Effentiall and Accidentall dignities, is moft powerfull in the whole Scheame of Heaven.

The Dragons Head we fometimes call   *Anabibazon*.
The Dragons Taile   *Catabibazon*.

The Longitude of a Planet is his diftance from the beginning of *Aries*, numbred according to the fucceffion of Signes, unto the place of the Planet.

Latitude is the diftance of a Planet from the Ecliptick, either towards the North or South, by which means we come to fay, a Planet hath either Septentrionall or Meridionall Latitude, when either he recedes from the Ecliptick towards the North or South.

Onely the Sun continually moveth in the Ecliptick, and never hath any latitude.

Declination of a Planet is his diftance from the Æquator, and as he declines from thence either Northward or Southward, fo is his declination nominated either North or South.

Chap. VII.
Of the twelve Houses, their Nature and signification.

AS before we have said there are twelve Signes, and also twelve Houses of Heaven, so now we are come to relate the nature of these twelve Houses; the exact knowledge whereof is so requisite, that he who shall learne the nature of the Planets and Signes without exact judgment of the Houses, is like an improvident man, that furnisheth himselfe with variety of Housholdstuffe, having no place wherein to bestow them.

There is nothing appertaining to the life of man in this world, which in one way or other hath not relation to one of the twelve Houses of Heaven, and as the twelve Signes are appropriate to the particular members of mans body; so also doe the twelve houses represent not onely the severall parts of man, but his actions, quality of life and living, and the curiosity and judgment of our Fore-fathers in Astrology, was such, as they have alotted to every house a particular signification, and so distinguished humane accidents throughout the whole twelve houses, as he that understands the Questions appertaining to each of them, shal not want sufficient grounds wheron to judge or give a rationall answer upon any contingent accident, and successe thereof.

Of the first House and its signification.

The first house, which containeth all that part of Heaven from the line where the figure one standeth, untill the figure two, where the second house beginneth.

It hath signification of the life of man, of the stature, colour, complexion, forme and shape of him that propounds the Question, or is borne; in Eclipses and great Conjunctions, and upon the ☉ his annuall ingresse into ♈; it signifieth the common people, or generall State of that Kingdome where the Figure is erected.

And as it is the first house, it represents the head and face of man, so that if either ♄ ♂ or ☋ be in this house, either at the time of a Question, or at the time of birth, you shall observe some

An Introduction to Astrlogie.

some blemish in the face, or in that member appropriate to the Signe that then is upon the cusp of the house; as if ♈ be in the Ascendant, the mark, mole, or scarre is without faile in the head or face; and if few degrees of the Signe ascend, the mark is in the upper part of the head; if the middle of the Sign be on the cusp, the mole, mark or sear is in the middle of the face, or neer it; if the later degrees ascend, the face is blemished neer the chin, towards the neck: This I have found true in hundreds of examples.

Of colours, it hath the White; that is, if a Planet be in this house that hath signification of white, the complexion of the Party is more pale, white or wan; or if you enquire after the colour of the cloaths of any man, if his significator be in the first house, and in a Signe corresponding, the parties apparell is white or gray, or somewhat neer that colour, so also if the Question be for Cattle, when their Significators are found in this house, it denotes them to be of that colour or neer it: The house is Masculine.

The Consignificators of this house are ♈ and ♄; for as this house is the first house, so is ♈ the first Signe, and ♄ the first of the Planets, and therfore when ♄ is but moderately well fortified, in this house, and in any benevolent aspect of ♃ ♀ ☉ or ☽, it promiseth a good sober constitution of body, and usually long life: ☿ doth also joy in this house, because it represents the Head, and he the Tongue, Fancy and Memory: when he is well dignified and posited in this house, he produceth good *Orators*: it is called the Ascendant, because when the ☉ commeth to the cusp of this house, he ascends, or then ariseth, and is visible in our Horizon.

Questions concerning the second Houses.

From this house is required judgment concerning the estate or fortune of him that asks the Question, of his Wealth or Poverty, of all moveable Goods, Money lent, of Profit or gaine, losse or damage; in suits of Law, it signifies a mans Friends or Assistants; in private Duels, the Querents second; in an Eclips or great Conjunction, the Poverty or Wealth of the people: in the ☉ his entrance into ♈, it reprefents the Ammunition, Allies and fupport the Common-wealth fhall have; it imports their Magazines.

It reprefents in man the neck, and hinder part of it towards the fhoulders, of colours the green.

So that if one make demand concerning any thing fpecified above in this houfe, you muft look for fignification from hence: It's a Feminine houfe and Succedant, called in fome Latin Authors *Anaphora*.

It hath Confignificators ♃ and ♉; for if ♃ be placed in this houfe, or be Lord hereof, it's an argument of an eftate or fortune; ☉ and ♂ are never well placed in this houfe, either of them fhew difperfion of fubftance, according to the capacity and quality of him that is either borne or asks the queftions.

The third Houfe

Hath fignification of Brethren, Sifters, Cozens or Kindred, Neighbours, fmall Journeys, or inland-Journeys, oft removing from one place to another, Epiftles, Letters, Rumours, Meffengers: It doth rule the Shoulders, Armes, Hands and Fingers.

Of Colours, it governeth the Red and Yellow, or Croceall, or Sorrell colour: It hath Confignificators, of the Signes ♊, of the Planets ♂; which is one reafon why ♂ in this houfe, unleffe joyned with ♄ is not very unfortunate, it is a Cadent houfe, and is the joy of the ☽; for if fhe be pofited therein, efpecially in a moueable Signe, it's an argument of much travell, trotting and trudging, or of being feldome quiet: The houfe is Mafculine.

The fourth Houfe

Giveth Judgment of Fathers in general, and ever of his Father that enquires, or that is borne; of Lands, Houfes, Tenements, Inheritances, Tillage of the earth, Treafures hidden, the determination or end of any thing; Townes, Cities or Caftles, befieged or not befieged; all ancient Dwellings, Gardens, Fields, Paftures, Orchards; the quality and nature of the

ground

An Introduction to Astrologie.

grounds one purchaseth, whether Vineyards, Cornfields, &c. whether the ground be Wooddy, Stony or barren.

The Signe of the fourth denoteth the Town, the Lord thereof, the Governour: It ruleth the Brest, Lungs.

Of Colours, the Red: It's Consignificator is ♋, and of Planets the ☉; we call it the Angle of the Earth, or *Imum Cœli*; it is Feminine, and the North Angle: In Nativities or Questions, this fourth house reseprefents Fathers, so doth the ☉ by day and ♄ by night; yet if the ☉ be herein placed, he is not ill, but rather shewes the Father to be of a noble disposition, &c.

The fifth House

By this house we judge of Children, of Embassadours, of the state of a Woman with child, of Banquets, of Ale-houses, Tavernes, Playes, Messengers or Agents for Republicks; of the Wealth of the Father, the Ammunition of a Towne besieged; if the Woman with child shall bring forth man or woman; of the health or sicknesse of his Son or Daughter that asks the Question.

It ruleth the Stomack, Liver, Heart, Sides and Back, and is masculine.

Of Colours, Black and White, or Honey-colour, and is a Succedant house: it's Consignificators are ♌ and ♀, who doth joy in this house, in regard it's the house of Pleasure, Delight and Meriment; it's wholly unfortunate by ♂ or ♄, and they therein shew disobedient children and untoward.

The sixth House.

It concerneth Men and Maid-servants, Gallislaves, Hogges, Sheep, Goats, Hares, Connies, all manner of lesser Cattle, and profit or losse got thereby; Sicknesse, its quality and cause, principal humor offending, curable or not curable, whether the disease be short or long; Day-Labourers, Tenants, Farmers, Shepherds, Hogheards, Neatherds, Warriners; and it signifieth Unkles, or the Fathers Brothers and Sisters.

It ruleth the inferiour part of the Belly, and intestines even to to the Arſe: this houſe is a Feminine and Cadent houſe, unfortunate, as having no aſpect to the Aſcendant.

Of Colours, black colour, ♂ rejoyceth in this houſe, but his Conſignificator is of the Signes ♍, of Planets ☿; we uſually find that ♂ and ♀ in Conjunction in this houſe, are arguments of a good Phyſitian.

The ſeventh Houſe.

It giveth judgement of Marriage, and deſcribes the perſon inquired after, whether it be Man or Woman, all manner of Love queſtions, our publique enemies; the Defendant in a Lawſuit, in Warre the oppoſing party; all Quarrels, Duels, Lawſuits; in Aſtrology the Artiſt himſelfe; in Phyſicke the Phyſitian; Theeves and Thefts; the perſon ſtealing, whether Man or Woman, Wives, Sweethearts; their ſhape, deſcription, condition, Nobly or ignobly borne: in an Annuall ingreſſe, whether Warre or Peace may be expected: of Victory, who over-comes, and who worſted; Fugitives or run-awayes; Baniſhed and Out-lawed-men.

It hath conſignificator ♎ and ☾, ♄ or ♂ unfortunate herein, ſhew ill in Marriage.

Of colour, a darke Blacke colour.

It ruleth the Haunches, and the Navill to the Buttocks; and is called the Angle of the Weſt: and is Maſculine.

The eighth Houſe.

The Eſtate of Men deceaſed, Death, its quality and nature; the Wils, Legacies and Teſtaments of Men deceaſed; Dowry of the Wife, Portion of the Maid, whether much or little, eaſie to be obtained or with difficulty. In Duels it repreſents the Adverſaries Second; in Lawſuits the Defendants friends. What kinde of Death a Man ſhall dye. it ſignifies feare and anguiſh of Minde. Who ſhall enjoy or be heire to the Deceaſed.

It rules the Privy-parts. Of colours, the Green and Black.

Of Signes it hath ♏ for conſignificator, and ♄, the Hemoroids, the Stone, Strangury, Poyſons. and Bladder are ruled

by

An Introduction to Astrologie.

by this House; and is a succedant House, and Feminine.

The ninth House.

By this House we give judgement of Voyages or long journies beyond Seas of Religious men, or Clergy of any kinde, whether Bishops or inferiour Ministers; Dreames, Visions, forraigne Countries, of Books, Learning, Church Livings, or Benefices, Advowsions; of the kindred of ones Wife, *& sic è contrario.*

Of colours it hath the Greene and White.

Of mans body it ruleth the Fundament, the Hippes and Thighes, ♐ and ♃ are consignificators of this House; for if ♃ be herein placed, it naturally signifies a devout man in his Religion, or one modesly given; I have oft observed when the Dragons tayle, or ♂ or ♄ have been infortunately placed in this House; the Querent hath either been little better then an Atheist or a desperate Sectarist: the ☉ rejoyceth to be in this House, which is Masculine, and Cadent.

The tenth House.

Commonly it personateth Kings, Princes, Dukes, Earles, Judges, prime Officers, Commanders in chiefe, whether in Armies or Townes; all sorts of Magistracy and Officers in Authority, Mothers, Honour, Preferment, Dignity, Office, Lawyers; the profession or Trade any one useth; it signifies Kingdomes, Empires, Dukedomes, Counties.

It hath of colours Red and White, and ruleth the Knees and Hammes.

Its called the *Medium Cœli*, or Mid-heaven, and is Feminine. Its consignificators are ♑ and ♂; either ♃ or the ☉ doe much Fortunate this House when they are posited therein, ♄ or ☋ usually deny honour, as to persons of quality, or but little esteeme in the world to a vulgar person, not much joy in his Profession, Trade or Mystery, if a Mechanick.

The

The eleventh House.

It doth naturally represent Friends and Friendship, Hope, Trust, Confidence, the Praise, or Dispraise of any one; the Fidelity or falseness of Friends; as to Kings it personates their Favourites, Councellours, Servants, their Associates or Allyes, their Money, Exchequer or Treasure; in Warre their Amunition and Souldiery; it represents Courtiers, &c. in a Common-wealth governed by a few of the Nobles and Commons, it personates their assistance in Councell: as in *London* the tenth House represents the Lords Major; the eleventh the Common-Councell; the Ascendant the generality of the Commoners of the said City.

Of members it ruleth the Legs to the Ancles.

Of colours, it ruleth the Saffron or Yellow.

It hath of the Signes ♒, and ☉ of the Planets, for consignificators ♃ doth especially rejoyce in this House; its a succedant House, and masculine, and in vertue is equivalent either to the seventh or fourth Houses.

The Twelfth House.

It hath signification of private Enemies, of Witches, great Cattle, as Horses, Oxen, Elephants, &c. Sorrow, Tribulation, Imprisonments, all manner of affliction, self-undoing, &c. and of such men as maliciously undermine their neighbours, or informe secretly against them.

It hath consignificators ♓ and ♀; *Saturne* doth much joy in that House, For naturally *Saturne* is author of mischiefe; and it ruleth in Mans body the Feet.

In colour it presents the Green.

Its a Cadent House, Feminine, and vulgarly sometines called *Cataphora*, as all Cadent Houses may be. This is the true Caracter of the severall Houses, according to the *Ptolomeian* Doctrine, and the experience my selfe have had for some yeers: I must confesse the *Arabians* have made severall other divisions of the Houses, but I could never in my practise finde any verity in them, wherefore I say nothing of them. Of

Chap. VIII.
Of the Planet Saturne, *and his signification.*

HE is called usually *Saturne*, but in some Authors *Chronos*, *Names.*
Phœnon, *Falcifer*.

He is the supreamest or highest of all the Planets; is placed betwixt *Jupiter* and the Firmament, he is not very bright or glorious, or doth he twinckle or sparkle, but is of a Pale, Wan *Colour.* or Leaden, Ashy colour, slow in Motion, finishing his Course through the twelve Signes of the Zodiack in 29 yeers, 157 dayes, or thereabouts; his middle motion is two minutes and *Motion.* one second; his diurnall motion sometimes is three, four, five, or six minutes, or seldome more; his greatest North latitude *Latitude.* from the Eclipstick is two degrees 48 minutes; his South latitude from the Ecliptick is two degrees 49 minutes; and more then this he hath not.

In the Zodiack he hath two of the twelve Signs for his Hou- *Houses.* ses, *viz. Capricorne* ♑ his Night-house, *Aquarius* ♒ his Day-house; he is Exaltation in ♎, he receives his Fall in ♈; he rejoyceth in the Signe *Aquarius.*

He governeth the Aiery Triplicity by day, which is compo- *Triplicity* sed of these Signes, ♊ ♎ ♒; in all the twelve Signes he hath these degrees for his Termes, alotted him by *Ptolomy*. *Terme.*

In ♈, 27 28 29 30.
In ♉, 23 24 25 26.
In ♊, 22 23 24 25.
In ♋, 28 29 30.
In ♌, 1 2 3 4 5 6.
In ♍, 19 20 21 22 23 24.
In ♎, 1 2 3 4 5 6.
In ♏, 28 29 30.
In ♐, 21 22 23 24 25.
In ♑, 26 27 28 29 30.
In ♒, 1 2 3 4 5 6.
In ♓, 27 28 29 30:

The meanng whereof is, that if ♄ in any Question be in *Face.* any

H

58 *An Introduction to Astrologie.*

any of these degrees wherein he hath a Terme, he cannot be said to be peregrine, or void of essentiall dignities; or if he be in any of those degrees alotted him for his Face or Decanate, he cannot then be said to be peregrine: understand this in all the other Planets.

He hath also these for his Face or Decanate.

In ♉, 21 22 23 24 25 26 27 28 29 30.
In ♌, 1 2 3 4 5 6 7 8 9 10.
In ♎, 11 12 13 14 15 16 17 18 19 20.
In ♐, 21 22 23 24 25 26 27 28 29 30.
In ♓, 1 2 3 4 5 6 7 8 9 10.

He continueth Retrograde 140 dayes.
He is five dayes in his first station before Retrogradation, and so many in his second station before Direction.

Nature.   He is a Diurnall Planet, Cold and Dry (being farre removed from the heat of the Sun) and moyst Vapours, Melancholick, Earthly, Masculine, the greater Infortune, author of Solitarinesse, Malevolent, &c.

Manners & Actions, when well dignified   Then he is profound in Imagination, in his Acts severe, in words reserved, in speaking and giving very spare, in labour patient, in arguing or disputing grave, in obtaining the goods of this life studious and solicitous, in all manner of actions austere.

When ill.   Then he is envious, covetous, jealous and mistrustfull, timorus, sordid, outwardly dissembling, sluggish, suspitious, stubborne, a contemner of women, a close lyar, malicious, murmuring, never contented, ever repining.

Corporature.   Most part his Body more cold and dry, of a middle stature; his Complexion pale, swartish or muddy, his Eyes little and black, looking downward, a broad Forehead, black or sad Haire, and it hard or rugged, great Eares; hanging, lowring Eye-browes, thick Lips and Nose, a rare or thin Beard, a lumpish, unpleasant Countenance, either holding his Head forward or stooping, his Shoulders broad and large, and many times crooked, his Belly somewhat short and lank, his Thighs spare, leane and not long; his Knees and Feet indecent; many times

An Introduction to Astrologie. 59

times shoveling or hitting one against another, &c.

You must observe, if *Saturne* be Orientall of the *Sun*, the stature is more short, but decent and well composed. ♄ *Orientall*

The man is more black and leane, and fewer Hairs; and againe, if he want latitude, the body is more leane, if he have great latitude, the body is more fat or fleshy; if the latitude be Meridionall or South, more fleshy, but quick in motion. *Occidentall*

If the latitude be North, hairy and much flesh.

♄ in his first station, a little fat.

In his second station, fat, ill favoured Bodies, and weak; and this observe constantly in all the other Planets.

In generall he signifieth Husbandmen, Clownes, Beggars, Day-labourers, Old men, Fathers, Grandfathers, Monks, Jesuits, Sectarists. *Quality of men.*

Curriers, Night-farmers, Miners under ground, Tinners, Potters, Broom-men, Plummers, Brick-makers, Malsters, Chimney-sweepers, Sextons of Churches, Bearers of dead corps, Scavengers, Hostlers, Colliers, Carters, Gardiners, Ditchers, Chandlers, Diers of black Cloth, an Herdsman, Shepheard or Cow-keeper. *Profession.*

All Impediments in the right Eare, Teeth, all quartan Agues proceeding of cold, dry and melancholly Distempers, Leprosies, Rheumes, Consumptions, black Jaundies, Palsies, Tremblings, vaine Feares, Fantasies, Dropsie, the Hand and Foot-gout, Apoplexies, Dog hunger, too much flux of the Hemoroids, Ruptures if in *Scorpio* or *Leo*, in any ill aspect with *Venus*. *Sicknesses*

Sower, Bitter, Sharp, in mans body he principally ruleth the Spleen. *Savours.*

He governeth Bearsfoot, Starwort, Woolf-bane, Hemlock, Ferne, Hellebor the white and black, Henbane, Ceterach or Finger-ferne, Clotbur or Burdock, Parsnip, Dragon, Pulse, Vervine, Mandrake, Poppy, Mosse, Nightshade, Bythwind, Angelica, Sage, Box, Tutsan, Orage or golden Hearb, Spinach, Shepheards Purse, Cummin, Horstaile, Fumitory. *Hearbs.*

Tamarisk, Savine, Sene, Capers, Rue or Hearbgrace, Polipody, Willow or Sallow Tree, Yew-tree, Cypresse-tree, Hemp, Pine-tree. *Plants and Trees.*

H 2

An Introduction to Astrologie.

Beasts, &c. — The Asse, Cat, Hare, Mouse, Mole, Elephant, Beare, Dog, Wolfe, Basilisk, Crocodile, Scorpion, Toad, Serpent, Adder, Hog, all manner of creeping Creatures breeding of putrifaction, either in the Earth, Water or Ruines of Houses.

Fishes. — The Eele, Tortoise, Shel-fishes.

Birds, &c. — The Bat or Blude-black, Crow, Lapwing, Owle, Gnat, Crane, Peacock, Grashopper, Thrush, Blackbird, Ostritch, Cuckoo.

Places. — He delights in Deserts, Woods, obscure Vallies, Caves, Dens, Holes, Mountaines, or where men have been buried, Chnrch-yards, &c. Ruinous Buildings, Cole-mines, Sinks, Dirty or Stinking Muddy Places, Wells and Houses of Offices, &c.

Minerals. — He ruleth overLead, the Load-stone, theDrosse of all Mettals, as also, the Dust and Rubbidge of every thing.

Stones. — Saphire, Lapis Lazuli, all black, ugly Country Stones not polishable, and of a sad, ashy or black colour.

Weather. — He causeth Cloudy, Darke, obscure Ayre, cold and hurtfull, thick, black and cadense Clouds: but of this more particularly in a Treatise by it selfe

Winds. — He delighteth in the East quarter of Heaven, and causeth EasterneWinds, at the time of gathering anyPlantbelonging to him, the Ancients did observe to turne their faces towards the East in his hour, and he, if possible, in an Angle, either in the Ascendant, or tenth, or eleventh house, the ☽ applying by a △ or ✶ to him.

Orbe. — His Orbe is nine degrees before and after; that is, his influence begins to work, when either he applies, or any Planet applies to him, and is within nine degrees of his aspect, and continueth in force untill he is seperate nine degrees from that aspect.

In Generation he ruleth the first and eighth moneth after Conception.

Yeers. — The greatest yeers he signifies---465.
His greater----57.
His mean yeers----43 *and a half*.
His least----30.

The meaning whereof is this; Admit we frame a new Building,

An Introduction to Astrologie. 61

ding, erect a Towne or City, or a Family, or principality is begun when *Saturne* is essentially and accidentally strong, the Astrologer may probably conjecture the Family, Principality, &c. may continue 465 yeers in honour &c. without any sensible alteration: Againe, if in ones Nativity *Saturne* is well dignified, is Lord of the Geniture, &c. then according to nature he may live 57 yeers, if he be meanly dignified, then the Native but 43; if he be Lord of the Nativity, and yet weak, the child may live 30 yeers, hardly any more; for the nature of *Saturne* is cold and dry, and those qualities are destructive to man, &c.

As to Age, he relates to decreped old men, Fathers, Grand-fathers, the like in Plants, Trees, and all living Creatures.

Late Authors say he ruleth over *Bavaria, Saxony, Stiria, Ro-* *Countries* *mandiola, Ravenna, Constantia, Ingoldstad.*

Is *Cassiel*, alias *Captiel*. *Angel.*

His Friends are ♃ ☉ and ☿, his enemies ♂ and ♀.

We call *Saturday* his day, for then he begins to rule at ☉ rise, and ruleth the first hour and eighth of that day.

CHAP. IX.

Of the Planet Jupiter, *and his signification.*

JUpiter is placed next to *Saturne* (amongst the Ancients) you shall sometimes finde him called *Zeus*, or *Phaeton:* He is the greatest in appearance to our eyes of all the Planets (the ☉ ☽ and ♀ excerted:) in his Colour he is bright, cleer, and of an *Colour.* Azure colour. In his Motion he exceeds *Saturne*, finishing his *Motion.* course through the twelve Signes in twelve yeeres: his midle motion is 4 min. 59 seconds: his Diurnall motion is 8 10 12, or 14 min. hardly any more.

His greatest North latitude is   1   38 *Latitude*
His greatest South latitude is   1   40
He hath two of the twelve Signs of the Zodiack for his hou- *Houses.* ses, viz. ♐ his Day-house, and ♓ his Night-house.

H 3   He

An Introduction to Astrologie.

He receives Detriment in ♊ and ♍: He is Exalted in ♋, hath his Fall in ♑.

Triplicity. He ruleth the Fiery Triplicity by night, viz. ♈ ♌ ♐.

Terms. He hath also these degrees alotted for his Tearmes, viz.

In ♈, 1 2 3 4 5 6.
In ♉, 16 17 18 19 20 21 22.
In ♊, 8 9 10 11 12 13 14.
In ♋, 7 8 9 10 11 12 13.
In ♌, 20 21 22 23 24 25.
In ♍, 14 15 16 17 18.
In ♎, 12 13 14 15 16 17 18 19.
In ♏, 7 8 9 10 11 12 13 14.
In ♐, 1 2 3 4 5 6 7 8.
In ♑, 13 14 15 16 17 18 19.
In ♒, 21 22 23 24 25.
In ♓, 9 10 11 12 13 14.

He hath assigned him for his Face or Decanate,

Of ♊, 1 2 3 4 5 6 7 8 9 10.
Of ♌, 11 12 13 14 15 16 17 18 19 20.
Of ♎, 21 22 23 24 25 26 27 28 29 30.
Of ♑, 1 2 3 4 5 6 7 8 9 10.
Of ♓, 11 12 13 14 15 16 17 18 19 20.

He is Retrograde about 120 dayes, is five dayes in his first station before retrogradation, and four dayes stationary before Direction.

Nature. He is a Diurnall, Masculine Planet, Temperately Hot and Moyst, Aiery, Sanguine, the greater Fortune, author of Temperance, Modesty, Sobriety, Justice.

Manners & Actions when well placed. Then is he Magnanimous, Faithfull, Bashfull, Aspiring in an honourable way at high matters, in all his actions a Lover of faire Dealing, desiring to benefit all men, doing Glorious things, Honourable and Religious, of sweet and affable Conversation, wonderfully indulgent to his Wife and Children, reverencing Aged men, a great Reliever of the Poore, full of Charity and Godlinesse, Liberll, hating all Sordid actions, Just, Wise, Prudent, Thankfull, Vertuous: so that when you find

♃

An Introduction to Astrologie. 63

♃ the Significator of any man in a Question, or Lord of his Ascendant in a Nativity, and well dignified, you may judge him qualified as abovesaid.

When ♃ is unfortunate, then he wastes his Patrimony, suffers every one to cozen him, is Hypocritically Religious, Tenacious, and stiffe in maintaining false Tenents in Religion; he is Ignorant, Carelesse, nothing Delightfull in the love of his Friends; of a grosse, dull Capacity, Schismaticall, abasing himselfe in all Companies, crooching and stooping where no necessity is. *When ill.*

He signifies an upright, straight and tall Stature; browne, ruddy and lovely Complexion; of an ovall or long Visage, and it full or fleshy; high Forehead; large gray Eyes; his Hair soft, and a kind of aburne browne; much Beard; a large, deep Belly: strong proportioned Thighs and Legs; his Feet long, being the most indecent parts of his whole Body; in his Speech he is sober, and of grave Discourse. *Corporat.*

The Skin more cleer, his Complexion Honey-colour, or betwixt a white and red, sanguine, ruddy Colour; great Eyes, the Body more fleshy, usually some Mole or Scarre in the right Foot. *Orientall.*

A pure and lovely Complexion, the Stature more short, the Haire a light Browne, or near a dark Flaxen; smooth, bald about the Temple or Forehead. *Occidentall.*

He signifies Judges, Senators, Councellours, Ecclesiasticall men, Bishops, Priests, Ministers, Cardinals, Chancellours, Doctors of the Civill Law, young Schollers and Students in an University or Colledge, Lawyers. *Men & their quality in generall.*

Clothiers, Wollen-Drapers.

Plurisies, all Infirmities in the Liver, left Eare, Apoplexies, Inflamation of the Lungs, Palpitation and Trembling of the Heart, Cramps, paine in the Back-bone, all Diseases lying in the Vaines or Ribs, and proceeding from corrution of Blood, Squinzies, Windinesse, all Putrifaction in the Blood, or Feavers proceeding from too great abundance thereof. *Diseases*

He governeth the Sweet or well sented Odours, or that Odour which in smell is no way extream or offensive. *Savours*

Sea-green or Blew, Purple, Ash-colour, a mixt Yellow and Green *Colours*

Cloves

Hearbs and Drugs.   Cloves and Clove-Sugar, Mace, Nutmeg, Gilly-flower, the Straw-bury, the herb Balfam, Bettony, Centory, Flax, Ars fmart, Fumitory, Lung-wort, Pimpernell, Walwort, Organy or Wild Majorane, Rubbard, Self heale, Borage, Bugloffe, Wheat, Willow-hearb, Thorough-Leafe, Violets, Laskwort, Liverwort, Bazil, Pomegranets, Pyony, Liquorifh, Mynt, Maftix, the Dazy, Feverfend, Saffron.

Plants, Trees.   Cherry-tree, Birch-tree, Mulbury-tree, Corall-tree, the Oae, Baburies, Olive, Goosburies, Almond tree, the Jvy, Manna, Mace, the Vine, the Fig-tree, the Afh, the Pear-tree, the Hazle, the Beech-tree, the Pyne, Rayfons.

Beafts.   The Sheep, the Hart or Stag, the Doe, the Oxe, Elephant, Dragon, Tygar, Unicorne, thofe Beafts which are Mild and Gentle, and yet of great benefit to Mankind, are appropriate to him.

Birds.   The Stork, the Snipe, the Lark, the Eagle, the Stock-dove, the Partridge, Bees, Pheafant, Peacock, the Hen.

Fifhes.   The Dolphin the Whale, Serpent, Sheath-fifh or River-Whale.

Places.   He delighteth in or neer Altars of Churches, in publick Conventions, Synods, Convocations, in Places neat, fweet, in Wardrobes, Courts of Juftice, Oratorie.

Minerall.   Tyn.

Precious Stones.   Amethift, the Saphire, the Smarage or Emrald, Hyacinth, Topaz, Chryftall, Bezoar, Marble, and that which in *England* we call the Free-ftone.

Weather.   He ufually produceth ferenity, pleafant and healthful North Winds, and by his gentle Beams allayes the ill weather of any former Malignant Planet.

Winds.   He governeth the North Wind, that part which tendeth to the Eaft.

Orbe.   His Radiation or Orbe, is nine degrees before and after any of his afpect.

Generation.   He governeth the fecond and tenth Moneth; his proper feat in man is the Liver; and in the Elements he ruleth the Ayre.

Yeers.   His greateft yeers are 428. his greater 79. his meane 45. leaft 12.

Age.   Men of middle age, or of a full Judgment and Difcretion.

He

An Introduction to Astrologie.

He governeth the second Climate.
Babylon, Persia, Hungaria, Spaine, Cullen.
The number of three is attributed to him.
Zadkiel.
Thursday, and rules the first hour after ☉ rise, and the eighth; the length of the Planetary hour you must know by the rising of the ☉, and a Table hereafter following.

Climate.
Countries.
Number.
Angel.
Day of the weeke.

All the Planets except ♂ are friends to ♃. In gathering any Hearb appropriated to ♃, see that he be very powerfull either in Essentiall or Accidentall Dignities, and the ☽ in some manner in good aspect with him, and if possible, let her be in some of his Dignities, &c.

CHAP. X.

Of the Planet Mars, *and his severall significations.*

MARS doth in order succeed *Jupiter*, whom the Ancients sometimes called *Mavors, Aris, Pyrois, Gradivus*; he is lesse in body then *Jupiter* or *Venus*, and appeareth to our sight of a shining, fiery, sparkling colour, he finisheth his course in the Zodiack in one yeer 321 dayes, or thereabous; his greatest latitude North is 4 31 min. his South is 6 degr. and 47.

Colour in Element.
Latitude

His mean motion is 31 degr. 27 min.
His diurnall motion is sometimes 32 34 36 38 40 42 44 min. a day, seldome more.

Motion.

He hath ♈ for his Day-house, and ♏ for his Night-house; he is exalted in 28 degr. of ♑, and is depressed in 28 ♋, he receiveth detriment in ♎ and ♉; he is retrograde 80 dayes; stationary before he be retrograde, two or three dayes, &c. He is stationary before direction two dayes; after, but one day

He governeth wholly the Watry Triplicity, *viz.* ♋ ♏ ♓.
In the whole twelve Signs, *Ptolomy* assigneth him these degrees for his Termes, *viz.*

Triplicity
Termes.

In

66   *An Introduction to Astrologie.*

In ♈, 22 23 24 25 26.
In ♉, 27 28 29 30.
In ♊, 26 27 28 29 30.
In ♋, 1 2 3 4 5 6.
In ♌, 26 27 28 29 30.
In ♍, 25 26 27 28 29 30.
In ♎, 25 26 27 28 29 30.
In ♏, 1 2 3 4 5 6.
In ♐, 26 27 28 29 30.
In ♑, 20 21 22 23 24 25.
In ♒, 26 27 28 29 30.
In ♓, 21 22 23 24 25 26.

He hath alotted him for his Face these degrees.

In ♈, 1 2 3 4 5 6 7 8 9 10.
In ♊, 11 12 13 14 15 16 17 18 19 20.
In ♌, 21 22 23 24 25 26 27 28 29 30.
In ♏, 1 2 3 4 5 6 7 8 9 10.
In ♑, 11 12 13 14 15 16 17 18 19 20.
In ♓, 21 22 23 24 25 26 27 28 29 30.

Nature.   He is a Masculine, Nocturnall Planet, in nature hot and dry, cholerick and fiery, the lesser Infortune, author of Quarrels Strifes, Contentions.

Manners when well dignified.   In feats of Warre and Courage invincible, scorning any should exceed him, subject to no Reason, Bold, Confident, Immoveable, Contentious, challenging all Honour to themselves, Valiant, lovers of Warre and things pertaining thereunto, hazarding himselfe to all Perils, willingly will obey no body, or submit to any; a large Reporter of his owne Acts, one that slights all things in comparison of Victory, and yet of prudent behaviour in his owne affaires.

When ill placed.   Then he is a Pratler without modesty or honesty, a lover of Slaughter and Quarrels, Murder, Theevery, a promoter of Sedition, Frayes and Commotions, an Highway-Theefe, as wavering as the Wind, a Traytor, of turbulent Spirit, Perjured, Obscene, Rash, Inhumane, neither fearing God or caring for man, Unthankful, Trecherous, Oppressors, Ravenous, Cheaters, Furious, Violent.   Gen-

An Introduction to Astrologie. 67

Generally Martialists have this forme; they are but of mid- *Corporature*
dle Stature, their Bodies strong, and their Bones big, rather
leane then fat; their Complexion of a brown, ruddy colour, or
of an high colour, their Visage round, their Haire red or sandy
flaxen, and many times crisping or curling, sharp hazle Eyes,
and they piercing, a bold confident countenance, and the man
active and fearlesse.

When ♂ is Orientall, he signifies Valiant men, some white *Orientall.*
mixed with their rednesse, a decent talnesse of Body, hairy of
his Body.

Very ruddy Complexion'd, but mean in Stature, little Head, *Occidentall*
a smooth Body, and not hairy; yellow Hair, stiffe, the naturall
humours generally more dry.

Princes Ruling by Tyranny and Oppression, or Tyrants, *Qualities*
Usurpers, new Conquerours. *men and pro-*
Generals of Armies, Colonels, Captaines, or any Souldiers *fession.*
having command in Armies, all manner of Souldiers, Physi-
tians, Apothecaries, Chirurgions, Alchimists, Gunners, Butchers, Marshals, Sergeants, Bailiffs, Hang-men, Theeves, Smiths,
Bakers, Armourers, Watch-makers, Botchers, Tailors, Cutlers
of Swords and Knives, Barbers, Dyers, Cooks, Carpenters,
Gamesters, Bear-wards, Tanners, Curriers.

The Gall, the left Eare, tertian Feavers, pestilent burning *Diseases.*
Feavers, Megrams in the Head, Carbunckles, the Plague and
all Plague-sores, Burnings, Ring-wormes, Blisters Phrensies,
mad sudden distempers in the Head, Yellow-jaundies, Bloody-
flux, Fistulaes, all Wounds and Diseases in mens Genitories, the
Stone both in the Reins and Bladder, Scars or smal Pocks in the
Face, all hurts by Iron, the Shingles, and such other Diseases as
arise by abundance of too much Choller, Anger or Passion.

He delighteth in Red colour, or Yellow, fiery and shining *Colour and*
like Saffron; and in those Savours which are bitter, sharp and *Savours.*
burn the Tongue; of Humours, Choller.

The Hearbs which we attribute to ♂ are such as come neare *Hearbs.*
to rednesse, whose leaves are pointed and sharp, whose taste
is costick and burning, love to grow on dry places, are corro-
sive and penetrating the Flesh and Bones with a most subtill
heat: They are as followeth. The Nettle, all manner of Thi-
I 2 stles,

68   *An Introduction to Astrologie.*

stles, Rest-harrow or Cammock, Devils-milk or Petty spurge, the white and red Brambles, the white called vulgarly by the Hearbalists Ramme, Lingwort, Onions, Scammony, Garlick, Mustard-feed, Pepper, Ginger, Leeks, Ditander, Hore-hound, Hemlock, red Sanders, Tamarindes, all Hearbs attracting or drawing choller by Sympathy, Raddish, Castoreum, Arsmart, Assarum, Carduus, Benedictus, Cantharides.

Trees. All Trees which are prickly, as the Thorne, Chesnut.

Beasts and Animals. Panther, Tygar, Mastiffe, Vulture, Fox; of living creatures, those that are Warlike, Ravenous and Bold, the Castor, Horse, Mule, Ostritch, the Goat, the Wolfe, the Leopard, the wild Asse, the Gnats, Flyes, Lapwing, Cockatrice, the Giffon, Beare.

Fishes. The Pike, the Shark, the Barbell, the Fork-fish, all stinking Wormes, Scorpions.

Birds. The Hawke, the Vultur, the Kite or Glead, (all ravenous Fowle) the Raven, Cormorant, the Owle, (some say the Eagle) the Crow, the Pye.

Places. Smiths Shops, Furnaces, Slaughter-houses, places where Bricks or Charcoales are burned, or have been burned, Chimneys, Forges.

Minerals. Iron, Antimony, Arsenick, Brimston, Ocre.

Stones. Adamant, Loadstone, Blood-stone, Jasper, the many coloured Amatheist, the Touch-stone, red Lead or Vermilion.

Weather. Red Clouds, Thunder, Lightning, Fiery impressions, and pestilent Aires, which usually appear after a long time of drinesse and faire Weather, by improper and unwholesome Mysts.

Winds. He stirreth up the Westerne Windes.

Orbe. His Orbe is onely seven degrees before and after any of his aspects.

Yeers. In man he governeth the flourishing time of Youth, and from 41 to 56; his greatest yeers are 264, greater 66, meane 40, lesse 15.

Countries. Saromatia, Lumbardy, Batavia, Ferraria, Gotholand, and the third Climate.

Day of the week. He governeth Tuesday, and therein the first hour and eighth from ☉ rise, and in Conception the third moneth.

Angel. Samael. His Friends are onely ♀; Enemies all the other Planets.

C H A P.

An Introduction to Astrologie.

Chap. XI.
Of the Sun, and his generall and particular significations.

THe *Sun* is placed in the middle of all the Planets, and is *Sol.* called amongst the Ancients, both Poets and Historians, *Sol, Titan, Ilios, Phebus, Apollo, Pean, Osyris, Diespiter:* It's needlesse to mention his Colour, being so continually visible to all mortall men: He passeth through all the twelve Signes of the Zodiack in one yeer, or in 365 dayes and certaine hours: His meane motion is 59 8; yet his diurnall motion is sometimes *Motion.* 57ᵐ 16 seconds, sometimes more, never exceeding 61 minutes and six seconds.

He alwayes moves in the Ecliptick, and is ever voyd of latitude, so that it is very improper in any Astrologian to speak of the ☉ his latitude.

He hath onely the Signe of ♌ for his House, and ♒ for his *House.* Detriment.

He is Exalted in the 19 degree of ♈, and receives his Fall in 19 ♎.

The *Sunne* governeth the fiery Triplicity, *viz.* ♈, ♌, ♐ *Triplicity* by day.

He hath no degrees of the twelve Signs admitted him for his *Termes.* Termes, though some affirme, if he be in the six Northerne Signes, *viz.* ♈, ♉, ♊, ♋, ♌, ♍, he shall be said to be in his Termes, but because there is no reason for it, I leave it as Idle.

In the twelve Signes he hath these degrees for his Decanate or Faces.

In ♈, the 11 12 13 14 15 16 17 18 19 20
In ♊, the 21 22 23 24 25 26 27 28 29 30.
In ♍, the 1 2 3 4 5 6 7 8 9 10.
In ♏, the 11 12 13 14 15 16 17 18 19 20.
In ♑, the 21 22 23 24 25 26 27 28 29 30.

The ☉ is always direct, and never can be said to be Retrograd; it's true, he moveth more slowly at one time then another.

He

Nature.   He is naturally Hot, Dry, but more temperate then ♂, is a Masculine, Diurnall Planet, Equivalent, if well dignified to a Fortune.

Manners when well dignified.   Very faithfull, keeping their Promises with all punctuality, a kind of itching desire to Rule and Sway where he comes: Prudent, and of incomparable Judgment; of great Majesty and Statelinesse, Industrious to acquire Honour and a large Patrimony, yet as willingly departing therewith againe; the Solar man usually speaks with gravity, but not many words, and those with great confidence and command of his owne affection; full of Thought, Secret, Trusty, speaks deliberately, and notwithstanding his great Heart, yet is he Affable, Tractable, and very humane to all people, one loving Sumptuousnesse and Magnificence, and whatsoever is honorable; no sordid thoughts can enter his heart, &c.

When ill dignified.   Then the Solar man is Arrogant and Proud, disdaining all men, cracking of his Pedegree, he is Pur-blind in Sight and Judgment, restlesse, troublesome, domineering, a meer vapour, expensive, foolish, endued with no gravity in words, or sobernesse in Actions, a Spend-thrift, wasting his Patrimony, and hanging on other mens charity, yet thinks all men are bound to him, because a Gentleman borne.

Corporature.   Usually the ☉ presents a man of a good, large and strong Corporature, a yellow, saffron Complexion, a round, large Forehead: goggle Eyes or large, sharp and piercing; a Body strong and well composed, not so beautifull as lovely, full of heat, their haire yellowish, and therefore quickly bald, much Haire on their Beard, and usually an high ruddy Complexion, their bodies fleshy, in conditions they are very bountifull honest, sincere, wel-minded, of great and large Heart, High-minded, of healthfull Constitution, very humane, yet sufficiently Spirited, not Loquacious.

In the ☉, we can onely say he is Orientall in the Figure, or in the Orientall quarter of the Figure, or Occidentall, &c. all other Planets are either Oriental when they rise, or appeare before him in the morning.

Occidentall, when they are seen above the Earth after he is set.

An Introduction to Astrologie. 71

He signifieth Kings, Princes, Emperours, &c. Dukes, Marquesses, Earles, Barons, Lieutenants, Deputy-Lieutenants of Counties, Magistrates, Gentlemen in generall, Courtiers, desirers of Honour and preferment, Justices of Peace, Majors, High-Sheriffs, High-Constables, great Huntsmen, Lieutenants, Deputy-Lieutenants, Stewards of Noble-mens houses, the principall Magistrate of any City, Towne, Castle or Country-Village, yea, though a petty Constable, where no better, or greater Officer is; Goldsmiths, Brasiers, Pewterers, Coppersmiths, Minters of Money. *Quality of men and their professions*

Pimples in the Face, Palpitation or Trembling, or any Diseases of the Braine or Heart, Timpanies Infirmities of the Eyes, Cramps, sudden swoonings, Diseases of the Mouth, and stinking Breaths, Catars, rotten Feavers; principally in man he governeth the Heart, the Braine and right Eye, and vitall Spirit, in Women the left Eye. *Sicknesse.*

Of Colours he ruleth the Yellow, the colour of Gold, the Scarlet or the cleer Red, some say Purple: In Savours, he liketh well a mixture of Sower and Sweet together, or the Aromatical savour, being a little Bitter and Stiptical, but withall Confortative and a little sharp. *Colours and Savours.*

Those Plants which are subject to the ☉ doe smell pleasantly, are of good savour, their Flowers are yellow or reddish, are in growth of Majestical forme, they love open and Sunshine places, their principall Vertue is to strengthen the Heart, and comfort the Vitals, to cleer the Eye-sight, resist Poyson, or to dissolve any Witchery, or Malignant Planetary Influences; and they are Saffron, the Lawrell, the Pomecitron, the Vine, Enula, Campana, Saint Johns-wort, Ambre, Musk, Ginger, Hearb-grace, Balme, Marigold, Rosemary, Rosasolis, Cinamon, Celendine, Eye-bright, Pyony, Barley, Cynqfoile, Spikenard, Lignum Aloes, Arsnick. *Hearbs and Plants.*

Ash-tree, Palm, Lawrel-tree, the Myrrhe-tree, Frankinsence, the Cane tree or plant, the Cedar, Heletropion, the Orange and Lemon-tree. *Trees.*

The Lyon, the Horse, the Ram, the Crocodile, the Bul, Goat, Night-wormes or Glow-wormes. *Beasts.*

The Sea-Calf or Sea-Fox, the Crabfish, the Starfish. *Fishes.*

The

Birds.   The Eagle, the Cock, the Phœnix, Nightingale, Pecock, the Swan, the Buzzard, the flye Cantharis, the Goshawke.

Places.   Houses, Courts of Princes, Pallaces, Theators, all magnificent Structures being clear and decent, Hals, Dining-Rooms.

Minerals or Mettals.   Amongst the Elements ☉ hath dominion of fire and cleere shining flames, over mettals he ruleth Gold.

Stones.   The Hyacinth, Chrisolite, Adamant, Carbuncle, the Etites stone found in Eagles nests, the Pantaure if such a stone be the Ruby.

Weather.   He produceth weather according to the season; in the Spring gentle moysting Showers; in the Summer heat in extremity if with ♂: in Autum mists; in Winter small Raine.

Winds.   He loves the East part of the World; and that winde which proceeds from that quarter.

Orbe.   Is 15. degrees before any aspect; and so many after separation.

Yeers.   In age he ruleth youth, or when one is at the strongest; his greatest yeers are 1460. greater 120. mean 69. least 19.

Countries.   Italy, Sicilia, Bohemia; and the fourth Climate, Phenicia, Chaldea.

Angel.   Michael.

Day of the weeke.   He ruleth Sunday the first houre thereof, and the eight; and in numbers the first and fourth; and in conceptions the fourth moneth. His Friends are all the Planets except ♄, who is his Enemy.

Chap. XII.

Of the Planet Venus and her severall significations and nature.

Name.   After the Sunne succeedeth Venus; who is sometimes called *Cytherea, Aphrodite, Phosphoros, Desperugo, Ericina,*

Colour in the Element.   She is of a bright shining colour, and is well known amongst the vulgar by the name of the evening Starre or *Hesperus*; and that is when she appeares after the Sunne is set: common people call her the morning Starre, and the learned *Lucifer*, when she is seen long before the rising of the Sunne: her meane motion is 59. min. and 8. seconds: her diurnall motion is sometimes

Motion.

Latitude.

An Introduction to Astrologie. 73

times 62. min. a day 64.65.66. or 70.74.76. minutes; but 82. min. she never exceedeth; her greatest North or South lati- *Latitude.* tude is nine degr. and two min. in *February* 1643. she had eight degr. and 36 min. for her North latitude.

She hath ♉ and ♎ for her houses, she is exalted in 27 ♓, *Houses.* she receiveth detriment in ♈ and ♏, and hath her fal in 27 ♍.

She governeth the Earrhly Triplicity by day *viz.* ♉ ♍ ♑; *Triplicity.* she is two dayes stationary before retrogradation, and so many before direction, and doth usually continue retrograde 42 dayes.

She hath these degrees in every Sign for her Terms. *Her Terms.*

In ♈, 7 8 9 10 11 12 13 14.
In ♉, 1 2 3 4 5 6 7 8.
In ♊, 15 16 17 18 19 20.
In ♋, 21 22 23 24 25 26 27.
In ♌, 14 15 16 17 18 19.
In ♍, 8 9 10 11 12 13.
In ♎, 7 8 9 10 11.
In ♏, 15 16 17 18 19 20 21.
In ♐, 9 10 11 12 13 14.
In ♑, 1 2 3 4 5 6.
In ♒, 13 14 15 16 17 18 19 20.
In ♓, 1 2 3 4 5 6 7 8.

These degrees are allowed for her Face.

In ♈, 21 22 23 24 25 26 27 28 29 30.
In ♋, 1 2 3 4 5 6 7 8 9 10.
In ♍, 11 12 13 15 16 17 18 19 20.
In ♏, 21 22 23 24 25 26 28 29 30.
In ♓, 1 2 3 4 5 6 7 8 9 10.

She is a Feminine Planet, temperately Cold and Moyst, *Element.* Nocturnal, the lesser Fortune, author of Mirth and Jolity; *Nature.* the Elements, the Ayre and Water are Venerial; in the Humours, Flegme with Blood, with the Spirit and Genital seed.

She signiffes a quiet man, not given to Law, Quarrel or *Manners &* Wrangling, not Vitious, Pleasant, Neat and Spruce, loving *quality when Mirth, well placed*

K

Mirth in his words and actions, cleanly in Apparel, rather Drinking much then Gluttonous, prone to Venery, oft entangled in Love-matters, Zealous in their affections, Musicall, delighting in Baths, and all honest merry Meetings, or Maskes and Stage-playes, easie of Beliefe, and not given to Labour, or take any Pains, a Company-keeper, Cheerful, nothing Mistrustful, a right vertuous Man or Woman, oft had in some Jealousie, yet no cause for it.

When ill. Then he is Riotous, Expensive, wholly given to Loosnesse and Lewd companies of Women, nothing regarding his Reputation, coveting unlawful Beds, Incestuous, an Adulterer, Fantastical, a meer Skip-jack, of no Faith, no Repute, no Credit; spending his Meanes in Ale houses, Taverns, and amongst Scandalous, Loose people; a meer Lazy companion, nothing careful of the things of this Life, or any thing Religious; a meer Atheist and natural man.

Corporature. A man of faire, but not tall Stature, his Complexion being white, tending to a little darknesse, which makes him more Lovely; very fair Lovely Eyes, and a little black; a round Face, and not large, faire Haire, smooth, and plenty of it, and it usually of a light browne colour, a lovely Mouth and cherry Lips, the Face pretty fleshy, a rolling wandring Eye, a Body very delightfull, lovely and exceeding well shaped, one desirous of Trimming and making himself neat and compleat both in Cloaths and Body, a love dimple in his Cheeks, a stedfast Eye, and full of amarous enticements.

Orientall. When Orientall the Body inclines to talnesse, or a kind of upright straightnesse in Person, not corpulent or very tall, but neatly composed. A right Venerian person, is such as we say, is a pretty, compleat, handsome Man or Woman.

Occidentall. When she is Occidental, the Man is of more short stature, yet very decent and comely in Shape and Forme, well liked of all.

Qualities of men and profession. Musitions, Gamesters, Silk-men, Mercers, Linnen-Drapers, Painters, Jewellers, Players, Lapidaries, Embroiderers, Women-tailors, Wives, Mothers, Virgins, Choristers, Fidlers, Pipers, whē joyned with the ☽ Ballad-singers, Perfumers, Semsters, Picture-drawers, Gravers, Upholdsters, Limners, Glovers, all such as

sell

An Introduction to Astrologie. 75

fell thofe Commodities which adorne Women, either in Body (as Cloaths) or in Face, (as Complexion-waters.)

Difeafes by her fignified, are principally in the Matrix and members of Generation; in the reines, belly, backe, navill and thofe parts; the Gonorrea or running of the Reines, French or Spanifh Pox; any difeafe arifing by inordinate Iuft. Prihpifme, impotency in generation, Hernias, &c. the Diabetes or piffing difeafe. *Sickneffe.*

In colours fhe fignifieth White, or milky Skie colour mixed with browne, or a little Greene. In Savours fhe delights in that which is pleafant and toothfome; ufually in moyft and fweet, or what is very delectable; in fmels what is unctious and Aromaticall, and incites to wantonneffe. *Savonrs colours.*

Myrtle alwayes greene; all hearbs which fhe governeth have a fweet favour, a pleafant fmell, a white flower; of a gentle humour, whofe leaves are fmooth and not jagged. She governeth the Lilly white and yellow, and the Lilly of the valley, and of the water. The Satyrion or Cuckoe pintle, Maidenhaire, Violet; the white and yellow Daffadil. *Herbs and Plants.*

Sweet Apples, the white Rofe, the Fig, the white Sycamore; wilde Afh, Turpentine-tree, Olive, fweet Oringes, Mugwort, Ladies-mantle, Sanicle, Balme, Vervin, Walnuts, Almonds, Millet, Valerian, Thyme, Ambre, Ladanum, Civet or Musk, Coriander, French Wheat, Peaches, Apricocks, Plums, Raifons. *Trees.*

The Hart, the Panther, fmall cattle, Coney, the Calfe, the Goat. *Beafts.*

Stockdove, Wagtayle, the Sparrow, Hen, the Nightingale, the Thrufh, Pellican, Partridge, Ficedula, a little Bird Feeding on Grapes; the Wren, Eagle, the Swan, the Swallow, the Owfel or Black bird, the Pye. *Birds.*

The Dolphin. *Fifhes.*

Gardens, Fountaines, Bride-chambers, faire lodgings, Beds, Hangings, Dancing-Schooles, Wardrobes. *Places.*

Copper, efpecially the Corinthian and White; Braffe, all Latten ware. *Mettals an Minerals.*

Cornelian, the Sky-colour'd Saphyre, white and red Coral, Margafite, Alablafter, *Lapis lazuli* becaufe it expels Melancholy, the Berill, Chrifolite. *Stones.*

K 2 Sea

Winde and Weather. She governeth the South-winde being hot and moyst; in the temperament of the Ayre, she ruleth the *Etesia*; she foretelleth in Summer, Serenity or cleer weather; in Winter, rain or snow.

Orbe. Her Orbe is 7. before and after any aspect of hers.

Yeers. Her greatest yeers are 151. her greater 82. her mean 45. her least 8. In Man she governeth Youth from 14. to 28.

Countries. *Arabia, Austria, Campania, Vienna, Polonia* the greater, *Turing, Parthia, Media, Cyprus,* and the six climate.

Angel. Her Angel is *Anael.*

Day of the week. Her day of the week Friday, of which she rules the first and eight houre; and in conception the fift Month. Her Friends are all the Planets except ♄.

CHAP. XIII.

Of Mercury, *and his signification, nature and property.*

Name. HE is called *Hermes, Stilbon, Cyllenius, Archas.* *Mercury* is the least of all the Planets, never distant from the Sun above 27. degrees; by which reason he is seldom visible to our sight:

Colour. He is of a dusky silver colour; his mean motion is 59. min. and 8. seconds; but he is sometimes so swift that he moveth one degree and 40. min. in a day, never more; so that you are not to marvaile if you finde him sometimes goe 66. 68. 70. 80. 86. or 100. in a day: he is Stationary one day, and retrograde 24. dayes.

Latitude. His greatest South Latitude is 3. degr. 35. min. His greatest North Latit. is 3. deg. 33. min.

House. He hath ♊ and ♍ for his Houses, and is exalted in the 15 of ♍: he receives detriment in ♐ and ♓, his fal is in ♓.

Triplicity. He ruleth the aery triplicity by night, *viz.* ♊ ♎ ♒.

Terms. He hath these degrees in every Sign for his Terms.

In ♈, 15 16 17 18 19 20 21.
In ♉, 9 10 11 12 13 14 15.
In ♊, 1 2 3 4 5 6 7.
In ♋, 14 15 16 17 18 19 20.
In ♌, 7 8 9 10 11 12 13.
In ♍, 1 2 3 4 5 6 7.

An Introduction to Astrologie. 77

In ♎, 20 21 22 23 24.
In ♏, 22 23 24 25 26 27.
In ♐, 15 16 17 18 19 20.
In ♑, 7 8 9 10 11 12.
In ♒, 7 8 9 10 11 12.
In ♓, 15 16 17 18 19 20.

These subsequent degrees are his Faces or Decanate :   *Face.*

In ♉, 1 2 3 4 5 6 7 8 9 10.
In ♋, 11 12 13 14 15 16 17 18 19 20.
In ♍, 21 22 23 24 25 26 27 28 29 30.
In ♐, 1 2 3 4 5 6 7 8 9 10.
In ♒, 11 12 13 14 15 16 17 18 19 20.

We may not call him either Masculine or Feminine, for he is *Nature.* either the one or other as joyned to any Planet; for if in ☌ with a Masculine Planet, he becomes Masculine; if with a Feminine, then Feminine, but of his own nature he is cold and dry, and therefore Melancholly; with the good he is good, with the *Elements.* evil Planets ill : in the Elements the Water; amongst the humours, the mixt, he rules the animal spirit : he is author of subtilty, tricks, devices, perjury, &c.

Being wel dignified, he represents a man of a subtil and *Manners* politick brain, intellect, and cogitation; an excellent dispu- *when well* tant or Logician, arguing with learning and discretion, and *placed.* using much eloquence in his speech, a searcher into all kinds of Mysteries and Learning, sharp and witty, learning almost any thing without a Teacher ; ambitious of being exquisite in every Science, desirous naturally of travel and seeing foraign parts : a man of an unwearied fancy, curious in the search of any occult knowledge ; able by his own *Genius* to produce wonders ; given to Divination and the more secret knowledge ; if he turn Merchant, no man exceeds him in way of Trade or invention of new wayes whereby to obtain wealth.

A troublesome wit, a kinde of Phrenetick man, his tongue *Manners,* and Pen against every man, wholly bent to fool his estate and *when ill* time in prating and trying nice conclusions to no purpose ; a *placed or* great lyar, boaster, pratler, busibody, false, a tale-carrier, *dignified.* given to wicked Arts, as Necromancy, and such like ungodly

K 3   know-

knowledges; easie of beleefe, an asse or very ideot, constant in no place or opinion, cheating and theeving every where; a newes-monger, pretending all manner of knowledge, but guilty of no true or solid learning; a trifler; a meere frantick fellow; if he prove a Divine, then a meer verball fellow, frothy, of no judgement, easily perverted, constant in nothing but idle words and bragging.

Corporature. Vulgarly he denotes one of an high stature and straight thin spare body, an high forehead and somewhat narrow long face, long nose, fair eyes, neither perfectly black or gray, thin lips and nose; little haire on the chin, but much on his head, and it a sad browne inclining to blacknesse; long armes, fingers and hands; his complexion like an Olive or Chesnut colour. You must more observe ☿ then all the Planets; for having any aspect to a Planet, he doth more usually partake of the influence of that Planet then any other doth: if with ♄ then heavy, with ♃ more temperate, with ♂ more rash, with ☉ more genteele, with ♀ more jesting, with ☽ more shifter.

Orientall. When he is Orientall, his complexion is honey colour, or like one well Sun-burnt; in the stature of his body not very high, but well joynted, small eyes, not much haire; in very truth, according to the height of body, very well composed, but still a defect in the complexion, *viz* swarty brown, and in the tongue, *viz.* all for his owne ends.

Occidentall. When Occidentall, a tawny visage, lanke body, small slender limbs, hollow eyes, and sparkling and red or fiery; the whol frame of body inclining to drinesse.

Quality of men and professions. He generally signifies all literated men, Philosophers, Mathematicians, Astrologians, Merchants, Secretaries, Scriveners, Diviners, Sculptors, Poets, Orators, Advocates, Schoolmasters, Stationers, Printers, Exchangers of Money, Atturneys, Emperours Embassadours, Commissioners, Clerks, Artificers, generally Accomptants, Solicitors, sometimes Theeves, pratling muddy Ministers, busie Sectaries, and they unlearned; Gramarians, Taylors, Carriers, Messengers, Foot-men, Userers.

Sicknesse. All Vertigoe's, Lethargies or giddinesse in the Head, Madnesse, either Lightnesse, or any Disease of the Braine; Ptisick, all

stammering

An Introduction to Astrologie. 79

stammering and imperfection in the Tongue; vaine and fond Imaginations, all defects in the Memory, Hoarcenesse, dry Coughs, too much abundance of Spettle, all snaffling and snuffling in the Head or Nose; the Hand and Feet Gout, Dumnesse, Tongue-evil, all evils in the Fancy and intellectuall parts.

Mixed and new colours, the Gray mixed with Sky-colour, such as is on the Neck of the Stock-dove, Linsie-woolsie colours, or consisting of many colours mixed in one: Of Savours an hodg-podge of all things together, so that none can give it any true name; yet usually such as doe quicken the Spirits, are subtill and penetrate, and in a manner insensible. *Colours and Savours.*

Herbs attributed to ☿, are known by the various colour of the flower, and love sandy barren places, they bear their seed in husks or cods, they smell rarely or subtilly, and have principall relation to the tongue, braine, lungs or memory; they dispell winde, and comfort the Annimall spirits, and open obstructions. Beanes, three leaved grasse, the Walnut and Walnut-tree; the Filbert-tree and Nut; the Elder-tree, Adders tongue, Dragon-wort, Twopenny-grasse, Lungwort, Annifeeds, Cubebs, Marioran. What hearbs are used for the Muses and Divination, as Vervine, the Reed; of Drugs, Treacle, Hiera, Diambra. *Hearbs and Plants.*

The Hyæna, Ape, Fox, Squirrel, Weasel, the Spider, the Grayhound, the Hermophradite, being partaker of both sexes; all cunning creatures. *Beasts.*

The Lynnet, the Parrot, the Popinian, the Swallow, the Pye, the Beetle, Pismires, Locusts, Bees, Serpent, the Crane. *Birds.*

The Forke-fish, Mullet. *Fishes.*

Tradesmens-shops, Markets, Fayres, Schooles, Common-Hals, Bowling-Allyes, Ordinaries, Tennis-Courts: *Places.*

Quicksilver. *Minerals.*

The Milstone, Marchasite or fire-stone, the Achates, Topaz, Vitriol, all stones of divers colours. *Stones.*

He delights in Windy, Stormy and Violent, Boistrous Weather, and stirs up that Wind which the Planet signifies to which he applyes; sometimes Raine, at other times Haile, Lightning, Thunder and Tempests, in hot Countries Earthquakes, but this *Winds and Weather.*

must

must be observed really from the Signe and Seafon of the yeere.

His Orbe is seven degrees before and after any afpect.

Orbe. His greateft yeers are 450; his greater 76; his meane 48; his *Yeers.* little or leaft 20: in Conceptions he governeth the fixth moneth,

Countries. He hath *Grecia, Flanders, Ægypt, Paris.*
Angel. His Angel is named *Raphael.*
Day of the week. He governeth Wednefday, the firft hour thereof, and the eight. His Friends are ♃ ♀ ♄, his Enemies al the other Planets.

Chap. XIIII.
Of the Moon her properties and fignifications.

Name. THE *Moon* we find called by the Ancients, *Lucina, Cynthia, Diana, Phœbe, Latona, Noctiluca, Proferpina*; fhe is neereft to the Earth of all the Planets; her colour in the Element is vulgarly knowne: fhe finifheth her courfe through the whole *Motion.* twelve Signs in 27 days, 7 hours and 43 min. or thereabouts: her meane motion is 13 degr. 10 min. and 36 feconds, but fhe moveth fometimes leffe and fometimes more, never exceeding 15 degr. and two min. in 24 hours fpace.

Latitude. Her greateft North latitude is 5 degr. and 17 min. *or thereabouts.*
Her greateft South latitude is 5 degr, and 12 min.

She is never Retrograde, but alwayes direct; when fhe is flow in motion, and goeth leffe in 24 hours then 13 degr. and 10 min. fhe is then equivalent to a Retrograde Planet.

Houfe. She hath the Signe ♋ for her houfe, and ♑ for her detriment; fhe is exalted in 3 ♉, and hath her fall in 3 grad. ♏; fhe governeth the Earthly Triplicity by night, *viz.* ♉ ♍ ♑:
Triplicity. The *Sun* and fhe have no Termes affigned them.

In the twelve Signes fhe hath thefe degrees for her Decanate or Face.

In ♉, 11 12 13 14 15 16 17 18 19 20.
In ♋, 21 22 23 24 25 26 27 28 29 30.

In

An Introduction to Astrologie. 81

In ♎, 1 2 3 4 5 6 7 8 9 10.
In ♐, 11 12 13 14 15 16 17 18 19 20.
In ♒, 21 22 23 24 25 26 27 28 29 30.

She is a Feminine, Nocturnall Planet, Cold, Moyst and Flegmatique. *Nature.*

She signifieth one of composed Manners, a soft, tender creature, a Lover of al honest and ingenuous Sciences, a Searcher of, and Delighter in Novelties, naturally propense to flit and shift his Habitation, unstedfast, wholly caring for the present Times, Timorous, Prodigal, and easily Frighted, however loving Peace, and to live free from the cares of this Life; if a Mechannick, the man learnes many Occupations, and frequently will be tampering with many wayes to trade in. *Manners or Actions when well placed dignified.*

A meer Vagabond, idle Person, hating Labour, a Drunkard, a Sot, one of no Spirit or Forecast, delighting to live beggarly and carelesly, one content in no condition of Life, either good or ill. *When ill.*

She generally presenteth a man of faire stature, whitely coloured, the Face round, gray Eyes, and a little louring; much Haire both on the Head, Face, and other parts; usually one Eye a little larger then the other; short Hands and fleshy, the whole Body inclining to be fleshy, plump, corpulent and flegmatique: if she be impedited of the ☉ in a Nativity or Question, she usually signifies some blemish in, or neer the Eye; a blemish neer the Eye, if she be impedited in Succedant Houses; in the Sight, if she be unfortunate in Angles and with fixed Starres, called *Nebulosæ*. *Corporature*

She signifieth Queens, Countesses, Ladies, all manner of Women; as also, the common People, Travellers, Pilgrims, Sailors, Fishermen, Fish-mongers, Brewers, Tapsters, Vintners, Letter-carriers, Coach-men, Hunts-men, Messengers, (some say the Popes Legats) Marriners, Millers, Ale wives, Malsters, Drunkards, Oister-wives, Fisher-women, Chare-women, Tripe-women and generally such Women as carry Commodities in the Secrets; as also, Midwives, Nurses, &c. Hackney-men, Water-men, Water-bearers. *Qualities Men and Women.*

Apoplexies, Palsie, the Chollick, the Belly-ake, Diseases *Sicknesses*

L

cafes in the left Side, Stones, the Bladder and members of Generation, the Men-ftrues and Liver in Women, Dropfies, Fluxes of the Belly, all cold rheumatick Difeafes, cold Stomack, the Gout in the Rifts and Feet, Sciatica, Chollick, Wormes in Children and men, Rheumes or Hurts in the Eyes, *viz.* in the Left of Men, and Right of Women: Surfets, rotten Coughs, Convulfion fits, the Falling fickneffe, Kings-evil, Apoftems, fmall Pox and Meafels.

Colours and Savours.
Of Colours the White, or pale Yellowifh white, pale Green, or a little of the Silver colour. Of Savours, the Frefh, or without any favour, fuch as is in Hearbs before they be ripe, or fuch as doe moyften the Braine, &c.

Hearbs, Plants and Trees.
Thofe Hearbs which are fubject to the *Moon* have foft and thick juicy leaves, of a waterifh or a little fweetifh tafte, they love to grow in watry places, and grow quickly into a juicy magnitude; and are

The Colwort, Cabbage, Melon, Gourd, Pompion, Onion, Mandrake, Poppy, Lettice, Rape, the Linden-tree, Mufhromes, Endive, all Trees or Hearbs who have round, fhady, great fpreading Leaves, and are little Fruitfull.

Beafts or Birds.
All fuch Beafts, or the like, as live in the water; as Frogs, the Otter, Snailes, &c. the Weafell, the Cunny, all Sea Fowle, Coockoe, Geefe and Duck, the Night-Owle.

Fifhes.
The Oyfter and Cockle, all Shel-fifh, the Crab and Lobfter, Tortoife, Eeles.

Places.
Fields, Fountaines, Baths, Havens of the Sea, Highwayes and Defert places, Port Townes, Rivers, Fifh-ponds, ftanding Pools, Boggy places, Common-fhoares, little Brooks, Springs, Harbonrs for Ships or Docks.

Minerals. Silver.
Stones. The Selenite, all foft Stones, Chriftals.
Weather. With ♄ cold Ayre; with ♃ Serene; with ♂ Winds red Clouds; with the ☉ according to the Seafon; with ♀ and ☿ Showres and Winds.

Winds.
In Hermeticall operation, fhe delighteth towards the North, and ufually when fhe is the ftrongeft Planet in the Scheame, *viz.* in any Lunation, fhe ftirs up Wind, according to the nature of the Planet fhe next applies unto.

An Introduction to Astrologie. 83

Is 12. degrees before and after any Aspect. *Orbe.*
Her greatest yeers are 320. greater 108. meane 66, least 25. *Yeers.*
in conceptions she ruleth the seventh moneth.
Holland, Zealand, Denmarke, Nornnberge, Flanders, *Countries.*
Gabriel. *Angel.*
Her day is Monday the first hour and the eight, after the rise *Day of the*
of the Sun are hers. Her Enemy is ♄, and also ♂. *weeke.*

The Head of the Dragon is Masculine, of the nature of ♃ *The Head of*
and ♀, and of himselfe a Fortune; yet the Ancients doe say, *the Dragon.*
that being in ☌ with the good he is good, and in ☌ with the
evill Planets they account him evill.

The Tayle of the Dragon is Feminine by nature, and cleane *The Taile.*
contrary to the Head; for he is evill when joyned with good
Planets, and good when in conjunction with the malignant
Planets. This is the constant opinion of all the Ancients, but
upon what reason grounded I know not; I ever found the ☊
equivalent to either of the Fortunes, and when joyned with
the evill Planets to lessen their malevolent signification; when
joyned with the good to increase the good promised by them
For the Tayle of the Dragon, I alwayes in my practise found
when he was joyned with the evill Planets; their malice or the
evill intended thereby was doubled and trebled, or extreamly
augmented, &c. and when he chanced to be in conjunction with
any of the Fortunes who were significators in the question,
though the matter by the principall significator was fairely
promised, and likely to be perfected in a small time; yet did
there ever fal out many rubs and disturbances, much wrangling
and great controversie, that the businesse was many times given
over for desperate ere a perfect conclusion could be had; and
unlesse the principall significators were Angular and well fortified with essentiall dignities, many times unexpectedly the
whole matter came to nothing.

CHAP. XV.
Another briefe Description of the shapes and formes of the Planets.

♄ Signifieth one of a swart colour, palish like lead, or of a blacke earthly browne; one of rough skin, thicke and very hairy on the body, not great eyes, many times his complexion is betwixt blacke and yellow, or as if he had a spice of the black or yellow Jaundies: he is leane, crooked, or beetle-browed, a thin whay Beard, great lips, like the black-Moores; he lookes to the ground, is slow in motion, either is bow-legged, or hits one leg or knee against another; most part a stinking breath, seldome free from a Cough: he is crafty for his owne ends, seducing people to his opinion, full of revenge and malice, little caring for the Church or Religion; its a foule nasty, slovenly knave, or a whore; a great eater, or one of a large stomacke, a brawling fellow, big great shoulders, covetous, and yet seldome rich, &c.

This where he is peregrine or unfortunate.

♃ We must describe ♃ and a Jovialist, to be one of a comely stature, full faced, full eyed, a sanguine complexion, or mixed with white and red, a large space betwixt his eye-browes, usually his Beard is of a flaxen or sandy-flaxen colour: sometimes also when ♃ is combust very sad or blacke, his haire thicke, his eyes not blacke, his teeth well set, good broad teeth, but usually some mark of difference in the two fore-teeth, either by their standing awry, or some blacknesse or imperfection in them; his haire gently curls (if he be in a fiery Signe:) A man well spoken, religious, or at least a good morall honest man; a person comely and somewhat fat (if ♃ be in moyst Signes) fleshie; if in Aery Signes, bigge and strong; if in earthly Signes, a man usually well descended; but if he be significator, of an ordinary clowne, as sometimes he may be, then is he of more humanity then usually in such kinde of men

♂ A Martiall Man, is many times full faced with a lively high colour like Sunne-burnt, or like raw tanned-Leather, a
fierce

An Introduction to Astrologie. 85

fierce countenance, his eyes being sparkling or sharpe and darting, and of yellow colour; his haire both of head and beard being reddish (but herein you must vary according to the Sign, in fiery signs and aery where ♂ fals to be with fixed Stars of his owne nature, there he shewes a deepe sandy red colour, but in watery signes, being with fixed Starres of his owne nature, he is of a flaxenish or whitish bright hayre ; if in earthly Signes, the haire is like a sad browne, or of a sad Chesnut colour.) He hath a marke or scar in his face, is broad-shouldered, a sturdy strong body, being bold and proud, given to mocke, scorne, quarrell, drinke, game and wench : which you may easily know by the Signe he is in ; if in the house of ♀ he wencheth, if in ☿ s he steals, but if he be in his owne house he quarrels, in *Saturnes*, is dogged; in the *Sunnes*, is lordly; in the *Moones*, is a drunkard.

☉ The Sunne doth generally denote one of an obscure white colour mixed with red; a round face, and short chin, a faire stature, and one of a comely body; his colour sometimes betwixt yellow and blacke, but for the most part more sanguin then otherwayes : a bold man and resolute, his hayre curling ; he hath a white and tender skin, one desirous of praise, fame and estimation amongst men ; he hath a cleere voyce and great head, his teeth somewhat distort or obliquely set, of slow speech but of a composed judgement ; using outwardly a great *decorum* in his actions, but privately he is lascivious and inclinable to many vices.

♀ Who is signified by *Venus*, whether Man or Woman, hath a goodly and faire round visage, a full eye, usually we say goggle-eyed, red ruddy lips, the nether more thicke or bigger then the upper, the eye-lids blacke, however lovely and gracefull, the hayre of lovely colour (but most part according to the Signe as before repeated) in some its coll-blacke, in others a light browne, a soft smooth hayre, and the body extreame well shaped, ever rather inclining to shortnesse then talnesse.

☿ We describe *Mercury*, to be a man neither white or black
but

but betwixt both, of a fad brown or dark yellowish color, long visaged, high-forehead, blacke or gray eyes, a thin long sharpe nose, a thin spare beard (many times none at all) of an aburne sad colour next to blacke, slender of body, small legs, a pratling busie fellow, and in walking he goes nimbly, and alwayes would be thought to be full of action.

☽ She by reason of her swiftnesse, varieth her shape very oft, but in the generall, she personates one having a round visage and full faced, in whose complexion you may perceive a mixture of white and red, but palenesse overcomes; if she be in fiery signes, the Man or Woman speaks hastily; in watery signes, he or she hath some freckles in his or her face, or is blub cheeked; no very handsome body, but a mudling creature, and unlesse very well dignified, she ever signifies an ordinary vulgar person.

The colours of the Planets and Signes.

♄ Giveth black colour : ♃ a colour mixed with red and greene : ♂ red, or iron colour : ☉ yellow or yellow Purple : ♀ white or purple colour : ☿ sky-colour or blewish : ☽ a colour spotted with white and other mixt colours.

♈ White mixed with red : ♉ white mixed with Citrine : ♊ white mixed with red : ♋ greene or russet : ♌ red or green : ♍ blacke speckled with blew : ♎ black or darke crimson, or tawny colour : ♏ browne : ♐ yellow or a greene sanguine : ♑ blacke or russet, or a swart browne : ♒ a skye-colour with blew : ♓ white glistering colour.

CHAP. XVI.
Of the twelve Signes of the Zodiack, and their manifold Divisions.

THe whole Zodiack is divided into twelve equall parts, which we call Signes, and give them the names of living Crea-

An Introduction to Astrologie. 87

Creatures, either for their proprieties they hold with living Creatures, or by reason of the situation of the Starres in those places which somewhat resemble that effigies and similitude of living creatures: Their names and characters follow.

1	2	3	4	5	6
♈	♉	♊	♋	♌	♍

7	8	9	10	11	12
♎	♏	♐	♑	♒	♓

Every one of these Signes containes thirty degrees or parts in longitude: Hence it comes to passe that the whole Zodiack doth consist of 360 degrees, every degree containes 60 minutes, which we also call scruples, every minute containes 60 seconds, and so further if you please, &c. but in Astrology we onely make use of degrees, minutes and seconds.

These Signes are againe divided many wayes; as first, into four Quadrants or quarters, answering to the four quarters of the yeare.

The Vernall or Spring quarter, is sanguine, Hot and Moyst, and containes the first three Signes, *viz.* ♈ ♉ ♊.

The Æstival or Summer quarter is Hot, Dry and Cholerick, and containes the fourth, fifth and sixth Signes, *viz.* ♋ ♌ ♍.

The Autumnal or Harvest quarter is Cold, Dry and Melancholly, and contains the seventh, eighth and ninth Signes, *viz.* ♎ ♏ ♐:

The Hyemnal, Brumal or Winter quarter is Cold, Moyst and Phlegmatique, and contains the tenth, eleventh and twelft Signes, *viz.* ♑ ♒ ♓.

They are againe divided in division of the Elements, for some Signes in nature are Fiery, Hot and Dry, *viz.* ♈ ♌ ♐, and these three Signes constitute the *Fiery Triplicity.*

Others are Dry, Cold and Earthly, *viz.* ♉ ♍ ♑, and make the *Earthly Triplicity.*

Others are Airy, Hot and Moyst, *viz.* ♊ ♎ ♒, which make the *Aiery Triplicity.*

Others are Watry, Cold and Moyst, *viz.* ♋ ♏ ♓, and are called the *Watry Triplicity.* Againe,

Againe, some Signes are Masculine, Diurnal, and therefore Hot, as ♈ ♊ ♌ ♎ ♐ ♒.

Some are Feminine, Nocturnal, therefore Cold, viz. ♉ ♋ ♍ ♏ ♑ ♓.

The use whereof is this, That if you have a Masculine Planet in a Masculine Signe, it imports him or her more manly; and so if a Masculine Planet be in a Feminine Signe, the man or woman is lesse couragious, &c.

Some Signes againe are called Boreal, Septentrional or Northerne, because they decline from the Equinoctial Northward, and these are ♈ ♉ ♊ ♋ ♌ ♍; and these six Signes containe halfe the Zodiack, or the first semi-circle thereof.

Some Signes are called Austral, Meridional or Southerne, for that they decline Southward from the Equinoctial, and these are ♎ ♏ ♐ ♑ ♒ ♓.

Moveable.   The Signes againe are divided into Moveable, Fixed and Common, ♈ ♋ ♎ ♑ are called moveable and Cardinall: moveable, because when the ☉ enters into ♈ and ♎, the Weather and Season of the yeer quickly varies and changes; they are called Cardinal, because when the ☉ enters into any of those Signes from that time we denominate the Quarters of the yeer.

For from the ☉ entring into ♈ and ♎ the Equinoctial or the Spring and Autumne arise; from the ☉ his entrance into ♋ and ♑ ariseth the Solstice of Summer and Winter.

    So then the Equinoctial Signes are   ♈ ♎.
    Solstitial and Tropicks   ♋ ♑.

Fixed Signs.   The Fixed Signes doe in order follow the Equinoctial and Tropicks; and they are called fixed, for that when ☉ enters into them, the season of the yeer is fixed, and we doe more evidently perceive either Heat or Cold, Moysture or Drinesse.

The fixed Signes are these, ♉ ♌ ♏ ♒.

Common.   Signes are constituted between moveable and fixed, and retaine a property or nature, pertaking both with the preceding and consequent Signe: and they are ♊ ♍ ♐ ♓.

They are called Bycorporeall or double bodied, because they represent two Bodies: as ♊ two Twinnes, ♓ two Fishes.

An Introduction to Astrologie.

The right knowledge of these in Astrology is much, and you must understand it thus; In the Question or Figure of Heaven, if the Planet who is Lord of the Ascendant be in a moveable Signe, and the Signe ascending be also one, it denotes the person to be unstable, and of no resolution, easily, mutable, perverted, a wavering unconstant man.

Let us admit the Ascendant to be fixed, and the Lord of that Signe also in a fixed Signe, you may judge the party to be of firme resolution, no changling; or as we say, one that will stand to maintaine what he hath said or done, be it good or ill.

If the Signe ascending be common, and Lord of that Signe also in a Common Signe, you may judge the man or woman to be neither very wilfull or easily variable but betweene both.

The Signes also are divided into

Bestial or Quadrupedian, viz. ♈ ♉ ♌ ♐ ♑; these have representation of Four-footed Creatures.

Fruitful or prolifical, viz. ♋ ♏ ♓.

Barren Signes, ♊ ♌ ♍.

Manly or humane, curteous Signes, ♊ ♍ ♎ ♒.

Ferall Signes are ♌ and last part of ♐.

Mute Signes or of slow Voice, ♋ ♏ ♓; the more if ☿ be in any of them, in ☌ ☐ or ☍ of ♄

The use hereof is, that if your Significator or Lord of the Ascendant be in ♈ ♉ ♌ ♐ ♑, there's in the conditions of that party something of the nature of that Beast which represents that Signe he is in; as if he be in ♈, the man is rash, hardy and lascivious; if in ♉, stedfast and resolved, and somewhat of a muddy condition, vitiated, with some private imperfection, &c. and so of the rest.

Let us admit, one propounds his Question, if he shall have children, then if the ☽ and principall Significators be in Prolificall Signes, and strong, there's no question but he shall; the same doe, if the Question concerne Barrennesse, viz. if the Ascendant or fifth house be of those Signes we call barren Signes, it generally represents few or no children.

In Questions, if ♊ ♍ ♎ or ♒ ascend, or the Lord of the Ascendant

M

cendant be in humane Signes, then we may judge the man to be of civill carriage, very affable and easie to be spoken withall, &c.

Antiscion of the Planets. Besides these and many other divisions of the Signes, I thought good to be plaine in setting downe the Antiscions of the Planets.

Ptol. Apho. Stellæ irratio The Antiseion Signes are those, which are of the same vertue and are equally distant from the first degree of the two Tropick Signes ♋ ♑, and in which degrees whilest the ☉ is, the dayes and nights are of equall length; by example it will be plaine; when the ☉ is in the tenth degree of ♉, he is as farre distant from the first degree of ♋ as when in the twentieth degree of ♌; therefore when the ☉ is in the tenth of ♉, he hath his Antiscion to the twentieth of ♌; that is, he giveth vertue or influence to any Star or Planet that at that time either is in the same degree by Conjunction, or casteth any Aspect unto it.

But that you may more fully and perfectly know where your Antiscion fals in degrees and minutes, behold this following Table.

A generall Table of the Antiscions in Signes.

$$\left\{\begin{array}{c}\text{♊}\\\text{♌}\\\text{♍}\\\text{♎}\\\text{♏}\\\text{♐}\end{array}\right\} \quad \left\{\begin{array}{c}\text{♋}\\\text{♉}\\\text{♈}\\\text{♓}\\\text{♒}\\\text{♑}\end{array}\right\}$$

Any Planet in ♊ sends his Antiscion into ♋, or being in ♌ into ♉.

If you would know the exact degrees and minutes, you must work as followeth.

Let us suppose ♄ in twenty degrees and thirty five minutes of ♌, I would know in what part of the Zodiack he hath his Antiscion.

Over against ♌ I find ♉, so then I conclude his Antiscian is in ♉. To know the degree and minute, work thus:

See what degree and minute the Planet is in, substract that from

An Introduction to Astrologie. 91

from 30 degrees, and the remainder tels yon both the degree and minute.

As ♄ being in 20 degrees and 35 minutes of ♌, I subtract
from   30   0
           20 35
       9^{deg} 25 *Substacted.*

Here I subtract 25 min. from one whole degr. or from 60 min. which I borrow, and there rests 25 min. one degr. I borrowed, taken frm 10, and there rest 9 degr. one that I borrowed and two are three, taken from three, then nothing remains, so then I find my Antiscian of ♄ fals to be in 9 degr. and 25 min. of ♉, which Signe as you see is over against ♌; but this Table expresseth the work more quickly.

The Antiscions in degr.		Antiscions of the Planets in minutes.					
1	29	1	59	16	44		
2	28	2	58	17	43		
3	27	3	57	18	42		
4	26	4	56	19	41		
5	25	5	55	20	40		
6	24	6	54	21	39		
7	in 23	7	53	22	38		
8	22	8	in 52	23	in 37		
9	21	9	51	24	36		
10	20	10	50	25	35		
11	19	11	49	26	34		
12	18	12	48	27	33		
13	17	13	47	28	32		
14	16	14	46	29	31		
15	15	15	45	30	30		

The use is easie if you enter with the whole degrees of your Planet, the two first columns serve you, as ♂ supposed to be 14 degr. of a Signe, look 14 in the first column, over against it is 16, to that degree he sends his Antiscian.

If you have minutes, enter the four last columns; as if you enter with 17 min. in the fift column, over against it you find 43. or first look the Sign where the Antiscion fals, then subtract the number of degr. and minutes the Planet is in from 30, what remaines is the degree and minute where the Antiscion is; and as there are

Antiscions

Antiscions, which of the good Planets we think are equall to a ✶ or △; so are there Contrantiscions, which we find to be of the nature of a □ or ☍: and to know where it is, you doe no more then observe in what Signe and degree the Antiscion is, in the Signe and degree opposite to that place the Contrantiscion is: as in the former examples, the Antiscion of ♄ is in nine degr. and 25 min. of ♉, his Contrantiscion must then be in 9 degr. and 25 min. of ♏.

There are also many other divisions of the Signes: as into signes commanding, *viz.* ♈ ♉ ♊ ♋ ♌ ♍

And Signes obeying ♎ ♏ ♐ ♑ ♒ ♓.
And into Signs of right or long ascention, *viz.* ♋ ♌ ♍ ♎ ♏ ♐
And into Signs of short or oblique ascentio, *viz.* ♑ ♒ ♓ ♈ ♉ ♊

Signes of long ascention continue two houres and more in the ascendant: and Signes of short ascentions, doe arise in little more then an houre, and some in lesse, as you may experiment by the table of Houses:

I would know how many houres the Signe of ♌ continues in the Ascendant or Horizon?

In the first column of the Table of Houses, I looke for the signe ♌, under the title of the first House, and in the fourth line, I finde 00 ♌ 21, *viz.* no degree, 21 min. of ♌.

Over against that number on the left hand, under the title of houres and min. or time from noon, I finde 00 18 min. or no houres, 18 min. I then continue with my signe ♌ in the same column untill I finde 29 40. by which I perceive that the signe ♌ is removing out of the Ascendant: I seeke under the title of houres and minutes from noon over against the said 29 40 of ♌: on the left hand, what houres and min. stand there. I finde the number of 3 ho. 6. min. I subduct my former number of 00 18 min. from 3 hours and 6 min.

    3 h. 6
    00   18
    ―――――
    2   48. there remaines two houres and 48 min. of an houre, which is all the space of time that ♌ continues in the Ascendant, and in this regard it is called a signe of long ascentions.

You shall see the difference now in a signe of short Ascenti-
tion

An Introduction to Astrologie. 93

tion. I would know how long the signe of ♒ continues in the Ascendant. See in the ninth column, and under the title of the first house: in the third line I finde 00 ♒ 57. *viz.* 0 degree, 57. min. of ♒, over against it under houres and min. I finde 16ʰ 4 min. in the tenth line under the first house I find 29 28. against it on the left hand 17 8 *viz.* 17 houres, 8 min. I substract my former houres and min. from the latter

  17 8
  16 4

   1 4. the difference is one houre and 4 min. and so long time the signe of ♒ rests in the Ascendant: without exact knowledge hereof, one cannot attaine to any exactnesse in naturall Magick, *viz.* in gathering Hearbs, or perfecting many other rarities.

That which is most necessary for every Student in the Art is, that he know and be expert in the following Chapter.

CHAP. XVI.

The Nature, Place, Countries, generall Description, and Diseases signified by the twelve signes.

♈ IS a Masculine, Diurnall Signe, movable, Cardinall, Equinoctiall; in nature fiery, hot and dry, cholericke, bestial, luxurious, intemperate and violent, : the diurnall house of ♂ of the Fiery Triplicity, and of the East.   *Quality.*

All Pushes, Whelks, Pimples in the Face, small Pocks, hare Lips, Polypus, (*noli me tangere*) Ringwormes, Falling-sicknesse, Apoplexies, Megrims, Tooth-ach, Head-ach and Baldnesse.   *Diseases.*

Where Sheep and small Cattle doe feed or use to be, sandy and hilly Grounds, a place of refuge for Theeves, (as some unfrequented place;) in Houses, the Covering, Seeling or Plaistring of it, a Stable of small Beasts, Lands newly taken in, or newly plowed, or where Bricks have been burned or Lyme.   *Places ♈ nifieth.*

A dry Body, not exceeding in height, leane or spare, but lusty Bones and the party in his Limmes strong; the Visage long;   *Descript of the Body shape ♈ presents*

M 3

long; black Eye-browes, a long Neck, thick Shoulders, the Complexion dusky browne or swartish.

Kingdomes subject to ♈. — Germany, Swevia, Polonia, Burgundy, France, England, Denmarke, Silesia the higher, Judea, Syria.

Cities. — Florence, Capua, Naples, Ferrara, Verona, Utretcht, Marselles, Augusta, Cæsarea, Padua, Bergamo.

Qualities of the Signe ♉. — ♉ Is an Earthly, Cold, Dry, Melancholy, Feminine, Nocturnal, Fixed, Domestical or Bestial Signe, of the Earthly Triplicity, and South, the Night-house of *Venus*.

Diseases. — The Kings Evil, sore Throats, Wens, Fluxes of Rheumes falling into the Throat, Quinzies, Impostumes in those part.

Places. — Stables where Horses are, low Houses, Houses where the implements of Cattle are laid up, Pasture or Feeding grounds where no Houses are neer, plaine grounds, or where Bushes have bin lately grub'd up, and wherin Wheat and Corn is sowed, some little Trees not far off, in Houses, Sellars, low Rooms.

Shape and description. — It presents one of a short, but of a full, strong and wel-set stature, a broad Forehead, great Eyes, big Face; large, strong Shoulders; great, mouth and thick Lips; grosse Hands; black rugged Haire.

Kingdomes subject to ♉. — Polonia the great, North part of *Sweatbland*, *Russia*, *Ireland*, *Switzerland*, *Lorraine*, *Campania*, *Persia*, *Cyprus*, *Parthia*.

Cities. — Novograde, Parma, Bononia, Panormus, Mantua, Sena, Brixia, Carolstad, Nants, Liepsig, Herbipolis.

Quality and Property of ♊. — ♊ It's an aerial, hot, moyst, sanguine, Diurnal, common or double-bodied humain Signe; the diurnall house of ☿ : of the aery triplicity, Westerne, Masculine.

Diseases. — He signifies all Diseases or infirmities in the Armes, Shoulders, Hands, corrupted Blood, Windinesse in the Veines, distempered Fancies.

Places. — Wainscot Roomes, Plaistering and Wals of Houses, the Hals, or where Play is used, Hils and Mountaines, Barnes, Storehouses for Corne, Coffers, Chests, High Places.

Kingdomes Countries. — Lumbardy, Brabant, Flanders, the West and Southwest of England, Armenia.

Cities. — London, Lovaine, Bruges, Norrimberg, Corduba, Hasford, Mont, Bamberg, Cesena.

Description. — An upright, tall, straight Body either in Man or Woman, the

An Introduction to Astrologie.

the Complexion sanguine, not cleer, but obscure and dark, long Arms, but many times the Hands and Feet short and very fleshy; a dark Haire, almost black; a strong, active Body, a good piercing hazle Eye, and wanton, and of perfect sight, of excellent understanding, and judicious in worldly affaires.

♋ Is the onely house of the *Moon*, and is the first Signe of the Watry or Northerne Triplicity, is Watry, Cold, Moyst, Flegmatick, Feminine, Nocturnal, Moveable, a Solstice Signe, mute and slow of Voyce, Fruitful, Northerne. *Quality and property of* ♋.

It signifies Imperfections all over, or in the Brest, Stomack and Paps, weak Digestion, cold Stomack, Ptisick, salt Flegms, roten Coughs, dropsicall Humours, Impostumations in the Stomack, Cancers which ever are in the Brest. *Diseases.*

The Sea, great Rivers, Navigable Waters; but in the Inland Countries it notes places neer Rivers, Brooks, Springs, Wels, Sellars in Houses, Wash-houses, Marsh grounds, Ditches with Rushes, Sedges, Sea banks, Trenches, Cisternes. *Places.*

Generally a low and small stature, the upper parts of more bignesse then the lower, a round Visage; sickly, pale, a whitely Complexion, the Haire a sad browne, little Eyes, prone to have many Children, if a Woman. *Shape and description.*

Scotland, Zealand, Holland, Prusia, Tunis, Algier, Constantinople, Venice, Millan, Genoa, Amsterdam, Yorke, Magdeberg, Wittenberg, Saint Lucas, Cadiz. *Kingdoms Countries and Cities.*

♌ Is the onely house of the *Sun*, by nature, Fiery, Hot, Dry, Cholerick, Diurnal, Commanding, Bestial, Barren, of the East, and Fiery Triplicity, Masculine. *Quality and property of* ♌.

All sicknesses in the ribs and sides, as Plurifies, Convulsions, paines in the backe, trembling or passion of the heart, violent burning-feavers, all weaknesse or diseases in the heart, sore eyes, the Plague, the Pestilence, the yellow-Jaundies. *Diseases.*

A place where wilde Beasts frequent, Woods, Forrests, Desert places, steep rocky places, unaccessable places, Kings Palaces, Castles, Forts, Parks, in houses where fire is kept, neer a Chimney. *Places.*

Great round Head, big Eyes starting or staring out, or goggle-eyes, quick-sighted, a full and large body and it more then of middle stature, broad Shoulders, narrow Sides, yellow or darke flaxen haire and it much curling or turning up, a fierce *Shape and form.*

Coun-

countenance, but ruddy, high sanguine complexion, strong, valiant and active.

Kingdoms, Countries, Cities.
Italy, Bohemia, the *Alpes*, Turkie, Sicilia, Apulia, Rome, Syracusa, Cremona, Ravenna, Damasco, Prague, Lintz, Confluentia, Bristol.

Quality and property.
♍ It's an earthly, cold, melancholly, barren, feminine, nocturnall, Southerne Signe; the house and exaltation of ☿, of the earthly triplicity.

Places.
It signifies a Study where Books are, a Closet, a Dairy-house, Corne fields, Granaries, Malt-houses, Hay-ricks, or of Barley, Wheat or Pease, or a place where Cheese and Butter is preserved and stored up.

Diseases.
The Wormes, Winde, Chollicke, all Obstructions in the bowels and miseraicks, croking of the Guts, infirmenesse in the Stones, any disease in the belly.

Kingdoms, Countries, Cities.
Greece, the South part thereof, Croatia, the *Athenian* territory, Mesopotamia, Afftica, the South-west of France, Paris, Hierusalem, Rhodes, Lyons, Tholous, Basil, Heidelburge, Brundusium.

Shape and form.
A slender body of meane height, but decently composed; a ruddy browne complexion, blacke hayre, well-favoured or lovely, but no beavtifull creature, a small shrill voyce, all members inclining to brevity; a witty discreet foule, judicious and excellently well spoken, studious and given to History, whether Man or Woman; it produceth a rare, understanding, if ☿ be in this Signe, and ☽ in ♋, but somewhat unstable.

Nature and property.
♎ Is a Signe aeriall, hot and moyst, Sanguine, Masculine, Moveable, Equinoctiall, Cardinall, Humaine, Diurnall, of the Æriall Triplicity, and Westerne, the chiefe House of ♀.

Diseases.
All Diseases, or the Stone or Gravell in the reines of the Backe, Kidnies, heats and diseases in the Loynes or Hanches, Impostumes or Vlcers in the Reines, Kidneys or Bladder, weaknesse in the Backe, corruption of Blood.

Places.
In the Fields it represents ground neere Winde-mils, or some stragling Barne or out-house, or Saw-pits, or where Coopers worke or Wood is cut, sides of Hils, tops of Mountains, grounds where Hawking and Hunting is used, sandy and gravelly Fields, pure cleere Ayre and sharpe, the upper rooms in Houses, Chambers, Garrets, one Chamber within another.

Shape and form.
It personates a well framed body, straight, tall and more
subtill

An Introduction to Astrologie. 97

subtill or slender then grosse; a round, lovely and beautifull Visage, a pure sanguine colour; in Youth, no abundance or excesse in either white or red, but in Age usually some pimples, or a very high Colour, the Haire yellowish, smooth and long.

The higher *Austria, Savoy* its Dukedome, *Alsatia, Livonia, Kingdom Lisbone* in *Portugal, Frankeford, Vienna, Placentia,* the Territory in *Greece* where sometimes the City *Thebes* stood, *Arles, Friburge, Spires.* *Kingdom Countries. Cities.*

♏ Is a cold, watry, nocturnal, flegmatick, feminine Signe, of the watry Triplicity, fixed and North, the house and joy of *Mars,* feminine; usually it doth represent subtill, deceitfull men. *Quality and property of* ♏.

Gravell, the Stone in the Secret parts, Bladder, Ruptures, Fistulaes, or the Pyles in *Ano,* Gonorrhea's, Priapismes, all afflicting the Privy parts either in man or woman; defects in the Matrix. *Diseases.*

Places where all sorts of creeping Beasts use, as Beetles, &c. or such as be without wings, and are poysonous; Gardens, Orchards, Vineyards, ruinous Houses neer Waters; muddy, moorish Grounds, stinking Lakes, Quagmires, Sinks, the Kitchin or Larder, Wash-house. *Places.*

A corpulent, strong, able Body, somewhat a broad or square Face, a dusky muddy Complexion, and sad, dark Haire, much and crisping; an hairy Body, somewhat bow-legged, short necked, a squat, wel-trussed Fellow. *Forme and Description*

North part of *Bavaria,* the Wooddy part of *Norway, Barbary,* the Kingdome of *Fez, Catalonia* in *Spaine, Valentia, Vrbine* and *Forum Julij* in *Italy, Vienna, Messina* in *Italy, Gaunt, Frankeford* upon *Odar.* *Kingdome Countries Cities.*

♐ Is of the fiery triplicity, East, in nature fiery, hot, dry, Masculine, Cholericke, Diurnall, Common, bycorporall or double bodied, the House and joy of ♃. *Quality a nature of* ♐

It ruleth the Thighes and Buttocks in the parts of mans body and all Fistulaes or Hurts falling in those members, and generally denoteth blood heated, Feavers Pestilentiall, fals from Horses, or hurts from them or four-footed Beasts; also prejudice by Fire, Heat and intemperatenesse in Sports. *Diseases.*

N A

An Introduction to Astrologie.

Places. A Stable of great Horses, or Horses for the Wars, or a House where usually great foure-footed Beasts are kept; it represents in the Fields, Hils, and the highest places of Lands or Grounds that rise a little above the rest; in houses upper rooms, neer the fire.

Shape and form of body. It represents a wel-favoured Countenance, somewhat long Visage, but full and ruddy, or almost like Sun-burnt; the Haire light Chesnut colour, the Stature somewhat above the middle Size; a conformity in the Members, and a strong able body.

Kingdoms, Countries, Cities. Spaine, Hungary, Slavonia, Moravia, Dalmatia, Buda in Hungary, Toledo, Narbon, Cullen, Stargard.

Quality and nature of ♑. ♑ It's the House of *Saturn*, and is Nocturnal, Cold, Dry, Melancholly, Earthly, Feminine, Solsticiall, Cardinall, Moveable, Domesticall, Fourfooted, Southerne; the exaltation of ♂.

Diseases. It hath government of the Knees, and all Diseases incident to those places, either by Straines or Fractures; it notes Leprosie, the Itch, the Scab.

Places. It shewes an Oxe-house, or Cow house, or where Calves are kept, or Tooles for Husbandry, or old Wood is laid up; or where Sailes for Ships and such Materials are stored; also Sheep-Pens, and grounds where Sheepe feed, Fallow-grounds, barren-Fields Bushie and Thorny; Dunghils in Fields, or where Soyle is laid; in houses low, dark places, neer the ground or threshold.

Corporature. Usually dry Bodies, not high of Stature, long, leane and slender Visage, thin Beard, black Haire, a narrow Chin, long small Necke and narrow Brest, I have found many times ♑ ascending, the party to have white Hair, but in the seventh ever Blacke, I conceive the whitenesse proceeded from the nature of the Family rather then of the Signe.

Kingdoms, Countries, Cities. Thrace, Macedon in Greece now Turkie, Albania, Bulgaria, Saxony the South-west part, West-Indias, Stiria, the Isles Orcades, Hassia, Oxford, Mecklin, Cleves, Brandenburge.

Nature and property of ♒. ♒ Is an aieriall, hot and moyst Signe, of the aiery Triplicity, diurnal, sanguine, fixed, rational, humane, masculine, the principall house of ♄, and house wherein he most rejoyceth; Westerne.

Sicknesse. ♒ Governeth the Legs, Ancles, and all manner of infirmities

An Introduction to Astrologie.   99

tes incident to those members, all melancholy Winds coagulated in the Veines, or disturbing the Blood, Cramps, &c.

Hilly and uneven places, places new digged, or where quarries of Stone are, or any Minerals have been digged up; in Houses, the roofs, eaves or upper parts; Vineyards, or neer some little Spring or Conduit-head. *Places.*

It presents a squat, thick Corporature, or one of a strong, well composed Body, not tall; a long Visage, sanguine Complexion; if ♄ who is Lord of this house, be in ♑ or ♒, the party is black in Haire, and in Complexion sanguine, with distorted Teeth; otherwayes, I have observed the party is of cleer, white or faire Complexion, and of sandy coloured Haire, or very flaxen, and a very pure Skin. *Shape and form.*

Tartary, Croatia, Valachia, Muscovia, Westphalia in *Germany, Piemont* in *Savoy,* the West and South parts of *Bavaria, Media, Arabia, Hamborough, Breme, Montsferat* and *Pisaurum* in *Italy, Trent, Ingolstad.* *Kingdoms. Countries, Cities.*

♓ Is of the Watry Triplicity, Northern, cold Signe, moyst, Flegmatick, feminine, nocturnal, the house of *Jupiter,* and exaltation of *Venus,* a Bycorporeal, common or double-bodied Signe, an idle, effeminate, sickly Signe, or representing a party of no action. *Property and quality of* ♓.

All Diseases in the Feet, as the Gout, and all Lamenesse and Aches incident to those members, and so generally salt Flegms, Scabs, Itch, Botches, Breakings out, Boyles and Ulcers proceeding from Blood putrifacted, Colds and moyst diseases. *Sicknesse.*

It presents Grounds full of water, or where many Springs and much Fowle are, also Fish-ponds or Rivers full of Fish, places where Hermitages have been, Moats about Houses, Water-Mils; in houses neer the water, as to some Well or Pump, or where water stands. *Places.*

A short Stature, ill composed, not very decent, a good large Face, palish Complexion, the Body fleshy or swelling, not very straight, but incurvating somewhat with the Head. *Corporature.*

Calabria in *Sicilia, Portugall, Normandy,* the North of *Egipt, Alexandria, Rhemes, Wormes, Ratisbone, Compostella.* *Kingdoms, Countres, Cities.*

N 2   CHAP.

Chap. XVII.

Teaching what use may be made of the former Discouse of the twelve Signes.

IF one demand of the *Artist*, of what condition, quality or stature the person quesited, or enquired of is, then observe the Signe of that house whereby he is signified, the Signe wherein the Lord of that house is, and wherein the *Moone* is, mix one with another, and by the greater testimonies judge; for if the Signe be humane, aierial, that ascends or descends, and the Lord of that Signe or the ☽ in any Sign of the same triplicity or nature, you may judge the Body to be handsome, and the conditions of the party to be sociable, or he very courteous, &c.

If the *Quere* be concerning a Disease, and ♈ be either on the cusp of the Ascendant, or descending in the sixt, you may judge he hath something in his Disease of the nature of ♈, but what it is, you must know by the concurrence of the other significators.

If a Country man or Citizen hath lost or misseth any Cattle, or any materiall thing in his house, let him observe in what Signe the Significator of the thing is in; if in ♈, and it be a Beast strayed, or the like, let him see what manner of places that Signe directs unto, and let him repaire thither to search, considering the quarter of heaven the Signe signifies: if it be an unmoveable piece of Goods, that without man or woman cannot be removed, then let him look into such parts of his house, or about his house as ♈ signifies.

If one aske concerning Travell, whether such a Country, City or Kingdome will be healthfull or prosperous unto him, yea or no; see in the Figure in what Signe the Lord of the Ascendant is in, if the significator be fortunate in ♈, or if ♃ or ♀ be therein, he may safely travell or sojourne in such Cities or Countries as the Signe of ♈ represents, which you may easily discerne in the abovenamed Catalogue: Those Countries subject to the Signe wherein the *Infortunes* are posited, unlesse

themselves

An Introduction to Astrologie.

selves be significators, are ever unfortunate: where remember, that a Gentleman enquires usually, if he shall have his health and live jocundly in such or such a Country or *City*; the Merchant he wholly aimes at Trade, and the encrease of his Stock, therefore in the Merchants Figure you must consider the Country or City subject to the Signe of the second house, or where the *Part of Fortune* is, or Lord of the second is, and which is most fortified, and thither let him Trade.

Chap. XVIII.
Of the Essentiall Dignities of the Planets.

THe exact way of judicature in Astrology is, first, by being perfect in the nature of the Planets and Signes.

Secondly, by knowing the strength, fortitude or debility of the Planets, Significators, and a well poysing of them and their aspects and severall mixtures, in your judgment.

Thirdly, by rightly applying the influence of the positure of Heaven erected, and the Planets aspects to one another at the time of the Question, according to naturall (and not enforced) maximes of Art; for by how much you endeavour to straine a judgment beyond nature, by so much the more you augment your Errour.

A Planet is then said to be really strong when he hath many Essential dignities, which are knowne, by his being either in his House, Exaltation, Triplicity, Terme or Face, at time of erecting the Figure. As for Example:

In any Scheame of Heaven, if you find a Planet in any of those Signes we call his house or houses, he is then essentially strong, and we allow for that five dignities; as ♄ in ♑, ♃ in ♐, &c. *Essential dignity by House*

In *judgment*, when a Planet or Significator is in his owne house, it represents a man in such a condition, as that he is Lord of his owne house, estate and fortune; or a man wanting very little of the Goods of this world, or it tels you the man is in a very happy state or condition: this will be true, unlesse the significator be retrograde, or combuſt, or afflicted by any other malevolent Planet or aſpect.

Exaltation. If he be in that Signe wherein he is exalted, you may allow him four dignities eſſentiall, whether he be neer the very degree of his exaltation, yea or not; as ♂ in ♑ or ♃ in ♋.

If the ſignificator be in his exaltation, and no wayes impedited, but Angular; it preſents a perſon of haughty condition, arrogant, aſſuming more unto him then his due; for it's obſerved, the Planets in ſome part of the Zodiack doe more evidently declare their effects then in others; and I conceive this to be in thoſe Signes and degrees where fixed Starres of the ſame nature with the Planet, are more in number, and neerer the Ecliptick.

Triplicity. If he be in any of thoſe Signes which are alotted him for his Triplicity, he hath allowed him three dignities: but herein you muſt be cautious; as for example: In a Queſtion, Nativity, or the like, if you find the ☉ in ♈, and the Queſtion, or Nativity, or Scheame erected be by night, and you would examine the ☉ his fortitudes, he ſhall have four dignities for being in his exaltation, which continues through the Signe; but he ſhall not be allowed any dignity, as being in his triplicity; for by night the ☉ ruleth not the fiery Triplicity, but ♃; who had he been in place of the ☉, and by night, muſt have had allowed him three dignities: and this doe generally in all the Planets, ♂ excepted, who night and day ruleth the watry Triplicity.

A Planet in his triplicity, ſhewes a man modeſtly indued with the Goods and Fortune of this world, one prettily deſcended, and the condition of his life at preſent time of the Queſtion, to be good; but not ſo, as if in either of the two former dignities.

Tearme. If any Planet be in thoſe degrees we aſſigne for his Termes, we allow him two dignities; as whether day or night, if ♃ be in one, two, three or four, &c. degrees of ♈, he is then in his owne Termes, and muſt have two dignities therefore; and ſo ♀ in any of the firſt eight degrees of ♉, &c.

A Planet fortified, only as being in his own Termes, rather ſhewes a man more of the corporature and temper of the Planet,

An Introduction to Astrologie. 103

net, then any extraordinary abundance in fortune, or of eminency in the Common-wealth.

If any Planet be in his *Decanate, Decurie* or *Face*, as ♂ in *Face*. the first ten degrees of ♈, or ☿ in the first ten degrees of ♉, he is then allowed one essentiall dignity; for being in his owne Decanate or Face, cannot then be called peregrine.

A Planet having little or no dignity, but by being in his *Denate* or *Face*, is almost like a man ready to be turned out of doores, having much adoe to maintaine himselfe in credit and reputation: and in *Genealogies* it represents a Family at the last gasp, even as good as quite decayed, hardly able to support it selfe.

The Planets may be strong another manner of way, *viz.* Accidentally; as when Direct, swift in Motion, Angular, in △ or ✶ aspect with ♃ or ♀, &c. or in ☌ with certaine notable fixed Stars, as shall hereafter be related; Here followeth a Table of Essentiall Dignites, by which onely casting your Eye thereon, you may perceive what essentiall dignity or imbecility any Planet hath.

There hath been much difference between the *Arabians, Greeks* and *Indians* concerning the *Essentiall* Dignities of the Planets; I meane how to dispose the severall degrees of the Signes fitly to every *Planet*; after many Ages had passed, and untill the time of *Ptolomey*, the *Astrologians* were not well resolved hereof; but since *Ptolomey* his time, the *Grecians* unanimously followed the method he left, and which ever since the other Christians of *Europe* to this day retaine as most rationall; but the *Moores* of *Barbary* at present and those *Astrologians* of their Nation who lived in *Spaine* doe somewhat at this day vary from us; however I present thee with a Table according to *Ptolomey*.

A

A Table of the Essentiall Dignities of the PLANETS according to *Ptolomy*.

Signes.	Houses of the Planets.		Exaltation	Triplicity of Plan. Di.	Noc.	The Termes of the Planets.					The faces of the Planets.			Detriment	Fall.
♈	♂	D	☉ 19	☉	♃	♃ 6	♀ 14	☿ 21	♂ 26	♄ 30	♂ 10	☉ 20	♀ 30	♀	♄
♉	♀	N	☽ 3	♀	☽	♀ 8	☿ 15	♃ 22	♄ 20	♂ 30	☿ 10	☽ 20	♄ 30	♂	
♊	☿	D	☊ 3	♄	☿	☿ 7	♃ 14	♀ 21	♄ 25	♂ 30	♃ 10	♂ 20	☉ 30	♃	
♋	☽	N D	♃ 15	♂	♂	♂ 6	♃ 13	☿ 20	♀ 27	♄ 30	♀ 10	☿ 20	☽ 30	♄	♂
♌	☉	N D		☉	♃	♄ 6	☿ 13	♀ 19	♃ 25	♂ 30	♄ 10	♃ 20	♂ 30	♄	
♍	☿	N	☿ 15	♀	☽	☿ 7	♀ 13	♃ 18	♄ 24	♂ 30	☉ 10	♀ 20	☿ 30	♃	♀
♎	♀	D	♄ 21	♄	☿	♄ 6	♀ 11	♃ 19	☿ 24	♂ 30	☽ 10	♄ 20	♃ 30	♂	☉
♏	♂	N		♂	♂	♂ 6	♃ 14	♀ 21	☿ 27	♄ 30	♂ 10	☉ 20	♀ 30	♀	☽
♐	♃	D	☋ 3	☉	♃	♃ 8	♀ 14	☿ 19	♄ 25	♂ 30	☿ 10	☽ 20	♄ 30	☿	
♑	♄	N	♂ 28	♀	☽	♀ 6	☿ 12	♃ 19	♂ 25	♄ 30	♃ 10	♂ 20	☉ 30	☽	♃
♒	♄	D		♄	☿	♄ 6	☿ 12	♀ 20	♃ 25	♂ 30	♀ 10	☿ 20	☽ 30	☉	
♓	♃	N	♀ 27	♂	♂	♀ 8	♃ 14	☿ 20	♂ 26	♄ 30	♄ 10	♃ 20	♂ 30	☿	☿

The Use of the Table.

Every Planet hath two Signes for his Houses, except *Sol* and *Luna*, they but one apiece : ♄ hath ♑ and ♒ ; ♃ ♐ and ♓ ; ♂ ♈ ♏ ; ☉ ♌ ; ♀ ♉ ♎ ; ☿ ♊ ♍ ; ☽ ♋. The one of these Houses is called *Diurnall*, noted in the second Column by the Letter *D*. The other is *Nocturnall*, noted by the Letter *N*. In these Signs the Planets have their Exaltations, which the third Column points out ; as the ☉ in 19 ♈ ; ☽ in 3 ♉ ; ☊ in 3 degr. ♊, &c. are exalted.

These twelve Signes are divided into four Triplicities : The fourth Colum tels you which Planet or Planets both night and day governe each Triplicity : As over against ♈ ♌ ♐, you find ☉ ♃, *viz.* ☉ governeth by day in that Triplicity, and ♃ by night : Over against ♉ ♍ ♑, you find ♀ and ☽ ; *viz.* that ♀ hath domination by day, and ☽ by night in that Triplicity : Over against ♊ ♎ ♒ you find ♄ ☿ ; which rule as aforesaid :

Over

An Introduction to Astrologie.   105

Over against ♋ ♏ ♓, you find ♂, who, according to *Ptolomy* and *Naibod*, ruleth onely that Triplicity both day and night.

Over against ♈, in the fift, sixt, seventh, eighth, ninth columns, you find ♃ 6. ♀ 14. which tels you, the first six degrees of ♈ are the Termes of ♃; from six to fourteen, the Termes of ♀, &c.

Over against ♈, in the tenth, eleventh and twelfth columns, you find ♂ 10. ☉ 20. ♀ 30. *viz.* the first ten degrees of ♈ are are the Face of ♂; from ten to twenty the Face of ☉; from twenty to thirty the Face of ♀, &c.

In the thirteenth column, over against ♈, you find ♀ *Detriment*; *viz.* ♀ being in ♈, is in a Signe opposite to one of her owne Houses, and so is said to be in her Detriment.

In the fourteenth column, over against ♈, you find ♄, over his head *Fall*; that is, ♄ when he is in ♈ is opposite to ♎ his Exaltation, and so is Infortunate, &c. Though these things are expressed in the nature of the Planets already, yet this Table makes it appeare more evidently to the eye.

Chap. XIX.

Of severall Termes, Aspects, words of Art, Accidents, and other materiall things happening amongst the Planets; with other necessary Rules to be well known and understood before any Judgment can be given upon a Question.

THe most forcible or strongest Rayes, Configurations or Aspects, are onely these (nominated before) the Sextil ✶, Quadrate ☐, Trine △, Opposition ☍, we use to call the Conjunction ☌, an Aspect, but very improperly.

A *Sextil* aspect is the distance of one Planet from another by the sixt part of the Zodiack or Circle; for six times sixty degr. doe make 360. degr. this aspect you shall find called sometimes a *Sexangular* aspect, or an *Hexagon*.

A *Quadrate* aspect, or *Quadrangular*, or *Tetragonall*, is the distance of two Points, or two Planets by a fourth part of the *Circle*, for four times ninety doe containe three hundred and sixty degrees.   O   The

The *Trine* aspect confifts of 120 degrees, or by a third part of the *Circle*, for three times an hundred and twenty degrees make the whole *Circle*, or 360 degrees: It's called a *Triangular* afpect, or *Trigonall*, and if you find fometimes the word *Trigonocrator*, it's as much as a Planet ruling or having dominion in fuch a Triplicity or Trygon; for three Signes make one Trygon or Triplicity.

An *Oppofition* or Diametrall Radiation is, when two Planets are equally diftant 180 degrees, or halfe the *Circle* from each other.

A *Conjunction*, *Coition*, *Synod* or *Congreffe* (for fome ufe all thefe words) is, when two Planets are in one and the fame degree and minute of a Signe: Other new Afpects I have formerly mentioned in the beginning of this Difcourfe. You muft underftand amongft thefe Afpects, the *Quadrate Afpect* is a figne of imperfect emnity; and that the *Oppofition* is an afpect or argument of perfect hatred; which is to be underftood thus: A Queftion is propounded, *Whether two perfons at variance may be reconciled?* Admit I find the two *fignificators* reprefenting the two *Adverfaries*, in □ afpect; I may then judge, becaufe the afpect is of imperfect hatred, that the matter is not yet fo farre gone, but there may be hopes of reconciliation betwixt them, the other *fignificators* or Planets a little helping. But if I find the maine *fignificators* in oppofition, it's then in nature impoffible to expect a peace betwixt them till the fuit is ended, if it be a fuit of *Law*; untill they have fought, if it be a *Challenge*.

The *Sextill* and *Trine* afpects are arguments of Love, Unity and Friendfhip; but the △ is more forcible, (*viz.*) if the two *fignificators* are in ✶ or △, no doubt but peace may be eafily concluded.

Conjunctions are good or bad, as the Planets in ☌ are friends or enemies to one another.

There is alfo a *Partill* and *Platick* afpect: *Partill* afpect is when two Planets are exactly fo many degrees from each other as make a perfect afpect: as if ♀ be in nine degrees of ♈, and ♃ in nine degrees of ♌, this is a Partill △ afpect: fo ☉ in one degree of ♉, and ☽ in one degree of ♋, make a Partil ✶, and this is a ftrong figne or argument for performance of any

thing

An Introduction to Astrologie. 107

thing, or that the matter is neer hand concluded when the aspect is so partill, and signifies good; and it's as much a signe of present evill when mischiefe is threatned.

A *Platick* Aspect is that which admits of the *Orbs* or *Rayes* of two Planets that signifie any matter: As if ♀ be in the tenth degree of ♉, and ♄ in eighteen degrees of ♍, here ♀ hath a Platick △, or is in a Platick △ to ♄, because she is within the *moiyty* of both their *Orbs*; for the *moity* of ♄ his Rayes or Orbs is five, and of ♀ 4, and the distance betwixt them and their perfect aspect is eight degrees; and here I will againe insert the Table of the quantity of their Orbs, although I have in the Planets severall descriptions mentioned them; they stand thus as I have found by the best Authors and my owne Experience.

	deg	min		deg	m	
♄	10	0	According to others	9	0	I sometimes use
♃	12	0	As some have wrote	9	0	the one, and
♂	7	30	All consent	7	0	sometimes the
☉	17	0	Most say	15	0	other, as my
♀	8	0	Many write but	7	0	Memory best
☿	7	0	All consent onely	7	0	Remembereth
☽	12	30	Generally but	12	0	them, and this without error.

Application Application of Planets is three severall wayes: First, when a Planet of more swift motion applies to one more slow and ponderous, they being both direct; as ♂ in ten degrees of ♈, ☿ five: here ☿ applies to ☌ of ♂.

Secondly, when both Planets are retrograde, as ☿ in ten degrees of ♈, and ♂ in nine of ♈; ☿ being not direct untill he hath made ☌ with ♂: this is an ill Application and an argument either suddenly perfecting, or breaking off the businesse, according as the two Planets have signification.

Thirdly, when a Planet is direct, and in fewer degrees, and a retrograde Planet being in more degrees of the Signe, as ♂ being direct in 15 ♈: and ☿ retrograde in 17 ♈; this is an ill application, and in the Ayre shewes great change; in a Question sudden alteration: but more particularly I expresse Application as followeth.

Application. It is when two Planets are dawring neere together either by ☌ or Aspect, viz. to a ✶ △ □ or ☍; where you must understand, that the superiour Planets doe not apply to the inferiour (unlesse they be Retrograde, but ever the lighter to the more ponderous; as if ♄ be in the 10. degree of ♈, and ♂ be in the seventh degree of ♈ the same Signe, here ♂ being in fewer degrees, and a more light Planet then ♄, applies to his ☌; if ♂ had been in the seventh degree of ♊, he had then applyed to a ✶ Aspect with ♄: had ♂ been in the seventh degree of ♋, he had then applyed to a □ of ♄; had he been in the seventh of ♌, he had applyed to a △ of ♄; had ♂ been in the seventh degree of ♎, he had applied to an ☍ of ♄, and the true Aspect would have been when he had come to the same degree and minute wherein ♄ was: And you must know that when ♄ is in ♈ and casteth his ✶ □ or △ to any Planet in the like degrees of ♊ or ♋ or ♌, this Aspect is called a Sinister ✶ □ or △, and it is an Aspect according to the succession of the Signes; for after ♈ succeeds ♉, then ♊, then ♋, &c. and so in order. Now if ♄ he in ♈, he also casteth his ✶ □ or △ to any Planet that is in ♒ ♑ or ♐, and this is called a Dexter Aspect, and is against the order of Signes; but this Table annexed will more easily informe you.

A Table of the Aspects of the Signes amongst one another.

	✶	□	△	☍		✶	□	△	☍		✶	□	△	☍
Dexter. ♈	♒	♑	♐		Dexter. ♌	♊	♉	♈		Dexter. ♐	♎	♍	♌	
				♎					♒					♊
Sinister:	♊	♋	♌		Sinister.	♎	♏	♐		Sinister.	♒	♓	♈	
Dexter. ♉	♓	♒	♑		Dexter. ♍	♋	♊	♉		Dexter. ♑	♏	♎	♍	
				♏					♓					♋
Sinister.	♋	♌	♍		Sinister.	♏	♐	♑		Sinister.	♓	♈	♉	
Dexter. ♊	♈	♓	♒		Dexter. ♎	♌	♋	♊		Dexter. ♒	♐	♏	♎	
				♐					♈					♌
Sinister.	♌	♍	♎		Sinister.	♐	♑	♒		Sinister.	♈	♉	♊	
Dexter. ♋	♉	♈	♓		Dexter. ♏	♍	♌	♋		Dexter. ♓	♑	♐	♏	
				♑					♉					♍
Sinister.	♍	♎	♏		Sinister.	♑	♒	♓		Sinister.	♉	♊	♋	

An Introduction to Astrologie. 109

The use of the Table aforesaid.

You may see in the 2, 3, 4, and fifth column, in the upper part of the Table, ✶ ☐ △ ☍.   {Dexter.
You may see in the second line and first Column { ♈
{Sinister.
and in the four Columns over against them { ♒ ♑ ♐
♎
{ ♊ ♋ ♌

The meaning is thus; a Planet posited in ♈, and another in ♒ in like degrees, he in ♈ doth behold the other in ♒ with a ✶ dexter Aspect.

A Planet in ♈ and another in ♑, he in ♈ beholds the Planet in ♑ with a ☐ dexter.

A Planet in ♈ beholding another in ♐, casts his △ dexter thither.

A Planet in ♈ beholding another in ♎, casts his opposite Aspect unto him.

Againe, over against Sinister, and under ♈ you finde ♊ ♋ ♌; that is, ♈ beholds ♊ with a ✶ Sinister: ♋ with a ☐ Sinister, ♌ with a △ sinister: Observe the dexter aspect is more forcible then the Sinister: this understand in the other Columns, *viz.* that Dexter Aspects are contrary to the succession of Signes, Sinister in order as they follow one another.

Signes not beholding one another.

♈	♉	♊	♋	♌	♍	♎	♏	♐	♑	♒	♓
♉	♈	♉	♌	♋	♌	♌	♎	♏	♎	♑	♌
♏	♊	♏	♒	♍	♒	♉	♐	♉	♒	♓	♒
				♑		♐					
	♎			♓		♈		♋			
	♐					♊					

These are called Signes inconjunct, or such as if a Planet be in one of them, he cannot have any aspect to another in the signe underneath: as one in ♈ can have no aspect to another in ♉ or ♏, or one in ♉ to one in ♈ ♊ ♎ or ♐, so understand of the rest.   **Sepera-**

An Introduction to Astrologie.

Separation.   Separation, it is in the first place; when two Planets are departed but six minutes distance from each other, as let ♄ be in 10. degr. and 25. of ♈ and ♃ in 10. degr. and 25.min.of ♈: now in these degrees and minutes they are in perfect ☌; but when ♃ shall get into 10. degr. and 31. or 32. minutes of ♈, he shall be said to be separating from ♄; yet because ♄ hath 9. degr. allowed him for his rayes, and ♃ hath also the same number allowed him, ♃ cannot be said to be totally seperated or cleere from the rayes of ♄, untill he hath got 9. whole degrees further into ♈, or is fully 9. degrees distant from him, for the halfe of ♃ his orbe is 4. degr. 30.min. and the halfe of ♄ his orbe is 4. degr. 30. min. added together they make 9. whole degrees; for every Planet that applies is allowed halfe his owne orbs and halfe the orbs of that Planet from whom he seperates: As if ☉ and ☽ be in any aspect, the ☽ shall then be seperated from the ☉, when she is fully distant from the ☉ 7.degr. and 30.min. *viz.* half the orbs of the ☉, and 6. degr. the moity of her owne orbes; in all 13.degr. and 30.minutes.

     The exact knowledge hereof is various and excellent: For admit two Planets significators in Marriage at the time of the question, are lately seperated but a few minutes; I would then judge there had been but few dayes before great probability of effecting the Marriage, but now it hung in suspence, and there seemed some dislike or rupture in it; and as the significators doe more seperate, so will the matter and affection of the parties more alienate and vary, and according to the number of degrees that the swifter Planet wanteth ere he can be wholly seperated from the more ponderous, so will it be so many weekes, dayes, moneths, or yeers ere the two Lovers will wholly desist or see the matter quite broke off: The two *significators* inmoveable Signes, Angular and swift in motion, doth hasten the times; in common signes, the time will be more long; in fixed, a longer space of time will be required.

Probibition.   Prohibition is when two Planets that signifie the effecting or bringing to conclusion any thing demanded, are applying to an Aspect; and before they can come to a true Aspect, another Planet interposeth either his body or aspect, so that thereby the matter propounded is hindered and retarded; this is called

An Introduction to Astrologie.

led Prohibition. For Example, ♂ is in 7. degr. of ♈, and ♄ is in the 12. ♂ signifies the effecting my businesse when he comes to the body of ♄, who promises the conclusion, the ☉ is at the same time in 6. degr. of ♈ : Now in regard that the ☉ is swifter in motion then ♂, he will overtake ♂, and come to ☌ with ♄ before ♂, whereby whatever ♂ or ♄ did formerly signifie, is now prohibited by the ☉ his first impediting ♂ and then ♄, before they can come to a true ☌. This manner of prohibition is called a Conjunctionall or Bodily prohibition; and you must know that the combustion of any Planet is the greatest misfortune that can be.

The second manner of Prohibition is by Aspect, either ✶ □ △ ☍, viz. when two Planets are going to Conjunction; as ♂ in 7. degr. of ♈, ♄ in 15 of ♈; let us admit the ☉ in 5. degr. of ♊; he then being more swift then ♂ in his diurnall motion, doth quickly over-take and passe by the ✶ dexter of ♂) and comes before ♂ can come to ☌) to a ✶ dexter of ♄ : This is called a Prohibition by Aspect, in the same nature judge if the Aspect be □ △ ☍.

Refrenation — There's another manner of Prohibition; by some more properly called Refrenation; as thus, ♄ in 12. degr. of ♈, ♂ in 7. degr. here ♂ hastens to a ☌ of ♄, but before he comes to the tenth or eleventh degree of ♈ he becomes Retrograde, and by that meanes refraines to come to a ☌ of ♄, who still moves forward in the Signe, nothing signified by the former ☌ will ever be effected.

Translation — Translation of light and nature is, when a light Planet seperates from a more weighty one, and presently joynes to another more heavy; and its in this manner, Let ♄ be in 20. degr. of ♈ : ♂ in 15. of ♈, and ☿ in 16. of ♈; here ☿ being a swift Planet seperates from ♂, and translates the vertue of ♂ unto ♄. Its done also as well by any Aspect as by ☌. And the meaning hereof in judgement, is no more then thus; That if a matter or thing were promised by ♄, then such a man as is signified by ☿ shall procure all the assistance a *Mars* man can doe unto *Saturne*, whereby the businesse may be the better effected; in Marriages, Lawsuits, and indeed in all vulgar questions Translation, is of great use, and ought well to be considered.

Reception

Reception. Reception is when two Planets that are significators in any Question or matter, are in each others dignity; as ☉ in ♈, and ♂ in ♌; here is reception of these two Planets by Houses; and certainly this is the strongest and best of all receptions. It may be by triplicity terme or face, or any essentiall dignity; as ♀ in ♈, and ☉ in ♉; here is reception by triplicity, if the Question or Nativity be by day: so ♀ in the 24. of and ♂ in ♈, the 16. of ♊; here is reception by terme, ♂ being in the terms of ♀, and she in his termes.

The use of this is much; for many times when as the effecting of a matter is denyed by the Aspects, or when the significators have no Aspect to each other, or when it seemes very doubtfull what its promised by □ or ☍ of the significators, yet if mutuall Reception happen betwixt the principall significators, the thing is brought to passe, and that without any great trouble, and suddenly to the content of both parties.

Peregrine. A Planet is then said to be Peregrine, when he is in the degrees of any Signe wherein he hath no essentiall dignity: As ♄ in the tenth degree of ♈, that Signe being not his House, Exaltation, or of his Triplicity, or he having in that degree either Terme or Faces, he is then said to be Peregrine; had he been in 27, 28, &c. of ♈, he could not be termed Peregrine, because then he is in his owne Terme.

So the ☉ in any part of ♋ is Peregrine, having no manner of dignity in that Signe.

This is very much materiall in all Questions to know the Peregrine Planet, especially in questions of Theft; for euer almost the significator of the Theefe is known by the Peregrine Planet posited in an Angle, or the second House.

Void of course. A Planet is voyd of course, when he is seperated from a Planet, nor doth forthwith, during his being in that Signe, apply to any other: This is most usually in the ☽; in judgements doe you carefully observe whether she be voyd of course yea or no; you shall seldome see a businesse goe handsomely forward when she is so.

Frustration. Frustration is, when a swift Planet would corporally joyne with a more ponderous, but before they can come to ☌, the more weighty Planet is joyned to another, and so the ☌ of

the

An Introduction to Astrologie. 113

the first is frustrated, as ☿ in ten degrees of ♈, ♂ twelve, ♃ in thirteen of ♈; here ☿ strives to come to ☌ with ♂, but ♂ first gets to ☌ with ♃; whereby ☿ is frustrated of the ☌ of ♂: in Questions is signifies as much as our common Proverb, *Two Dogges quarrell, a third gets the Bone.*

Hayz. is, when a Masculine and Diurnal Planet is in the day time above the earth, and in a Masculine Sign, and so when a Feminine, Nocturnal Planet in the night is in a Feminine Sign and under the earth: in Questions it usually shews the content of the Querent at time of the Question, when his *significator* is so found.

Saturn, Jupiter and *Mars* being placed above the Orbe of the *Sun*, are called the superiour, ponderous and more weighty Planets; *Venus, Mercury* and *Luna* are called the inferiour Planets, being under the Orbe of the *Sun*.

A Planet is said to be *Combust* of the ☉, when in the same Sign where the ☉ is in, he is not distant from the ☉ eight degrees and thirty minutes, either before or after the ☉; as ♃ in the tenth degree of ♈, and ☉ in the eighteenth of ♈; here ♃ is *combust*: or let the ☉ be in eighteen of ♈, and ♃ in twenty eight degrees of ♈, here ♃ is *combust*: and you must observe a Planet is more afflicted when the ☉ hastens to ☌ of him, then when the ☉ receds from him; in regard it's the body of the ☉ that doth afflict. I allow the moyity of his own Orbs to shew the time of *combustion*, and not of ♃; for by that rule ♃ should not be *combust* before he is within four degrees and a half of the ☉. I know many are against this opinion.

Use which you find most verity in: the *significator* of the Querent combust, shews him or her in great fear, and overpowred by some great person.

A Planet is said to be still under the Sun-beams, untill he is fully elongated or distant from his body 17. degr. either before or after him.

A Planet is in the heart of the Sun, or in Cazimi, when he is not removed from him 17. min. or is within 17. min. forward or backward, as ☉ in 15. 30. ♉, ☿ in 15; 25. of ♉: here ☿ is in Cazimi, and all Authors doe hold a Planet in Cazimi to be fortified thereby; you must observe all Planets may be in Combustion

Hayz.

Superior & inferiour Planets.

Combustion.

Under the ☉ beams.

Cazimi, or in the heart of the ☉.

P

bustion of the ☉, but he with none, and that Combustion can onely be by personall ☌ in one Signe, not by any aspect, either ✶ □ △ or ☍, his □ or opposite aspects are afflicting, but doe not Combure or cause the Planet to be in Combustion.

Orientall.   ♄ ♃ and ♂, are Orientall of the ☉, from the time of their ☌ with him, untill they come to his ☍: from whence untill againe they come to ☌, they are said to be Occidentall; to be *Occidentall.* Orientall is no other thing then to rise before the ☉: to be Occidentall is to be seen above the Horizon, or to set after the ☉ is downe: ☿ and ♀ can make no ✶ □ △ or ☍ to the ☉: their Orientality is when they are in fewer degrees of the Signe the ☉ is, or in the Signe preceding; their Occidentality, when they are in more degrees of the Signe the ☉ is in, or in the next subsequent: for you must know ☿ cannot be more degrees removed from the ☉ then 28. nor ♀ more then 48. though some allow a few more. The ☽ is Orientall of the ☉ from the time of her ☍ to her conjunction, and Occidentall from the time of her Conjunction to Opposition; and the reason hereof is, because she farre exceeds the Sunne in swiftnesse of motion, and so presently gets further into the Signe, &c.

Besieging.   Besieging is, when any Planet is placed betwixt the bodies of the two Malevolent Planets ♄ and ♂: as ♄ in 15. ♈, ♂ in 10. of ♈, ♀ in 13 ♈: here *Venus* is besieged by the two infortunes, and it represents in questions, a Man going out of Gods blessing into the warme Sunne; I mean if ♀ be a significatrix that time in the figure.

There are other accidents belonging to the Planets one amongst another mentioned by the Ancients, but of so little purpose in judgement, that I have cleerly omitted them.

Direction is.   When a Planet moveth forward in the Signe, as going out of 13. degr. into 14. and so along.

Retrogradation is.   When a Planet goeth backward, as out of 10. degr. into 9, 8, 7, &c.

Stationary is.   When he moves not at all, as the superiours doe not 2, 3, or 4, dayes before Retrogradation.

Already

An Introduction to Astrologie.

A ready TABLE whereby to examine the *Fortitudes* and *Debilities* of the Planets.

Essentiall Dignities.		Debilities.	
A Planet in his owne house, or in mutual reception with another Planet by house, shall have Dignities	5	In his Detriment	5
		In his Fall	4
		Peregrine	5
In his exaltation, or reception by exaltation	4		
In his owne Triplicity	3		
In his owne Terme	2		
Decanate or Face	1		

Accidentall Fortitudes.		Accidental Debilities.	
In the Mid-heaven or Ascendant	5	In the twelfth House	5
In the seventh, fourth & eleventh houses	4	In the eighth and sixth	2
In the second and fifth	3	Retrograde	5
In the ninth	2	Slow in motion	2
In the third house	1	♄ ♃ ♂ Occidentall	2
Direct (the ☉ and ☽ are alwayes so, as to them this is voyd)	4	♀ ☿ Orientall	2
		☽ decreasing in light	2
Swift in motion	2	Combust of the ☉	5
♄ ♃ ♂ when Orientall	2	Under the ☉ Beames	4
♀ and ☿ when Occidentall	2	Partill ☌ with ♄ ♂	5
The ☽ encreasing, or when she is Occidentall	2	Partill ☌ with ☋	4
		Besieged of ♄ and ♂	5
Free from Combustion and ☉ Beams	5	Partill ☍ of ♄ or ♂	4
In the heart of the ☉, or Cazimi	5	Partill □ of ♄ or ♂	3
In partill ☌ with ♃ and ♀	5	In ☌ with Caput Algol in 20. ♉, or within five degrees	5
In partill ☌ with ☊	4		
In partill △ to ♃ and ♀	4		
In partill ✶ to ♃ and ♀	3		
In ☌ with Cor Leonis, in 24. degr. ♌	6		
Or in ☌ with Spica ♍, in 18. ♎	5		

P 2

An Introduction to Astrologie.

I forbeare here to explaine the Table, because I shall doe it better hereafter, upon some Example.

Two necessary TABLES *of the Signes, fit to be understood by every Astrologer or Practitioner.*

	Degrees masculine and feminine.	Degr. light, darke, smoakie, voyd.	Degr. deepe or pitted.	Degr. lame or deficient.	Degr. encreasing fortune.
♈	mas. 8. 15. 30. fem. 9. 22.	d. 3. l. 8. d. 16. l. 20. v. 24. l. 29. v. 30.	6 11 16 23 29		19
♉	mas. 11. 21. 30 fem. 5. 17. 24.	d. 3. l. 7. v. 12. l. 15 v. 20. l. 28. d. 30.	5 12 24 25	6 7 8 9 10	3 15 27
♊	mas. 16. 26. fem. 5. 22. 30.	l. 4. d. 7. l. 12. v. 16 l. 22. d. 27. v. 30.	2 12 17 26 30		11
♋	m. 2. 10. 23. 30 fem. 8. 12. 27.	l. 12. d. 14. v. 18. sm. 20. l. 28. v. 30.	12 17 23 26 30	9 10 11 12 13 14 15	1 2 3 4 15
♌	mas. 5. 15. 30. fem. 8. 23.	d. 10. sm. 20. v. 25. l. 30.	6 13 15 22 23 28	18 27 28	2 5 7 19
♍	mas. 12. 30. fem. 8. 20.	d. 5. l. 8. v. 10. l. 16 sm. 22. v. 27. d. 30	8 13 16 21 22		3 14 20
♎	mas. 5. 20. 30. fem. 15. 27.	l. 5. d. 10. l. 18. d. 21. l. 27. v. 30.	1 7 20 30		3 15 21
♏	mas. 4. 17. 30. fem. 14. 25.	d. 3. l. 8. v. 14. l. 22 sm. 24. v. 29. d. 30.	9 10 22 23 27	19 28	7 18 20
♐	mas. 2. 12. 30. fem. 5. 24.	l. 9. d. 12. l. 19. sm. 23. l. 30.	7 12 15 24 27 30	1 7 8 18 19	13 20
♑	mas. 11. 30. fem. 19.	d. 7. l. 10. s. 15 d. 19 d. 22. v. 25. d. 30.	7 17 22 24 29	26 27 28 29	12 13 14 20
♒	mas. 5. 21. 27. fem. 15. 25. 30.	sm. 4. l. 9. d. 13. l. 21. v. 25. l. 30.	1 12 17 22 24 29	18 19	7 16 17 20
♓	mas. 10. 23. 30. fem. 20. 28.	d. 6. l. 12. d. 18. d. 22. v. 25 l. 28 d 30	4 9 24 27 28		13 20

The

An Introduction to Astrologie.

The use of the Table.

Many times it happens, that it is of great concernment to the Querent to know, whether a Woman be with childe of a Male or Female; or whether the Theefe be Man or Woman, &c. When it shall so chance that neither the Angles, or the sex of the Planet, or the Signes doe discover it, but that the testimonies are equall; then if you consider the degrees of the Signe wherein the ☽ is, and wherein the Planet significator of the thing or party quesited is, and the degree of the Cuspe of the House signifying the person quesited after; and see by the second Column whether they be in Masculine or Feminine Degrees, you may poyse your judgement, by concluding a Masculine party, if they be posited in Masculine degrees; or Feminine, if they be in Feminine degrees. You see the first eight degrees of ♈ are Masculine, the ninth degree is Feminine, from nine to fifteene is Masculine, from fifteen to two and twenty is Feminine, from two and twenty to thirty is Masculine; and so as they stand directed in all the Signes.

The third Columne tels you there are in every Signe certain Degrees, some called Light, Darke, Smoakie, Void, &c. the use hereof is thus:

Let a Signe ascend in a Nativity or Question, if the Ascendant be in those Degrees you see are called Light, the Childe or querent shall be more faire; if the degree ascending be of those we call Darke, his Complexion shall be nothing so faire, but more obscure and darke; and if he be borne deformed, the deformity shall be more and greater; but if he be deformed when the light degrees of a Signe ascend, the imperfection shall be more tolerable.

And if the ☽ or the Degree ascending be in those degrees we call Voyd, be the Native or Querent faire or foule, his understanding will be small, and his judgement lesse then the world supposeth, and the more thou conferrest with him, the greater defect shalt thou finde in him. If the Ascendant, the ☽, or either of them be in those degrees we call Smoakie, the person inquiring or Native, shall neither be very faire nor very

foule,

118   *An Introduction to Astrologie.*

foule, but of a mixt Complexion, Stature or condition, betwixt faire and foule, betwixt tall and of little Stature, and so in condition neither very judicious or a very Asse.

You see the three first Degrees of ♈ are Darke, from three to eight are light from eight to sixteen are Darke, from sixteen to twenty are Light, from twenty to four and twenty are Voyd, from foure and twenty to nine and twenty are Light, the last Degree is Voyd.

Degrees, deep or pitted.   Degrees deep or pitted presented in the fourth Column have this signification, that if either the ☽ or the Degree ascending or Lord of the Ascendant be in any of them, it shews the Man at a stand in the question he askes, not knowing which way to turn himselfe, and that he had need of helpe to bring him into a better condition; for as a man cast into a Ditch doth not easily get out without helpe, so no more can this querent in the case he is without assistance.

Called by some Azimene degrees.   Degrees lame and deficient are those mentioned in the fifth Columne; the meaning whereof is thus, If in any question you finde him that demands the question, or in a Nativity, if you finde the Native defective in any member, or infected with an inseperable disease, halting, blindnesse, deafnesse, &c. you may then suppose the native hath either one of these Azimene degr. ascending at his birth, or the Lord of the Ascendant, or the ☽ in one of them: in a Question or Nativity, if you see the Querent lame naturally, crooked, or vitiated in some member, and on the sodain you can in the figure give no present satisfaction to your selfe, doe you then consider the Degree ascending, or Degree wherein the ☽ is in, or the Lord of the Ascendant, or principall Lord of the Nativity or Question, and there is no doubt but you shall finde one or more of them in Azimene degrees.

Degrees increasing fortune.   These Degrees are related in the fifth Column, and tend to this understanding, that if the Cuspe of the second House, or if the Lord of the second house, or ♃, or the part of fortune be in, any of those degrees, its an argument of much wealth, and that the Native or Querent will be rich.

A

An Introduction to Astrologie.

A TABLE shewing what members in Mans Body every Planet signifieth in any of the twelve SIGNES.

	♄	♃	♂	☉	♀	☿	☽
♈	Brest, Arme.	Neck, Throat, Heart, Belly.	Belly, Head.	Thighes.	Reines, Feet.	Secrets, Legs.	Knees, Head,
♉	Heart, Brest, Belly.	Shoulders Armes, Belly, Neck.	Reines, Throat.	Knees.	Secret-members, Head.	Thighs, Feet.	Legs, Throat,
♊	Belly, Heart.	Brest, Reines, Secrets.	Secrets, Armes, Brest.	Legs. Ancles.	Thighs, Throat.	Knees, Head.	Feet, Shoulders Armes, Thighs,
♋	Reines, Belly, Secrets.	Heart, Secrets, Thighs.	Feet.	Knees, Shoulder Armes.	Knees, Shoulders Armes.	Legs, Throat, Eyes.	Head, Brest, Stomack.
♌	Secrets, Reines.	Belly, Thighs, Knees.	Knees, Heart, Belly.	Head.	Legs, Brest, Heart.	Feet, Armes, Shoulders Throat.	Throat, Stomacke Heart.
♍	Thighs, Secrets, Feet.	Reines, Knees.	Legs, Belly.	Throat.	Feet, Stomacke Heart, Belly.	Head, Brest, Heart.	Armes, Shoulders Bowels.
♎	Knees, Thighs.	Secrets, Legs, Head, Eyes.	Feet, Reines, Secrets.	Shoulders Armes.	Head, smal guts	Throat, Heart, Stomacke Belly.	Brest, Reines Heart, Belly.
♏	Knees, Legs.	Thighs, Feet.	Head, Secrets, Armes, Thighs.	Brest, Heart.	Throat, Reines, Secrets.	Shoulders Armes, Bowels, Back.	Stomack, Heart, Secrets, Belly.

♄

	♄	♃	♂	☉	♀	☿	☽
♐	Legs, Feet,	Knees, Head, Thighs.	Throat, Thighs, Hands, Feet.	Heart, Belly.	Shoulder, Armes, Secrets. Thighs,	Brest, Reines, Heart, Secrets.	Bowels, Thighs, Back.
♑	Head Feet.	Legs, Neck. Eyes, Knees.	Armes, Shoulders Knees, Legs.	Belly, Back.	Brest, Heart, Thighs,	Stomack Heart, Secrets.	Reines, Knees, Thighs.
♒	Neck, Head.	Feet, Armes, Shoulder, Brest.	Brest, Legs, Heart.	Reines, Secrets.	Heart, Knees.	Bowels, Thighs, Heart.	Secrets, Legs, Ancles.
♓	Armes. Shoulders Neck.	Head, Brest, Heart.	Heart, Feet, Belly, Ancles.	Secrets, Thighs.	Belly, Legs, Neck, Throat.	Reines, Knees, Secrets, Thighs.	Thighs, Feet.

The Use and Reason of the former Table.

IT was well neere foure yeeres after I had studied Astrology, before I could finde any reason, why the Planets in every of the Signes should signifie the members as mentioned in the Table: at last, reading the 88. *Aphorisme* of *Hermes*, I understood the meaning of it, viz. *Erit impedimentum circa illam partem corporis quam significat signum, quod fuerit nativitatis tempore impeditum.* There wil be some impediment in or neer that part of the body, which is signified by the Signe that shall be afflicted at time of the Birth The use of all comes to thus much:

That if you would know where any Disease is, I meane in what member of the body, see in what Signe the *significator* of the sick Party is, and what part of mans body that Planet signifies in that Signe, which you may doe by the former Table, in that member or part of body shall you say the sick party is grieved or diseased.

As if ♄ be Significator of the sick party, and at time of your

Question

An Introduction to Astrologie. 121

Question in ♊, have recourse to your Table, and you see ♄ in ♊ signifieth a Disease in the Belly or heart, &c. Do so in the rest.

Now the reason of this signification of every Planet in such or such a Signe is this:

Every Planet in his owne House or Signe, governeth the Head; in the second Signe from his House, the Neck; in the third Signe from his House, the Armes and Shoulders; and so successively through the twelve Signes: as ♄ in ♑ ruleth the Head, in ♒ the Neck, in ♓ Armes and Shoulders: so ♃ in ♐ ruleth the Head, in ♑ the Neck, in ♒ the Armes and Shoulders.

The ☽ observes the same order as the rest; yet the *Arabians*, from whom this learning is, doe allow her in ♈ the Head as well as the Knees: The Head, because *Aries* signifies so much: The Knees, because *Aries* is the ninth Sign from *Cancer*.

You may observe this in the marks of mans Body, and many other judgments, and make singular use of it; ever remembring this, the more the Signe is vitiated, the greater mole or scarre; or the neerer to an *Azimene*, *Pitted* or *deficient* degree of the Signe, the stronger is the deformity, sicknesse, &c.

CONSIDERATIONS before Judgment.

ALL the *Ancients* that have wrote of Questions, doe give warning to the *Astrologer*, that before he deliver judgment he well consider whether the Figure is radicall and capable of judgment; the Question then shall be taken for radicall, or fit to be judged, when as the Lord of the hour at the time of proposing the Question, and erecting the Figure, and the Lord of the Ascendant or first House, are of one Triplicity, or be one, or of the same nature.

As for *example*; let the Lord of the houre be ♂, let the Signe of ♏ ♋ or ♓ ascend, this Question is then radicall, because ♂ is Lord of the hour, and of the Watry Triplicity, or of those Signes ♋ ♏ or ♓.

Againe, let the Lord of the hour be ♂, and ♈ ascend, the Question shall be radicall, because ♂ is both Lord of the hour and Signe ascending.

Q   Let

An Introduction to Astrologie.

Let the Lord of the hour be ♂, and let the Signe ♌ ascend, here, although the ☉ is one of the Lords of the fiery Triplicity, and sole Lord of the Signe ♌, yet shall the Question be judged; because the ☉, who is Lord of the Ascendant, and ♂ who is Lord of the hour, are both of one nature, *viz.* Hot and Dry.

When either 00. degrees, or the first or second degrees of a Signe ascend (especially in Signes of short ascentions, *viz.* ♑ ♒ ♓ ♈ ♉ ♊, you may not adventure judgment, unlesse the Querent be very young, and his corporature, complexion and moles or scarres of his body agree with the quality of the Signe ascending.

If 27, 28, or 29 degrees ascend of any Signe, it's no wayes safe to give judgment, except the Querent be in yeers corresponding to the number of degrees ascending; or unlesse the Figure be set upon a time certaine, *viz.* a man went away or fled at such a time precise; here you may judge, because it's no propounded question.

It's not safe to judge when the ☽ is in the later degrees of a Signe, especially in ♊ ♏ or ♑; or as some say, when she is in *Via Combusta*, which is, when she is in the last 15 degrees of ♎, or the first fifteen degrees of ♏.

All manner of matters goe hardly on (except the principall *significators* be very strong) when the ☽ is voyd of course; yet somewhat she performes if voyd of course, and be either in ♉ ♋ ♐ or ♓.

You must also be wary, when in any question propounded you find the Cusp of the seventh house afflicted, or the Lord of that house Retrograde or impedited, and the matter at that time not concerning the seventh house, but belonging to any other house, it's an argument the judgment of the Astrologer will give small content, or any thing please the Querent; for the seventh house generally hath signification of the *Artist*.

The *Arabians*, as *Alkindus* and others, doe deliver these following rules, as very fit to be considered before a Question be judged.

Viz. if ♄ be in the Ascendant, especially Retrograde, the matter of that Question seldome or never comes to good.

♄ In

An Introduction to Astrologie. 123

♄ In the seventh either corrupts the judgement of the *Astrologer*, or is a Signe the matter propounded will come from one misfortune to another.

If the Lord of the Ascendant be Combust, neither question propounded will take, or the Querent be regulated.

The Lord of the seventh unfortunate, or in his fall, or Termes of the Infortunes, the *Artist* shall scarce give a solid judgment.

When the testimonies of Fortunes and Infortunes are equal, deferre judgment, it's not possible to know which way the Ballance will turne: however, deferre you your opinion till another question better informe you.

Chap. XX.

What Significator, Querent and Quesited are; and an Introduction to the Judgment of a Question.

THE Querent is he or she that propounds the question, and desires resolution: the Quesited is he or she, or the thing sought and enquired after.

The *significator* is no more then that Planet which ruleth the house that signifies the thing demanded: as if ♈ is ascending, ♂ being Lord of ♈, shal be *significator* of the Querent, *viz.* the Sign ascending shall in part signifie his corporature, body or stature, the Lord of the Ascendant, the ☽ and Planet in the Ascendant, or that the ☽ or Lord of the Ascendant are in aspect with, shall shew his quality or conditions equally mixed together; so that let any Signe ascend, what Planet is Lord of that Signe, shall be called Lord of the House, or Significator of the person enquiring, &c.

So that in the first place therefore, When any Question is propounded, the Signe ascending and his Lord are alwayes given unto him or her that asks the question.

2ly. You must then consider the matter propounded, and see to which of the twelve houses it doth properly belong: when you have found the house, consider the Sign and Lord of that Sign,

Q 2 how,

how, and in what Signe and what part of Heaven he is placed, how dignified, what aspect he hath to the Lord of the Ascendant, who impedites your *Significator*, who is friend unto him, *viz.* what Planet it is, and what house he is Lord of, or in what house posited; from such a man or woman signified by that Planet, shall you be furthered or hindered; or of such relation unto you as that Planet signifies; if Lord of such a house, such an enemy, if Lord of such a house as signifieth enemies, then an enemy verily; if of a friendly house, a friend: The whole naturall key of all Astrology resteth in the words preceding rightly understood: By the Examples following I shall make all things more plain; for I doe not desire, or will reserve any thing whereby the Learner may be kept in suspence of right understanding what is usefull for him, and most fit to be knowne.

In every question we doe give the ☽ as a *Cosignificator* with the querent or Lord of the Ascendant (some have also allowed the Planet from whom the ☽ separated as a *significator*; which I no way approve of, or in my practice could ever find any Verity therein.)

In like manner they joyned in judgment the Planet to whom the ☽ applyed at time of the question, as *Cosignificator* with the Lord of the house of the thing quesited, or thing demanded.

Having well considered the severall applications and separations of the Lords of those houses signifying your question, as also the ☽, the Scite of Heaven and quality of the aspect the ☽, and each *Significator* hath to other, you may begin to judge and consider whether the thing demanded wil come to passe yea or no; by what, or whose meanes, the time when, and whether it will be good for the querent to proceed further in his demands yea or no.

CHAP. XXI.
To know whether a thing demanded will be brought to perfection yea or nay.

THE *Ancients* have delivered unto us, that there are four wayes or means, which discover whether one question

or

or the thing demanded shall be accomplished yea or not.

First, by *Conjunction*; when as therefore you find the Lord of *Conjunction* the Ascendant, and Lord of that house which signifies the thing demanded, hastening to a ☌, and in the first house, or in any Angle, and the *significators* meet with no *prohibition* or *refrenation*, before they come to perfect ☌; you may then judge, that the thing sought after, shall be brought to passe without any manner of let or impediment, the sooner, if the *Significators* be swift in motion, and Essentially or Accidentally strong; but if this ☌ of the *Significators* be in a Succedant house, it will be perfected, but not so soon: if in Cadent houses, with infinite losse of time, some difficulty, and much strugling.

Things are also brought to a passe, when as the principall *Aspect of* ✶ signifiers apply by ✶ or △ aspect out of good Houses and pla- *or* △. ces where they are essentially well dignified (and meet with no malevolent Aspect to intervene ere they come to be in perfect ✶ or △; I meane to the partill Sextill or Tryne.

Things are also produced to perfection, when the Signifi- *Aspects of* ▢ cators apply by ▢ aspect, provided each Planet have dignity *and* ☍. in the Degrees wherein they are, and apply out of proper and good Houses, otherwise not. Sometimes it happens, that a matter is brought to passe when the Significators have applyed by ☍, but it hath been, when there hath been mutuall reception by House, and out of friendly Houses, and the ☽ seperating from the Significator of the thing demanded, and applying presently to the Lord of the Ascendant; I have rarely seen any thing brought to perfection by this way of opposition; but the Querent had been better the thing had been undone: for if the Question was concerning Marriage, the parties seldome agreed, but were ever wrangling and jangling, each party repining at his evill choyce, laying the blame upon their covetous Parents, as having no minde to it themselves: and if the Question was about Portion or Monies, the querent did its true, recover his Money or Portion promised, but it cost him more to procure it in suit of Law, then the debt was worth, &c. and so have I seen it happen in many other things, &c.

Things are brought to perfection by Translation of Light *Translation.* and Nature, in this manner.

When

When the *Significators* both of *Querent* and *Quesited* are separated from ☌ or ✶ or △ aspects of each other, and some one Planet or other doth separate himselfe from one of the *Significators*, of whom he is received either by House, Triplicity or Terme, and then this Planet doth apply to the other *Significator* by ☌ or aspect, before he meeteth with the ☌ or aspect of any other Planet, he then translates the force, influence and vertue of the first Significator to the other, and then this intervening Planet (or such a man or woman as is signified by that Planet) shall bring the matter in hand to perfection.

Consider what house the Planet interposing or translating the nature and light of the two Planets is Lord of, and describe him or her, and say to the party, that such a party shall doe good in the businesse of, &c. *viz.* if Lord of the second, a good Purse effects the matter; if Lord of the third, a Kinsman or Neighbour; and so of all the rest of the Houses: of which more shall be said in the following Judgments.

Collection.

Matters are also brought to perfection, when as the two principall Significators doe not behold one another, but both cast their severall Aspects to a more weighty Planet then themselves, and they both receive him in some of their essentiall dignities; then shall that Planet who thus collects both their Lights, bring the thing demanded to perfection: which signifies no more in Art then this, that a Person somewhat interessed in both parties and described and signified by that Planet, shall performe, effect and conclude the thing which otherwayes could not be perfected: As many times you see two fall at variance, and of themselves cannot think of any way of accommodation, when suddenly a Neighbour or friend accidentally reconciles all differences, to the content of both parties: And this is called *Collection*.

Lastly, things are sometimes perfected by the dwelling of Planets in houses, *viz.* when the *Significator* of the thing demanded is casually posited in the Ascendant; as if one demand if he shall obtaine such a Place or Dignity, if then the Lord of the tenth be placed in the Ascendant, he shall obtaine the Benefit, Office, Place or Honour desired: This rule of the Ancients holds not true, or is consentanious to reason: except they

An Introduction to Astrologie. 127

they will admit, that when the ☽, besides this dwelling in house, doth transferre the light of the *Significator* of the thing desired, to the Lord of the Ascendant; for it was well observed that the applictaion of the *Significators* shew inclination of the parties, but separation usually privation; that is, in more plaine termes, when you see the principall *Significators* of the *Querent*, and thing or party quesited after seperated, there's then little hopes of the effecting or perfecting what is desired, (notwithstanding this dwelling in houses) but if there be application, the parties seeme willing, and the matter is yet kept on foot, and there is great probability of perfecting it, or that things will come to a further treaty.

In all Questions you are generally to observe this Method following.

As the Ascendant represents the person of the Querent, and the second his Estate, the third his Kinred, the fourth his Father, the fifth his Children, the sixth his Servant or Sicknesse, the seventh his Wife, the eight the manner of his Death, the ninth his Religion or journeys, the tenth his Estimation or hnour, the eleventh his Friends, the twelfth his secret Enemies.

So you must also understand, that when one askes concerning a Woman or any party signified by the seventh House and the Lord thereof, that then the 7th House shall be her Ascendant and signifie her person, the eight House shall signifie her Estate and be her second, the ninth House shall signifie her Brethren and Kindred, the tenth shall represent her Father, the eleventh her Children or whether apt to have Children, the twelfth her Sicknesse and Servants, the first House her Sweetheart, the second House her Death, the third her Journey, the fourth her Mother, the fifth her Friends, the sixth her sorrow, care and private Enemies.

Let the Question be of or concerning a Churchman, Minister, or the Brother of the Wife or Sweet-heart, the ninth House shall represent each of these, but the tenth House shall be Significator of his Substance, the eleventh House of his Brethren, and so in order: and so in all manner of Questions the House signifying the party quesited shall be his Ascendant or first
House,

House, the next his second House, and so continuing round about the whole Heavens or twelve Houses.

If a question be made of a King, the tenth is his first house, the eleventh his second, and so orderly; but in Nativities, the Ascendant ever signifieth the party borne, whether King or Beggar: These things preceding being wel understood, you may proceed to judgment; not that it is necessary you have all that is wrote, in your memory exactly, but that you be able to know when you are in an errour, when not; when to judge a question, when not: I should also have shewed how to take the *Part of Fortune*, but that I will doe in the first Example, the use of the *Part of Fortune* being divers, but hardly understood rightly by any Author I ever met with: However note, if a King propound an *Astrologicall Question*, the Ascendant is for him, as well as for any meaner party; and all the houses in order, as for any vulgar person: For Kings are earth, and no more then men; and the time is comming, &c. when.

THE RESOLVTION
of all manner of QUESTIONS and DEMANDS.

CHAP. XXII.
Queſtions concerning the firſt Houſe.

If the QUERENT *is likely to live long yea or not.*

MANY Men and Women have not the time of their *Nativities*, or know how to procure them, either their Parents being dead, or no remembrance being left thereof; and yet for divers weighty conſiderations they are deſirous to know by a queſtion of Aſtrology, *Whether they ſhall live long or not? Whether any Sickneſſe is neer them? What part of their Life is like to be moſt happy?* together with many other ſuch *Queries* people doe demand incident to this houſe.

SIGNES *of Health or long Life.*

IN this *Queſtion* you muſt conſider if the Signe aſcending, the Lord thereof, and the ☽ be free from misfortune, *viz.* if the Lord of the Aſcendant be free from Combuſtion of the ☉, *Signes of Health.*

R   from

The Resolution of

from the □ ☍ or ☌ of the Lord of the eighth, twelfth, sixth or fourth house, if he be Direct, in Essentiall Dignity, swift in Motion, or Angular, especially in the first house, (for in this question he is best placed therein) or tenth, or else in the eleventh, or ninth houses, and in a good aspect with ♃ or ♀, or the ☉, or in the Termes of ♃ and ♀, it's an argument of Health and long life to the *Querent*, for the Lord of the Ascendant, or Ascendant it selfe unfortunate or ☽ in bad houses afflicted, shew mischiefe at hand; the aforesaid *significators* free, argue the contrary: for as you consider the Lord of the Ascendant, so the Ascendant is to be considered, and what aspect is cast unto it, *viz.* good or evill, and by what Planet or Planets, and of what house or houses they are Lords of.

Signs contrary, viz. of Sicknesse, Death, &c. Misfortune.

It's generally received, that if the Lord of the Ascendant be under the *Sun* beams, or going to Combustion, which is worse then when he is departing, or the ☽ cadent and unfortunated by any of those Planets who have dominion in the eighth or sixth, and either the ☋, ♄ or ♂ in the Ascendant or seventh house, peregrine or in their detriments, or retrograde, or if there be in the degree ascending, or in that degree of the Signe wherein the Lord of the Ascendant is, or with the ☽, or with that Planet who afflicts any of those; I say, any fixed *Starre* of violent influence or nature of the Planet afflicting, or nature of the Lord of the eighth or sixth house, then you may judge the *Querent* not long lived, but neer some danger, or shall undergoe some misfortune in one kind or other, according to the quality of the *significator* and signification of that or those houses they are Lords of.

The time when any of these ACCIDENTS *shall happen.*

YOU must see if the Lord of the Ascendant be going to Combustion, or to ☍ or ☌ of the Lord of the eighth or fourth, how many degrees he is distant from the ☉, or Lord of the eighth or fourth, and in what Signe either of them are in; if the space betwixt them be eight degrees, and in a common Signe, it denotes so many moneths; if in a fixed Signe, so many yeers; if in moveable, so many weeks: this is onely for example,

all manner of Questions. 131

example, and in generall; for the meafure of time muft be limited according to the other *significators* concurring in judgment herein.

Secondly, having confidered the Lord of the Afcendant, fee how many degrees the ☽ is alfo diftant from any Infortune, or from the Lords of the fixth or eighth, and in what Signe or Signes their Nature, Quality and Houfe wherein they are pofited.

Thirdly, confider if there be an Infortune in the Afcendant, how many degrees the Cufp of the houfe wants of that degree the unfortunate Planet is in, or if the unfortunating Planet be in the feventh, how many degrees the Afcendant wants of his true Oppofition, and compute the time of Death, Sickneffe or Misfortune according to the dimenfion of degrees in Signes moveable, common or fixed.

If you find the Lord of the Afcendant afflicted moft of all by the Lord of the fixt, and in the fixt, or if the Lord of the Afcendant come to Combuftion in the fixt, you may judge the *Querent* will have very many and tedious fickneffes, which will fcarce leave him till his death; and the more certaine the judgment will be, if the Lord of the Afcendant, and Lord of the eighth and the ☽ be all placed in the fixth.

if you find the Lord of the Afcendant, the Signe afcending, or ☽ moft principally impedited or unfortunated by the Lord of the eighth, or that Planet who afflicts your *significators* out of the eighth, then you may judge that the Sickneffe with which he is now afflicted, or is fhortly to be troubled withall, will end him, and that his death is approaching for that death is threatned.

But if you find that the Lord of the Afcendant, or Signe of the Afcendant, or the ☽ are chiefly afflicted by the Lords of fome other houfes, you fhall judge his misfortune from the nature of the houfe or houfes whereof the Planet or Planets afflicting are Lords; and the firft original thereof, or difcovery, fhall be fignified from fomething, Man or Woman, &c. belonging to that houfe wherein you find the Planet afflicting pofited, and thereby you fhall judge a misfortune and not death: The fixed Starres I mentioned, being of the nature of ♂, fhew fudden

R 2 diftempers

distempers of body, or Feavers, Murders, Quarrels, &c. of the nature of ♄, quartan Agues, Poverty, casuall hurts by Fals, &c. of the nature of ☿, they declare Consumptions, Madnesse, cozenage by false Evidence or Writings: of the nature of the ☽, Tumults, Commotions, Wind-chollick, danger by Water, &c. of the nature of the ☉, envy of Magistrates, hurt in the Eyes, &c. of the nature of ♃, oppression by domineering Priests, or by some Gentleman: of the nature of ♀, then prejudice by some Woman, the Pox, or Cards, Dice and Wantonnesse.

Caution. You must carefully avoid pronouncing Death rashly, and upon one single testimony; you must observe, though the Lord of the Ascendant be going to Combustion, whether either ♃ or ♀ cast not some ✶ or △ to the Lord of the Ascendant, ere he come to perfect Combustion, or any other infortune, for that is an argument that either Medicine or strength of Nature will contradict that malignant influence, or take off part of that misfortune; but when you find two or more of the rules aforesaid concurring to death, you may be more bold in your Judgment: yet concerning the absolute time of death of any party, I have found it best to be wary, and have as much as I could, refrained this manner of judgment; onely thus much by the Question may be knowne, that if you find the *significators*, as aforesaid, afflicted, you may judge the man or party inquiring to be no long lived man, or subject to many miseries and calamities, and this I know by many verified examples: the knowledge hereof is of excellent use for such as would purchase any Lease or Office, or thing for Life or Lives, &c. or for those who would carefully in a naturall way prevent those casualties their natures or inclinations would run them into.

To what part of Heaven its best the Querent direct his Affaires, or wherein he may live most happily.

You must know that the twelve Houses are divided into the East, West, North and South quarters of Heaven.

The Cuspe of the first House is the beginning of the East,

all manner of Questions. 133

and its called the East Angle, from the Degree of the first house to the Degree or Cuspe of the tenth House or *Medium Cœli*, containing the 12, 11, and tenth Houses, are East, inclining to the South: from the Cuspe of the tenth House to the Cuspe of the seventh House, containing the 9, 8, and 7, is South, verging towards the West: from the degree of the seventh House to the Cuspe of the fourth House, consisting of the 6, 5, and fourth houses, is the West, tending to the North: from the Degree of the fourth House to the Degree of the Ascendant, containing the 3, 2, and first Houses, is North inclining to the East.

Having viewed the severall quarters of Heaven, see in which of them you finde the Planet that promiseth the Querent most good, and where you finde ♃ ♀ ☽ or ⊗, or two or more of them, to that quarter direct your affaires; and if you have the part of Fortune and the ☽ free from Combustion and other misfortunes, go that wayes, or to that quarter of heaven where you finde her; for you must consider, that though ♃ and ♀ be Fortunes, yet casually they may be Infortunes, when they are Lords of the 8, 12, or 6. in that case you must avoyd the quarter they are in, and observe the ⊗ and the ☽ and Lord of the Ascendant; and as neere as you can avoyd that quarter of Heaven where the infortunes are, especially when they are significators of mischiefe, otherwayes either ♂ or ♄ being Lord of the Ascendant or second House, tenth or eleventh, may (being essentially strong) prove friendly. The generall way of resolving this Question is thus; If the Querent doe onely desire to live where he may enjoy most health, looke in what Signe and quarter of Heaven the Lord of the Ascendant and ☽ are in, and which of them are strongest, and doth cast his or her more friendly Aspect to the Degree ascending; to that quarter of Heaven repaire for Healths sake: If the *Querent* desire to know to what part he may steer his course for obtaining of an Estate or Fortune, then see where and in what quarter of Heaven the Lord of the second is placed, and the ⊗, and his *Dispositor* or two of them; for where and in what quarter they are best fortified, from thence may he expect his most advantage, &c. Of this I shall speak casually in subsequent Judgments.

R 3 *What*

What part of his LIFE is like to be best.

See either in what Angle or quarter of Heaven the fortunate and promising Planets are posited in; for in this way of Judicature, we give usually to every house five yeers, but sometimes more or lesse, according as you see the *significators* promising Life or Death, (but commonly five yeers we give) beginning with the twelfth, and so to the eleventh, then the tenth, then the ninth, &c. and so to the Ascendant; as if in your Question you find ♃ or ♀ in the eleventh or tenth house, you may judge the Man or Woman to have lived happily from the fift yeer of his age to the fifteenth, or in his youth: if they, or either of them, be in the eighth or seventh, they declare that from twenty to thirty he will, or hath lived, and may live contentedly: if ♃ or ♀ be in the 6. 5. or 4. then judge after his middle age, or from 30. to 45. he may do very well: if you find ♃ or ♀ in third, second or first, then his best dayes, or his greatest happinesse will be towards his old age, or after he is forty five untill sixty; if you find the *significators* of Life very strong, and signifying long Life, you may adde one yeer to every house, for it's then possible the *Querent* may live more then sixty yeers, or untill seventy, or more, as many we know doe.

Lastly, you must observe at the time of your **Question**, how the Lord of the Ascendant and the ☽ are separated, from what Planet, and by what aspect; the separation of those shew the manner of Accidents which have preceded the **Question**; their next application, what in future may be expected; if you consider what house or houses, the Planet or Planets they separated from are Lords of, it acquaints you with the matter, nature, person and quality of the thing already happened: ill, if the aspect was ill; Good, if the aspect was good; and if you observe the quality of the next aspect by application, and the well or ill being and position of the Planet or Planets applied unto, it delivers the quality of the next succeeding Accidents and Casualties, their nature, proportion, time when they will happen or come upon the *Querent*.

An

all manner of Questions. 135

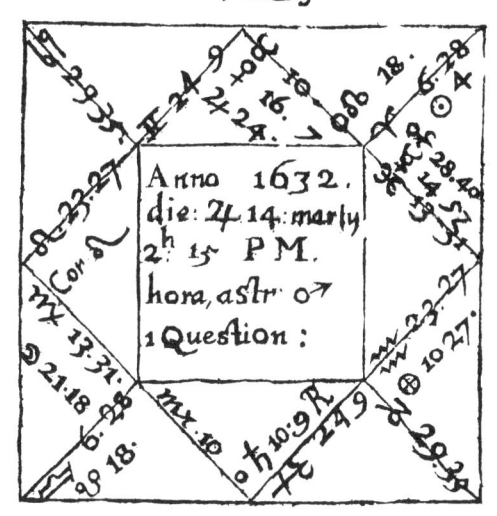

An ASTROLOGICALL Judgement concerning these demands propounded by the Querent.

1. *If he were like to live long, yea or not.*
2. *To what part of the World he were best direct his course of life.*
3. *What part of his life, was in probability like to be most fortunate.*
4. *He desired I would relate (if possible by a Figure) some of the generall Accidents had happened unto him already.*
5. *What Accidents in future he might expect, good or evill.*
6. *The Time when.*

The Stature of the Querent is signified by ♌, the signe ascending: there is a fixed Star called *Cor Leonis* neere the cuspe of the first house, viz. in 24. 34. of ♌, of the nature of ♂ and ♃, and first magnitude; both the Cuspe of the first house and degree of the signe wherein ☉ Lord of the Ascendant is in, are

the

the termes of ♃; the ☽ is in a △ aspect with both ♃ and ♀, and they in the tenth house: so that the forme and Stature of this *Querents* body was decent, of a middle stature, strongly compacted, neither fat or fleshy, but comely, wanting no gracefulnesse in its composure; a faire Visage, reddish Haire, cleere Skin, some cuts on his right Cheek, (for he was a Souldier;) but certainly the presence of the fixed Starre in the Ascendant, which represents the Face, occasioned those hurts or scarres.

As the Signe ascending is fiery, and as the Lord of the Ascendant is in a fiery Signe, and by nature is *Hot* and *Dry*, so was this Gentlemans temper and condition, being exceeding Valiant, Cholerick, high Minded, and of great spirit; for ☉ Lord of the Ascendant is in his *Exaltation*; yet in regard the ☽ is in △ with the two *Fortunes*, he was sober, modest, and by Education excellently qualified, and thereby had great command of his *Passion*; but as the ☽ was in ☍ to ☿, he had his times of *Anger* and *Folly*, whereby he much prejudiced his Affaires. But to our Question.

If live long, &c.

Finding the *Ascendant* not vitiated with the presence of either *Saturne*, who is Lord of the sixth, or of *Jupiter* who is Lord of the eighth.

Seeing the Lord of the *Ascendant* was in *Exaltation*, no wayes impedited, pretty quick in motion, in the ninth house, and in the *Termes* of ♃.

Observing the ☽ separated from △ of ♀ applying to △ of ♃, and he posited in the mid heaven, and thereby the malice of ♂ restrained by the interposition of ♃.

Considering the ☉ was above the earth, the fortunate Planets, *viz.* ♃ and ♀ Angular, and more potent then the infortunes, *viz.* ♄ or ♂: from hence I concluded, that according to naturall Causes, he might live many yeers; and that Nature was strong, and he subject to few Diseases. This hath hitherto proved true; he being yet alive this present, *March* 1646.

all manner of Questions.   137

To what Part of the WORLD, *or of this* KINGDOME, *he might best apply himselfe to Live in.*

The Lord of the *Ascendant* is ☉, who being neer the *Cuspe* of the ninth house,(signifying *long Journeyes*)and the Signe thereof Moveable; I intimated he was resolving sodainly upon a *Journey* South-east, or to those parts of the World which lye from *London* South-east: *South*, because the quarter of Heaven wherein the Lord of the *Ascendant* is in, is South: *East*, because the Signe where ☉ is in is East, [*this be confessed:*] And as the ☉ was but two degr.10 ♍. distant from the Cusp of the ninth, he went away within two moneths; for ☉ was 4. 18 ♈.

I judged those *Countries* subject to the Signe of ♈, might be suitable and propitious to his Affaires; which you may see in the nature of ♈, *pag.* 95. and what their Names are, to which I now refer you.

Had his resolution been to have staid in *England*, the ☊ and ☉ being both in ♈, shew it might have been good for him, for *England* is subject to ♈; I would have advised him to have steered his course of life towards *Kent, Essex, Sussex,* or *Suffolk*, for they lye East or by South from *London*; but if sometimes you find that a City, Towne or Kingdome subject to the *Cælestiall* Signe which promiseth you good, stands not, as to the quarter of Heaven, *directly* as you would have it, or as the Signe points it out; herein you must observe this generall rule; That if your occasions enforce you, or you shall and must live in that Country, City or Towne, so directed unto you in *Art*, that then you must lead your Life, or direct your actions, or manage your imployments to those parts of that City or Country which lye *East, West, North* or *South*, as in the Figure you were directed: as for Example; You may see *France* is subject to the Signe ♈, it lyeth from *London* South-west: had this Gentleman gone into *France*, it would have been best for him to have seated himselfe towards the South-east part, or East part of *France*, &c.

Now because the ☽ applied so strongly to the △ of ♃, and that he and ♀ were in ♉, and that Signe signifies *Ireland*; I
S   advised

advised him that *Ireland* would well agree with his Constitution, and that he might get *Honour* there, becauſe the Planet to whom the ☽ applies is in the houſe of *Honour*.

And verily the *Querent* did goe into *Ireland*, and there performed good ſervice and obtained a notable Victory againſt the *Rebels*; as I could manifeſt, but that I will not mention the Name of the Gentleman.

What part of his LIFE *would be beſt.*

Conſidering the two *Fortunes* were placed in the tenth houſe, and that ☊ and ☉ were in the ninth, I judged his younger yeers would be the moſt pleaſant of all his whole *life*; ſeeing alſo ♂ in the eighth houſe, which according to our owne direction of time comes to be about the 24, 25, or 26. of his age; I judged that about thoſe times he had many croſſes, or firſt of all his afflictions then began; and ſeeing further no fortunate Planet was either in the ſeventh, ſixth, fifth, fourth or third houſes, I judged the remainder of his *life* for many yeers would be little comfortable unto him, but full of labour and trouble; yet I judged thoſe Calamities or Misfortunes ſhould not ſuddenly come upon him, becauſe the ☽ was in application to a △ of ♃, and wanted almoſt three degrees of comming to his perfect aſpect; wherfore I conceived by means of ſome man in authority repreſented by ♃, or ſome Courtier or perſon of quality, for almoſt three yeers after the propoſall of the *Queſtion*, he ſhould be ſupported and aſſiſted in his affaires, or elſe get Imployment anſwerable to his deſires; had ♃ been Eſſentially fortified, I ſhould have judged him a more durable fortune.

What generall ACCIDENTS *had happened already.*

Although it is not uſuall to be ſo nice or inquiſitive, yet ſeeing the Queſtion ſo radicall, I firſt conſidered from what Planet or Planets the ☉, who is Lord of the *Aſcendant*, had laſt ſeparated; if you look into the *Ephemeris* of that yeere, you ſhall find, that the ☉ had lately, during his paſſage through the

Signe

all manner of Questions.

Signe ♓, been first in ☌ with ♂, then in □ of ♄, lately in ✶ of ♃; now, for that ♂ in our *Figure* is Lord of the fourth house, signifying *Lands*, &c. and was now locally in the eighth, which signifies the substance of *Women*, I judged he had been molested of late concerning some Lands, or the *Jointure* or *Portion* of his Wife, or a Woman: wherein I was confirmed the more, because the ☽ was also applying to an ☍ of ♂, in this Figure placed in the eighth house; for the ☽ being in the *Querents* house of substance, viz. the second, intimated the Quarrell or Strife should be for, or concerning *Money*, or such things as are signified by that house: [*And this was very true.*]

Because ☉ had lately been in □ of ♄, who is *Significator* of the *Querent's* Wife, I told him I feared his Wife and he had lately been at great variance; and because ♄ her *Significator* did dispose of his *Part of Fortune*, I judged she had no mind he should have any of her Estate, or manage it, but kept it to her owne use; for ♄ is Retrograde, a superiour Planet, and in a fiery Signe, and the Signe of the seventh is fixed; these shew her a *Virago*, or a gallant spirited Woman, and not willing to be curbed, or else to submit: [*This was confessed.*]

Lastly, because ☉ was lately in ✶ with ♃, and ♃ was in the tenth; I told him, either some great *Lawyer* or *Courtier* had endeavoured to reconcile the differences betwixt them; and forasmuch as both the ☉ who was his *Significator*, and ♄ who was hers, did now both apply to a △ aspect, there seemed to be at present a willingnesse in both Parties to be reconciled; nor did I see any great obstruction in the matter, except ☿ who is in □ aspect with ♄, did impedite it; I judged ☿ in the generall, to signifie either some *Attourney*, or *Lawyer*, or *Writings*; but as he is Lord of the *Querent's* second, it might be because the *Querent* would not consent to give or allow such a summe of Money as might be demanded, or that the *Querents* purse was so weak, he had not wherewithall to solicite his cause lustily; or as ☿ is Lord of the eleventh house, some pretended friend would impedite her, or advise the contrary, or some of her *Lawyers*; or as the eleventh is the fifth from the seventh, a Child of the *Querent's* Wife might be occasion of continuing the Breach. [*I beleeve every particular herein proved true: however, this was the way*

It was the Lord Coventry.

S 2

The Resolution of

to find the occasion or thing disturbing their unity or concord.] Observe as ♀ Lady of the tenth, doth dispose of ♃ Lord of the eighth, *viz.* the Wives Fortune, so she had entrusted her Estate to a great *Nobleman.*

What ACCIDENTS *in future he might expect*; *Time when.*

In this *Quere*, I first considered the ☉ Lord of the *Ascendant*, who being no wayes unfortunated, or in any evill aspect with any Planet, which might impeach or impedite him, but on the contrary excellently fortified, I judged, he had the wide world to ramble in, (for a Planet strong, and in no aspect with others shewes a man at liberty to doe what he will;) and that for many yeers he might (*quoad capax*) live in a prosperous condition (according to the preceding limitation) and traverse much ground, or see many Countries; because ♈, the Signe wherein the ☉ is in, is moveable, placed on the Cusp of the ninth, signifying long Journeys, which prenoted many turnings and shiftings, variety of action in sundry parts.

Secondly, I observed the ☽ in the *Querent's* house of substance, *viz.* the second, did apply to ♃ in the tenth house, and that ♃ was Lord of the fifth house and eighth: the fifth house signifies *Children*; the eighth denotes the substance of the Wife: From hence I gathered, that the *Querent* was very desirous to treat with some Nobleman (because ♃ is in the tenth) about the Education of his Child or Children, and that there might be a Salary payable for their so breeding and education, out of the Wives Jointure or annuall Revennue : [*Such a thing as this in one kind or other, he did settle before he went out of* England.]

Thirdly, I found the ☽ in the Signe ♍ (*Peregrine*) it being a Diurnal Question, else she hath a Triplicity in that Trygon by night.

Foarthly, I found ☿ Lord of his second house, *viz.* signifying his Fortune and Estate, in ♓, which is his Detriment, yet in his owne Termes, afflicted by ♂, from whose ☍ the ☽ lately had separated.

From hence I collected, that he had been in great want of Money a little before the Question asked; and if we look how

many

all manner of Questions. 141

many degrees there is diſtant betwixt ☽ and ☿, ſince their ☍ laſt paſt, we ſhall find them to be 6 d. 21 m. viz. ſix degrees, twenty one min. which noted, that he had been in ſome want of Money for about ſix moneths and ſomewhat more, or thereabouts, before the time of demanding the Queſtion: [*This was confeſſed.*]

Fiftly, ſeeing the ☽ was applying to a △ of ♃, of which ſignification I ſpoke before, and then before ſhe got out of the Signe ♍, did occurre the ☍ of ♂: I did acquaint the *Querent*, that after ſome yeers or times of pleaſure, he would be in great danger of loſing his Life, Goods, Lands and Fortune. His *Life*, becauſe ♂ is in the eighth: His *Goods* or *Eſtate*, becauſe ☽ is in the ſecond: His *Lands* or *Inheritance*, becauſe ♂ is Lord of the fourth, now placed in the eighth. For the fourth houſe ſignifies Lands, &c.

The Time When.

In this *quere* I conſidered the application of the ☽ to a △ of ♃, which wanting about three degrees from the true aſpect, I judged for ſome times ſucceeding the Queſtion, or for three yeers, he might live pleaſantly.

Secondly, ſeeing the ☉ Lord of his *Aſcendant*, during his motion through the Signe ♈, did not meet with any malevolent aſpect, and had 26 degrees to run thorough of the Sign, ere he got into ♉; I gave in this nature of judgment, for every degree one moneth, and ſo told him, That for about 26. moneths following, or untill after two yeers, or much about that time, I judged he ſhould live in a free condition in thoſe parts into which he intended his Journey, &c.

Laſt of all, I conſidered how many degrees the ☽ wanted ere ſhe came to the true ☍ of ♂.

Longitude of ♂		28	40
Of the ☽		21	18
Difference		7	22

The difference is ſeven degrees and twenty two minutes; which If I proportion into time, and neither give yeers, becauſe the *Significators* are in Common Signes, and not in Fixed; or moneths, becauſe the Signes doe ſignifie ſomewhat more; but doe proportion a *meane* between both: the time limited in this way of *Judicature*, will amount to about three yeers and three quarters from the time of asking the Queſtion, ere the malevolent ☍ of the ☽ to ♂ ſhall take effect: But in regard his *quere* was generall, I might have allowed for every degree one yeer: After, or about which time, he was in ſeverall actions both dangerous to his Perſon and Fortune; and ſince that time, till the time of publiſhing hereof, he hath had his *Intervals* of good and ill, but is now under the frowne of Fortune, &c.

But as the ☉ at time of the Queſtion was ſtrong, he did overcome all manner of difficulties for many yeers, and ſubſiſted, and hath in our unlucky differences had honourable Imployment on his Majeſties part: but as the ☽ is in ☍ to ♂, ſo it was not without the generall out-cry and exclamations of the people; nor was it his fortune, though in great Commands, ever to doe his Majeſty any notable piece of Service; yet is he now for ever, by juſt Sentence of the Parliament, deprived of ſo much happineſſe as to end his dayes in *England*; which, though in ſome meaſure, might have been foreſeen, by the ☽ her ☍ to ♂, being Lord of the fourth, *viz.* the end of all things.

Yet we muſt herein admire *Providence*, and acknowledge according to that ſtrong *Maxime of Aſtrologers*; *That the generall Fate of any Kingdome is more prevalent, then the private geniture or queſtion of any Subject or King whatſoever.*

Very little of this Judgment hath already failed; I have been herein ſomewhat large, becauſe young Students might hereby benefit the more; and if my Judgments doe vary from the common Rules of the ANCIENTS, let the Candid Reader excuſe me, ſith he may ſtill follow their Principles if he pleaſe; and he muſt know, that from my Converſation in their Writings, I have attained the Method I follow.

Chap. XXIII.
Of the Part of Fortune, and how to take it, either by Day or Night.

PTolomy doth not more confider a Planet then the *Part of Fortune*, thus charactered ⊗; it hath no afpect, but any Planets may caft their afpect unto it.

The greateft ufe of it, that hitherto I have either read or made of it for, is thus; That if we find it well placed in the heaven, in a good houfe, or in a good afpect of a Benevolent Planet, we judge the Fortun or eftate of the *querent* to be correfpondent unto its ftrength, *viz.* if it be wel pofited or in an angle, or in thofe figns wherein it's fortunated, we judge the eftate of the *querent* to be foundand firme, if ⊗ is otherwayes placed, we doe the contrary.

The manner either night or day to take it is thus:
Firft, confider the Signe, degree and minute of the ☽.
Secondly, the Signe, degree and minute of the ☉.
Thirdly, fubftract the place of the ☉ from the ☽, by adding twelve Signes to the ☽ if you cannot doe it otherwayes; what remaines, referve and adde to the Signe and degree of the Afcendant; if both added together make more then twelve Signes, caft away twelve, and what Signes, degrees and minutes remaine, let your *Part of Fortune* be there: For example in our prefent Figure.

The ☽ is in 21. 18. of ♏, or after 5. Signs, in 21. degr. 18. min. of ♏.
The ☉ is 00. Signs, 4. degr. 18. min. of ♈.
Set them together thus:

    Place of the ☽   5 s   21 d   18 m
    Of the ☉   00   4   18

I fubftract the ☉ from the ☽ thus: I begin with minutes, 18. min. from 18. remaines nothing.

Next I fubftract degrees, 4. degr. from 21. refts 17 degr.

Then 00. Signes from 5. remaines 5. Signes: All put together, there doth reft in Signes and degrees as followeth:

    5 s   17 d   00 m

To thefe 5. Signes 17. degrees, I adde the Signe afcending,
which

which is 4. Signes, 23. degrees, 27. minutes, or the 23. 27. of ♌.

       sig deg min
Then it is thus 5 17 00 *distance of* ☉ *from* ☽.
       4 23 27 *Signs and degr. of the Ascendant.*

Added together, they make } 10 10 27

Viz. 10. Signes, 10. degrees and 27. minutes, which direct you to know, that after ten Signes numbred from ♈, you must place the ⊗, *viz.* in 10. degr. and 27. min. of ♒, for ♈ ♉ ♊ ♋ ♌ ♍ ♎ ♏ ♐ ♑ are ten Signs, &c. and ♒ the eleventh in order.

Whether your Figure be by day or night, observe this Method; for how many degrees the ☉ is distant from the ☽, so many is the ⊗ from the Ascendant; but because this may not be throughly understood by every Learner upon a sudden, let him observe this generall rule, the better to guide him.

If the ⊗ be taken upon a new ☽, it will be in the Ascendant.

If upon the first quarter, in the fourth house.

If upon the full ☽, in the seventh house.

If upon the last quarter, in the tenth house.

After the change, and before the first quarter, you shall ever have her in the first, second or third house.

After the first quarter untill the full ☽, in the fourth, fift or sixth.

After the full ☽ untill the last quarter, in the seventh, eighth or ninth houses.

After the last quarter, either in the tenth, eleventh or twelfth.

So that if the Learner doe mistake, he may by this method easily see his errour; ever remembring, that the more dayes are passed after the change or quarter, &c. the more remote the ⊗ is from the Angle preceding.

Some have used to take ⊗ in the night from the ☽ to the ☉; which if you doe, you must then make the place of the ☉ your first place, and adde the Ascendant as in the former method. *Ptolomie*, day and night takes it as above directed, with whom al Practicioners at this day consent.

Here followeth a Table, by help whereof you may examine the strength of ⊗ in any Figure you erect. *The*

all manner of Questions. 145

The part of Fortune is strong and fortunate — In the Signes of	♉ ♓, wherin if it be, it hath allowed dignities	5
	♎ ♐ ♌ ♋, in these Signs	4
	♊, In this Signe	3
	♍, so it be in the Terms of ♃ or ♀	2
If in ☌ with ♃ or ♀, it hath dignities		5
In △ with ♃ or ♀		4
In ✶ with ♃ or ♀		3
In ☌ with ☊		3
⊗ is strong by being in houses, viz. If in	First or Tenth, it hath allowed dignities	5
	Seventh, Fourth, Eleventh,	4
	Second or Fifth,	3
	Ninth,	2
	Third,	1
In ☌ with any of these Fixed Starres	with Regulus in 24. 34. ♌	6
	with Spica Virginis in 18. 33. ♎	5
	Not Combust, or under the ☉ Beams	5
The part of fortune is weak in	♏ ♑ ♒, being in any of these signs it hath deblities	5
	In ♈ be neither gets or loses.	
⊗ is weak by ☌ or aspect,	In ☌ ♄ or ♂, hath debilities	5
	In ☌ with ☋	3
	In ☍ of ♄ or ♂	4
	In □ of ♄ or ♂	3
	In Termes of ♄ or ♂	2
As also by being in Houses, viz.	In the Twelfth	5
	In the Eighth	4
	In the sixth	4
With Caput Algol in 20. 54. ♉		4
Combust		5

There are many other Parts which the *Arabians* have mentioned frequently in their Writings, of which we make very little use in this Age: I shall, as occasion offers, teach the finding them out, and what they said, they did signifie: sometimes the ⊗ hath signification of Life, and sometimes of Sicknesse; which occasionally I shall teach, as matter and occasion offer, addhering to the true observation of the *Ancients*: but I am little hitherto satisfied concerning ⊗ its true effects; intending to take paines therein hereafter, and publish my intentions.

T

The preceding FIGURE *judged by a more short*
METHOD.

1. The *Ascendant* not afflicted, Lord of the *Ascendant* Essentially fortified, the ☽ in △ with both the *Fortunes*; Signes of long Life.

2. ♃ and ♀ in the South Angle, in ♉, a South-east Signe; ☉ in ♈, an Easterly Signe; ☽ in ♍, a Southerne or South-west Signe; best to travell Southward, or a little East.

3. ♃ and ♀ in the *Mid-heaven*, ☊ and ☉ in the ninth; his younger yeers are most full of Pleasure.

4. ☉ Lord of the *Ascendant*, lately separated from good and ill aspects; ☽ also separated as well from ☍ of ☿ as △ of ♀; shew both good and ill had happened of late: Good, because of the good aspects: ill, by reason of the malevolent: but the evill aspects being more in number then the good, and signified by superiour Planets; augment the Evill and lessen the Good.

5. ☽ applying to △ of ♃ the ☉ Lord of the *Ascendant* in Exaltation; promise Preferment.

☽ weak in the second, and after her △ with ♃ going to ☍ of ♂; shewes, after a little time of Joy, great danger.

6. The small distance of degrees between the △ of ☽ to ♃, and he Angular; denote a present happinesse or fortune neer to the *Querent*.

Her greater distance from ☍ of ♂, shew his miseries to succeed some yeers after his times of Honour are expired, &c. In such a nature I ever contract my Judgment.

I wish all young Beginners at first to write down their Judgments in length, and the reasons in *Art*, as fully as they can, and afterward to contract their opinions into a narrow compasse: by following these directions, they will have the Rules of *Art* perfectly in their memory: I also wish them in delivering their Judgment to the *Querent*, to avoid termes of *Art* in their Discourse, unlesse it be to one understands the *Art*.

If

all manner of Questions. 147

Chap. XXIV.
If one shall find the Party at home he would speak withall.

THE *Ascendant* and his Lord are for the *Querent*, the seventh house and his Lord for him you would speak withall; this is understood, if you goe to speak with one you familiarly deale withall, or are much conversant with, and is not allied unto you, &c. but if you would goe to speak with the Father, you must take the Lord of the fourth; if with the Mother, the Lord of the tenth; if the Father would speak with his Child, the Lord of the fifth, and so in the rest; vary your rule and it serves for all.

If the Lord of the seventh house be In any of the four Angles, you may conclude the party is at home with whom you would speak with; but if the Lord of the seventh, or Lord of that house from whom Judgment is required, be in any Succedant house, *viz.* the eleventh, second, fifth or eighth, then he is not far from home; but if his *Significator* be in a Cadent house, then he is far from home.

If you find the Lord of the Ascendant applying to the Lord of the seventh house by any perfect aspect, the same day that you intend to goe visit him, you may be assured either to meet him going to his house, or heare of him by the way where he is, for he cannot be farre absent; or if any Planet, or the *Moon*, separate from the Lord of the seventh house, and transferre his light unto the Lord of the Ascendant, he shall know where and in what place the Party is, by such a one as is signified by that Planet who transferres his light: describe the Planet, and it personates the Man or Woman accordingly: But whether it will be Man or Woman, you must know by the nature of the Planet, Signe and quarter of Heaven he is in, wherein plurality of masculine Testimonies argue a man, the contrary a Woman.

T 2 *Of*

Of a thing suddenly happening, Whether it signifieth Good or Evill.

Erect your Figure of Heaven at what time the Accident happened, else when you first heard of it; then consider who is Lord of that Signe wherein the *Sunne* is, and the Lord of that Signe wherein the *Moon* is, and the Lord of the house of Life, which is ever the Ascendant, and see which of these is most powerfull in the Ascendant, let his position be considered, and if he be in ✶ or △ with the ☉ ♃ or ♀, there will no evill chance upon the preceding Accident, Rumour or Report; but if you find that Planet weak in the Scheame, combust, or in □ ☍ or ☌ of ♂ ♄ ☿, there will some misfortune follow after that accident, in one kind or other; if you consider the Planet afflicting your *Significator*; his positure and nature, it may easily be discovered, in what nature the evill will chance or upon what occasion; as if the Lord of the third, from or by some Neighbour or Kinsman; if the Lord of the second impedite them, then losse in substance; if Lord of the fourth, expect discontent with one of your Parents, or about Land or Houses; if the Lord of the fifth, some difference or discord in an Ale-house or Taverne, or in Company keeping, or by meanes of some Child, &c. and so of the rest.

What Marke, Mole or Scarre the Querent hath in any Member of his Body.

I have many times admired at the verity hereof, and it hath been one maine argument of my engaging so farre in all the parts of Astrology, for very rarely you shall find these rules faile.

When you have upon any demand erected the *querents* Figure, consider the Sign ascending, what member of mans body it represents, and tell the *querent* he hath a Mole, Scar or marke on that part of his body represented by that Signe; as if the Signe ascending be ♉, it's on the Neck: if in ♊, on the Arms, &c. See also in which of the twelve Signes of the Zodiack the

Lord

all manner of Queſtions. 149

Lord of the Aſcendant is in, and in that member repreſented by that Signe, he or ſhe hath another.

Then obſerve the Signe deſcending on the Cuſp of the fixt houſe, and what part of mans body it perſonates, for in that member ſhall you find another ; ſo ſhall you diſcover another in that member which is ſignified by the Signe wherein the Lord of the fixt is.

Laſt of all, conſider what Signe the *Moon* is in, and what member of mans body it denotes, therein ſhall you alſo find a Mark, Mole or Scarre : if ♄ ſignifie the Mark, it's a darkiſh, obſcure, black one ; if ♂ , then it's uſually ſome Scarre or Cut if he be in a fiery Signe, or elſe in any other Signe, a red mole ; and you muſt alwayes know, that if either the Signe, or the Planet ſignifying the Mole, Mark or Scarre, be much afflicted, the Mark or Scarre is the greater and more eminent.

If the Signe be Maſculine, and the Planet Maſculine, the Mole or Scar is on the right ſide of the body.

The contrary judge, if the Signe be Feminine, and the Lord thereof in a Feminine Signe,

If the Significator of the Scarre or Mole be above the earth, (that is, from the Cuſp of the Aſcendant to the Cuſp of the ſeventh, as either in the twelfth, eleventh, tenth, ninth, eighth or ſeventh) the Mark is on the fore part of the body, or viſible to the eye, or on the out-ſide of the member ; but if the Significator be under the earth, *viz.* in the firſt, ſecond, third, fourth, fift, ſixt, the Mole or Scarre is on the back part of the body, not viſible, but on the inſide of the member.

If few degrees of a Signe doe aſcend, or if the Lord of the Signe be in few degrees, the Mole, Mark or Scarre is in the upper part of the member ; if the middle of the Signe aſcend, or the Lord thereof in the middle, or neer the middle of the Signe, the Mole or Mark is ſo in the member, *viz.* in the middle : If the latter degrees aſcend, or the *Moon*, or Lord of the firſt or fixt houſe be neer the laſt degrees of the Sign, the Mole, Mark or Scar is neere the lower part of the member.

If your Queſtion be radicill, the time rightly taken, and the party enquiring be of ſufficient age, or no Infant, you ſhall rarely find errour in this rule : I have many times upon a ſudden in company, tryed this experiment upon some of the company, and ever found it true, as many in this City well know. In *November* and *December*, when Signes of short ascensions are in the Ascendant, you must be wary, for in regard many times the ☉ is not then visible, and Clocks may faile, it's possible you may be deceived, and misse of a right Ascendant, for ♓ and ♈ doe each of them ascend in the space of three quarters of an hour, and some few minutes; ♒ and ♉ in one hour and some odde minutes; but if you have the time of the day exact, you need not ever mistrust the verity of your Judgment: which will infinitely satisfie any that are Students herein, and cause them to take great pleasure in the *Art*, and make them sensible, that there is as much sincerity in all the whole *Art of Astrologie*, when it is rightly understood and practized, which at this day I must confesse it is by very few.

As these rules will hold certaine upon the body of every *querent*, and in every question, so will they upon the body of the *quesited*, (*mutatis*, *mutandis*;) as if one enquires somewhat concerning his Wife, then the Signe of the seventh house, and the Signe wherein the Lord of the seventh is, shall shew the Womans Marks; so shall the Signe upon the Cusp of the twelfth, for that is the sixth from the seventh, and the Signe wherein the Lord of the twelfth is in, shew two more Moles or Marks of the Woman.

Usually an Infortune in the Ascendant blemishes the Face with some Mole or Scarre according to his nature, for the first house signifies the Face, the second the Neck, the third the Armes and Shoulders, the fourth the Brest and Paps, the fifth the Heart, &c. and so every house and Signe in order, according to succession; for what Signe soever is in the Ascendant, yet in every Question the first house represents the Face: Many times if the ☽ be in ☌ or ☍ of the ☉, the *querent* hath some blemish or the like near one of his Eyes; and this is ever true, if the ☍ or ☌ be in Angles, and either of them have any ill aspect to *Mars*.

Whether

all manner of Questions. 151

Whether one absent be dead or alive.

If a Question be demanded of one absent in a generall way, and the *querent* hath no relation to the party; then the first House, the Lord of that House and the ☽ shall signifie the absent party; the Lord of the eight House or Planet posited either in the House or within five degrees of the Cuspe of the 8th House shall shew his death or its quality.

In judging this Question, see first whether the Lord of the Ascendant, the ☽ and Lord of the eight House or Planet in the eight house be corporally joyned together; or that the ☽ Lord of the Ascendant and Lord of the eight are in opposition either in the eight and second, or twelfth and sixt, for these are arguments the party is deceased, or sick, and very neer death.

See also if there be any translation of the light of the Lord of the Ascendant unto the Lord of the eight, especially in degrees deepe, lame or deficient; or on the contrary, that there be any translation or carrying the vertue or influence of the Lord of the eight unto the Lord of the Ascendant; or if the Lord of the eight be posited in the Ascendant, or if the Lord of the Ascendant and the ☽ be placed in the fourth House, these are testimonies the party absent is dead.

If the Lord of the Ascendant be seperated from a bad Aspect of the Lord of the sixt, you may say the absent hath been lately sicke; if from the Lord of the eight, he hath been in danger of death, but is not dead; if from the Lord of the twelfth, he hath been lately much troubled in minde, in feare of imprisonment, arrests, &c. if from the Lord of the second, he hath been hard put to it for money, or in distresse for want; if from the Lord of the seventh, in some quarrell or contention; if from the Lord of the ninth or third, he hath been crossed in his journey (if he was at Sea by contrary windes, or Pyrats) if at Land by Theeves, bad Wayes, &c. and so of the rest. In judging this question, I have ever found, that if the Lord of the Ascendant be in the ninth, tenth, or eleventh (though many reports went the absent was dead) yet I found him to live. Now if you finde the absent alive, and you would know, when happily

152 The Resolution of

pily you may heare of him; see in your *Ephemerides* when the Lord of the eleventh and Lord of the Ascendant come to a △ or ✶ Aspect, and about that time, if not that day, newes will be had of him; or if the ☽ apply to a ✶ or △ of the Lord of the Ascendant, see how many degrees shee wants of the Aspect, and give dayes, weekes or moneths, *viz.* For every degree in moveable Signes a day, in common Signes weekes, in fixed Signes moneths.

A further EXPLANATION *of the preceding Judgments by the Figure succeeding.*

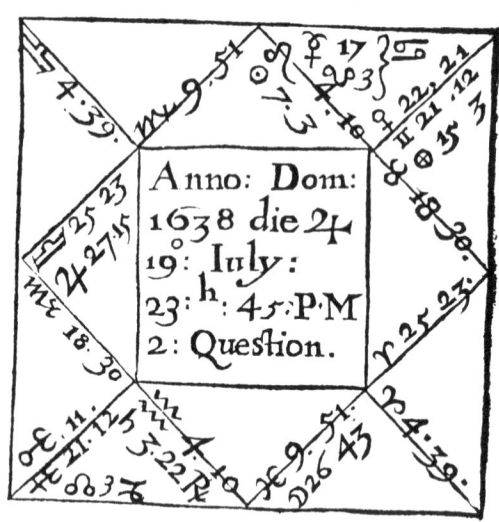

[Astrological figure: Anno: Dom: 1638 die ♃ 19°: July: 23ʰ: 45: P.M 2: Question.]

Resolution of these Questions following:

I finde the party inquired of at home.
A thing suddenly happening, whether good or bad is intended?
What Moles or Marks the Querent hath?
If one absent be dead or alive?

CHAP.

all manner of Questions. 153

Chap. XXV.

Viz. *A Woman being at my House in the Country, demanded if her Sonne were with his Master, or at her owne House.*

IN this Figure ♀ is Lady of the *Ascendant*, and shall signifie her that asked the Question; the matter quesited after must be required from that house which signifieth Children, and that is the fifth: I considered ♃ who is Lord of the Signe ♓, for ♓ is the house of ♃, and I found ♃, the Youths *Significator*, in the Angle of the East, or *Ascendant*; one argument, that the Party sought after was at home at his Mothers house at time of the Question: I observed further, that the ☽ did apply to a ✶ *dexter* of ♄, Lord of the fourth house, which signifies the house or dwelling place of the *Querent*: from which two testimonies, I judged the Youth was at his Mothers, and that she should find him there at her comming home, as indeed she did: now had I found ♃, Lord of the fift, in the tenth, because that is the house which signifies the Master, or had the ☽ separated from ♃, Significator of the Youth, and presently applyed to a good or indifferent aspect of the ☉, & she, *viz.* ☽ been in an Angle, I would have adjudged him at his Masters house, &c. I did further consider that the 25. of *July* following, at two hours after noon, ♃ and ♀, being both their *Significators, viz.* both the Mothers & the Sons came to a △ aspect, and therfore I judged she should see him that very day, but hardly any sooner, or before; (and indeed she staid in the country till that very morning; but whe the strength of the influence grew powerfull, and as well her *Significatrix*, as his, were so neer their perfect aspect, she could not be induced to stay any longer, and so (*volens nolens*) went awy, and it was about three in the afternoon the same day before she could get home, where she found her Sonne in her owne house, abiding her comming; for usually about that day when the *Significators* come to a ✶ or △ aspect (which you may know by your *Ephemeris*) it's very probable you shall have a Letter, or newes of the Party *quesited* after (if the distance of places betwixt you can afford it,) but if the Party enquiring, and Person inquired after be not farre asunder, without question they

V   meet

meet that very day, though neither of them formerly thought any such matter.

Had this Woman enquired, if she should have found a Neighbour or Brother or Sister at home, or not;

You must have taken signification from ♃, who is Lord of the third house; for you may see in the signification of the Houses, *pag.* 52. that the third house signifieth Brethren, Sisters, Kinred and Neighbours; you might safely have adjudged, she should have found any one of these at home, because ♃ their Significator is in an Angle.

But if she had enquired, whether she should have found a Party at home, yea or not, to whom she had no relation, but as to a stranger; then ♂ the Lord of the seventh, had been his *Significator*, whom I find to be in the Signe of ♐, and in the second house of Heaven, for wanting more then five degrees of the Cusp of the third, he is not admitted to have signification in that house. In the first place therefore, I find ♂ in the second house, and in a Northerne quarter of Heaven, (for from the Cusp of the fourth house to the Cusp of the first, or Ascendant, is so, as you may see *pag.* 48.) next I find ♂, who is *Significator* of the Party with whom shee would speak with, is in ♐, which is an Easterly Signe, as you may see *pag.* 97.

Being ♂ is not in an Angle, I say he is not at home; the second house wherein he is being a Succedant, I say he is not far from home.

The quarter of Heaven wherein at present he is, is Northeast, for so Signe and quarter import.

His distance from home may be a Furlong, or a Close or two, because his *Significator* is in a Succedant house.

The quality of the place or ground where you may expect to find him, must be judged from the Signe wherein ♂ his *Significator* is, *viz.* ♐, a fiery Signe; what manner of place that Signe signifies, see in *pag.* 98. and you shall there find, it represents in the Fields, Hils, or Grounds that rise a little: so that the Party enquired after being absent, you must direct a messenger to find him, in such or such a Ground, or part of the Ground, as is of the nature and quality described, and butting

or

all manner of Questions. 155

or lying to that quarter of Heaven, as is formerly directed, *viz.* North-east.

But had it been so, that you were informed, the man was in a Towne, and not in the Fields, then enquire in the Towne neer to some Smiths or Butchers shops, or the like, being North-east from his house, for you may read ♂ delights in such places. see *pag.* 68.

Of a Thing suddenly happening, whether good or ill, Resolution thereof by the last Figure.

Let us admit the Figure preceding to be set upon such an occasion; the ☉ is here Lord of the Signe wherein he is; ♃ is Lord of ♓, the Signe wherein the ☽ is, ♀ is Lady of the Ascendant, or house of Life; ♀ is here most powerfull in the Ascendant, ♎ being her house, and she having a Terme therein, and casting her △ *Sinister* unto the Cusp of the house; as also, being in △ with ♃, and he in the Ascendant; from hence one might have safely judged, had this been the very time of a sudden accident, or thing done, that it could not have redounded to the *Querent's* disadvantage, but rather good: Now had ♀ been neerer to the ☍ of ♂, he being in the second, which signifies Riches, I should have judged the *Querent* would have received some losse shortly; and so of the rest; or some falling out about Moneys.

What Marks the Querent had.

I find the 25. of ♎ ascending, and ♃ in the *Ascendant*; which as I acquainted you, signified the Face; this *Querent* had a Wart or Mole on the right side of her Face, neer her Mouth, for ♃ is masculine, so is the Signe ♎; and as the later degrees of ♎ ascend, so the *Querent* confessed a Mole on the lower part of her Reines, towards the Hanches; ♈ being the Signe of the sixth, shewed she had one on the Fore-head, neer the Haire, for you see the Cusp of the house is but four degrees; ♂ Lord of ♈, being in a masculine Sign, *viz.* in ♐ but under the earth, shewed a Mole on the right Thigh, towards the middle of it, on the

V 2   back

back part, or that part which is not visible; the ☽ being in ♓, *viz.* 26 deg. 43 min. in a Feminine Signe, and under the Earth, I told her she had one Mole under her Foot, towards the extremity of her left Foot.

The *Quesited* party being her Sonne, had ♓ the ninth degr. for his Ascendant, which denoted a Mole on the left side of his Cheek; and as ♓ signifies the Foot, so he had one on the left Foot, a little below the Ancle, for you see few degrees ascend. The sixt house from the sift, is the tenth in the Figure, where you see ♌ 4 deg. which signified, that neer his right Side, below his Brest, he had some Scarre, Mole or Marke, &c. follow these Directions, and they are sufficient Instructions in this kind of Judgment.

Whether one absent be dead or alive, by the preceding Scheame of Heaven.

In the Figure abovesaid, let us admit the Question to have been demanded for one absent:

The Ascendant ♎, ♃ therein, ♀ and ☽ are *Significators* of the absent Party.

The ascending Signe manifests his Stature, ♃ gives comlinesse unto it, ♀ ♃ and ☽ argue his Conditions.

Neither is the ☽ or Lord of the *Ascendant* joyned to any Planet in the eight by ☌ but are all free from the malignant beams and aspects of the Lords of the 8th or 6th, or is the Lord of the *Ascendant* or the ☽ in ☍ with the Lord of the eighth.

Or is there translation of light from the Lord of the eighth to the Lord of the *Ascendant*, or is the Lord of the eighth in the *Ascendant*, but a Benevolent Planet, or is ☽ or the Lord of the *Ascendant* in the fourth house: I should therefore pronounce the absent in health; but because ♀ Lady of the *Ascendant*, had not many dayes before been in ☍ with ♂, who is Lord of the second and sixt; I should adjudge he had been lately discontented for want of Money, and also inclinable to a Feaver; but by ♃ his positure in the Ascendant, and his △ to ♀, I should judge *Medicine*, or such a one as ♃ had relieved him: and because ☿ Lord of the eleventh, applies to a □ of ♃

in

all manner of Questions. 157

in the *Ascendant*, both of them being in Signes of long ascensions, which is equivalent to a △, I should judge the *Querent* to have newes of the absent about ten weeks from the time of the Question, because ☿ wants ten degrees of the □ of ♃ ; if the absent be known to be at a neer distance, I would have said in ten dayes they should heare of him, because the Signes are moveable.

Chap. XXVI.
Of a Ship, and whatever are in her, her Safety or Destruction:

THE *Ancients* doe put this Question to those concerning the ninth house, and I conceive for no other reason, then because it must be granted, that all Ships are made for Travell and Journeys: however, in regard the most part of the Judgment concerning its safety or ruine is derived from the Ascendant and his Lord, and the ☽, I thought fit to place this Judgment as belonging to the first house.

Generally, the Signe ascending and the ☽ are *Significators* of the *Ship*, and what Goods are in her, the Lord of the Ascendant of those that saile in her: if in the Question demanded you find all these unfortunate, that is, if a malevolent Planet by position be placed in the Ascendant, he having dignities in the eighth: or if you find the Lord of the Ascendant in the eighth, in any ill configuration with the Lord of the eighth, twelfth, fourth or sixth, or the ☽ combust, or under the earth, you may judge the Ship is lost and the men drowned, (unlesse you find reception betwixt themselves) for then the Ship was casually Shipwrackt, and some of the Sea-men did escape: but if you find the preceding *Significators* all of them free from misfortune, both Men and Goods are all safe; the more safe if any reception be. But if the Ascendant and the ☽ be infortunate, and the Lord of the Ascendant fortunate, the Ship is like to be drowned, but the men will be saved: Some for better knowledge and discovery of what part of the Ship was like to be freest from danger, have divided the severall parts of the Ship, and have assigned to every of the twelve Signes, a part or place

T 3 of

158   *The Resolution of*

of the Ship, by which if any damage was to come to the Ship, they could or might better prevent it.

Unto Aries *they give the Breſt of the Ship.*
To Taurus *what is under the Breſt a little towards the Water.*
To Geminis *the Roother or Sterne of the Ship.*
To Cancer *the Bottome or Floor of the Ship.*
To Leo *the top of the Ship above Water.*
To Virgo *the Belly of it.*
To Libra *that part which ſometimes is above, and ſometimes below the Water, or betwixt Wind and Weather.*
To Scorpio *that part where the Seamen are lodged, or doe their Office.*
To Sagitarius *The Mariners themſelves.*
To Capricornus *the ends of the Ship.*
To Aquarius *the Maſter or Captaine of the Ship.*
To Piſces *the Oares.*

At the time when the Queſtion is asked concerning the well or ill being of the Ship, ſee which of theſe Signes, or how many of them are fortunate, or hath the ☽ or the Lord thereof fortunate, it's an argument thoſe parts of the Ship ſo ſignified, will have no defect, or need repaire thereof, or the Ship will receive any detriment in thoſe parts : but which of theſe Signes you find unfortunate, or in what Signe you find the ☽ or Lord of the Signe where ſhe is, unfortunate, in that place or part of the Ship aſſigne impediment and misfortune, and thereof give warning.

But when the *Querent* ſhall demand of any Ship which is ſetting forth, and the State of that Ship ere ſhe returne, and what may be hoped of her in her Voyage, then behold the Angles of the Figure, and ſee if the fortunate Planets are therein poſited, or falling into Angles, and the Infortunes remote from Angles, Cadent, Combuſt or under the ☉ Beames, then you may judge the Ship will goe ſafe to the place intended, with all the Goods and Loading in her : But if you find the Infortunes in Angles, or ſucceeding Houſes, there will chance ſome hinderance unto the Ship, and it ſhall be in that part which the Signe ſignifies where the unfortunate Planet is ; if the ſame Infortune be ♄,
the

all manner of Questions.   159

the Ship will be split, and the men drowned, or receive hurt by some bruise, or running a ground: but if it be ♂, and he in any of his Essentiall Dignities, or behold a place where he hath any Dignity or be in an earthly Signe, he shall then signifie the same which ♄ did, or very great danger and damage to the Ship: But if the Fortunes cast their benevolent rayes or aspect to the places where ♂ or ♄ are, and the Lords of the four Angles of the Figure, and especially, or more properly, the Ascendant, and Lord of that house or Signe where the ☽ is in be free, then it's an argument, the Ship shall labour hard, and suffer much damage, yet notwithstanding the greater part both of Goods and Men shall be preserved. But if ♂ doe afflict the Lords of the Angles, and Dispositor of the ☽, the Mariners will be in great feare of their Enemies, or of Pyrates or Sea-robbers, shall even tremble for feare of them: and if there also unto this evill configuration chance any other affliction in the Signes, there will happen amongst the Mariners Blood-shed, Controversies, quarrelling one with another, theeving and robbing each other, purloyning the Goods of the Ship; and this judgment will prove more certaine if the unfortunate Planets be in the Signes which fall to be in the Division of the upper part of the Ship, towards the height or top of her.

If ♄ in the like nature doe afflict, as was before recited of ♂, there will be many thefts committed in the Ship, but no blood-shed; the Goods of the Ship consume, no body knowing which way.

If the unfortunate Signes (viz. those which are afflicted by the presence of ♄ ♂ or ☋) be those which signifie the bottome or that part of the Ship which is under Water, it's an argument of the breaking and drowning thereof, or receiving some dangerous Leak: if the Signes so unfortunate be in the Mid-heaven, and ♂ unfortunate them, it's like the Ship will be burnt by fire, thunder or lightning, or matter falling out of the Aire into the Ship; this shall then take place when the Signes are fiery, and neer violent fixed Stars.

If that Signe wherein ♂ or the unfortunate Planet be the Signe of the fourth house, it notes firing of the Ship in the bottome of her; but if ♂ be there, and the Signe humane, *viz.*

either

either ♊ ♎ or ♒, that fire or burning of the Ship shall proceed from a fight with Enemies, or they shall cast fire into her, or shall teare the Ship in pieces in grapling with her, and the fire shall in that part of the Ship first take hold, signified by the Signe wherein an Infortune was at time of asking the Question.

If ♄ instead of ♂ doe denunciate dammage, and be placed in the Mid-heaven, the Ship shall receive prejudice by contrary Winds, and by leaks in the Ship, by rending or using of bad Sailes; and this misfortune shall be greater or lesser, according to the potency of the *significator* of that misfortune, and remotenesse of the Fortunes.

If the same Infortune be in the seventh house, and he be ♄, the latter part of the Ship will be in danger of misfortune, and the Sterne of the Ship will be broke.

Moreover, if any Infortune be in the Ascendant, some losse will be in the fore-part of the Ship, greater or lesse, according to the quality or strength of the *significator* thereof; or if the Lord of the Ascendant be Retrograde, the Ship will proceed forward a while, but either returne or put into some Harbour within a little time after her setting forth; and if the Lord of the Ascendant be in a moveable Signe and Retrograde, and the Lord of the fourth also, *viz.* Retrograde, the Ship will returne againe crossed by contrary Winds, to the very Port from which she first set out: and if the Lord of the Ascendant have no other impediments then Retrogradation, there will be no losse by the returne of it; but if to Retrogradation some other misfortune happen, the Ship returnes to amend something amisse, and was also in danger.

Besides, if the Lord of the eighth shall infortunate the Lord of the Ascendant, especially if the Lord of the Ascendant be in the eighth, there will come hurt to the Ship according to the nature of the Planet afflicting: as if the same Planet that is Lord of the eighth house doe impedite the Lord of the house of the ☽, the Lord of the Ascendant and the ☽, it imports the death of the Master or Governour of the Ship, and of his Mate and principall Officers of the Ship: and if the *Part of Fortune* and the Lord of the second house be both unfortunate, it pronounceth

all manner of Queſtions. 161

nounceth loſſe in ſale of thoſe Goods in the Ship, or ill venting of them, or that they will not come to a good Market; but if either ☊ ♃ or ♀ be in the ſecond houſe, or Lords thereof, or Diſpoſitors of the Signe the ⊗ is in, there will good profit ariſe from the Voyage of that Ship, and ſale of Goods therein the more the *Significators* are eſſentially ſtrong, the more profit may be expected.

If the Lord of the Aſcendant and Lord of the houſe of the ☽ be ſlow of courſe, and thoſe Planets that diſpoſe of them, then it's probable the Ship will be ſlow in her motion, and make a long Voyage of it: but if the aforeſaid *Significators* be quick in motion, the Ship ſhall make good ſpeed to the Port intended, and will returne home againe in ſhorter time then is expected.

And if it happen that there be an ☍ or □ aſpect betwixt the Lord of the Aſcendant and Lord of that Signe who diſpoſeth the ☽, and this aſpect be without reception, then will there be much diſcord amongſt the *Saylors*, and much controverſie betwixt the Merchant and them; wherein, he ſhall prevaile that is moſt dignified; that is, the Sea-men if the Lord of the Aſcendant be ſtrongeſt; the Merchant, if the Lord of the houſe where the ☽ is be beſt fortified.

If the Lord of the ſecond be removed from his ſecond, (that is, if ♉ be the Cuſp of the ſecond, and ♀ further removed then ♊) or if the Lord of the ſecond be removed from the ſecond houſe wherein the ☽ is in, (as if ſhe be in ♍, and the Lord of the ſecond not in ♎, or if the Diſpoſer of the ⊗ be not with it, then the Ship-men will have ſcarſity of Proviſion of Victuals and Food: if theſe Planets or ⊗ be in Watry Signes, want of freſh Water will moſt annoy the Saylors: if the *Significators* be in Earthly or Aiery Signes, want of Food, Victuals and Fire will oppreſſe them: This is the manner by which the *Ancients* did judge of the good or ill ſucceſſe of a Ship, concerning her Voyage at her firſt going forth.

X   In

An Example of a Ship at Sea.

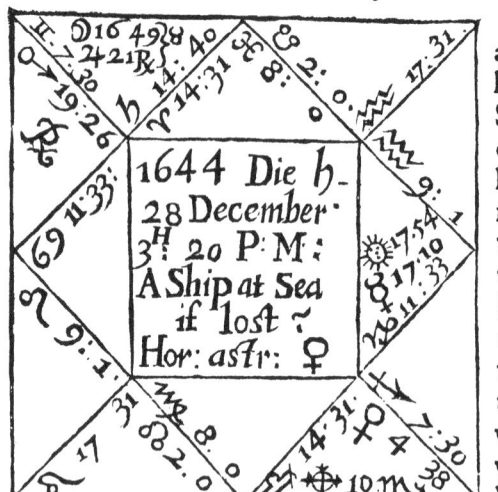

In *December* 1644. a *Merchant* in *London* having sent out a Ship to the Coasts of *Spaine* for Trade, had severall times newes that his Ship was lost or cast away, there having been a little before very Tempestuous weather, in so much that many Shippes were sunk and shipwrackt; he would have given 60 li. in the hundred for the assurance of her; but so generall was the report of her losse, that none of the *Ensurance* company would meddle, no not upon any tearmes. A Friend of the *Merchants* propounds the Question unto me, *What I thought of the Ship, if sunk or living?* whereupon I erected the Figure preceding, and having well considered what was requisite in this manner of Judgment, I gave my Opinion, That *the Ship was not lost, but did live, and though of late in some danger, yet was now recovered.* My Judgment was grounded upon the Considerations in *Art* following.

IN the first place, the *Ascendant* being the 11th. degr. and 33. min. of ♋, shewed the Bulk or Body of the Ship; there doth also ascend with these degrees of ♋ three fixed Starres in our *Horizon*, wholly almost of the nature of ♄ : I find ♄ casteth his □ *Sinister* out of the eleventh house, but from a Cardinall Signe to, or very neer the Cusp of the ascending degrees, thereby afflicting it: after his □ aspect, I found the ☽ in her Exaltation, casting a ✶ *Sinister* to the degree ascending, interposing her ✶ betwixt the Ascendant and the ☍ aspects of ☿ and ☉ in the seventh, which otherwise had been dangerous, for all opposite aspects to the Ascendant in this Judgment are dangerous.

From

all manner of Questions. 163

From the *Ascendants* affliction both by the □ of ♄, and presence of fixed Stars of his like nature, I judged the Ship was much of the nature of ♄, *viz.* a sluggish, heavy one, and of no good speed, or very sound; and ♋ being a weakly Signe, made me judge the condition, building and quality of the Ship was such; [*and it was so confessed.*]

From hence, and for that ☋ is in the ninth house, I judged the Ship had been in some affliction or distresse in her Journey, occasioned from such casualties as are signified by ♄, *viz.* had received some bruise, leak, dammage in or neer her Brest; because ♈, the Signe wherein ♄ is, represents that part, thereby afflicting it.

But in regard the ☽, who is Lady of the Ascendant, is posited in the eleventh house, and in her Exaltation, *is no manner of way impedited, but by a benevolent aspect applying to a △ of ☿ and ☉*, and is by bodily presence so neer unto ♃, and all the *Significators* above the Earth, (a thing very considerable in this Judgment.)

Besides, I observed no *Infortunes* in Angles, which was one other good argument; for these considerations, I judged the Ship was not cast away, but was living, and that the Saylors and Officers of the Ship were lively and in good condition.

The next *Quere* was, *Where the Ship was, upon what Coast, and when any newes would come of her?*

Herein I considered the ☽ was fixed, and locally in the eleventh house; ♉ is a Southerne Signe, but in an East quarter of Heaven, verging towards the South: her application to △ of ☿, and he in ♑, a South Signe and West Angle, made me judge the Ship was South-west from *London*, and upon our own Coast, or neer those which lye betwixt *Ireland* and *Wales*; I judged her at that time to be in some *Harbour*, because ♉ wherein the ☽ is, is fixed, and in the eleventh house, which is the house of *Comfort* and *Reliefe*; and that she was put into some *Harbour* to mend her Defects or Rents: [*It proved true that she was in the West, and in an Harbour.*]

Because the ☽ applyed to a △ of ☿ and ☉, and they in an Angle, and was her selfe as well as they, very swift in motion, and did want but a few minutes of their perfect △; I judged

X 2　　　　　　　　　　　　　　　there

there would be newes or Letters, or a certaine difcovery of the Ship in a very fhort time ; the *fignificators* fo neer afpect, I faid either that night, or in two dayes ; [*and fo it proved :*] And you muft obferve, that it gave me good encouragement when I faw ⊗ difpofed by ♂, and ☿ to whom the ☽ applyed to be in reception with ♂ : as alfo, that the ☽, by fo forcible an afpect, did apply to the ☉, who is Lord of the fecond houfe, or of *Subftance*, an argument, the *Merchant* fhould encreafe his Stock, and not lofe by that adventure : You fhall alfo obferve, that ♃ hath his *Antifcion* in the ninth of ♌, the very Cufp of the fecond houfe, and ♂ his *Antifcion* fals upon the very degree afcending : thefe were good teftimonies of fafety : ♂ as being Lord of the eleventh, and Difpofitor of ⊗ ; and ♃ as Lord of the tenth, *viz*. of *Trade* and *Commerce*.

Befides, ufually when the ☽ applies to a good afpect of a Retrograde Planet, it brings the matter to an end one way or other fpeedily, and when leaft fufpected : and it's a generall Maxime in fuch like cafes, if the ☽ apply to the *Fortunes*, or by good afpect to any Planet or Planets in Angles, then there is reafon we hope well, &c.

The Afcendant free from prefence of *Infortunes*, a good fign : Lord of the Afcendant above the Earth, and the ☽ and their Difpofitors, good fignes : Lord of the Afcendant in tenth, eleventh or ninth houfes, good : Lord of the Afcendant in △ or ✶ with ♃ or Lord of the eleventh, good.

Here

all manner of Questions:

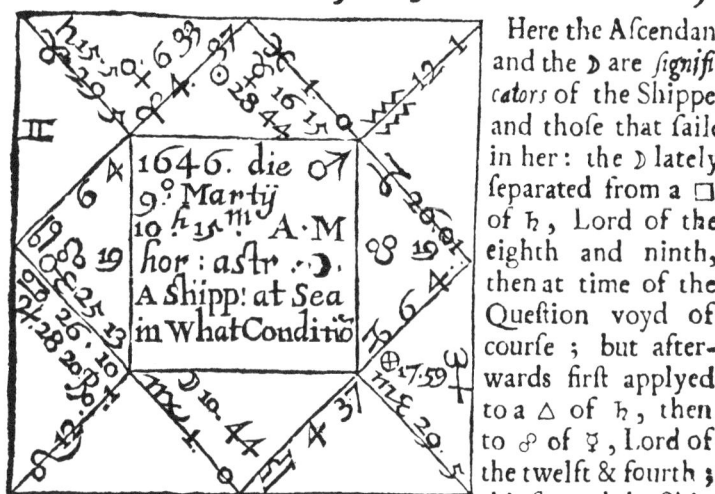

Here the Ascendant and the ☽ are *significators* of the Shippe, and those that saile in her: the ☽ lately separated from a ☐ of ♄, Lord of the eighth and ninth, then at time of the Question voyd of course ; but afterwards first applyed to a △ of ♄, then to ☍ of ☿, Lord of the twelft & fourth ; this shewed the Ship had lately been in danger (of Death) viz. shipwrack : and as the ☽ had been voyd of course, so had no newes been heard of her; because the ☽ was last in ☐ of ♄, in fixed Signes, tortuous or odiously and maliciously aspecting each other, and falling into Cadent houses, and then did not presently apply to the good aspect of any benevolent Planet, but was voyd of course, and then againe continued her application out of the fourth to ♄, who is still Lord of the eighth, although it was by good aspect ; and then after separation from him, applyed to ☍ ☿, and that ☿ her Dispositor was in his Detriment, and entring Combustion, and ♃ Dispositor of ☿ Subterranean and in ☌ with ♂, and termes of an *Infortune* ; and forasmuch as I found ♂ in his Fall, upon or neer the Cusp of the second house, I judged losse was at hand to the Merchant ; ⊕ being in the sixt house, disposed by ♃, and he Retrograde in the second, not beholding ⊗ ; the ☽ also casting her ☐ *Sinister* to the ⊗, and so ☿ his *Dexter* ☐ : by meanes therefore of so many evill testimonies of receiving losse rather then benefit; I judged that the Merchant should lose much, if not all that was adventured in this Ship, and so consequently I doubted the Ship was cast away ; [and so it proved.]

Principall Significators under the Earth, ill : worst of all, if

Example of another Ship.

in the fourth, for that is an assured testimony of sinking the Ship.

Of the time of receiving any QUESTION.

It hath been disputed largely amongst the *Arabians*, who were excellent in the resolution of Horary Questions, what time the *Astrologer* should take for the ground of his Question, whether that time when the *Querent* first comes into ones House or Closet, or first salutes the *Artist*, whether that is to be admitted for the most proper time of erecting a Figure, and giving Judgment thereupon.

Though some have consented to this opinion, yet I could never be satisfied herein either with reason or experience: for let us admit one comes to demands a Resolution of me, and we converse together a good while; but in the end, some occasion intervenes, and we depart: I hope no sound Judgment will allow of this time to be the *Radix* of a Question (whenas none is really demanded) *viz.* at what time he first saw me, or entred my house and spake with me.

Without doubt the true houre of receiving any Question is then, when the *Querent* propounds his desire unto the *Astrologer*, even that very moment of time, in my opinion, is to be accepted: for let us suppose a Letter is sent or delivered unto me, wherein I am desired to resolve some doubts; perhaps I receive the Letter into my hands at three of clock in any day of the week, but in regard of some occasions, doe not read it untill four or five hours after; that very hour and minute of hour when I break it open, and perceive the intention of the *Querent*, is the time to which I ought to erect my Figure, and from thence to draw mine *Astrologicall Judgment* : This way and manner have I practised, and found successe answerable : And whereas *Bonatus* and some others doe give warning that the *Astrologian* judge not his owne Question, and say he cannot tell how to accept of a question from himselfe; this I conceive was his reason, Because he thought the *Artist* would be partiall to himselfe in his judgment : Verily I am of a contrary opinion and have found by many experiments, that at what hour the

mind

all manner of Questions. 167

mind or intention of the *Astrologer* is heavily perplexed with, or concerning the succeffe of any matter wherein himfelfe is really concerned, I fay he may with great reafon accept of that hour for the true time of erecting his Scheame of Heaven, and he may (if not partiall) as well judge of that Figure erected by himfelfe, as of any other; but herein I advife him to lay afide all love and partiality unto his owne Caufe.

JUDGMENTS concerning the fecond HOUSE.

CHAP. XXVII.

Whether the Querent fhall be Rich, or have a competent Fortune? By what meanes attaine it? The time when? &c. and if it fhall continue?

WHoever interrogates, be his Condition what it will be, *King, Noble, Prieft* or *Lay-man*, the Afcendant, the Lord thereof and the ☽ are his *fignificators*: and if the Queftion be in generall termes, (*viz. Whether he fhall ever be rich yea or not?*) withou relation to any particular perfon from whom he may expect a Fortune, the refolution of it is in this nature:

Confider the Signe afcending on the Cufp of the fecond Houfe, the Lord thereof, the Planet or Planets therein pofited, or afpecting the Lord of that houfe or Cufp thereof; the *Part of Fortune*, the Signe and place of Heaven where it is placed, and how afpected by the Planets, (for ⊕ it felfe emitteth no rayes, or cafteth any afpect to any Planet, no more doe the ☊ or ☋.)

Firft, if you find the Planets all angular, it's one good Signe of Subftance; if they be in fuccedant houfes, direct and fwift in motion, it's a good figne.

If the Planets be in good houfes, direct, and but moderately

ly dignified in essentiall Dignities, it's an hopefull argument of an Estate: Those Rules are generall.

If the Lord of the Ascendant, or the ☽, and Lord of the second house, *viz.* of Substance, be corporally joyned together, or if they, *viz.* Lord of the Ascendant and ☽, have friendly aspect to the Lord of the second, or if ♃ and ♀ cast their △ or ✶, or be in ☌ with ⊗, or if the Lord of the second be in the Ascendant, or the ☽, or Lord of the Ascendant in the second, or if any Planet transfer the light and vertue of the Lord of the second to the Lord of the Ascendant, or if benevolent Planets cast their ✶ or △ to the Cuspe of the Ascendant or ⊗, or any fixed Starre of the nature of ♃ and ♀, doe ascend with the cuspe of the second or ⊗ be in ☌ with or neer to such a fixed Starre; or if ♃ who is naturall significator of substance, or ♀ who is naturally a fortune or ☊ be in the second, and no infortune cast his aspect unto them, or if you finde all the Planets direct and swift in motion *(viz.)* if their daily motion be more then what is assigned for their meane or middle motion, which you may perceive by Page 57. 61. 65. 69. 72. 76. 80. the querent shall not feare poverty, for he will be competently rich or have a sufficient fortune to subsist on, and this his estate shall be greater or lesser according to the Major testimonies, which you are carefully to examine of those significators which doe naturally resolve this question; and here in this demand you must remember to take notice of the quality of the person inquiring or demanding the question, for (*Quoad capax*) it shall happen to any Interrogant.

By what meanes attaine it.

When you have sufficiently examined your Figure, and perceive that the *Querent* shall have a subsistence or will come to have riches, it will be demanded, how? by whom, or what meanes it may be obtained?

Herein you must observe, that if the Lord of the second house be in the second, the *querent* shall obtain an Estate by his owne labour and proper industry; if the Lord of the second be placed in the Ascendant, he shall unexpectedly come to a Fortune, or

all manner of Questions. 169

or without much labour attaine it. If that the Lord of the second or the ☽ doe promise substance by any aspect they have to each other, you must consider from what House the aspect is, or of what House the ☽ is Lady of, or if neither of these promise substance; see to the ⊗ what house it is in, and what House of Heaven the *Disposer* is Lord of.

If the Planet assisting or promising encrease of Fortune be Lord of the Ascendant, the *Querent* himselfe will by his owne diligence advance his owne Fortune; if he be a meane man or Mechanicall that interrogates, then by the sweat and labour of his owne hands, his owne Invention, Care and Paines-taking shall put him into a Fortune: but if the Adjuvant Planet be Lord of the second, he will augment his Estate by advance of his owne Stock, and well managing his private Fortune, and adventuring to Buy and Sell in such things as naturally he is addicted unto, or fals in his way in the course of his life, or are of the nature of that Planet (the Signe he is in considered.)

If the Lord of the third fortunate the Lord of the second, or the Cusp of the house, or *Part of Fortune*, he will be assisted in procuring an Estate by some honest Neighbour, or some one of his Kinred, Brethren or Sisters, if he have any, or by some Journey he shall undertake, or removing to that quarter of Heaven from whence the Lord of the third casts his good aspect, or is corporally joined with the Significator of Substance.

If the fortunate Planet or Significator be Lord of the fourth, or placed in the fourth, the *Querent* will attaine Wealth by meanes of his Fathers assistance, (if he be living) or by some aged person, as Grandfather, &c. or by taking some Farme or Grounds, or purchase of Tenements, Lands or Hereditaments, or well managing the Stock his *Ancestors* have or shall leave him, or some Stock of Money his Kinred may lend him.

If the Lord of the fifth doe promise Wealth, then he obtaines meanes: if a Gentleman (by Play, Cards, Dice, Sports, Pastimes,) if of Capacity, and a Courtier, by some Embassage, Message, &c. If an ordinary man propounds the Question, by keeping a Victualling-house, as Ale-house, Inne, Taverne, Bowling-alley, or being a Door-keeper, Porter to some Gentleman;

Y

in the second, and the Lord of the second receive him, it's probable the businesse will be effected; but if the Lord of the seventh, or of the eighth be in the first or second, and neither have reception of the Lord of the first or second house, or of the ☽, it's an argument he shall not have his desire accomplished, but shall receive a deniall or more prejudice in the thing demanded.

If the Lord of the Ascendant and the ☽ be joyned to a *Fortune* that hath dignity in the Signe ascending, or Signe intercepted in the Ascendant, the matter will be effected; or if any of them be joyned to an *Infortune* who hath dignity in the Ascendant, and that *Infortune* receive the Lord of the Ascendant or the ☽, the businesse will be dispatched: Or if the Lord of the Ascendant or the ☽ be joyned to a fortunate Planet, and he well placed either in the tenth or eleventh, the matter shall be perfected, though there be no reception: The Judgments of this Chapter shall then have place and prove true, when as the the matter in question is amongst ordinary persons, or with such people as with whom there is a community, as Citizens with Citizens, Countrymen with Countrymen, one Tradesman with another; from this Judgment we exempt Kings, Princes, Noblemen and such, who pay Debts slowly, and on whom the Law takes little notice.

If one shall acquire that Gains or Profit, Wages or Stipend of the King or Nobleman, Generall or Common-wealth, Lieutenant-Generall, or any great Person which he Expects.

The resolution hereof will serve for any Question of the like nature, where the *Querent* is much inferiour to the *Quesited*, or the party or parties from whom he expects the accomplishment of his desires.

The Ascendant, Lord thereof and ☽ signifie him that askes the Question; the tenth house and Lord thereof, signifie the *Quesited*, or Person sought after, or from whom the matter is to be required; the second house and Lord thereof are to be considered for the *Querent*, the eleventh house and Lord thereof shall
signifie

all manner of Questions. 171

fignifie the Eftate, Money or Subftance of the King, Nobleman, Generall. &c. or Party enquired after : If in the Queftion you doe find the Lord of the Afcendant or the ☽ joyned to the Lord of the eleventh houfe, or if any of them be joyned to any Planet in the eleventh houfe, and that Planet be a *Fortune*, not in any meafure impedited, or ill difpofed, then you may afhrme that the *Querent* fhall obtaine what Salary, wages, debt, or money the great perfon of what quality foever owes unto him; or if it happen that the ☽ and Lord of the afcendant be joyned to an unfortunate Planet, and he receive them into fome of his effentiall dignities, the *querent* fhall obtaine his Monies, Wages, &c. but not without much folicitation, many weary addreffes, feares and diftrufts; if it happen any Afpect be betwixt the Significators, the one being an infortune and without reception, the *querent* will never obtaine what he defires. In this manner of Judgement be very carefull to obferve the Planets true effentiall dignities, and their mutuall receptions, and by which of their mutuall dignities they receive each other.

Of the time when the aforefaid accidents treated of in this Chapter may happen.

Herein you muft diligently obferve unto what Planet either the Lord of the Afcendant or ☽ applyes unto, or is joyned by body, and doth fignifie the effecting and performance of the matter quefited after, for if that Planet be in ✶ or △ with the Lord of the Afcendant or the ☽, whether he be a Fortune or not, or receive the Lord of the Afcendant or ☽ or not; confider well how both of them project their beames or rayes to each other, untill they come to their perfect afpect, or fee how many degrees at the time of the Queftion asking, they want of being in true partill afpect or ☌, and you may anfwer that it fhall be fo many dayes as are the number of degrees betwixt the Significators, if they be both in Cadent houfes : if they be in Succedant houfes of Heaven, it will be fo many weeks; if in Angles, the time will be fo many moneths : but herein the Aftrologer muft ufe difcretion, and confider if it be poffible that the matter enquired of may be effected in dayes, weeks the figne of the twelfth be humain; if the Signe be ♉ or ♑ or ♈ by Cattle; if ♍ by corne. And herein mix your judgement with reafon.

The moſt aſſured teſtimony in Aſtrology, and upon a Queſtion onely propounded, that the *querent* ſhall be rich and continue ſo, is this, If the Lord of the firſt and ſecond and ♃ be joyned together in the ſecond Houſe, firſt, tenth, ſeventh, fourth or eleventh; but if they be not in ☌, then that they apply by ✶ or △ with mutual reception: nay, although they apply by □ or ☍, yet if it be with reception, the party will thrive or have an eſtate, though with much labour, and many intervening difficulties, yet will he ever more abound then want.

Of the Reaſon, or from whence it proceeds, or what is the Cauſe, why the QUERENT *ſhall not obtaine Wealth.*

When in any Queſtion you find your Figure ſignifies the *Querent* ſhal come to an eſtate, the reſolution following is needleſſe; but if you find that he ſhall not obtaine any great fortune, and the *Interrogant* would know the cauſe why, or thing impediting, that ſo he may the better direct his affaires, and be more wary in the courſe of his life, for better prevention of ſuch difficulties: In this Judgment carefully obſerve the Planet obſtructing, or who doth moſt afflict the Lord of the ſecond, or ⊗, or the cuſp of the ſecond, the ☽, or Lord or Diſpoſitor of the ⊗; if the Lord of the firſt be that Planet, then the *Querent* himſelfe is the cauſe; if the Lord of the ſecond doe with □ or ☍ behold ⊗, or the Cuſp of the ſecond, then want of Money or a ſufficient Stock to ſet himſelfe in imployment is the cauſe: if Lord of the third, his own Kinred will doe nothing for him, or will prove burthenſome, or malicious Neighbours will get all the Trade from him, or ſo under-ſell him, that he will be much kept under thereby: and ſo run thorough the twelve Houſes, as in the Chapter before mentioned. I thought good here to give this generall caution, that if the Lord of the ſecond houſe, or Diſpoſitor of ⊗ be Infortunes, yet if they have Eſſentiall Dignities where they are, or aſpects to good Planets, or be placed in ſuch benevolent houſes as I formerly mentioned, they may be

Significa-

all manner of Questions. 173

Significators of Acquisition of Substance; and in like nature both ☿ and ♀ being afflicted or impedited, or Significators, as aforesaid, may be the Planets obstructing as well as any other, for every Planet must doe the work for which he is by divine Providence assigned unto: Doe you also ever remember that In what House you find *Cauda Draconis*, it prenotes detriment and impediment in such things as are signified by that house, as if he be in the second, he denotes consumption of Estate by the *Querents* owne folly or not theiving, by his owne proper neglect: in the third, hinderance by evill, beggarly or peevish Kinred, &c. and so judge in all the rest of the twelve Houses.

If the QUERENT *shall obtaine the Substance which he demands, or hath lent, or the Goods he hath pawned.*

If the Demand of the *Querent* be, *Whether or no he shall procure the Money or Substance from him of whom he intends to demand it?*

The Lord of the Ascendant and the ☽ are his Significators, the Lord of the second of his Substance.

The seventh House, and the Lord thereof signifie him or her of whom he intends to demand or borrow Money: In proceeding to Judgment,

See if the Lord of the Ascendant or the ☽ be joyned to the Lord of the eighth, who is Lord of the Substance of the party quesited after, or see if either of them be joyned, or in aspect to a Planet posited in the eighth, if the Planet in the eighth be a *Fortune*, or the aspect it selfe fortunate, he shall obtaine the money desired; or if he would borrow the money required will be lent him; if he have deposited any Pledge, it will be restored, whether the fortunate Planet in the eighth be received or not: yea, if an infortunate Planet be in the eighth, or Lord of the eighth, and receive either the Lord of the Ascendant or the ☽, the *Querent* shall obtaine his desire: but if no reception be, he will hardly or ever procure his demands, and if ever, with so much difficulty and labour, as he would rather wish the thing had been undone.

In like manner, if the Lord of the eighth be in the first, or
Y 3   in

tleman; or be he who he will that enquires, if the Lord of the fifth house be strong, he promises somewhat out of the Estate of the Father, or by making Matches, &c.

If the Lord of the sixth, or Significator, or assistant Planet be in the sixth, and the Signe of the sixth be humane, the Querent may expect good Servants, and profit by their labour: if a King or Prince propounds the Question (as sometimes they doe) you may judge, his Subjects will assist him with many tumbling Subsidies, Privy-Seales, Loanes of Money, &c.

If a Nobleman or Gentleman enquire, he shall augment his Estate by Letting Leases, and the discreet managing of his Estate by his Stewards, Bailiffs, and such as undertake for him.

If the Question come from a Country-man, as a Farmer or Husband-man, tell him he may thrive by dealing in little Cattle, as Sheep, Goats, Hogs, Conies, &c.

If a Scholler propound the Question upon the like occasion, advise him to turne Physitian, for he shall thrive by his Salary obtained from people infirme and diseased.

If the Lord of the seventh house fortunate the Lord of the second, or the Cusp of the house, or the ⊗, or that Planet which is posited in the second, let the Querent expect Gods blessing, by meanes of a rich and good Wife, or the assistance of some loving Woman: As also, if a Gentleman propound the Question, then by the Sword, or the Wars, or by Law recovering somewhat detained from him, by contracting of Bargains, by the common acquaintance he hath in his way of Trade or Commerce, if he be a Merchant.

If the Lord of the eighth be that Planet who fortunates the Significators above named, the Querent shall either have some Legacy bequeathed him by Testament of a deceased party, or a further encrease of his Wives Portion, little by him expected at time of his Question, or shall goe uncompelled, and reside in some Country, where encrease of substance shall happen unto him, viz. he shall unexpectedly settle himselfe where formerly he had no intention, and there shall thrive and grow rich.

If the Lord of the ninth give vertue or fortunate the ⊗ or Lord of the second, or Cusp of the House, the Querent may

thrive

all manner of Questions.

thrive by some Voyage to Sea, if ♋ or ♓ descend on the cusp of the ninth, and the Lord of the same Signe be therein, or one of his Wives Brothers, or some allied unto her, or a neer Nighbour, to the place where she did live when he first married her, or some religious man or Minister shall befriend him in the way of his Vocation or Calling, for the encrease of his Fortune.

If an Earthly Signe be on the cusp of the ninth, and the Lord of that house be therein posited, he may thrive by removing to that part of Heaven, or that Coast of the Kingdome or County signified by the Signe and quarter of Heaven, and by dealing in the native Commodities of that County, City or Country to which the Heavens direct him.

If the Lord of the second be fortunate in the tenth house, or the Lord of the tenth and second be in reception, or the Lord of the tenth doe behold the Lord of the second or Cuspe of the second house, or a Planet therein, or the ⊗ with any benevolent configuration; let the *Querent* endevour the service or imployment of some King, Prince, Nobleman, Gentleman, Master, or the like, and thereby he shall augment his estate or get a subsistence: if one inquires that is young and of small fortune, let him learne a Mechanicall trade, according to the nature of the signe of the tenth and Planet who is Lord thereof; for the heavens intimate he shall doe well in his Magistery or Trade, if he be capable and fit for it; or if he be a man of any education and desirous of preferment, let him expect an Office or Publique imployment in the Common wealth, in one kinde or other.

If the Lord of the eleventh be that benevolent Planet who is significator in the premises, *viz.* the Planet fortunating, then some friend shall commend the party inquiring to accept of some imployment very advantagious, or some Merchant, Courtier, or servant of a Nobleman, King, or great person shall be the meanes of raising the *Querent* to a Fortune, and then, things shall unexpectedly happen unto the *querent* which he never thought of: and this for good.

If the Fortunate Planet, who casts his Aspect as aforesaid; be in the twelfth, the *querent* shall advance his Fortune by great Cattle, Horse-races, by imprisonments, or men imprisoned, if weeks or moneths; for if it be a businesse that may require much time, instead of moneths you may adde yeers, and this especially if the Lord of the Ascendant, the ☽ and other Significators be in Angles; but if one Planet be in an Angle, and the other in a Succedant, then they shall signifie moneths; if one be in a Succedant and the other in a Cadent, then they shall denote weeks; but if one be in an Angle, and the other in a Cadent house, they prenote moneths.

Some of the Ancients have said, that if at the houre of the Question the Planet which signifies the perfection of the thing demanded be in one Signe with the Lord of the Ascendant, the matter shall then be brought to conclusion when that Planet and the Lord of the Ascendant come to corporall conjunction in Degree and Minute; if the Lord of the Ascendant be the more ponderous Planet, or whether there be reception yea or not; but if the Lord of the Ascendant be the more light Planet, so that he make haste to the conjunction of the Planet signifying the effecting of the matter, and that Planet receive the Lord of the Ascendant, the matter will be finished. But if that Planet shall not receive the Lord of the Ascendant, then the matter will not be effected, unlesse the foresaid significators be in an Angle when the Conjunction shall be, or in one of his owne Houses, and especially in that house which is called his joy; as ♒ is the joy of ♄, ♐ of ♃, ♏ of ♂, ♎ of ♀, ♍ of ☿. What I have observed in resolving Questions of this nature, is this, that single reception by exaltation without other testimonies profiteth not; that reception by essentiall dignities of House, when benevolent Planets are significators, though by □ or ☍ doe usually shew perfection, yea beyond expectation, and therefore very certainly when by ✶ or △ aspect it so fals out.

And *for the time when*, I observe, if a fortune, or the ☽ or Lord of the thing quesited be in the Ascendant, and have any essentiall dignity therein, the number of Degrees betwixt the Cusp of the Ascendant and body of the Planet, doth denote the time when, dayes if a moveable Signe, and the businesse capable of being perfected in dayes, moneths, or yeers, according to the Signe, its quality and nature of the businesse.

A

all manner of Questions. **177**

A Tradesman of this City in the yeer 1634. propounded these severall Demands unto me: because I have seen the experience of my Judgment, and his *Queries* were pertinent for Resolutions of the Demands of this second House; I have inserted his severall *Queries*, with the Reasons in Art of my so judging them. His *Queries* were;

    1. *If he should be rich, or subsist of himselfe without Marriage?*
    2. *By what meanes he should attaine Wealth?*
    3. *The time when?*
    4. *If it would continue?*

Z

Chap. XXVIII.
If the Querent shall be Rich or Poore.

IT's first necessary for more exact judgement in this question, that you examine the Diurnall motion of the Planets, which I finde here to be as followeth:

Viz. ♄ moveth in 24. houres, two minutes: and is therfore slow in motion.

♃ 13. min. *Ergo,* he moveth more in 24. houres, then his meane motion: which is 4. min. 59. sec. is reputed swift, as you may see fol. 61.

The Diurnall motion of ♂ is 35 min. this being more then his middle or meane motion, which you see in page 65. is 31. min. 27. seconds. He is reputed swift.

Diurnall motion of the ☉ 57. min. 00. sec. being lesse then his mean motion; he is slow.

Of ♀   1. degr. 13. min. very swift.
Of ☿   1. degr. 44. min. more swift.
Cf ☽   11. degr. 54. min.   slow.

In the next place I am to examine the fortitudes and debilities of the Planets: by the Table of essentiall dignities Page 104. and the other Table of Page 115. I doe this more willingly that young Learners may better understand the use of both these Tables, which they will frequently have occasion to use.

True place of ♄ is 15. 19 ♐, Essentiall dignities he hath none in that degree of ♐, where he is, as you may observe by the Table of essentiall dignities, Page 104.

♄ His Accidental Dignities.		♄ His Debilities.	
In the third House	1	Peregrine	5
Free from Combustion	5	Retrograde	5
	6	*Slow in motion*	2
		Occidentall	2
			14

♃ H

all manner of Questions. 179

♃ His Fortitudes.

In Exaltation	4
In the tenth House	5
Direct	4
Swift in motion	2
Free from Combustion	5
	20

He hath no Debilities, either Accidentall or Essentiall, yet some Detriment it is unto him, being in □ with ♂, though the aspect be Platick.

♂ In those degrees of ♎ he is in, hath no Essentiall Dignities.

His Accidentall Fortitudes.

In the Ascendant	5
Direct	4
Swift in motion	2
Free from Combustion	5
In ☌ with Spica ♍, or within five degrees	5
	21

His Debilities.

In Detriment	5
Peregrine	5
Occidentall of the ☉	2
	12

☉ His Fortitudes, Essentiall and Accidentall.

In his owne House	5
In Mid-heaven	5
	10

Debilities.

Slow in motion	2
	2

♀ Her Fortitudes.

In the eleventh house	4
Direct	4
Swift in motion	2
Occidentall of ☉	2
Free from Combustion	5
☌ with Regulus, viz. within six degrees of him	6
	23

Debilities of ♀.

Peregrine	5
	5

Z 2   His

180   *The Resolution of*

♀ His Fortitudes.		Debilities.	
In the tenth house	5	Peregrine	5
Direct	4		5
Swift in motion	2		
Occidentall	2		
Free from Combustion	5		
	18		

☽ Her Fortitudes		Debilities.	
In the tenth house	5	Slow in motion	2
Increasing in Light	2	Peregrine	5
Free from Combustion	5		7
	12		

☷ As you may observe *pag.* 145. in ♏ hath five Debilities, and as it is placed in our Figure, shall rather be admitted to be in the second house, then in the first; and hath therefore but three testimonies of strength, which taken from five of Debilities, ☷ is found weak by two testimonies : and though ☷ is some minutes more then five degrees removed from the Cusp of the second, yet were it absurd to think it had signification in the first.

The Testimonies of all the Planets collected into one, stand thus.

♄ *Is weak by Testimonies*	8	*And is therefore unfortunate.*
♃ *Hath Fortitudes*	20	*And no imbecillity.*
♂ *Is strong as having*	9	Dignities : *His Debilities substracted from his Fortitudes.*
☉ *Hath Dignities*	8	0
♀	18	0
☿	13	0
☽ *Hath*	5	0
☷ *Hath Debilities*	2	0

You

all manner of Questions. 181

You must ever consider, whether your Planet have more Fortitudes or Debilities, and having substracted the lesser number from the greater, make use of what remaines, whether they be Fortitudes or Debilities, and so judge.

The Antiscions of the Planets.

				Contrantiscions.			
♄ in	14	41	♑	♄ in	14	41	♋
♃	12	29	♊	♃ in	12	29	♐
♂	13	48	♓	♂	13	48	♍
☉	26	50	♉	☉	26	50	♏
♀	4	26	♉	♀	4	26	♏
☿	12	15	♉	☿	12	15	♏
☽	10	53	♉	☽	10	53	♏

If the Querent should be Rich or in a Capacity of subsistence without Marriage.

Herein first I considered the generall disposition of the Planets, and found that the Major number of them (especially the two fortunes) were swift in their motion, well posited in houses, no manner of wayes in a violent way, or by a forcible aspect afflicting each other. I also well considered that ♀ Lady of the ascendant was neere to *Cor Leonis*, a Star of great vertue and influence, the ☽ increasing in light, ♃ almost culminating: From hence I collected thus much in generall, that he should subsist in the Common-wealth, and live in good ranke and quality amongst his Neighbours, &c. (*quoad capax*) according to his calling.

Secondly, whether he should be rich or not? In resolving this Question, I considered, that the Lord of the second is posited in the Angle of the East, and that the Lord of the second, *viz.* ♂ is Lord of ♋ or Dispositor thereof, and is neere *Spica* ♍ in 18. of ♎. Then I observed that ♃ a generall significator of wealth, was in his exaltation and Angular, casting his □ sinister very neer to the degree ascending, which □ in signes of long ascensions, we usually repute a △. I also found the ☽ se-

Z 3   parated

perated newly from a ✶ of ♂ Lord of the second, and significator of the thing demanded, and immediately after seperated from ☌ of ☿, then instantly applying to the ☌ of ♀ significator of the *Querent*, transferring thereby both the vertue and influence of ☿ and ♂ to the proper significator of the *Querent*; the ☽ is also disposed by the ☉ and he is strong and powerfull, and as she hath a generall signification in every Question, so being no wayes unfortunate she promised the *Querent* much good. Lastly, I considered that ⊗ was in a fixed sign and in ♂ his own termes: from all which testimonies aforesaid, I judged that the Demandant would acquire an Estate, and have a competent fortune in this world, but attaine it with labour and care, because it is signified by an Infortune; so to the day hereof he hath: but because ♂ Lord of the seventh house (which is the house of Women and Wives) hath the most materiall signification of the thing demanded, *viz.* Wealth and Riches. I advized to marry, and acquainted him, that without Marriage he should nothing so well subsist.

By what meanes, or how attaine Riches.

Herein you must consider the Planet or Planets promising Wealth; ♂ in our Scheame being Lord of the second house and of ⊗ is the Planet we must principally consider; for in the second house you finde no Planet, as he is Lord of the second and placed in the ascendant, he intimates an estate to be got by the Querents owne industry, and because the Significator of the thing demanded is posited in the ascendant, it argues that an estate or increase thereof would come somewhat easily or with lesse labour then expected, but ♂ being an infortune something lessens that point in our positure at this time; and as ♂ is Lord of the seventh house, and thereby signifieth (Women, &c.) I acquainted him he would marry a Woman who would produce him a good fortune, and it fixed, and more then he could very well looke for; which I judged first by the Lord of the seventh his being in the ascendant and neer so eminent a fixed Starre; as also because ♀ who is Lady of his wives house of substance, *viz.* the eight, is so well fortified. I afterwards

all manner of Questions. 183

wards confidered the ☽ was Lady of the tenth houſe (which ſignified his Trade) that ſhe was transferring the light and nature of ☿ and ♂ to the *Querent*; wherefore I adviſed him to diligence in his profeſſion, and that he ſhould thereby attaine a very good or competent Eſtate. He hath, as he informes me, had a good fortune with his Wife, both Money and Land; and for his Trading it hath been very good; for ♃ in the tenth is a certaine and infallible argument (according to naturall cauſes) that the *querent* ſhall have plenty of Trading, or exerciſe a gainfull Profeſſion.

The Time When.

All the ſignificators either in the Aſcendant or Orientall quarter of heaven, and five of the Planets ſwift in their motion, promiſe Subſtance in a ſmall compaſſe of time, after the propoſall of the Queſtion. ♂ Lord of the ſecond houſe, and of ⊗, the principall thing inquired of, being ſwift in motion argues the ſame.

The diſtance of the Aſcendant from ♂ being about two degrees, did in this way of judgement ſignifie two yeers or thereabouts, at what time he had a Portion with his Wife: ſome may wonder why ♂ being peregrine ſhall ſignifie any good to the *querent*. I ſay to that, he being Lord of the ſecond houſe and of the ſeventh, and the promiſing Planet of the thing demanded, ſhall as well ſhew the time When, as alſo the performance of what he ſignifies, (but not without ſome manner of obſtruction;) and herein no queſtion ought to be made, ſith in civill ſocieties of men, the wicked or ungracious doe as well many good offices of love for their Friends, as others better qualified. In the next place, I obſerved what quantity of degrees the ☽ wanted of her perfect ☌ with ♀, & I found they were ſix degrees. 27. minutes; from hence and the former conſideration, I concluded, that about two yeers after the Queſtion propounded, or ſooner, he ſhould ſenſibly perceive a melioration in Eſtate by meanes of a Wife, or by his owne proper diligence and induſtry, and about 1640. which was ſix yeers after the Queſtion, he ſhould have very great trading, and live in excelent

lent repute, have many good Friends and Acquaintance, by whose meanes he should improve his Estate: And the reason why I judged augmentation of his Wealth by means of Friends was, because ♀ is seated on the cusp of the eleventh house, which signifieth Friendship, &c. for in all Judgments you must warily consider the nature of the house wherein the application of your *Significators* are, &c. as also, when you judge in this nature of things contingent, you must measure out the time when they shall happen according to reason, and mix Art and Reason together, and not too much rely upon the generall rules of Art, for *Abs te & a Scientia*.

Of that Planet or Planets impediting the effecting or performance of what is demanded in every Question.

It is considerable in all Demands, that you be carefull to know what that Planet is, who impedites the matter, or hinders it, that it shall take no effect, and we may justly call him *Strong, Hurtfull, Destroyor, Abscissor*, because he onely destroyes and perverts the nature of the Question, when otherwayes it would come to a good conclusion: We receive judgment herein from that Planet with whom the Lord of the Ascendant is joyned, or the *Significator* of the thing quesited after, whether it be the ☽ her selfe, or that she is partaker with the Lord of the Ascendant or no, or is *Significatrix* of the thing Demanded.

In resolving this you must consider the Planet unto whom the *Significator* of the *Querent* is joyned, or the *Significator* of the thing required, or the ☽, and observe how that Planet is disposed, and unto whom he is joyned; for if the Lord of the Ascendant, or ☽, or *Significator* of the matter propounded, is joyned to an evill Planet, evill disposed, without reception; or if he be not ill disposed, but joyned to an *Infortune*, and he ill disposed, and receive him not, it prenotes the destruction of the thing quesited.

We understand a Planet to be ill disposed, when *Peregrine, Retrograde, Combust, Cadent*, from the Ascendant or house of the thing demanded, so that he beholds not the house, or at least
the

all manner of Questions.

the Lord of the house, in this nature the aspect to the house is better then to the Lord thereof; so any Planet in his Fall or Detriment, may properly be called *Destroyer* or *Obstructor*, or Planet impediting.

Moreover, if the *Significator* of the Querent, or thing sought after, or ☽, or Planet to whom she is joyned, whether she is a *Significatrix*, or hath participation in the Question, be joyned to an unfortunate Planet, *viz. Retrograde, Combust, Cadent,* then observe if *Reception* intervene; which if there be, it signifies the perfection of the matter, though with wearinesse and much solicitation: If no reception be, the matter will come to nothing, though there have been much probability of its performance.

If the Planet who receives the Lord of the Ascendant, or the ☽, or Lord of the thing Demanded, or the Planet who receives any of them, be free from misfortunes, neither receiving or received, it perfects the matter with facility.

If the Planet to whom the Lord of the Ascendant, or the ☽, or Lord of the matter sought after, be free from the *Infortunes*, and is joyned to any benevolent Planet who is in aspect with a malevolent, and he impedited and not receiving the former Planet, the matter will not then be brought to perfection, or come to any good conclusion.

Doe you still materially consider if the Planets aspects be without reception, for when they are in reception, things are brought to passe, though with some trouble; ever considering whether any Planet doe cut off the light and vertue of the *Significators* before their perfect ☌ with an evill Planet; if such a thing happen, it hinders not, but that the matter may be perfected and accomplished: but if no abscission of light intervene, whereby the malevolence of the *Infortune* may be taken off, the matter is prohibited, and will not be effected.

You must notwithstanding judge if Reception doe intervene whether it be not by □ or ☍ aspect, for then if a Planet be evill disposed, then the reception profiteth nothing; the lesse when he that is received is impedited: but if reception be by ✶ or △, you may confide the matter will be effected; or if the Planet who receives be at that time well disposed, let the recep-

A a

tion be by any manner of aspect, the matter is performed, be the aspect □ or ☍; if the aspect be △ or ✶, it performes the thing, whether the *Significator* be received or not; but provided, the aspect be not separated, but applying; if the *Significator* be joyned with a *Fortune* not impedited, the thing will be perfected.

If any Planet translate the light or vertue betwixt one *Significator* and another, and he to whom the light is translated be an *Infortune*, and impedited, the Question or matter is destroyed, unlesse the *Infortune* be againe received.

If the *Significator* of the Querent, or the *Moon*, and *Significator* of the thing looked after, be joyned to any Planet who collects the light of both Planets, be he an *Infortune* or infortunate, he destroyes the matter, and permits it not to be accomplished, unlesse himselfe receive both the *Significators*; if he receive one onely of them, it matters not, the matter will not be performed.

Consider likewise, whether the *Significator* of the Querent be in the house of the thing desired, or going to ☌ of his Lord, this intimates the Querent is going to the thing quesited after; if the *Significator* of the thing demanded be found in the Ascendant, or hastening to the ☌ of the *Significator* of the Querent, it imports the matter enquired of, or thing desired shall come to the Querent, receptions notwithstanding, the ☽ and other aspects remaining in their proper being.

If the Querent should continue Rich.

This I resolved by the cusp of the second, which being a Sign fixed, and ⊗ in it, and ♃ in his exaltation and Angular, and ♀ the Dispositor of ♂, and the ☽ in ♌, a firme and stable Sign, I judged he would continue in a plentifull estate, and that the riches God should blesse him withall would be permanent; I meane, he would still have a competent fortune, and not be reduced to poverty or want.

The Antiscions of the Planets could be made little use of in this Figure, because none of them fell exactly either upon the cusp of any materiall house, or with the exact degree of any

Planet,

Planet; onely I obferve the Contrantifcion of ♄ fals neer to the degree of ♃; from whence I judged, no great unity betwixt him and his kindred, or Brothers and Sifters, for you fee ♄ perfonally in the third, and ♃ Lord of that houfe, difturbed by ♄ his Contrantifcion, nor did it promife leffe then prejudice by Servants, or fome vices or blemifhes at leaft in their behaviour, let their outward demeanour be what it will be; for though ♃ be in his exaltation, yet the forefaid Contrantifcion doth afflict him, and leaves a tincture of ♄ with ♃: Here are onely two things of which in the courfe of his life I advifed him friendly of, which materially arife out of the Figure, *viz.* becaufe ☉ Lord of the eleventh, beholds ⊗ with a □ *Siniſter*, as alfo, the cufp of the fecond houfe, and that the ☉ is Lord of the eleventh, which fignifies Friends, I dehorted him from engagements, or confiding in folar men, though of much friendfhip with him, for in all fuch cafes defcribe the Planet afflicting, and you give caution enough; what manner of men ☉ fignifies; fee *page* 71.

Of the third HOUSE, viz. *Of Brethren, Sifters, Kinred, fhort Journeys.*

MAny are the Demands which may be made concerning Queftions appertaining to this Houfe; but in effect, the moft principall and materiall of them, and which naturally doe arife from hence, concerne the Querents Brethren, Sifters, Kinred, or whether there is like to be Unity and Concord betwixt the Querent and them, yea or no; or if the Querent fhall live in peace with his Neighbours, or what are their condition good or bad; or of a fhort Journey, whether profperous, yea or not.

Chap. XXIX.
If the Querent and his Brother, Neighbour or Sister shall agree or love each other.

THe Lord of the Ascendant is for him that asks the Question, the Lord of the third for the Brother, Sister or Neighbour quesited after.

If the Lord of the third be a benevolent Planet, or if he be in the Ascendant, or if a fortunate Planet be in the third, or if the Lord of the third and Lord of the Ascendant be in ✶ or △ aspect within the orbs of either Planet, or if they be in mutuall reception, or if the Lord of the third cast his ✶ or △ to the cusp of the Ascendant, or Lord of the Ascendant cast his ✶ or △ to the third house; theres then no doubt but unity and concord will be betwixt the Querent and Brother, Sister, Neighbour or Kinsman quesited after; if a *Fortune* be in the Ascendant or the Lord of the Ascendant behold the cusp of the third, and the Lord of the third doe not aspect either the Ascendant, or be in aspect with the Lord thereof, you may judge the Querent to be of good condition, and that there will be no default in him, but that the defect will be in the Brother, Sister, Neighbour, or Kinsman quesited after; when either ♄ or ♂ or ☋ are locally placed in the Ascendant, it shewes the Querent to be evill conditioned, and the fault in him, but if you find either ♄ ♂ or ☋ in the third, unlesse in their owne essentiall Dignities, it's an assured evidence the Querent shall expect little good from his Brethren, Sister, Kinred or Neighbour, and lesse if they are Peregrine, Retrograde or Combust, or in any malevolent configuration with any other Planet; for though at the present time of the question, there is apparence of unity, yet will it not continue, but usually mortall hatred or untoward grumbling doth afterward arise.

When ♄ is in the third, or ☋, it signifies the Neighbours are Clownes, the Kinred covetous and sparing; if ♂, then Kinred are trecherous, Neighbours theevish; and this most assuredly when either of them are out of their Dignities essentiall.

Of a Brother that is absent.

The Ascendant and his Lord are the Querents Significator, the cusp of the third house shall be the Ascendant of the Brother that is absent, the fourth the absents house of Substance, and so in order.

Consider in what condition the Lord of the third is in, and in what house, and how the Planets do aspect him, and whether he be in the aspect of the good or evill Planets, and what that aspect is they have to each other, or whether they are in corporall Conjunction; for if the Lord of the third be in the third and the unfortunate Planets have no □ or ☌ aspect unto him, you may judge the Brother is in health; but if the malignant Planets behold him with a □ or ☍, without reception, you may say, the Brother lives, is in health, but he is in great perplexity, discontent and sorrow; but if they behold him with the aforesaid aspects, and be in reception, you may say, the Brother is in great distresse, but he will with ease evade it, and free himselfe from his present sad condition: but if the fortunate Planets behold him wth a ✶ or △ aspect, without reception, or with a □ or ☍ with reception, you may judge the Brother is in good health and is well content to stay in the place where he then is: if the fortunate Planets behold him with ✶ or △ and with reception, you may tell the Querent his Brother is in health, and wants nothing in this world to make him happy: But if the Lord of the third be in the fourth, which is his owne second house, without the aspect of the malignant Planets, he endeavours to get an Estate or fortune in that Country wherein he is at the time of the erecting the Scheame; but if the Lord of the third be in the fifth house, and is joyned with the Lord of the fifth house, with reception of a *Fortune* or not, as long as the Lord of the fifth house is not impedited in any grievous manner, it's an argument the absent Brother is in health, is jocund and merry, and well liketh the conversation of the men of that Country where he is: if he be a *Fortune* with whom the Significator of the Brother is in ☌ with, or in ✶ or △ with reception, you may then more safely pronounce the Brother to

be

be in a good condition; yet if the Lord of the third be in the fifth voyd of courſe, or in perfect ☌ with any of the infortunate Planets, without reception, and thoſe unfortunate Planets be themſelves impedited, it's an argument the abſent Brother is indiſpoſed in health, crazy and not contented in the place where he is: if you find the Brother's ſignificator in other houſes which are not naturally ill (as the ſixth, eighth and twelfth houſes are) then he is not well pleaſed, but yet no hurt will come of it.

If the Brother's Significator be found in the eighth houſe, and is either corporally or by ✶ or △ aſpect joyned to a *Fortune*, you may judge the Brother is not very well, yet not ſo ill, that he need any thing doubt of his wel-being; however, he is indiſpoſed.

If he be joyned to evill Planets by bad aſpects, and out of the ſixt houſe, the abſent Brother is infirme; the ſame you may judge if the Lord of the ſixt be in the third, unleſſe he have dignities in the Signe, and be in thoſe dignities.

If you find the Brother of the Querent to be ill, ſee if the Lord of the third be in ☌ with the Lord of the eighth, or is entring Combuſtion, it's likely then he will dye of that infirmity; but if you find his Significator in the ſeventh, ſay, he is in the ſame Country in which he we went, and not yet gone out of it, he continues there as a Stranger or Sojourner, is neither well or ill, but ſo ſo.

If the Significator be in the eighth, he doubts himſelf that he ſhall dye; and the more dubious he is, if his Significator be either combuſt, or in ☌ with the Lord of the eighth in the eighth, or in aſpect by □ or ☍ of the *Infortunes* out of the eighth.

If his ſignificator be in the ninth, then is he gone from the place to which he firſt went into a further Country, or if capable, he is entred into ſome religious Order, or is imployed by thoſe that are in Order, *viz.* Religious Men, or poſſibly according to his quality, is imployed in ſome journey far diſtant from his former aboad.

If his ſignificator be in the tenth, and joyned by ☌ or in aſpect with the fortunes by △ or ✶ aſpect, eſpecially with reception, he hath then got ſome imployment, Office or Command

all manner of Questions. 191

mand in the Country where he is, and is in good eſtimation and lives in a credible way: but if he be joyned to the infortunes, or in □ or ☍ of them, or any other wayes be impedited by them, or Combuſt in the tenth; it may be feared he is dead.

If he be in the eleventh Houſe, joyned to the Fortunes by any good aſpect; or if he be in ☌ with the Lord of the eleventh; he is then ſafe at the houſe of a friend, and is pleaſant and merry: but if evill Planets afflict him in that Houſe, or caſt their malevolent beames unto him; then is he malecontented, and not well pleaſed with his preſent condition.

If he be in the twelfth Houſe, joyned to the Fortunes with reception, and that or thoſe Fortunes not impedited; he then trucks for Horſes, or great Cattle, is turned Graſier, or is Maſter of a Horſe, an Hoſtler, a Drover of Cattle, or one that drives Cattle to Market, according to the quality of the perſon inquired after.

If he be unfortunate in the twelfth, or in bad aſpect with the infortunes, or in aſpect with the Lord of the eight, or Combuſt; the man is diſcontent, and doubts he ſhall never ſee his Country againe; and well he may, for its probable he will dye there.

If he be in the firſt, the abſent Brother is frolicke and merry, and extreame well pleaſed where he is; and they much love and reſpect him where he is.

If he be in the ſecond, its probable the man can by no means come away; either he is detained as priſoner, or hath done ſome ſuch act as that he is not capable of coming away; yet if the Significator be Retrograde, he will make hard ſhift to eſcape when ever opportunity is offered.

I have been ſomewhat more tedious in this judgement, becauſe it is as a Key to all the reſt: For if any aske of their Father being abſent, let the fourth Houſe be the Aſcendant of him, and ſo run round the twelve Houſes in your judgement for the Father as you have done for the Brother, ever having this Conſideration, that the ſecond Houſe from the Aſcendant of your Queſtion, is the ſubſtance of the queſited; the third from that ſhall ſignifie his Brethren; the fourth his Father: If

inquiry

inquiry be made for a Childe, or Sonne, or Daughter absent, the fift House is their ascendant; the fixt their second House, then the seventh their third, &c.

If one aske of a Servant, the fixt House is his first House or Ascendant; the seventh his second or House of Substance, and so orderly as is before specified: and you must understand that although every House hath his fixt, eight House and twelfth House, yet in every one quesited after, the fixt House of the figure shall signifie his infirmity, the eight his death, the twelfth his imprisonment; onely you must know how to vary your Rules, wherein principally consists the Master-peece of the Art.

Of Reports, Newes, Intelligence, or Feares, Whether true or false, or in what sence its best to take them? Whether they signifie good or evill?

The manner of understanding this Question, and taking it in its proper sence, is diversly related by the Ancients; for some would make these like Questions to belong to the fift House; others, to certain Lords of triplicities, having dominion in the Signes ascending or descending on the Cuspes of the third or fift House. That which I have found true by experience (in our wofull late sad times of Warre) was this; that if I found the ☽ in the ascendant, tenth, eleventh or third House, seperated by a benevolent aspect from any Planet (be he Lord of what House soever) and then applying by ✶ △ or ☌ to the Lord of the ascendant; I say, I did finde the report or rumour true, but alwayes tending to the good of the Parliament, let the report be good or ill; but if at the time of erecting the Figure, the ☽ applyed to the Lord of the seventh by any good aspect, I was sure we had the worst, and our enemies the victory: if the ☽ was voyd of course, the Newes proved of no moment, usually vaine or meer lyes, and very soon contradicted: if the ☽ and ☿ were in □ aspect or in opposition, and did not either the one or other, or both cast their favourable ✶ or △ to the degree ascending, the Newes was false, and reported of purpose to affright us. For the time when

all manner of Questions. 193

when to take the Question, I ever observed the houre when I first heard the newes of the rumour, and tooke that moment of time for the ground of my question; but if another propounded it, then that very particule of hour when it was proposed: however, if at any time upon the like occasion you heare some speech or have some intelligence or report of any thing, and would know whether it will be prejudiciall to you, yea or no, then see whether ♃ or ♀ be in the Ascendant, or the ☽ or ☿ in any of their essentiall Dignities, in △ or ✶ to the Lord of the eleventh; you may then judge, the newes is such as you or the party enquiring shall receive no detriment thereby: but if you find the Lord of the sixth, eighth or twelfth houses in the Ascendant, or in bad aspect to the Lord of the Ascendant, or ♂ or ♄ *Retrograde* in the Ascendant, or in an evill aspect with the Lord of the Ascendant, or casting their □ or ☍ rayes to the degree ascending, then the Querent shall receive prejudice by the newes he heares, if it concerne him or her selfe; or if it concerne the Common-wealth, some dammage hath happened to their Ministers or Parties: if ♄ signifie the mischiefe, their poor Country-friends have been plundered, lost their Corne and Cattle; if ♂, then some stragling parties of theirs is cut off; if ☿, some of their Letters have miscarried, or been intercepted; if the ☉ be the Signifitator, their principall Officer or Commander in chiefe is in some distresse, &c. if ♃ or ♀, the mischiefe fals on some Gentlemen, their friends, or such as take part with them. Herein vary your rules according to the Question.

If Rumours be true or false, according to the
ANCIENTS.

Consider the Lord of the Ascendant and the ☽, and see which of them is in an Angle, or if the Dispositor of the ☽ be in an Angle, and a fixed Signe, or if any of these be in any succedant house and fixed Signe, or in good aspect with the fortunate Planets, *viz.* in ✶ or △ of ♃ ♀ or ☉, you may then judge the Rumours are true and very good; but if you find the Lord of the Ascendant afflicted by the *Infortunes*, or cadent in house, you must judge the contrary though he strong in the

B b   Signe

Signe wherein he is. Rumours are for the moſt part true when the Angles of the Figure are of fixed Signs, *viz* ♉ ♌ ♏ ♒, and the ☽ and ☿ in fixed Signes, ſeparating from the *Infortunes*, and applying to a fortunate Planet, placed in any Angle. Ill Rumours hold true, if the Angles of the fourth and tenth houſe be fixed, and the ☽ received in them; I ſay, they will be in ſome ſort verified: If you heare evill newes or bad reports, or have unlucky intelligence, yet if either of the *Fortunes* be in the Aſcendant, or the ☽ ufortunate, it's a ſtrong argument the Rumours are falſe, and that they will turne rather to good than evil: The Retrogradation of ☿, or he any other way afflicted, or of that Planet to whom the ☽ applies, or to whom ☿ applies, and above all, if either of thoſe two be Lords of the Aſcendant, doe ſignifie the ill Rumours ſhall vaniſh to nothing, and ſhall be converted to good; if the Lord of the Aſcendant be under the ☉ Beames or Combuſt, the matter is kept ſecret, and few ſhall ever know the truth of them.

Of Councell or Advice given, whether it be for Good or Evill.

Sometimes a Neighbour, Kinſman or Friend takes occaſion to come viſit their Friends, with intention and pretenſion to give them good advice, or perſwade them to ſuch or ſuch a matter, &c if you would know, whether they inted really, yea or no, erect your Figure for the moment of time when firſt they begin to break their minds unto you; then conſider if there be in the *Medium Cœli*, or tenth houſe a fortunate Planet, *viz*. ☉ ♃ or ♀, or elſe ☊, or the ☽ applying to the Lord of the Aſcendant, then judge they come with an honeſt heart, and the advice they give is intended for your good: If an *Infortune*, *viz*. ♄ ♂ or ☋, they intend deceitfully, and are lyars. *Haly* doth further affirm, that if the Signe aſcending be a moveable Signe, and the Lord of the Aſcendant, and ☽ in moveable Signes, he is a trecherous Fellow, and comes with deceit to entrap thee.

Whether

all manner of Questions.

Whether the Querent have Brethren or Sisters.

Although this is better resolved from the proper Nativity of the Querent, then the Question; yet you may observe these rules, which I have found true by experience.

Viz. If you find upon the cusp of the third house a fruitfull Sign, as ♋ ♏ ♓ (♒ ♐ or ♊, though these are not so fruitfull as the other) yet you may judge he hath Brethren or Sisters; Brother or Brethren, if a Masculine Signe be there, and the Lord thereof in a Masculine Signe or house, or in aspect with a Masculine Planet: Sister or Sisters, if a Feminine Signe and Planet be in the third, or the *Significators* in Feminine Signes or Houses, and in ☌ or application to Feminine Planets; some say, so many Planets as are in the house, or that the Lord of the third is in aspect with, so many Brothers or Sisters the Querent hath; but I ever held it too scrupulous to require such particulars from a Question: the unity amongst Brethren or Kinred, either in the present or future, is discernable by the last aspect the Lord of the third, and Lord of the Ascendant were in, or by the happy positure of Benevolent or malignant Planets in the Ascendant or third; for where the *Fortunes* are placed, from thence it may be expected all unity and concord from that party: from the Querent, if they be in the Ascendant: from the Brother, Sister or Kinred in generall, if the *Fortunes* be in the third. The ill positure of ♄ or ♂ out of their essentiall Dignities in the third, or ☋ therein, is a strong argument of untoward and crosse Brethren, Sisters or Kinred, and of no unity betwixt them, but continuall discord, wrangling and jangling, &c.

Of a short Journey, if good to goe, yea or no; which way intended.

By a short Journey I intend twenty, thirty or forty miles, or so farre from ones home, as he may goe and come in a day, or at least on the next; now if you would know whether it will be best for you to goe, yea or not: herein consider the Lord of the Ascendant at the time of propounding the Question, and

The Resolution of

see if he be swift or slow in motion, or in any of the Dignities of the Lord of the third, or placed in the third, or in ✶ △ or ☌ either with the Lord of the third, or with a Benevolent Planet posited in the third, or if the ☽ apply to the Lord of the third, or to any Planet posited in the third, or be in the third, or cast her ✶ aspect to the Signe ascending, or her □ in Signs of short ascensions, in any house whatsoever, or if she be swift in motion, all, or any of these are arguments, that the party shall goe his short Journey, and with good successe; and if you would know to what part of Heaven the place lyeth whether he would goe, consider the Signe of the third house, the Signe wherein the Lord of the third is, and wherein the ☽ is, and judge by which of them is strongest in essentiall Dignities where he is; if the principall Significator be in a Northerne Signe, then his Journey is intended North; and so of the rest, with their due limitations.

Where an absent Brother was?

In

all manner of Questions. 197

In *November* 1645. a Citizen of *London* being gone into the West of *England*, and no newes for many weeks had where he was, his owne Brother with great importunity moved me to give my judgment concerning these Particulars.

1. *If living or dead? if dead, whether killed by souldiers? for at this time our miserable Kingdome was full of souldiery.*
2. *If living, when he should heare of him? and where he was?*
3. *When he would come home?*

CHAP. XXX.
Judgment upon the preceding Figure.

THE Ascendant doth here represent the shape and forme of him that asked the Question, with consideration had to ♄ Lord of the Signe; and as both the Signe ascending and Lord thereof are of a dry quality and nature, so was the *Querent*, leane, spare of body, and a reall *Saturnine* man, &c.

♉ Is the Ascendant of the third House, and ♀ being Lady of the signe, did represent the absent Brother, or party inquired after: the ☽ in regard she neither applyed to one significator or other, had not much to doe in this Question, I mean in description of the parties.

For as much as ♀ significatrix of the Quesited is no manner of way afflicted either by ☿ who is Lord of the eight in the figure, or by ♂ who is Lord of the eight as to the ascendant of the quesited, and that the separation of the ☽ was good, *viz.* from a △ dexter of ♃, and her next application to a ☌ of ☉, upon the Cuspe of *Medium Cæli*, I judged the absent Brother was alive and had no manner of casualty happened unto him, but was in good health. Having judged the man to be alive, there needs no proceeding to judgement of the rest of the first *Quere*.

Bb 3 *When*

The Resolution of

When heare of him.

You see ♀ is Lady of the third, and ♄ is Lord of the Ascendant; if you consider the Signes they are in, and the severall degrees of each planet in the Signe; you shall observe, that as well the Significator of the absent Brother, who is ♀, as ♄ Lord of the Ascendant doe apply to each other by a friendly △; for ♄ though a ponderous Planet, yet being Retrograde and in more degrees of the Signe then ♀, doth by Retrogradation apply to meet her: a very good argument that the Querent should heare newes of his Brother very suddenly; and if you looke into the *Ephemeris of Eickstadius* 1645 *Novemb.* 7. you shall finde the true time of the △ aspect betwixt ♄ and ♀ to be at five of the clocke the same day the Question was asked in the afternoon; but with reduction to our *London Meridian* a little after foure: I therefore advised the querent to goe to the *Carriers* of those Countries where he knew his Brother had been, and aske of them when they saw the quesited; for I told him, it was probable he should heare of him that very day; upon the reason onely because the Significators of both parties met by a friendly △. *He hath since confidently affirmed, that about the very moment of time, viz. about four, a Carrier came casually where he was, and informed him his Brother was in health and living.*

Where he was.

His Journey was into the *West*; at time of the question I find ♀ the quesited his *Significatrix*, leaving ♐ a Northeast Signe, and entring ♑ a South Signe: whereupon I judged he was in the Souh-east part of that County unto which he went; and because ♀ was not farre removed from the Ascendant, but was in the *Orientall* quarter of Heaven, I judged he was not above one or two dayes journey from *London*; and because ♀ was departing the Signe ♐, and entring the Signe ♑, wherein she hath essentiall Dignities by *Triplicity* and *Terme*, I judged the man was leaving the Country and place where he last was, and wherein he had no Possession or Habitation, and was coming
to

all manner of Questions. 199

to his owne house in *London*, wherein he had good propriety; in regard that ♀ wanted one degree of getting out of ♐, I judged he would be at home in lesse then one week; for ♐ is a *Bi-corporeall*, *Common* Signe, and one degree in that Signe, and in the nature of this question, might well denote a week.

But he came home the *Tuesday* following, when the ☽ came to the body of ♀, she being then got into ♑ to her owne *Termes*, and into her *diurnall Triplicity*.

There being an amicable aspect betwixt the two Brothers Significators, *viz.* ♄ and ♀, these two Brothers alwayes did, and doe agree lovingly: This which hath been said is enough concerning the judgment of this question; vary your judgment according to the position of your Significators and matter propounded, and by this method you may judge of any thing propounded belonging to this third house.

CHAP. XXXI.

If a Report or common Rumour were True or False.

In the yeer 1643. His Majesties Army being then *Rampant*, serverall Reports were given out, that his Majesty had taken *Cambridge*, &c. a wel-affected person enquires of me, if the Newes were true or false? Whereupon I erected the Figure ensuing, and gave Judgment, *All that we heard was untruth, and that the Towne neither was, or should be taken by Him or his Forces.*

The Resolution of

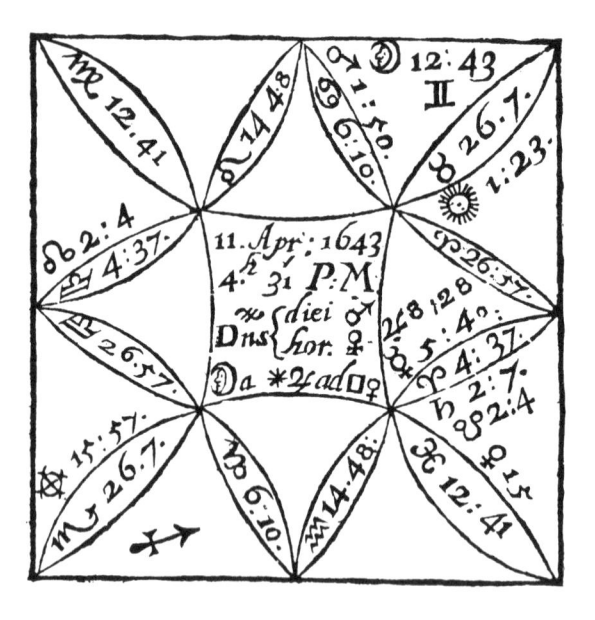

A Report that CAMBRIDGE *was taken by the King's Forces; if true?*

First, I confidered that the Angles were all moveable, and that ♂ did vitiate the cufp of the tenth, and ♄ the cufp of the feventh, one argument the Report was falfe.

Secondly, I found th ☽ cadent, and in ♊, a Signe wherein fhe nothing delights; a fecond ftrong evidence of a falfe Rumour.

Thirdly, I found ☊ on the cufp of the Afcendant, a Signe of good to the Parliament, for the firft houfe fignified that honourable *Society*: I found ♀ Lady of the Afcendant, and our *Significatrix*, in her Exaltation; but ♂, Lord of our Enemies Afcendant, *viz.* the feventh, entring his Fall, *viz.* ♋, and afflicted by □ of ♄; I faw the ☽ feparating from ♃, placed in the feventh and transferring his light and vertue to ♀, which gave me reafon to expect, that there would come good to us or

ou

all manner of Questions. 201

our fide from this report or Rumor, and no benefit to our Enemies: I faw ♂ and ♄ in a □, which affured me our Enemies were fo full of divifion and treafon, and thwarting one anothers Defignes, that no good fhould come unto them upon this Report; and fo in fhort, I judged *Cambridge* was not taken, and what we heard of its taking were lyes.

Had this Queftion been propounded, *Whether the Querent fhould have Brethren or Sifters?* then you fhould have converted the Judgment thus:

♍ The Signe of the third is a fruitfull Signe.

♋ Wherein the Lord of the third is pofited, is a fruitfull Signe.

☽ Applies to ♀ who is placed in a friutfull Sign, as you may fee *page* 89. where all thefe Signes are noted Prolifical, or Signs arguing fruitfulneffe; from hence you might have affured the Querent, he might have expected both Brothers and Sifters, or a plentifull numerous Kinred; but more Sifters then Brothers, becaufe all the Signes are Feminine, as you may fee *page* 88. and ♂, Lord of the third, is in a Feminine Signe yet in regard the ☽ who is Difpofitor of ♂, is in ♊, a Mafculine Signe, and in ✶ platick with ♃, a Mafculine Planet, Angular, and in a Mafculine Signe and Houfe, it's an argument of the *Demandant's* having a Brother or Brethren.

It were too nice a poynt in *Art*, to predict of the certain number, fith we onely intend to fatisfie our felfe in generall, leaving the difpofing and determination of their certaine number to divine *Providence*.

The third houfe no wayes afflicted, or any ill afpect betwixt ♀, *Significatrix* of the Querent, and ♂ Lord of the third, both being in Signes of the fame nature, and ☽ applying by a □ *dexter* in Signes of fhort afcenfions, to ♀; ☽ having been lately, and yet being within Orbs of the ✶ of ♃; thefe argue an agreement, concord and unity betwixt this Querent Kinred and him, and betwixt him and fuch Brothers or Sifters as he fhould infuhave ture.

Cc Of

Of the fourth HOUSE, and the JUDGMENT depending thereupon.

This is the House of Parents, of Lands, Tenements, Hereditaments, Cities, Towns, Villages, Farmes, Mannours, Castles, Treasure-trove, or of any thing hid in the ground, &c.

CHAP. XXXII.
To find a thing hid or mislaid.

BE carefull to take your Ascendant exactly, and consider the nature of the Question, *viz.* whose Goods, or to whom the thing missing, or lost, or enquired after, did appertaine; if the Goods be the Querents owne Commodity, then see to the Lord of the second; if it belong to his Brother or Sister, then have regard to the Lord of the fourth; if to the Father, the Lord of the fifth; if to the Mother, the Lord of the eleventh, &c. and so in order, according to the nature of the Party who proposeth the Question.

If you find the Lord of the second in any Angle, you may judge the thing lost, hid or missing, is within the house of him that demands the Question; and if the Lord of the second be in the Ascendant, or in the Sign wherin the Lord of the Ascendant is, or in one of his houses, you may judge the thing is in that part of the house which he himselfe most frequents, or wherein he doth most abide, or is conversant, or where himselfe layeth up his owne Commodities, or such things as he most delights in; but if the Lord of the second be in the tenth house, it's then in his Shop, if he be a *Mechanick*; if a *Gentleman*, in his Hall or Dinining-room; if a Husband-man, in the ordinary common room of his house, or first room after entrance into his house: If the Lord of the second be in the seventh, it's in that part of the house where his Wife, or his Maid-servants have most to

doe

all manner of Questions.   203

doe in: If the Lord of the second be in the fourth, it's where the most aged of the house doth lodge, or formerly did most frequent, or in the middle of the house, or in the most ancient part of the house, where either his Father or some ancient man lodged: the nature and quality of the place is knowne by the Signes the *Significators* are in; for if the Signe of the second be aiery, or the greater number of the *Significators* and Signe wherein ⊗ is, doth concurre, the thing is hid in the Eaves or top, or upper part of that house or roome where it is, or on high from the ground: and if the thing hid be in the Field, or in a Garden or Orchard, it's higher then the ordinary ground, or upon the highest hill or part of that ground, or hangs upon some stalk of a Plant or Tree.

If the former *Significators* be strong, and in watry Signes, it's in the Buttery, Dairy or Wash house, or neer Water.

If in fiery Signes, it's neer the Chimney, or where Iron is, or in, or neer the Wals of the house.

If in earthly Signes, the thing hid is on the ground or earth, under or neer some Pavement or Floor, and if you find the thing to be mislaid out of the house in any ground, it notes neer the Bridge or Stile where people come into the ground.

If your *Significator* be going out of one Signe and entring another, the thing is behind something or other, or is carelessly fallen downe betwixt two rooms, or neer the Threshold, or joyning together of two rooms, and is higher or lower in the place, according to the nature of the Signe, &c.

The *Ancients* have delivered many rules, and doe say, that to judge in what part of the house or ground the thing is in, you must see to the Lord of the hour, and if he be in the tenth house or eleventh, you may say the thing is in the South part of the house, towards the East; and if he be between the fourth house and Ascendant, then North-east: if between the fourth and seventh, then North-west: if between the tenth house and the seventh, then South-west. *What part of the house or ground.*

This is and was the opinion of the former *Astrologians*, however, I have not found this judgment very exact, therefore I laboured to find a more certaine manner, and a more exact way for the ready discovery or finding out any thing mislaid or mis-

Cc 2   sing missing in a house, and not stolen; and it was thus:

First, I considered the Signe ascending, it's nature, the quarter of Heaven it signified.

Secondly, what Signe the Lord of the Ascendant was in.
The Signe of the fourth house.
The Signe the Lord of the fourth was in.
What Signe the ☽ was in.
The Signe of the second.
The Signe the Lord of the second was in.
The Signe ⊕ was in.

I considered the quality of the Signe, as to shew what part of the house it was in; I meane, what quarter, whether East, West, North or South, according to the greater number of testimonies: and you must know, for things lost, mislaid, or fugitives, these are the true quarters of Heaven the Signes signifie.

♈ *East*, ♌ *East and by North*, ♐ *East and by South*.
♎ *West*, ♊ *West by South*, ♒ *West by North*.
♋ *North*, ♏ *North by East*, ♓ *North by West*.
♑ *South*, ♉ *South by East*, ♍ *South by West*.

Having found the quarter of Heaven, the nature of the Signs shewed me also the quality of the place in the house, *viz.* aiery Signes, above ground; fiery Signes, neer a Wall or Partition; earthly Signes, on the Floor; watry, neere a moyst place in the roome, &c. A few experiments I know may better this Judgment: I have sometimes in merriment set a present Figure, and by that discovered in what part of the house the Glove, Book, or any thing else was hid, and found the rule very true.

Chap. XXXIII.
Of Buying and Selling Lands, Houses, Farmes, &c.

GIVE the Ascendant and Lord thereof, and Planet from whom the ☽ is separated to the *Querent* or *Buyer*.

Give the seventh house the Lord thereof, and the Planet to whom the ☽ applyes to the *Seller*.

Give

all manner of Questions. 205

Give the fourth house, the Planet therein placed, and the ☽ and Lord of the fourth house to the *House, Ground* or *Mannour* to be bought or purchased.

Let the tenth house, a Planet or Planets posited therein, and Lord of that house signifie the *Price*, that is, *Whether it will be sold cheap or deer.*

If you find the Lord of the Ascendant and Lord of the se- *If agree.* venth in any amicable aspect, the Lord of the seventh applying to the Lord of the Ascendant, you may judge the *Seller* hath good will to *sell* and to deale with the *Querent* or *Buyer*: and if the *Significators* be in any essentiall Dignities upon this their application or translation of light; or their application be by ☌, it's then probable they will agree and conclude upon the *Purchase* with little labour: if the application or translation of light be by □ or ☍, the two Parties will at last bargaine, but with many words and probabilities of breaking off, and after much expence of time.

Consider also, if the Lord of the Ascendant or the ☽ apply to the Lord of the fourth, or the Lord of the fourth or the ☽ to the Lord of the ascendant, and whether onely the Lord of the fourth apply to the Lord of the ascendant, and he receive him in any of his Dignities, or if the Lord of the ascendant be in the fourth, or the ☽, or the Lord of the fourth in the ascendant, then shall the Party enquiring buy the House or Inheritance at that time in question.

But if this dwelling in houses be not, yet if the ☽ transferre the vertue or light of the Lord of the fourth to the Lord of the ascendant, the *Bargaine* will be concluded, but rather by Messengers or Brokers, then by the personall treaty of the two principall *Agents*.

If there be no application or translation, or transferring the light of one Planet to another, it's not like there will be any *Bargaine* concluded.

Of the goodnesse or badnesse of the Land or House.

If you find in the fourth house the two *Infortunes*, very po- *House or land* tent, or peregrine, or if the Lord of the fourth be Retrograde *good or ill.*
Cc 3 or

or unfortunate, or in his Fall or Detriment, 'twill never continue long with your Posterity.

But if either ♃ ♀ or ☊ be in the fourth, or the Lord of the fourth in his owne house, *viz.* in the fourth, the *Purchaser* may expect good successe in the Land or House now in buying, and that it may continue a long time with his Posterity, and it's an argument he shall have good encrease for his Money by that Bargaine.

Quality of the ground. If it be arrable Land, and you would know the nature of it, make the ascendant the *Significator* of the Tenants, Husbandmen and Farmers occupying it.

The fourth house shall signifie the condition and nature of the Soyl, its form and condition; or of a House or Houses, when the Question is for them.

The Angle of the West shall signifie the Herbage thereof, and the quality and quantity, but the *Medium Cœli* is signifier of the Wood, Trees and Plants growing thereupon.

Tenants good or ill. If an *Infortune* possesse the Ascendant, the Tenants or Occupiers are ill, deceitfull and unwilling the goodnesse of the ground should be discovered: if a *Fortune* be in the Ascendant judge the contrary, *viz.* the Tenants are honest men, and doe give, and will give the Land-lord content, and will love him besides, and are content to hold what they have already, and to occupy the Land still: but if an infortunate Planet be in the ascendant, and direct, the Tenants will purloyne the Woods, or weare out the vertue of the land; but if he be retrograde, the Tenants wil put the land upon the Landlord, or will run away or throw up their Leases.

Wood on the Ground. If a fortunate Planet be in the *Mid-heaven*, and direct, say, there is good Timber upon the ground, and good store; if the *Fortune* be retrograde, judge there are many Trees, but little Timber, and those lopt, or that of late the *Seller* hath sold many, or made much spoyle thereof, or that the Trees are much decayed, &c. if an *Infortune* be in the *Medium Cœli*, direct, there's then but few Trees; if he be retrograde, say, the Country people have stolne, or made great wast thereof.

But if no Planet be in the *Mid-heaven*, see to the Lord of that house, if he behold it with a good aspect, and be in any of his owne

all manner of Questions.

owne Dignities, fay, there is fome Wood on the ground; if he doe not behold the Mid-heaven, either there is little or no Wood, or it is worth nothing; if the Lord of the tenth be *Orientall*, and behold his owne houfe, the Trees are young ones, or the Wood of fmall growth, or there are Copfes: but if the Lord of the tenth be *Occidentall*, and in the condition beforefaid, the Trees are of more growth, and the Wood is ancient; and if the Lord of the tenth be then direct, the Trees are found, and will continue fo a long time; but if he be retrograde, there's many Trunks and hollow Trees amongft them.

Having confidered what precedes, confider the Angle of the Weft, or the feventh houfe which will declare unto thee the ftate and quality of the Herbage, or fmaller Plants of the ground, for if you find either ♃ or ♀, or the Lord of the feventh in the feventh, it's an argument the Land yeelds plenty of Graffe, Corne, or what is feafonably required from it, if an *Infortune* be there, judge the coutrary, &c.

In confideration of the property of the earth, have refpect *Quality of* to the fouth houfe and Signe of the fourth, for if ♈ ♌ or ♐ be *the ground.* on the cufp of the houfe, it's a hilly, mountainous, dry and hard piece of ground, or a great part of it is fo; if either ♉ ♍ or ♑ be on the cufp of the fourth, the ground is plaine, champion, and excellent Paftorage, or good for Grazing or Tillage.

If ♊ ♎ or ♒, it's neither very hilly or very plaine, but there is grounds of both forts, and in nature part of it is good, and part not fo: if ♋ ♏ or ♓, then there is no doubt but there is fome pretty River, Rivolet, or good ftore of Water.

You muft for the perfect knowledge of the quality and nature of the Soyle, obferve this generall rule, That if an *Infortune* be in the Signe of the fourth, Retrograde, or in his Fall or Detriment, the Land fhall partake highly in the infelicity that Planet fignifies; as if ♏ be the cufp of the fourth, and ♄ is placed therein, and is either Retrograde or afflicted by fome other Misfortune, you may confidently averre, the ground is troubled with too much Water, or it's Boggy and unwholfome, full of long rufhy Graffe, &c.

And if the Land lye neer the Sea, you may feare the excurfion of the Sea, or a decay in the Sea banks, or it is fubject to be

over-

overflowne with the River or Water, &c. if ♄ afflict a fiery Signe in the fourth, the Land is barren, stony hungry, mountainous, yeelds no profit without infinite labour, wants water, for it's naturally barren, produces little Grasse: If ♄ afflict the Signe of ♊, by his presence there, or any of the humane Signs, *viz.* ♎ or ♒, by his retrogradation, that Signe being the cusp of the fourth, there's yet defect in the goodnesse of the Land, and ill Husbands have formerly managed it unthriftily: If he be unfortunate in an earthly Signe, upon the Signe of the fourth, the Land is good, but the present Occupiers give it not its due Tillage, or are not in the right way in their managing it, they are idle, lazy, slothfull, penurious, and unwilling to bestow cost upon it; besides, it's an heavy clay ground, and the *Farmers* understand not the nature of the Soyle, &c.

Cheap or dear   This is knowne by the Lord of the tenth, for if he be Angular, Direct, and strong in essentiall Dignities, the price will be high, and the *Seller* will put it off at deare rates; but if the Lord of the tenth be cadent, combust, retrograde, slow of motion, afflicted, then the price will not rise high.

If it be good to hire or take the Farme, House or
Land desired.

Give the ascendant and his Lord to the person of him that would hire a House, or take Lands.

Let the seventh house and his Lord signifie him or her that hath the letting or selling of this House or Farme.

Let the tenth house and the Lord thereof signifie the Profit which may arise by that undertaking.

The fourth house, and Planets therein placed shall shew the end which shall ensue upon taking, or not taking the House, Land or Farme, &c. be it what it will be.

If the Lord of the ascendant shall be in the ascendant or Sign ascending, or shall have a ✶ or △ aspect unto the Signe ascending, but more properly to the degree ascending, within the moyity of his owne Orbs, or if in the ascendant there be a *Fortune*, whether essentially dignified or not, or if ⊗ be therein placed, and not impedited, it's an argument or testimony the
Farme

all manner of Questions.

Farmer shall take the House, Land or Farme, and is full of hopes to doe good thereby, or that it will be a good Bargaine, and he obtaine much profit thereby, and that he hath much liking to the thing, and is well pleased therewith.

But if an *Infortune* be in the ascendant (it's no matter which of them) if the man have taken the thing ere he come unto you, it now repents him; if he have not taken it already, he hath no will thereunto; or if he doe take it, he will presently post it off to some other party, for he nothing at all cares for the Bargaine.

Having considered what belongs to the party intending to buy or take a Lease, have now recourse to the seventh house, and Lord thereof, for him that shall let it: If you find the Lord of the seventh in the seventh, or casting a benevolent aspect to the cusp of the house, or find a fortunate Planet therein, the man will keep his word with you, you shall have what you bargaine with him for, but he will porfit by the bargaine.

If an *Infortune* be in the seventh, and not Lord of the seventh, have great care of the Covenants and Conditions to be drawne betwixt you, the Landlord will be too hard for you, he minds nothing but his owne ends in dealing with you.

Consider the tenth house afterwards, and if a fortunate Planet be therein, or behold the tenth house, the parties notwithstanding some rubs, will proceed in their Bargaine, and the House, Farme or Lands will be let to the *Querent*.

But if you find an unfortunate Planet in the tenth, or behold that house with an ☍ or □ aspect, there will be no house or Lands taken; and if it be Land that is in agitation to be let, it's probable they differ about the Wood or Timber on the ground, or upon the new erecting of some houses or building upon the ground; or if it be a house, they differ upon the repaires thereof.

As to the end of the businesse, see to the fourth house, and let that signifie the end thereof; if there be a *Fortune* therein, or if the Lord of the fourth be there, or behold the house with ✶ or △, there will come a good end of the matter in hand, both parties will be pleased: but if an *Infortune* be there, in conclusion, the Matter, bargain or thing demised will neither please the one party or otrhe   Dd   If

CHAP. XXXIV.
If the Querent shall enjoy the Estate of his Father.

YOU must in this Question give the ascendant and Lord therof to the Querent; the fourth house, Lord thereof and Planet posited in the fourth for the *Significator* of the Father; the personall Estate or Goods moveable of the Father, are signified by the fift house, his Lord, and any Planet accidentally placed in the fifth; if in this Question you find the Lord of the second and Lord of the fifth in reception, the Lord of the fifth being in the second, and the Lord of the second in the fifth, there's no doubt to be made but the Querent shall have a competent fortune out of the Estate of his Father; but if it happen that the Lord of the fifth house be Retrograde, or in some bad aspect of any malevolent Planet, then some part of that Estate the Father intends for the Querent, will be wasted or otherwayes disposed of by the Father; and if you enquire wherefore or upon what grounds, or who shall be the occasion of it? then see what Planet it is that impedites the Lord of the fifth, either by □ or ☍, or if it be the ☉ by Combustion, what house he is Lord of; if it be the Lord of the sixt, it's probable it is one of he Fathers Brothers or Sisters, or some of his Tenants or Neighbours that will perswade the Father to alter his intention, and to diminish part of what he did formerly intend to doe: If it be the Lord of the seventh, it is some Woman or Sweethart, or one the Querent hath been sometimes at variance with, that will withdraw the Parents intention: If it be the Lord of the twelfth, it's some sneaking *Parson* or Parish *Priest*, or some or other of the Mothers Kinred; now if upon the description of the Party, the Querent is well informed of him or her who it is, and he is desirous to obtaine this parties favour or good will, that so he may be lesse malicious unto him, let him then observe, when that Planet who impedite and the Lord of the ascendant, are approaching to a ✶ △ or ☌, and that day that in the *Ephemeris* he shall find the ☽ separating from the one, and applying to the other, let him, I say, about or at that time endeavour a reconcilement, and it's not to be

doubted

all manner of Questions.

doubted but he may obtaine his defires, as I have found many times by good experience.

If the Lord of the fift difpofe of ⊗, and be in the Afcendant or fecond, the Querent fhall obtain his defires which he expects from his Father.

If ♃ or ♀ out of the fifth houfe caft their benevolent afpects to any Planet in the Querents fecond, it argues the fame.

If the ☽ feparate from the Lord of the fifth, and either have prefently after a ✶ or △ to the Lord of the fecond, or of the afcendant, it fhewes ftrong and affured hopes of acquiring the thing demanded of the Father.

If you find an *Infortune* in the fourth, not having Dignities there, then you may fay the Father hath little lift to part with his Money, nor will it be good to move him much, untill that unfortunate Planet be tranfited out of that Signe; but if you cannot ftay fo long, obferve when that unfortunate Planet is Direct, fwift in Motion, Orientall, and in ✶ or △ with ♃ or ♀, or with the Lord of the afcendant, and then let the Father be moved in the bufineffe: This I write, where the Querent would have prefent meanes, and cannot conveniently ftay the Fathers leizure: nor doe I write, that the obfervation of thofe times doe of themfelves enforce the mind or will of the Father, but that then at thofe times there's more benevolent inclinations.

If you find the Lord of the fecond and of the fifth, applying by Retrogradation to any good afpect, the Querent will receive fome Eftate from his Father fuddenly, ere he be aware, or when he leaft thinks of it: now to know, whether the Father love the Querent better then any of his Brothers or Sifters, you muft obferve, whether the Lord of the third, or any Planet in the third be neerer to, or in a better afpect with the Lord of the fourth, then the Lord of the afcendant is, or if there be any reception betwixt them, *viz.* the *Significators* of Brethren and Sifters, or tranflation of light, and none betwixt the Lord of the afcendant and Lord of the fourth, You may then be affured, the Fathers affection ftands more to another then to the Querent; the Planet neereft in afpect to the Lord of the fourth, fhewes the party or perfon beloved, fo doe the moft powerfull reception of *Significators*.

The Resolution of

Chap. XXXV.
If good to remove from one house or place to another, or to stay or abide in any place or not?

SEE to the Lords of the ascendant, the fourth house and seventh house, for if the Lord of the fourth be in the seventh, and be a good Planet, and the Lord of the first and seventh be good Planets, or strong in that part of Heaven where they are, or in the whole Figure, if they be Direct, and of swift motion, and in aspect with good Planets, it is good then to abide still and not remove from the place where the Querent is; but if the Lord of the seventh be with a good Planet, and the Lord of the fourth with an evill one, it is then not good to stay, for if he doe, he shall receive much damage there: That which I have observed in this manner of Judgment was this; That if the Lord of the ascendant did lately separate from the □ or ☍ of the Lord of the sixth, eighth or twelfth, and the ☽ also did concurre in judgment, *viz.* if she did separate from any evill aspect of the *Infortunes*, they being Lords of either the seventh or fourth, &c. and not Friends or Significators in the person of the Querent; or if I found an *Infortune* in the ascendant, Peregrine or Retrograde, or if a Peregrine or unfortunate Planet was in the fourth, or if the Lord of the second was weak or ill posited, I advised the Querent to remove his Habitation, and gave him reason why he should; for if I found the Lord of the sixt house in the ascendant, or afflicting the Lord of the ascendant, I judged he had his health very bad there, was sickly, or was tormented with ill servants, by whose meanes he did not thrive in his Vocation.

If the Lord of the twelfth afflicted the Lord of the ascendant or the ☽, I said he had backbiting, evill or slanderous Neighbours, or people that lived not very farre from him did scandalize him; if the Lord of the second was unfortunate, or in □ or ☍ to the Lord of the ascendant, or if ⊗ was in the twelfth eighth or sixth, I judged he went back in the world, and his Estate consumed.

If his Significator, *viz.* if the Lord of the ascendant was
afflicted

all manner of Questions.

afflicted by the Lord of the tenth, I acquainted him, his Reputation was lost, his Trade decayed, or had no Trading; and if the Lord of the fourth was unfortunate, or the fourth house it selfe, I judged the house was unlucky, and few that had lived therein did thrive, or that the Repaires of the house had much weakned him * : If the Lord of the seventh afflicted the Lord of the ascendant or second, his overthwart Neighbours had all the Trade, were better furnished with Commodities, &c. Now in giving direction which way to steer his course, in hops of better Trading, I observed what Planet in the Scheame was most fortunate and strongest, and had the most friendly aspect either to the Lord of the ascendant or Lord of the second, look what quarter of Heaven the Signe that Planet was in did signifie, to that part did I ever advise the Querent to remove; and I remember not, that any ever repented their following my advise; many have afterwards returned me thanks and rewards.

* *Or the house stood not conveniently for his Trade.*

And whereas I mention these words [*perhaps the house was unluckie*] some may cavill at the words, and say, *God's blessing is alike in all places, and it's superstition to judge, a house that is not a living thing, can be made unsuccesfull,* ‖ *&c.* let these enjoy their opinion still; there's not a man in this world lesse superstitious then my selfe, yet what I have found by experience, I freely communicate, and doe remaine of this opinion ; That in what house any execrable facts are committed, the ministring Angels of God seeing the villany done in that house, and the dishonour done to God therein, doe accurse that place or house; which continues so long, as there is not a full expiation made by some godly person, for the sinnes committed in that house; or untill the time limited by the angry Angel be expired, the house shall remaine a most unfortunate house for any to live in : And this which I write, and is inflicted upon houses which are insensible, I assuredly know is performed to the full upon the great and smaller Families of this world, &c. How in a naturall way to discharge these curses, *Sunt sigilla & lamina quæ nec scripta sunt, & ego novi.*

‖ *Or unfortunate.*

But some for resolution of this Question, say, if the ☽ separate at time of the Question from ♃ or ♀, then stay; if she

separate

The Resolution of

separate from an *Infortune*, remove; or a *Fortune* in the ascendant bids you stay; an *Infortune* remove: This heedfully considered with the preceding Judgment, will instruct any indifferent *Astrologer* to resolve the preceding Question concerning removing from one place to another.

CHAP. XXXVI.
Of turning the course of Rivers, or bringing Water into ones Ground or House, either by Conduit or Pipes.

IN this manner of judgment, you must principally consider the position and strength of ♄ and the ☽, and in what aspect they or either of them are in, either with ♃ or ♀; for if you find ♄ Direct, swift in Motion, Orientall, and the ☽ in the third, eleventh or fifth house, without any aspect either good or evill to ♂, it's an argument, the Work that is to be undertaken will have good successe, be brought to a good conclusion, and that the Querent will have prosperity and credit by it, and the matter easily performed; and this the rather, if the ☽ apply to that Planet who is Lord of that Signe wherein she is, and he receive her in any of his Dignities; and if that Planet who is receiver of the ☽ be a *Fortune*, and is ascending in his latitude, and in a fixed Signe, the Querent shall not need to feare, but that there will be water enough, and that it will runne plentifully, and the Water-course will long continue: if there be in the tenth house either ♃ or ♀, but especially ♃, it's a sure argument the River, Channell, Conduit, Pipe, or Water-work shall remaine many a yeer.

In further consideration of this judgment, if you find ♄ in the eleventh, very strong and potent, and the ☽ in ✶ or △ unto him, and the Dispositor of the ☽ in a fixed Signe, or a common one, or the ☽ her selfe in one of those Signes producing Raine, which are ♋ ♌ ♒ ♓.

All these are arguments, that in the work you are in hand with, you shall have a good Current, and plenty of Water; but if you find an infortunate Planet in the tenth, it's probable your

all manner of Questions. 215

your Pipes will break, your Water-courſe be ſubject to ruptures or breaking downe of the Banks, the Water will not run currantly, that thePlot is ill laid, nor is there any ſucceſſe promiſed to the undertaker or undertakers, by that preſent imployment.

CHAP. XXXVII.

Of Treaſure lying hid in the Ground, or to be digged out of the Earth.

THE reſolution of this Queſtion is various, according to the nature of its propoſall, or according to the nature and quality of the thing enquired after, *viz.* whether Money, Plate or Jewels, or things eaſily moveable, or for Treaſure long ſince obſcured or hid, the Querent not knowing what it is: or if it be, Whether there be any Mine of Gold, Silver or Iron, or any other Minerals in the Ground, Mannor or Lordſhip now queſtioned; then it is requiſite to know whether the Querent did hide or obſcure this Treaſure now enquired after, or whoſe it was, or what relation the party that did ſo had unto him, or whether that he aske in a generall way of Treaſure hid, not being able to diſcover either when, where, or whoſe, or what it is?

If the Querent did hide his owne Plate, Money or Jewels in any part of his Ground, or in his houſe, and hath forgotten whereabouts, you muſt herein obſerve the Signe of the ſecond houſe, the Lord thereof, what Signe and quarter of Heaven he is in, as alſo, the Signe of the fourth and his Lord, and what quarter of Heaven they ſignifie: the Lord of the ſecond and of the fourth in Angles, the Plate is ſtill in the houſe, or in the ground, and not removed; but if theſe Planets be not in Angles, but an *Infortune,* without dignities, be either in the fourth or ſeventh, there's then either part of it, or all removed and made away; and if your Figure promiſe, that your Goods are not removed, to find in what part they are, have recourſe to the firſt Chapter of this houſe concerning things hid, &c.

If the Queſtion be concerning Treaſure abſolutely, without
knowledge

knowledge whose or what it was, *viz.* whether there be any in the place or ground suspected, yea or no; observe in the Figure whether ♃ or ♀ or ☊ be in the fourth house, there's then probability of Treasure being there; if they be there and in their owne houses, the matter is without dispute, and you may be sure there is Treasure, or something of value in the house or ground suspected; or if you find either ♄ or ♂ in any of their owne houses, Direct, and without Impediment, and in the fourth, there is also Treasure, or if you find ♀ in ♉ in the fourth, not labouring with any misfortune, it's probable there is Treasure there, for you must know there is no Planet unfortunate, when he is in his owne house, or essentially dignified, and a Significator.

If you are ignorant of the nature and quality of the Treasure, or thing obscured, then see to the Planet who signifieth the Treasure, and consider if he be Lord of the seventh house, and examine his nature and property, if he be so; if he be not Lord of the seventh, joyne the Lord of the seventh in judgment with him, and so frame a mixture for the quality of the thing.

But if that Planet who is Significator of the Treasure be not Lord of the 7th or have affinity with him, then absolutely take the Lord of the seventh to signifie the nature and *Species* of the Treasure; who if he be the ☉, and he in his house or exaltation, there is Gold there, or precious Stones or Jewels of that colour, or neer to the colour of the ☉.

And if the Question were, Whether there were a good Mine yea or not? the place considered, it's like there is; if the ☉ be not so well dignified, and yet signifie the Treasure, it's then somewhat very precious, and neere to Gold in goodnesse.

If the ☽ be in her owne house or exaltation, and be Lady of the seventh, the Treasure is Silver, Plate, Chrystal or Jewels, &c. of the colour she is of, &c.

If ♂ be Lord of the seventh, and so dignified, he shewes, the thing sought after may be Brasse or Glasse, or some Curiosities or Engines of Iron, &c. but if he be weak, perhaps you may find some old rusty Iron, Candlesticks, Kettles, &c. If the Question were about Iron-stone, it's probable it will prove good Iron-
stone

all manner of Questions. 217

stone, and make good Iron. If ♄ be Lord of the seventh, and fortified as before specified, there's some *Antiquities* of great account, or ancient Monuments of men long since deceased, some *Urne*, &c. or there are some things wrapt up in old blacke Cloaths, or old woodden Boxes: and if the Question were concerning any Mine or quarrey of Stone, then it's very probable there is a rich Mine of Coles, if the Question were concerning Coles; or of good Stone, if the Question were of it: but if ♄ be weak, and ill dignified, then neither is the Mine a rich one, or can it be wrought without much expence of Treasure; whether it be full of water, or what may be the impediment, you must require from the Signe he is in, well considering what was formerly said in this Chapter.

If ♃ be Lord of the seventh and essentially fortified, there is Silver or very rich Cloth, and great store of it, or Tyn, &c.

If ♀ be Lady of the seventh, she intimates curious Houlholdstuffe, costly Jewels, or that fine Linnen is there hid.

If ☿ be Significator, he prenotes some Pictures, Meddals, Writings, Books, some pretty Toyes are obscured, or are the Treasure looked after.

If the Querent shall obtaine the Treasure hid.

If the Planet who signifies the Treasure or thing hid, doth apply to the Lord of the ascendant, or if there be mutuall reception or translation, or collation of light and nature betwixt them, it's probable the Querent shall obtaine the matter sought after; if the aspect be by □ or ☍, then not without difficulty and much labour; the ☌ of both Significators best of all performes the businesse, and the more assuredly, if they be in a fixed Signe, and posited in the Querents second house, or in the ascendant, either of the *Luminaries* placed in the ascendant and not unfortunated, gives great facility in the Work; but if neither of them be in the ascendant, or behold it, but be both in cadent houses, there remaines little hopes in the matter: When ⊗ is in the ascendant, and also his Lord or Disposer, it promiseth acquisition of the Treasure: but if the Lord of ⊗ be cadent, and both the Lights, especially the ☽, and have no aspect to

E e   the

the ⊗, or the Lord of the afcendant behold not the afcendant, I can give the Querent then no hopes of obtaining the Treafure or thing hid: *Alkindus* giveth this generall rule concerning Treafure, or any thing obfcured in the ground; Erect your Figure aright, confider the feverall afpects of the Planets, if there be in the afcendant, or in any Angle a *Fortune*, fay, there is Treafure in the ground, and that the thing hid is ftill in the ground, the quantity, price, efteem thereof, fhall be according to the potency, vertue or debility of the *Fortune*.

If you find the thing hid to be unremoved, then he proceeds and faith, Behold the Lord of the afcendant & the ☽, if there be any good afpect betwixt them, and that *Fortune* which fignified the Treafure to be there, *viz.* a good afpect and reception, he that demands the queftion fhall then have the thing enquired after, &c. He further faith, that fixed Signes fhew the thing is hid in the Earth, common Signes in or neer a Wall, moveable Signes on high, or in the covering of houfes: whether it lye deep in the earth or not, confider if the Planet Significator, be in the beginning, middle, or neer the end of the Signe; if he be newly entred the Signe, the Commodity is not deep, but fhallow, neer the upper part of the earth; the further the Planet is in the Signe, the deeper, &c. when you would dig, let not the *Infortunes* be angular, but if poffible, the Significators applying by ✶ or △ to the Lord of the fecond houfe, or the ☽ feparating from the Significator of the Treafure, and applying to the Lord of your afcendant.

CHAP.

Chap. XXXVIII.
If I should purchase Master B. his houses.

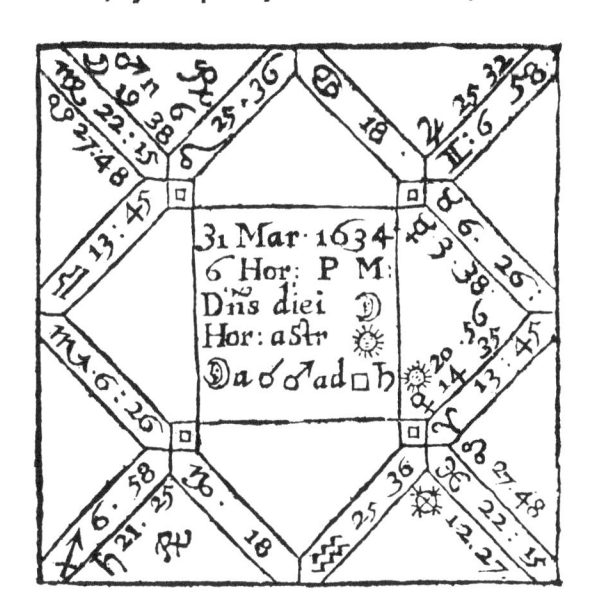

The *Inheritance* of the house wherein at this present 1647. *I* live, and some others being proffered me to buy 1634. *I had a desire to know if I should deal with the seller and procure Moneys in convenient time to pay for the Purchase,* (*my owne Money being in such hands as I could not call it in under six moneths warning*) *being desirous, I say, to purchase the said houses, and fully resolved upon it, I took my owne Question my selfe, at what time I found my mind was most perplexed and solicitous about it;* the time of my *Quere to my selfe fell out according to the position of Heaven aforesaid.*

The Resolution of

THE Signe ascending is ♎, the degree of the Signe is the same wherein ♃ was in my *Radix*; I looked upon that as a good *Omen* in the first place.

♀ Is for my selfe, the ☉ locally placed in the seventh is for the Seller; the ☉ receives ♀ in his Exaltation; besides, ♀ is neer the cusp of the seventh, and no other Planet in the seventh ☉ excepted, which signified, there was at present no other purchaser about it but my selfe: the ☉ so exalted and angular prenoted the Seller to be high in his Demands, [*and so he was;*] nor was he necessitated to depart with it: finding, I say, my *Significator* received of ☉, and so neer to the cusp of the Angle of the West, it was an argument I should proceed further in the matter, notwithstanding ♀ her many Debilities; for as I found ☉ Lord of the seventh, so also was he Lord of the eleventh, signifying my hopes should not be frustrated: besides, ♀ was applying to a △ of ♄, Lord of the fourth, *viz.* the houses enquired after, and had no abscission or frustration ere the perfect aspect; a maine strong argument that I should buy the houses: and indeed both *Significators* strongly applyed to a △ aspect, *viz.* ♄ and ♀, for ♄ is Retrograde: I also considered the ☉ was in perfect △ with ♄, the ☉ being, as I said, Lord of my eleventh, and he of the fourth; ♄ hath also signification of me, as Querent, because he beholds the ascendant, and therein hath exaltation: now whether you consider him, as having Dignities in the ascendant, or as Lord of the fourth, the Lord of the eleventh and he applying unto each other by a △, argued, assuredly I should proceed further in the matter, and in the end conclude for them. The ☽ in the next place translating the influence of ♂, who hath Dignities in the seventh, to ♄, having vertue in the ascendant, though by a □ aspect (yet out of Signes of long ascensions) did much facilitate the matter, and argued my going on, and probability of contracting, but with some leizure, and slowly, because of the □ aspect; for as the ☽ is afflicted, and ♀ unfortunate, so had I much to doe, and many meetings about it; the Seller not abating one penny of five hundred and thirty pounds, being the first penny he demanded. As the ☉ is neer to a ✶ aspect of ♃, so did a joviall man endeavour to procure the purchase unto himselfe *; but ♃ is cadent, and in

* *This was after I begun, and before I concluded.*

detriment

all manner of Questions. 221

detriment, shewing he should not prevaile, ♀ angular and in
aspect with ♄ Lord of the thing sought after; and as ☉ is
Lord of the eleventh, which is the fift from the seventh, so a
Daughter of the Sellers was my very good friend in this businesse, and suffered no interloper to intervene, though some offered fair*; for ♂ Lord of my second house Retrograde, argued   * *To hinder*
I should get none of my owne Monies to supply my occasions;   *me.*
nor did I: ♃ Lord of ⊗ in ✶ with ☉ no wayes impeded,
but by being in detriment, in ✶ platick with ♀ Lady of my
ascendant, shortly entring his exaltation, gave me such hopes
as I doubted not of procuring Monies when he entred ♋, and
♂ became direct, which he did twelve dayes after, at what time
a friend lent me 500 ˡ. the qualities of the Houses are signified
by ♑ the Signe of the fourth, and ♄ Lord thereof, who having
no materiall debilities, except Retrogradation and Cadency,
being also in △ with ☉; the Houses were really old, but strong
and able to stand many yeers. When ♀ and ☉ came to ☌ in
♉, that day I bargained, *viz.die* ♀ 25. *Aprill* following; the seventeenth of *May* ♀ and ☽ in ☌; I paid in 530 ˡ. and my Con-
veyance was Sealed. So that as ♀ wanted fix degrees of the
body of the ☉, so was it fix weekes and some dayes from the
time of the Question ere I perfected what the Figure promised; as to the Moles and Scars of my body it doth exactly a-
gree: for as ♀ is in ♈, which represents the face, so have I a
Mole on my cheeke about the middle of it; and as ♎ ascends,
I have one on the reines of my backe, the ☽ in ♍ afflicted by
♂, I have a red Mole below my Navell, ♃ Lord of the sixt in
♊ a Masculine Signe, I have a Mole neer my right hand visible
on the outside; so have I on the left foot, as ♓ the Signe of the
sixt doth represent. Many things might be considered herein,
besides what is written; but I feare this Booke will increase
beyond my first intention: *Ergo.* The truth of the matter is, I
had a hard bargaine, as the Figure every way considered doth
manifest, and shall never live to see many of the Leases yet in
being, expired; and as ♀ is in ♈, *viz.* opposite to her owne
House, so did I doe my selfe injury by the Bargaine, I meane
in matter of Money; but the love I bore to the House I now
live in, wherein I lived happily with a good Master full seven
E e 3 yeers,

yeers, and therein obtained my first Wife, and was bountifully blessed by God with the Goods of this World therein, made me neglect a small hinderance, nor now, I thanke God, doe I repent it; finding Gods blessing in a plentifull measure upon my Labours: yet was I no Taylor or Scrivener, as *Wharton* affirmes, or indeed any profession at all; nor was my Master a Taylor, or my Wife a Scriveners Widdow.

Of the fifth House, and its Questions.

Chap. XXXIX.
If one shall have Children, yea or no?

WHEN this question is demanded by a man or woman, long before marriage, or by some ancient Batchelour, or Maid, *Whether they shall ever have any Child or Children, yea or not?* herein generally you are to consider, whether the Signe upon the fifth, or ascending, be of those we call Fruitfull, yea or no, (*viz.* ♋ ♍ ♓) and whether the Lord of the ascendant (be the Signe what it will) or the ☽ be in aspect with the Lord of the fifth house, and that aspect be either ☌ ✶ △ or □ (though ☌ is not properly an aspect) which if it be so, and the Planet to whom the Lord of the fifth doth apply, or is in aspect with, be free from Combustion, and other Accidentall or Essentiall misfortunes, it's an argument the good old Batchelour or stale Maid, or whoever propounds the Question, shall have Children or Issue ere they dye; In like case judge, if the Lord of the fifth be in the ascendant, or else the ☽, or the Lord of the ascendant in the fifth, for this is a strong argument of having Issue or Children; but if neither the Lord of the ascendant or the ☽ apply to the Lord of the fifth. yet if there be rendring of vertue or light one unto another, or translation or collection by or from the principall *Significators*, you may still continue your judgment, that

the

all manner of Questions. 223

the Querent shall have issue, but not so soone, as if it had been foreseen by the first manner of judgement. After all this, have respect to that Planet who is receiver of the Disposition of the Significators; who if he be cleer from misfortune or affliction, viz. from Retrogradation, Combustion, or Cadency in House, it gives great hopes of issue. See also if that Planet from whom the ☽ is seperated be Lord of the fift Signe from the Signe wherein the Planet is to whom the ☽ applies, and both these Planets have any aspect to each other; that also doth testifie the party shall have Children or a Childe. If no Aspect happen betwixt them, its not then likely he will have any; and yet some say, that if the above named Planets or Significators be not in any Aspect, yet if the Planet to whom the ☽ applies be in an Angle, the Querent may have Issue.

If a Woman aske, whether she may conceive?

Many times a Woman married, having been long without Children, may inquire, whether she is like to Conceive, yea or no? In this Question you are to consider:

If the Lord of the Ascendant be in the seventh, or the Lord of the fift in the first, or the Lord of the first in the fift, or if the Lord of the fift be in the seventh, or the Lord of the seventh in the fift, or the ☽ with him, or good Planets in the Ascendant, or with the Lord of the fift, or in any of the Angles; she may then conceive: but if none of these testimonies concurre and you find barren Signs and ill Planets to be in the former places, she neither is at present concieved, or will hereafter conceive. If good and bad Planets be mixed together, she may perhaps conceive or have children, but they will not live: if ♋, ♏ or ♓ be in the Ascendant or fift, she may have children; but if ♌ or ♍ be there, she neither is at present, or hardly after will be with Child. When women have bin long without children, and propound such a question, see if their Nativity did not originally deny children.

At what time, or how long it may be ere she have a Childe?

If you finde that according to naturall causes she may have a Childe or Children; and the Querent is desirous to know neer
what

what time: see then where thou findest the Lord of the fift house, *viz*. if in the Ascendant or first house; then judge the first yeere; if in the second house, the second yeere; if the tenth house, the third yeer; if in the seventh, the fourth yeer; if in the fourth house, the fift yeer. And herein you must be carefull in considering what signe the Lord of the fift house is in; for the swiftnesse of a Planet in a moveable sign doth somewhat hasten the time; a double bodied Signe doth not manifest so soone; fixed Signes prolong the matter; however, this is worthy of your cosinderation, that let the Significator be in what Signe he will be, yet if he be swift in motion and direct, he doth make the more haste in performance of the businesse he is a significator in, and causeth the matter sooner to be accomplished.

Whether the Querent shall have Children, be he Man or Woman that asketh?

Behold the Ascendant, and if fortunate Planets behold the same, and the Lord thereof be in the Ascendant, or in the tenth, eleventh or fift House, and you finde ♃ also well placed together with that Planet who is Lord of the Triplicity ascending, and he be not Combust or Retrograde; judge then, if the Man aske the Question, he may have Children, or is capable of getting them. If a Woman inquire, say, she may Conceive, and is not naturally barren. If the Lord of the ascendant be in the fourth or seventh, and ♃ in a good House of heaven, doe you say, the party shall have a Childe a long time after the asking of the Question.

But if you finde the Ascendant afflicted, or infortunated by the Malevolent Planets, and the Lord of the Ascendant in an evill place or House of heaven, and ♃ Cadent, or in the eight or Combust, or not fully elongated from the Sunne-beames; then shall you judge he will have few Children, and they sickly, hardly any to live. Its also a great signe of non conception, or no capacity to conceive, when the ☽ is unfortunate. If you finde a fortunate Planet in the fift House, or having a benigne aspect to the Cuspe thereof, it gives hopes and strong
testi-

all manner of Questions.

testimony of having a Childe in a little compasse of time; but if an infortune be in the fift ill dignified, Combust, Retrograde, slow of motion, &c. the Querent will have no Children; but if the Infortune be direct and swift, Orientall, and in any of his essentiall dignities, he shall signifie Children; the more Children if ♃ ♀ or ☉ be in ✶ or △ with him out of good houses: you must ever remember, that the neerer a Fortune is to the Ascendant, the sooner the Querent may expect Children, the more remote the longer time must be allowed. Others observe this rule following That if ♃ be in the Ascendant or fift, and in a Signe which is not barren, its an argument the Querent may have a Childe; there is also much strength in the Lord of the houte; for if he be angular with reception of the Lord of that Angle where he is, or in the eleventh or fift with the like reception, it is a sure testimony of having Children. In all Questions concerning Children, be carefull of the age of the Querent, or some other natural or hereditary infirmity incident to the Querent, and seldome conclude wtihout two testimonies.

If a Man shall have Children by his Wife yea or not, or of any other Woman whom he nominates.

When it is demanded of you by any Man, *Whether he shall have any Children by the Wife he hath, or the Woman he mentions*; or if a Woman aske if she shall have Issue or Children by such a Man. Behold the Ascendant, his Lord and the ☽, and if the Lord of the Ascendant or the ☽ be joyned to the Lord of the fift, you may judge he or she shall have Issue by the party inquired of; if this be not, then see if any translation be from the Lord of the fift to the Lord of the ascendant; that's an argument of having Children after some space of time: if the Lord of the ascendant or the ☽ be in the fift House, he or she may have children, or the Lord of the fift in the ascendant: if none of these be, consider if the Lord of the ascendant, the ☽, and Lord of the fift be not joyned to a Planet more ponderous then themselves; for he collecting both their lights, shall be the receiver of their disposition, and shall signifie whether the Childe

Ff

or Children (if any be) shall live or not; if he be not impedited the Children then shall live, but if he be Retrograde, Combust, Peregrine, or otherwise unfortunate, neither will the Children live long, or will the Parents take comfort of these Children. After this, consider ♃, who naturally signifieth Children, if he be in the ascendant, third, fift, ninth or eleventh house, free from all manner of misfortune; you may affirme the Woman shall shortly conceive, perhaps upon the first congresse or coition after the asking of the question, or a little after, and the matter seems as good as done.

If ♀ be in the fifth no way impedited, and some other *Fortune* be there besides, it hastens the time, and she will conceive very suddenly. But if ♃ be in the aforesaid places impedited, say, that either she is not conceived, or if she be, it will not come to perfection, for the Woman shall suffer abortion. In like manner if ♀ be unfortunate by ♄ or ♂, or be under the ☉ beames, or Combust, the Woman is not conceived, unlesse a *Fortune* be in the fifth house, and then she is more assuredly with childe, or shall be shortly; yet you may justly feare she will suffer mischance ere the birth.

If either ♄ or ♂, or especially ☋ be in the fifth, or the two former malevolents cast their ☍ to the fifth, it seemes the Woman is not with childe; and verily the □ of the *Infortunes* to the fifth house seems to hinder conception.

Whether she is with Childe or not.

She is.   A Woman mistrusting her selfe to be with Childe, and desirous to know the truth; if she aske the Question of thee, then give Answer, having well considered your Figure, erected according to the time of her demand, *viz.* as these following rules direct you.

If the Lord of the ascendant or ☽ behold the Lord of the fifth with any aspect or translation.

If the Lord of the ascendant and the ☽ be in the fifth house
*I meane ♄ free from the malevolent aspect of the *Infortunes* and direct; and
and ♂ for herein you must not wholly rely upon ♄ and ♂ or the ☋ to be
Planets, not the onely *Unfortunate* Planets, * you must consider the position
☊.   of

all manner of Questions. 227

of heaven at time of erecting your Scheame, and take any evill aspect of the Lord of the sixth, eighth or twelfth, be he what Planet he will, to be an affliction, if he have ☐ or ☍ to the Lord of the fifth, or Lord of the ascendant, or the ☽.

♃ generally in the first, fifth, eleventh or seventh, not in aspect to ♄ or ♂, they being slow in motion or Retrograde.

The Lord of the ascendant, or Lord of the fifth house aspecting a Planet in an Angle with reception, and rendring up his vertue unto him; if the ☽ be in reception with any Planet in an Angle, that is, essentially Fortified, else not; for accidentall dignities in this manner of judgement, giveth hopes, but not reall assurance.

If the Lord of the Ascendant behold the Ascendant with an amicable aspect, out of any good House; or if the ☽ be in the seventh, and behold the Lord of the seventh in the eleventh, or if the ☽ be in the eleventh, and behold the Lord of the seventh in the seventh.

The Lord of the Ascendant received in either House, Triplicity or Exaltation, and the receiver of the Lord of the Ascendant having alike dignity in the House, *Triplicity, Exaltation,* or Term of the received, *viz.* Lord of the Ascendant.

The ☽ giving vertue, or rendring her light to a Planet in the fifth house, or having essentiall dignities in the fifth.

The ☽ applying to the Lord of the ascendant or Lord of the fifth in the first or tenth House, and he not Cadent from his owne House or exaltation; * where you must understand this generall rule concerning a Planet his being Cadent from his owne House, is this, *viz.* if ♂ be in ♈, it being his own House, let him then be in any of the twelve Houses, he shall be said to be Angular as to his being in ♈: if ♂ be in ♉ he is succeeding or in a succedant House in that way: if ♂ be in ♊ he is then Cadent as from his owne House; and so doe in the rest: for ever a Planet is Angular in any of his owne Houses. *A Planet cadent from his owne house.*

* The *Dispositor* of the ☽ and Lord of the houre in Angles; ♂ in the Signe of the seventh House, she is newly conceived (this is to be understood if he be well Fortified:) ♄ in the seventh, the party is quicke, or her Infant moveth: ♃ in the seventh, she is impregnated of a male childe: ♐ or ♓ in the *These added to other testimonies.*

Ff 2 seventh

228   *The Resolution of*

seventh, she is with childe of a Girle; this must be understood when all the rest of the Significators are equall, and ballance not the judgement, then if you finde ♐ or ♓ in the seventh, you may judge the party shall have a Girle. Besides, the ☽ in the fifth applying to ♃ or ♀ argue the same. You may ever predict true Conception, if the Signe ascending be fixed, and a Fortune therein placed, or the Lord of the fift strong in the ascendant or tenth House.

If the Man aske unknowne to the Woman.

Shee is.

If the Lord of the fifth behold a Planet in an Angle with reception, or if the Lord of the Houre, Lord of the fifth, ♃ ♀ ☉ ☽ ☿ or ☊ be in the fifth Fortunate; or if the Lord of the fifth be in the seventh, or Lord of the seventh in the fifth.

Shee is not.

If ♃ or ♀ be impedited, if ♀ be joyned to ♄ or ♂, and they either Combust, Retrograde, or slow in motion, or in ♌ ♍ or ♑, ♄ or ♂ in the fifth, in □ or ☍ to the Lord of the fifth, denotes no conception, or danger of abortion, if other significators be more prevalent then they, and give testimony of conception.

The Lord of the ascendant joyned to a Retrograde Planet, or one in a Cadent House, or received by a Retrograde or Combust Planet, no aspect or translation of light betwixt the Lord of the fifth and Lord of the ascendant; judge by the major testimonies.

Male or Female.

The Lord of the ascendant, Lord of the fifth, Lord of the Houre Masculine, and the ☽ in a Masculine Signe, degrees, or quarter, doe note a Male, the contrary a Female.

The Lord of the fifth Retrograde, Combust, or Cadent from his House or Exaltation, is a presage of Death, *& e contra*.

Whether it shall live?

The Lord of the Ascendant, Lord of the Houre, Lord of the fifth, all or most of them unfortunate, is an argument of death; ♄ ♂ or ☋ in the first or fifth House, and Retrograde, denote the same.

Where

all manner of Questions. 229

Where suspition is had of Twins: if upon that Question you finde the Signe ascending Common, and a Fortune in it, or the fifth or first House, and ☉ and *Luna* in common Signes, or the Sign of the fifth one, and Lord of the fifth in a common Sign, you may judge Twins.

Other Judgements concerning Womens being with chide or not.

CHAP. XL.

Whether a Woman be with Childe or not.

WHEN a Woman asks this Question, have respect to the Lord of the ascendant and the ☽ who shall signifie the person of the *Querent*, the fifth house and Lord thereof shall shew the Conception, if any be: If the Lord of the ascendant be in the fifth, or Lord of the fifth in the ascendant, free from all manner of impediments, it argues the Woman is conceived with child; so also if the Lord of the ascendant his vertue or disposition be translated to any Planet in an Angle, the more certain you may judge: if he to whom the Lord of the ascendant commits his Disposition, be received of the Lord of the ascendant, or the Lord of the ascendant by him; but if the Planet to whom the Lord of the ascendant hath committed his Disposition, be in a cadent house, it notes the Woman hath taken griefe; and whereas she thinks she may be conceived of a Child, it's more like to be a Sicknesse; and if the Conception should hold, 'twill come to no good end, especially if the ascendant be ♈ or ♋, ♎ or ♑, or if any of the malevolent Planets be in an Angle, or else ☋, for usually ☋ in the fifth, shewes abortion, in the ascendant extreame feare and mistrust of it; but if the ponderous Planet to whom the Lord of the ascendant commits his Disposition be in a good house, *viz.* in the second, eleventh or ninth, not in ☌ with the *Infortunes*, and the ☽ be free, it notes the Conception shall come to a good end, and the Woman safely delivered: so as

Ff 3   also

also if the Lord of the fifth, who is naturall *Significator* of children, be in the ascendant free from misfortune, *viz.* Retrogradation or Combustion, or not with ☋.

If a Woman doe Conceive with Childe of more then one?

To resolve this Question, see if either ♊ ♍ ♐ or ♓ be ascending, then see if both ♃ and ♀ be in the Signe ascending, or in the Signe of the fifth, or be in any of the twelve Signes (except ♌) it's probable she goeth with two children ; and if the ☊ be with ♃ and ♀ in the ascendant or fifth, it's possible she may have three ; but if none of these be in the ascendant or fifth, behold if these Planets cast their ✶ or △ to the degree ascending, or to the cusp of the fifth house ; it's also probable she may conceive, or is with child with more then one : but if a fixed Signe possesse the ascendant or fifth house, or any moveable Signes, and the ☉ and ☽ be therein, *viz.* either in fixed or moveable Signes, and in the fifth or first house, it's a certain argument the Woman is with child but with one : The *Astrologer* must not rashly adventure his Judgment without well considering his rules, or without knowledge had, whether it be not naturall or usuall for some of her Family to bring at one Birth more then one.

If Male or Female.

See to the ascendant, the Lord that Signe, the Signe of the fifth and Lord of the fifth, and whether the Signes be ♈ ♊ ♌ ♎ ♐ ♒ ; these Signes import a Male, the other six Signes a Female : If the Lord of the ascendant be in a Masculine Signe, and the Lord of the fifth in a Feminine, then have recourse to the ☽, and see what Signe she is in, and if she apply to a Planet in a Masculine Signe, then she gives her testimony to that *Significator* who is in a Masculine Signe, and you may judge the party is with child of a Boy or Man child.

Masculine Planets. Masculine Planets are ever ♄ ♃ ♂ and ☉, ♀ and the ☽ Feminine, and ☿ as he is in aspect or ☌ with a Masculine or
Feminine

all manner of Questions. 231

Feminine Planet, so is he of either sex accordingly ; but when he is *Orientall* of the ☉, he is reputed Masculine ; when *Occidentall*, then Feminine.

How long the Woman hath been Conceived ?

In this case have regard to the ☽ and the Lord of the fifth, and Lord of the hour and see which of all these is neerest from the separation of any Planet, and well consider him, and from what manner of aspect this separation is ; if he be separated by a △ aspect, say, she is in the fifth moneth of her Conception, or the third ; if the aspect was a ✶, say, she is in the second or sixt moneth of her conception ; if the separation was by a □ aspect, she is in the fourth of her Conception ; if it was by an *Opposition*, she hath been Conceived seven moneths, if it were by a *Conjunction*, then she hath beene Conceived one moneth.

Of the time when the Birth will be ?

In judging about what time the *Querent* may be delivered, you are to consider, When ♂ and ☉ are in ☌ with the Lord of the fifth, and with the ☽ and Lord of the houre, or the more part of them, and that time of their ☌ shall shew the hour of Birth ; help your selfe herein by that *Fortune* which in the Question shall behold the *Part of Children*, viz. when he shall apply to that Quarter of Heaven where the *Part of Children* is, and direct that *Part of Children*, by the ascensions to the degree of the fifth house, and to the degree of ♃, and to his aspects, especially if ♃ be between the *Part of Children* and the fift house, because when that *Part* doth apply it self to the degrees of ascensions, and when it is within the *Orbes* of those degrees, is the time of delivery, giving to every degree one day.

Behold also the Disposition or application of that Planet to whom the *Part of Children* is directed, before the ☌ of the Lord of the fifth with the Lord of the ascendant, in the ascendant or in the fifth house, because about that time will be the time of birth. See also when the *Significator* of the Question
doth

doth change his forme, *viz.* when he removes out of one Signe into another, then is alſo like to be the time of the Birth : or behold the Lord of the fifth, how farre he is removed from the cuſp of the fifth, and give to every Signe one moneth, and help your ſelfe with your other teſtimonies, and judge according to the major part of thoſe *Significators* that doe moſt neerly concurre.

The *Part of Children* is taken day and night from ♂ to ♃, and projected from the aſcendant.

Whether the Birth ſhall be by day or by night?

In this manner of Judgment, behold the aſcendant and his Lord, the *Moon*, Planet in the aſcendant, Lord of the fifth, Sign of the fifth ; if the major part of the *Significators* be in Diurnall Signes, the Birth will be by day ; if the contrary happen, then in the night. If the *Significators* diſagree amongſt themſelves, take him that is Eſſentially moſt ſtrong, and judge by him ; or elſe conſider the number of degrees that the Planet you judge by is diſtant from the cuſp of the fifth houſe, ſo many degrees as is their diſtance each from other, doe you project from the degree aſcending, and ſee where your number determines ; and if it end in a Diurnall Signe, ſhee will be brought to bed by day ; if contrary then in the night : by this meanes alſo you may judge of the quality of the Sex, by conſidering the Lord of the fifth, the *Moone* the Lord of the Houre, and the Part of Children before mentioned, and his Diſpoſitor ; if the major part hereof be in Maſculine Signes, its a Male the Woman goes with, and the birth will be by day ; but if the teſtimonies be equall, the birth will be by twilight.

Some ſay, if the Queſtion be, *Whether a Woman be with Childe or not*; conſider the Lord of the Aſcendant, Lord of the fifth, and Diſpoſitor of the *Moone*, and the *Moone* her ſelfe ; if any application be betwixt theſe Planets, and the *Moon* be in a common Signe, and the Aſcendant one, and the *Significators* in Angles, or if in the aſcendant or ſecond there be a fortunate Planet, ſhe is with child, otherwiſe not.

Or if by chance a Planet Direct be in ☌ with the *Moon*, it
ſhewes

all manner of Questions.

shewes the same; ♃ or ♀ in the fifth, or ☽ in the fifth, applying to ♃ or ♀, or a Planet in *Cazmi* of the ☉, the Planet being a *Fortune*, is a strong argument of being with Child; but if instead of *Fortunes* you find the *Infortunes* so placed as abovesaid, it's no signe of Conception; or if there be assurance of Conception before the Question be asked, it's a pregnant proofe of abortion, and if you find ♂ to be the infortunate Planet afflicting, she will miscarry by a Flux of blood; if ♄ afflict, then by Sicknesse, Feare, Frights, or by too much aboundance of wind and water.

If you are demanded of the state of the Mother, and how, or in what case she shall be in after the Birth? behold the ☽, and observe to what Planet she applies, and according to the last application she hath before she goe out of the Signe she is in, it shall be with the Mother; so that observe that Planet she last applies unto, his Nature, place in the Heaven and Fortitude, so shall it be with the Mother after Birth: I have in my pactice observed this concerning the safety of the Mother, and her condition at the Birth, if it were evident she were with Child; and I found the ascendant free, and the Lord of the ascendant neither separated from a bad aspect of the Lord of the eighth or fourth, or applying to any bad aspect of the Lord of those two houses, or if I found the ☽ fortunately applying to either of the *Fortunes*, or to the ☉, or indeed to any good aspect of the *Infortunes*, I never doubted the life of the Mother, and I remember not that I ever failed.

If the Lord of the fifth were in the eight, and had no essential dignities in the Sign, and had any aspect good or ill to the Lord of the eight or fourth, I usually judged the *Infant* would not live long after the Birth, and I ever found the prediction true; and you shall very seldome observe my Infant borne upon the very change of the ☽, but he dyes shortly, seldome outlives the next full ☽; or if he or she be borne at the moment of the full *Moon*, it's very probable the Infant dyes upon the next new *Moon*; for as there is no light in earth but what these two Planets give, so neither doe I beleeve any life can be permanent, when both these at the time of birth are either of themselves, or by the *Infortunes* afflicted. &c.

G g   *Whether*

The Resolution of

Whether Unity is like to be betwixt the Infant and the Parent, or betwixt the Parent and any of his Children of elder Yeers.

This were better resolved from the Nativity, but becaufe few among us are capable of judging one, I adventure fomewhat by an *Horary Queſtion:* The *Queſion* being then demanded as aforefaid, behold the Lord of the afcendant, the *Moon*, the Lord of the fifth ; if you find reception and application betwixt the Lord of the fift, and Lord of the afcendant, and this in the tenth, eleventh, fift, third, ninth, firft or fecond houfes, there will be Love and Unity betwixt them ; or if ♃ or ♀ doe behold the cufps of both houfes, there will be Unity and Concord betwixt them.

I doe in thefe manner of demands obferve onely thus much ; I prefently confider if either ♄ ♂ or ☋ be in the fift, for if thofe two Planets, or any Planet who is pofited in the houfe be Peregrine ; I fay, that the Childe will be untoward, very averfe, and not eafily regulated by his Parents directions, and that the fault is wholly in the Child, or young Man or Maid, according to the Queftion propounded. If I find ♄ ♂ or ☋ in the afcendant, I tell the Parents that enquires, the fault is their owne, that the Child is not more obfervant unto them ; and if ♂ be there, I fay, they are too much lordly over him or her, or their Children, and over-awe them, and keep them in too much fujection ; if ♄ be the Planet impediting, I fay, they are too auftere, dogged, and too much clofe fifted, and expect more fervice, duty, obedience or attendance from them then is fitting in a Chriftian liberty, that they give their Children no encouragement, or fhew them any countenance, &c. If ☋ be there in the afcendant, I blame the Parent enquiring, and tell him, he is too too jealous, and too miftruftfull of the actions of his or their Children, that he beleeves lyes and calumnies againft his or their Children, that fimple people foole him in his numour, and befot him with vaine reports, &c.

You may apply the laft part of Judgment to any other Queftion as well as this, with very good fucceffe, as I have done

many

many times, and thereby have reconciled the Father or Mother and their Child.

But by all meanes I desire all *Astrologians* to deale fairly and really, let the fault be where it will be, &c.

Chap. XLI.
Of Embassadours or Messengers.

THE Lord of the fift shall represent the person of the *Embassadour*, the *Moon* shall herein be admitted to have signification, that Planet to whom either the Lord of the fift house or the *Moon* doe apply unto, shall shew the cause of his Embassage, or you may take judgment from both those Planets to whom they apply.

If you find the application is from a *Fortune* by a □ or ☍ or ☌, and if there be reception betwixt them, or collection or translation of light by any Planet, and that Planet be either Lord of the tenth, or in the tenth, you may say, the cause of his Embassage is unto the King upon a meer point of honour, or upon some high and great Businesse, or concerning a very great and urgent occasion: If the Planet who is received, or who collects or translates the vertue of one to another, be Lord of the eleventh, he comes to renew the League of Friendship betwixt the two Nations: If the Lord of the fift be unfortunate in the seventh, and the Lord of the ascendant and he be in □ or ☍, and ♂ have any malicious aspects to them both, or to either of them, there is then no likelihood of Unity, or to be any content in the Embassage to be delivered, or both parties will find triviall meanes to discontent one another, so that no solid peace may be expected from any act performed or to be performed by this Treaty or Embassage, rather probability of falling at varience; whether the *Embassadour* will deale fairly or prove false, or shuffle in his Undertakings, you must know that Judgment from the well or ill affection of the Lord of the fift house, and from that aspect he shall cast to the ascendant or Lord thereof, or to the Lord of the eleventh; observe also in

The Resolution of

what house the Lord of the fift is in, for if he be in the tenth, and there dignified essentially, the *Embassadour* will stand too much npon the Honour of his owne Prince, and hath an overweening conceit of his owne abilities: If ☿ and the Lord of the fift be in □ or ☍, the *Embassadour* hath not a *Commission* large enough, or shall be countermanded or contradicted either by some Missive from his Prince, or the Secretary playes the knave with him, &c. or his Message will be ill taken.

Observe this generally, if the *Significator* of the *Embassadour* have any ✶ or △ aspect (or be he well dignified or not) either to the Lord of the ascendant, or Lord of that Signe under which the Kingdome you are in is subject, the *Embassadour* himselfe wishes well to the Kingdome, and will peforme his trust with much sincerity.

Of a Messenger sent forth upon any Errand for Money.

Herein give the ascendant and his Lord to him that sends, the seventh house and his Lord unto him to whom the *Messenger* is sent, the Message to the ☽, the Lord of the fifth to the Messenger and managing of the Businesse: If you find the Lord of the fifth separated from the Lord of the seventh, and applying to the Lord of the ascendant, you may judge the *Messenger* hath effected the thing he went about, is departed from him, and returning home againe: If the Lord of the fift be separated from the Lord of the second house, he brings Money with him, whether a *Fortune* or *Infortune* be Lord of that house; and you must understand, that the answer which the *Messenger* brings is of the nature of that house, whose Lord is the Planet from whom the Lord of the fift is separated, and of the Planet himselfe; so that if you find his separation from a good Planet, it gives hopes of a good Answer, the contrary when separation is from the *Infortunes*: If the *Significator* of the *Messenger* doe apply by □ or ☍ to an *Infortune*, before he is separated from the Lord of the seventh, you may then acquaint the *Querent*, that his *Messenger* hath had some impediment in effecting his Businesse by the party to whom he was sent, and that he also sustained some hinderance in his Journey, ere he

came

all manner of Questions. 237

came to the place to which he was sent: but if this application to an *Infortune* happen after that the Lord of the fift was separated from the Lord of the seventh, the *Messenger* will have delayes or misfortune in his returning home againe; if you find an *Infortune* in the ninth, he will hardly travell safe for Theeves; if a *Fortune* be in the ninth, judge his going and returning will be safe.

Concerning the sending of *Foot-Posts, Lackeys*, &c. about any Message or Errand, whether they shall come to their Journeys end, or safe to the place unto which they are sent, behold the Lord of the ascendant and the ☽, and if either the one or the other be in the seventh, or one or both apply to the Lord of the seventh, he then went safe to his journeys end; ever judge in this manner of Question according to the nature of the *Fortune* or *Infortune*, and how he is dignified in the Heavens, what is his Vertue, what his Debility, and accordingly frame your judgment according to *Fortunes*, or they dwelling or being in Significant Houses, portend good, the *Infortunes* the contrary.

If there be reception between the Lord of the fift and seventh, and any amicable aspect, your *Messenger* was well received and entertained by him to whom he went, yea though the application be by □ or ☍, yet he was well received; but the party sought after, framed some excuse, or framed some matter in his owne defence, concerning the thing sent unto him for. For your Messengers returne when it shall be; behold if the Lord of the fift be receded from the Lord of the seventh, or applying to the Planet who is his Dispositor, say, he commeth; the time when, is found out thus; according to the number of degrees of the application, give Days, Weeks or Moneths, according to the nature & length of the Journey, and according to the nature of the Signs, *viz.* either Fixed, Common or Moveable; if the *Significator* be Retrograde, the Messenger will returne when he comes to be Direct, or according to the number of degrees he wants ere he prove Direct. I doe usually observe this generall rule, when he Lord of the fift comes to a ✶ or △ of the Lord of the ascendant, that day, or neer it, the Messenger is heard of; or when the ☽ separates from the Lord of the fift to the Lord of

Gg 3 the

238   *The Resolution of*

the afcendant, the *Querent* fhall have intelligence of his Meffenger: You muft know, the application of the *Significator* to a ponderous Planet, fhewes more certainly the day; ufe defcretion in knowing the length or brevity of the Journey, and by what precedes you may be fatisfied,

---

If the Querent fhould ever have Children?

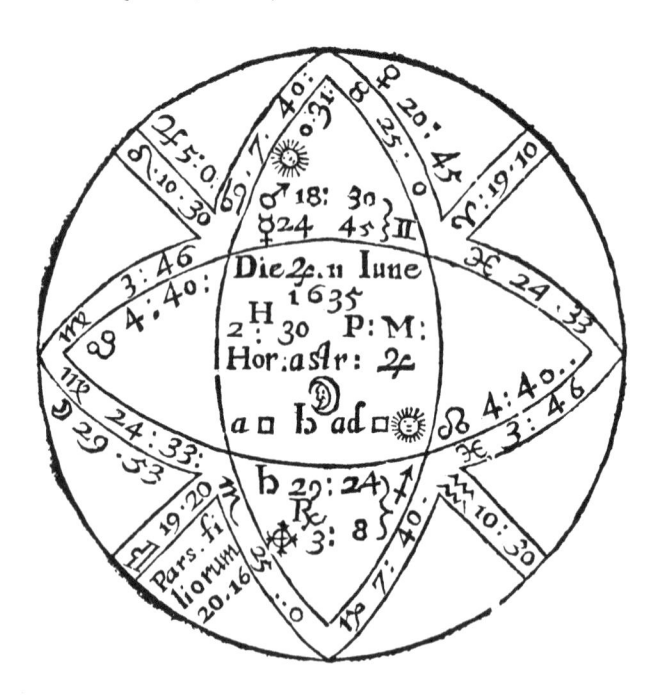

[astrological figure]

CHAP. XLII.
Judgment upon the preceding Figure.

THE afcendant is here ♍ a barren Signe, as you may fee *page* 89. and 96. the Signe of the fift is ♑, a Signe of indifferency in this nature of judgment; the ☽ is in a barren Signe;

all manner of Questions. 239

Signe; ♄ Lord of the fift house is Retrograde, and in ♐; ☿ Lord of the ascendant in ♊; both ♄ and ☿ being in Signes rather barren then fruitfull: the ☽ in the Termes of ♂, in □ of ♄ Lord of the fift, ☿ Lord of the ascendant in the Termes of ♄, afflicted by the presence of ♂, and going to ☍ of ♄, who is Lord of the sixt, as well as of the fift; ☋ also possesseth the ascendant; a strong argument of barrennesse: for these reasons in *Astrologie* above recited, I delivered this Judgment, *viz.* That the *Querent* neither had been ever yet conceived, or for any reason in *Art* that I could find, ever would conceive, and that she was naturally barren; for finding the first, tenth and fourth houses, being the principall Angles of the Figure, afflicted, I was certaine, the evill impediting her Conception had been long upon her, and would also continue.

Had I found ♃ either fortunating the cusp of the fift house, or in any aspect to the Lord of the ascendant, or unto ♄, or if any reception had been betwixt ♄ and ♃, or ♃ and ☿, or any collection of light from ☿ to ♄, and that Planet so collecting had received ♄ or ☿, I would not have been so peremptory; but when I found no one promising testimony, I gave my judgment in the negative, *viz.* she should not conceive or ever have any children; for whoever considers the positure of Heaven exactly, shall find it is a most unfortunate Figure for having children: as the ☽ was in □ of ♄, Lord of the sixt, and ☿ Lord of the ascendant, applying to his ☍, so was the *Querent* very sickly, and extreamly afflicted with the Wind and Chollick in her Belly and small Guts; the ☋ in the ascendant shewed very great paine in the Head, so did ☿ in ♊, being afflicted by both the Malevolents, represent extreame griefe in the Head, for ☿ in ♊ signifies the Head, *vide page* 119.

Shee affirmed, that the Moles of her Body did correspond exactly to the Figure of Heaven, *viz.* one Mole close by the Navill, one upon the right Ancle, signified by ♒ on the cusp of the sixt; one towards the right Knee on the inner side of the Thigh, represented by ♄, Lord of the sixt in ♐; one in or neer the member signified by the ☽ in ♍; and as ☿ Lord of the ascendant is in ♊, so had the *Querent* a Scarre or Mole on her right Arme, on the outside thereof, &c.

When

When you find a Question that is so peremptory in the negative, you shall deale discreetly to enquire the time of Birth, and set the Figure thereof, and see what correspondency there is betwixt the *Radix* and the Question propounded, and help your selfe in your judgement by discretion; for if the *Radix* affirme Barrennesse, it's impossible any promising Horary Question can contradict its signification: and usually I have found, that whoever propounds a Question to the *Astrologer*, I meane in their first Question, they have a Signe of the same Triplicity ascending in their Question, agreeable to the nature of the ascendant in their Nativity, and many times the very selfsame Signe and degree is ascending upon an Horary Question which was ascending in the Nativity, as I have many times found by experience; for if ♊ ascend in the Nativity, it's probable upon an Horary Question, either ♎ or ♒ may ascend, which are Signes of the same Triplicity.

If one were with Child of a Male or Female, and about what time she should be delivered.

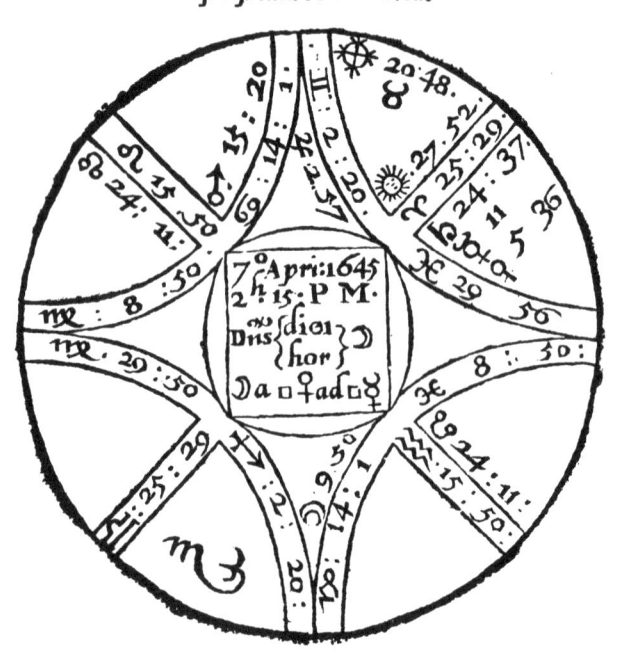

Judg.

all manner of Questions. 241

Chap. XLIII.
Judgment upon the Figure beforegoing.

YOU may see in the judgments appertaining to this house how to judge of this question; however, I did follow the Method succeeding, and considered onely the plurality of testimonies, Masculine or Feminine, of the proper *Significators*, and thereby gave resolution.

Arguments of a Girle.

♍ Signe ascending,	Feminine.
♑ Signe of the fifth,	Feminine.
☽ In a Signe	Feminine.
☿ Lord of the ascendant with ♀, a Planet	Feminine.

Significations of a Male Child.

☿ Lord of the ascendant in a Signe	Masculine.
♄ Lord of the fift a Planet	Masculine.
♄ Lord of the fift in a Sign	Masculine.
☽ Iu a house	Masculine.
♄ In a house	Masculine.
♃ Lord of the Houre	Masculine.
♃ In a Signe	Masculine.
☿ Applying to ♂ his □, and ♂ a Planet	Masculine.

You see here are eight testimonies of a Male Conception, or of Being wth child of a Sonne, and but four of a Female; I therefore affirmed, that the *Lady* was impregnated of a Man child, [*and so it proved.*]

H h *How*

How long ere she should be Delivered.

The Signe of the fift, viz. ♑, is moveable, so is ♈, wherein both the Lord of the ascendant and fift are posited; these argued but a short time: but because ♄ Lord of the fift is a ponderous Planet, and of slow motion, I much valued him in this Judgment, so did I the ☽, because she was posited in the Signe of the fift; I took their proper difference in degrees and minutes each from other:

Locus ♄ in 24 37 ♈ .⎱ Both Cardinall Signes.
Locus ☽ in 9 50 ♑ .⎰

The distance of the ☽ from the □ aspect of ♄ is, as you may find by subduction of the ☽, from ♄ 14. degrees, 47. minutes.

I then substacted ☿ his distance from the body of ♄, because he was Lord of the ascendant, and ♄ Lord of the fift.

♄ 24 37 ♈
☿ 11 00 ♈

Distance 13. degr. 37. min. so that finding no greater difference betwixt the distance of the ☽ to the □ of ♄, and the ♂ of ☿ with ♄, then one degree and ten minutes; I gave for every degree one week, and so judged, that about fourteen weeks from the time of the Question, she should be delivered.

The truth is, she was delivered the eleventh of *July* following, at what time ♂ transited the degree ascending, and ☿ Lord of the ascendant, the opposite place of the ☽, viz. the ninth of ♋: You may further observe that the ☉ the same day is in 27.48. ♋, viz. in perfect □ to his place in our Figure, and the ☽ in ♋ in ♂ with ☿.

Of

Of the sixt House, and its Questions.
Viz. Sicknesse, Servants, small Cattle.

Chap. XLIV.
Judgment of Sicknesse by Astrology.

THAT which I hold convenient to write of *Sicknesses*, is thus much:

That in the first place, we ought carefully to take the exact time of the parties first falling sick, *viz.* the houre as neer as can be had, not that moment when first the Patient felt a smatch of it, but that very time when first he was so ill, or so extreamly oppressed, that he was enforced to take his Bed, or to repose.

Secondly, if that cannot be had, then accept of that time when the sick parties *Urine* was first carried to somebody, to enquire of the Disease, whether the party enquired of was Physitian or not.

Thirdly, if no such thing can be had, let the Physitian take the time of his owne first speaking with, or accesse to the Patient, or when first the *Urine* was brought unto him, let a Figure be erected accordingly, and the place of the ☽ exactly rectified to the very houre; and then to know where the Disease is, let him carefully observe:

First, the ascendant, what Planet or Planets are therein placed. Secondly, the sixt house, and what Planet or Planets are therein posited. Thirdly, the Signe and house wherein the ☽ is. Fourthly, how she is affected or afflicted, by what Planet, in what house that Planet is, what house of the Figure that Planet is Lord of.

What part of the Body is afflicted; wherein you consider:

If the first house be afflicted by the presence of an evill Planet and he Retrograde, Combuſt, Peregrine, flow in motion, or in □ or ☍ to any Planet who is Lord of the fourth, ſixt, eighth or twelfth, the Diſeaſe is then in the Head, or in that or thoſe parts of the Body which the Planet or Planets ſignifie in that Sign then aſcending, which you may ſee by the Table beforegoing *page* 119. as if the Signe aſcending be ♋, and ♄ therein, you may judge, the ſick party is afflicted in the Head, or ſuch Diſeaſes as are incident to the Head, becauſe that firſt honſe ſignifies in mans Body the Head, and is now afflicted by the poſition of ♄ in that houſe: but you ſhall alſo judge the ſick party is Diſeaſed with a Looſneſſe or Flux in the Belly, or an imperfection in the Reynes or Secrets, or troubled with cold, raw Matter in his Stomack, becauſe ♄ in ♋ doth ſignifie thoſe members, or elſe with ſome rotten Cough; and your Judgment herein ſhall be more certaine, and I dare ſay infallible, if either the Lord of the aſcendant, the ☽, or Lord of the ſixt be in a Signe, and therein ſignifie that very member which ♄ doth, or if the Signe of the ſixt repreſent that member.

The ſame courſe and manner which I have directed in the aſcendant, I would have obſerved in the ſixt houſe, *viz.* the Signe of the ſixt, the Planet or Planets therein placed, what member of mans Body they repreſent in the Signe wherein they are poſited, from whom the Lord of the ſixt laſt ſeparated, to whom he next applyes: Together with theſe, obſerve carefully the Signe and houſe wherein the ☽ is, her ſeparation and application, and you may then deſcend to give judgment in what part of the Body the ſick party is grieved, and of what nature and quality the Sickneſſe is of, or what humour is moſt predominant and peccant.

From what cauſe the Sickneſſe is. Generally obſerve:

The *Significators* in Signes fiery, and the Signes aſcending in the firſt, and deſcending in the ſixt of the ſame nature, ſhew Hectick Feavers, and that Choller principally is predominant in this Sickneſſe.

The *Significators* in earthly Signes, argue long and tedious Agues, or Feavers of great continuance, or ſuch Diſeaſes as may occaſionally proceed from Melancholly, Conſumptions, &c.

The

all manner of Questions. 245

The *Significators* in ayery Signes, shew the Blood putrified or corrupted, Gouty Diseases, Leprosies, the Hand and Foot Gout.

The *Significators* in moyst Signes, declare the Disease to proceed from some cold and moyst cause or causes, and shewes Coughs, rottennesse in the Stomack, and that those parts are disaffected, &c.

Diseases signified by the Houses.

House
1 The Head, the Eyes, the Face, Eares, stinking Breath, sore Mouth, and *Noli me tangere*.
2 The Throat, Neck, Kings-Evill.
3 Shoulders, Armes, Hands.
4 The Stomack, Brest, Lungs.
5 The Back, hinder part of the Shoulders, Stomack, Liver, Heart, Sides.
6 Lower part of the Belly, Guts, Liver and Reynes.
7 Hammes, Flank, small Guts, Bladder, Matrix, members of Generation.
8 The Back-bone, Arse, Groine.
9 The Huckle-Bone, *or*, the Hips.
10 The Knees, the Hamme of ones Leg behind the Knee.
11 The Shank, Legge from the Knee to the Ancle, Shin-Bone.
12 The Feet, and all Diseases incident to them.

Diseases signified by the Signes.

♈ All Diseases incident to the Head (as in the first house is signified) and such as proceed or have originall from Choller, small Pocks Pushes, Pimples.

♉ Diseases in the Neck and Throat, having their beginning from Melancholly, as in the second House.

♊ Shoulders, Armes, Hands, proceeding from Blood distempered.

♋ Scabbinesie, Cancers in the Brest, Hurts in the Brest, ill Digestion in the Stomack, Spleen, Lungs, upper part of the Belly,

Belly, Cold and Moisture being the cause, Surfets, &c.

♌ Back-bone, Sides, Ribs, Heart, lower part of the Breſt, ſuch infirmities as proceed from Choller and exceſſe of Blood.

♍ Shewes Melancholly, Diſeaſes in the Guts, and Belly-akes, Fluxes, &c. impediments in the Miſeraicks, Wind-chollick.

♎ Great Heats in the Back, or the Stone in the Reines or Kidneys, Surfets by drinking or eating, or from too much Venery, Diſeaſes in the Buttocks, Joints, Hammes and Hanches.

♏ The Groin and parts about the privy Members, the Arſe, Bladder, Pyles, Stone in the Bladder, Strangury.

♐ The Hippes, Hammes, Buttocks, Fiſtula's, Itches, Sciatica's.

♑ The Knees, back part of the Hammes, Scurfs and Itches in and about the Knees, proceeding of Melancholly.

♒ The Legs, Shin-bone and Calves of the Legs, with the Ancles.

♓ The Ancle-bone and Feet, Gouts, Swellings in thoſe parts.

Diſeaſes of the Planets.

♄ Is ſignificator of theſe Diſeaſes; of noyſe or rumbling in the right Eare and Head, Deafneſſe, the Tooth-ach, paine in the Bones, in the Bladder, all cold Diſeaſes proceeding from a deflux of the Humours, the Gout, Scab, Melancholick infirmities, Leproſie, Palſie, Conſumptions, black-Jaundies, quartan Agues, the Iliack-paſſion, Dropſie, Chin-coughs, Catarres of Rheums falling upon the Lungs and Pectorals.

♃ The Lungs, Ribs, Griſſels, Liver, the Pulſe, the Seed, Arteries, Apoplexies, Plureſies, wringings at the Heart, Convulſions, Inflamations of the Liver, Diſeaſes in the Head, prickings and ſhootings neer or upon the Ridgebone, all windineſſe in the Veines and Body, or any Diſeaſes ariſing from putrifaction in the Blood, &c.

♂ The left Eare, Gall, Reines, Privities and Stones, the Plague, wounds in the Face, Impoſthumations, burning-Feavers, yellow-Jaundies, Carbuncles, Fiſtula's, Epilepſies, bloody-Flux, Calentures, St. Anthonies fire.

☉ The

all manner of Questions.

☉ The Braine, Heart, Eye-fight, right Eye of a man, left of a woman, Cramps, Swoonings or sudden tremblings at the Heart, the Cardiack Passion, Fluxes in the Eyes, Catarres, red Choller.

♀ The Matrix, Genitals, Paps, Throat, Liver, Sperme, or Seed in man or woman, Suffocations or Defections in the Matrix, Pissing Disease, Gonorrhea, Debility in the Act of Generation, Strangury, weaknesse of Stomack and Liver, French or Spanish Pocks, imbecility or desire to vomit, or that Disease when presently after eating, all comes up againe.

☿ The Braine, Spirit, Fancy, Imagination, Speech, Tongue, Fingers, Hands, privation of Sense, Madnesse, Lethargy, Stammering, Hoarcenesse, Coughes, falling Evill, aboundance of Spettle, &c.

☽ Left Eye of man, right Eye of a woman, the Braine, the Intestines or small Guts, the Bladder, Taste, falling Sicknesse, Palsie, Collick, Menstrues in women, Apostems, Fluxes of the Belly, *viz.* Loosnesse, and all coagulated, crude Humours in any part of the Body.

From what precedes, it's easie to discover both the member afflicted, quality of the Disease, its cause and originall rise; which being well considered, it's requisite you be able to acquaint the sick party of the length or shortnesse of his Disease, and its time of accesse or recesse, the better to comfort him if life be ordained, or to make him more penitent and prepared for Heaven, if you see apparent testimonies of death.

Whether the Disease will be long or short.

Herein you must have respect to the time of the yeer in the first place, and to consider, that Sicknesses happening in the Winter are usually more long, and of long continuance; in the Summer more short; in the Spring they are reputed healthfull; in the Autumne, for the most part Diseases mortall and pernicious are stirred up.

Also cold and dry Diseases which proceed from ♄, or which
he

he ftirres up,, or is the Author of, are more permanent and long, and generally are regulated by the ☉ : hot and dry Difeafes, which are procreated from the influence of ♂ and the ☉ are but fhort, and are determined by the motion of the ☽ : ♄ produceth chronick Infirmities ; ♃ and ☉ fhort ; ♂ more fhort, violent and quick ; ♀ a meane betwixt both ; ☿ divers and unconftant ; the ☽ fuch as do againe revert, as the Falling-ficknefſe, Giddineſſe, Swimming of the Head, Gouts, &c.

Signes of a long or fhort Sickneſſe.

If the Signe of the fixt be fixed, expect a long Difeafe ; a moveable Signe, fhort continuance ; a common Signe, a mediocrity, neither too long or fhort, but for the moſt part, an alteration of the Difeafe, and returne of it againe.

The laſt degrees of any Signe being upon the cufp of the fixt houfe, the difeafe is almoſt at an end, or is either altering for better or worſe : fixed Signes doe argue the humour not to be expulſed without much time and difficulty.

When the Lord of the fixt is of evill influence, and placed in the fixt, it's an ill *Omen*, or an unlucky figne of a durable and great fickneſſe : but if in the like nature a *Fortune* be there, the Difeafe will ſoon be cured, nor is it mortall : When the Lord of the fixt is ſtronger then the Lord of the afcendant, the Difeafe is like to encreaſe, adviſe the Patient to take fit remedies, for Nature is weaker then the Difeafe ; but if the Lord of the fixt houfe be more weak then the Lord of the afcendant, then be aſſured nature will be able to overcome the malignity of the Difeafe, without much affiſtance of the Phyſician : When ♄ is Lord of the fixt houſe, and fixed in the Signe he is in, he extreamly prolongs the Difeafe ; if he be Retrograde or flow in motion, he performes the fame ; but if he be in a moveable Sign and in any of his Termes, or fwift in motion, he is not then much unfortunate, or will he greatly prolong the Difeafe : a moveable Signe in the fixt, and the ☽ likewiſe, and no impediment otherwayes appearing, the Difeafe continues but a while ; common Signes doe more long continue any infirmity, except ♓, for that being upon the cufp of the fixt, I ever found

it

all manner of Questions.

it equivalent to a moveable Signe: If the ☽ apply by ill aspect to the Lord of the ascendant, the Disease encreases; if the ☽ be in the sixt in ill aspect with ♀, the sick may thank himselfe for his Disease, he is a disorderly fellow, and of ill Dyet; and if ♀ be in ♏,&c. he hath got a clap of some uncleane woman; if a woman ask, she hath too great Flux of the Whites or Reds, or the Disease is occasioned by her owne Folly, &c.

If the Lord of the sixt apply to the Lord of the ascendant by □ or ☍, the Disease is encreasing, and is not yet at his height or full growth; so also the Lord of the sixt in the eighth or twelfth, is an ill argument and great presumption, that the party sick must be more afflicted ere his Disease leave him: If an infortunate Planet be in the sixt, and is removing out of one Sign into another, the Disease will speedily alter: if it's desired *When, or how long it may be before it doe so?* then see how many degrees the malevolent Planet wants ere he can get out of the Signe, and thereby judge so many Moneth, Weeks or Dayes according to the nature and quality of the Signe: if the Lord of the sixt be Retrograde, Combust in the eighth or twelfth, and and in □, ☍ or ☌ with ♄, ♂, or Lord of the eighth or fourth of the Figure, he prenotes much infirmity, a long continued and sudden alteration of the Disease from better to worse, if not Death it selfe; the Lord of the sixt in the eighth, and Lord of the eighth in the sixt, there being also a ✶ or △ aspect betwixt both *Significators*, you shall not doubt of the death of the Patient at that time, for the Heavens doe declare, that Nature is not yet so overcome, or so weak, but that the sick shall overcome it: if there happen any △ ✶ or ☌ betwixt the Lord of the sixt and ♃, and he in the ninth, and the ☽ separate from the Lord of the sixt to ♃, so in the ninth house posited, it's an assured argument, that the Medicines which the Phisician prescribes, or which the Patient hath already taken, have caused the party to be very sick at time of their taking, and whilest they operated, and that the Medicines wrought effectually in the outward parts of the Body, but afterwards the sick felt great comfort, and hath found great emendation in the parts of his Body, afflicted at time of his first being ill; either ♄ or ♂, or any unfortunate Planet in the sixt, threatens great danger in the Sicknesse, yet if he be well affected or essentially fortified, he hurts little; and you may rather judge, the Disease is happened casually and suddenly, then upon any prepared matter in the Body beforehand, therefore let the sick be of good comfort: so likewise when you find a Benevolent Planet well fortified in the sixt, and he not author of the Disease, you may safely judge, the Disease is not, or will be permanent.

Many times it happens that in some Country townes, people are afraid of *Witches*; If the Lord of the twelfth be in the sixt when mistrust is had by any such Querent, it's a strong argument the supposition is true, that the party is vexed by an evill Spirit, or by Fascination; when you find in the Question of a sick party, the Lord of the sixt in the ascendant, and the Lord of the ascendant in the sixt, you may give judgment the Disease hath been of long continuance, and will continue untill one of the *Significators* get out of the Signe wherein he is; and if it happen, at the time of the Planets transit out of one Signe into another, he meet with the □ or ☍ of the Lord of the fourth or eighth, or with the oppressing or malicious aspect of ♄ or ♂, and they flow in motion, in Signes odiously beholding or aspecting one another, it's a very great signe the sick will then depart this Life; when you find the Lord of the sixt afflicted by the □ or ☍ of the Lord of the ascendant in *Azimen* degrees, a fig for the Physitian, the Disease is uncurable, and the sick party continually pained: When the Lord of the sixt is in the ascendant, the Disease will continue, but the paine doth slacken and seems quite removed at some times, or the Patient sometimes is not sensible of paine: but if he be in a Cadent house, the Disease is neither very grievous, or will it endure any long space of time; so also good Planets in the sixt do promise a good end of the Disease; evill the contrary: usually a malignant Planet in the sixt, shew the Disease unsetled, so doth also the Lord of the sixt if he be in the sixt, eighth or twelfth, denote a Disease not easily curable; if the Lord of the ascendant and ☽ be free from the □, ☍ or ☌ of ♄ or ♂, or any infortunate Planet, and be Direct, free from Combustion, swift in Motion, not Peregrine, or in his Fall or Detriment, or in the eighth or sixt, or in any aspect with the Lord of the twelfth,

sixt

all manner of Questions.

fixt or eighth, it's a faire fignification of health and recovery; when the Lord of the afcendant is in the fourth or eighth, and is not afflicted, he fhall not fignifie death, but recovery; but if he be unfortunate in the fourth, it notes great difficulty ere the party be cured; but if the Lord of the afcendant be himfelfe unfortunate, either in his houfe, or by Retrogradation, Peregrination, Combuftion, or be in his Fall or Detriment, it's poffible he may be cured, but within a fhort time after he will relapfe, dye, or fall into fome defperate infirmity; when alfo the Lord of the afcendant is infortunated by the Lord of the fixt or twelfth, and in a bad afpect of the ☽, there's danger in the Difeafe threatned; above all, have a care if ♄ be Lord of the afcendant, and in his Dignities, flow, diminifhed in light, Retrograde, for then the Patient or Querent will be long fick; judge the contrary of the fignification of ♄ when otherwayes qualified.

The Lord of the afcendant in an Angle, having no configuration to any malevolent Planet, but being in a benevolent houfe of Heaven, and not under the ☉ beames, or Retrograde, you may judge the *Querent* is in no danger at this time: when the Lord of the afcendant is fwift in motion, and entring into another Signe, or going out of his owne houfe into another, fo it be not into the Signe of the fixt or twelfth, the Difeafe will quickly determine: if the Lord of the afcendant be not afflicted in himfelfe, or by any ill afpect of the malevolent Planets, or Planets of a contrary nature unto himfelfe, but is fwift in motion, and in fome good afpect with the fortunate Planets, it's a ftrong argument that the nature of the Difeafed or *Querent* is nothing diminifhed, but is able to overcome the malignity of the Difeafe, and that in a very fhort time; but if the *Significator* of the fick be afflicted powerfully, it's a figne of a ftrong fit of ficknefle; the greater it will be, when the *Significator* of life is more weak then the Planet afflicting: if all the *Significators* of the Difeafe be in Signes fixed, it prenotes a great fpace of time ere the Patient can be cured, nor will the cure be eafily perfected; when the Lord of the afcendant is applied unto by a malevolent Planet, it retards the cure, prolongs the infirmity, though at prefent great hopes appeare; fo doth alfo the ☽

when she is slow in motion, and goeth in twenty four hours lesse then her meane motion, and be in any aspect or ☌ with the Lord of the ascendant; but if she be swift the cure is performed presently, or effected in a little time; for the most part when the ☽ decreases in light and motion, and comes to the ☌, □ or ☍ of ♄, unlesse the disease be in its decrease and leaving the Patient or *Querent*, it's I say, very mortall and dangerous: when the ☽ is in ☌ with a Planet that is Orientall Direct and Swift, expect a short sicknesse; joyned to a Retrograde or Planet Occidentall, look for the contrary.

When you find ♏ ascending, you may for the most part judge, the party was cause of his owne infirmnesse, either by peevishnesse, folly, choller or the like; and your judgment will be more firme, if ♂ be then placed in ♏: if both the *Luminaries* be in Cadent houses, and the Planet or Planets that are their Dispositors be unfortunate, the *Querent* may expect a terrible sicknesse; if the *Fortunes* assist in judgment, yet will the sicknesse be of long continuance, and of a sharp Disease, prove chronick, yet beyond all expectation, the sick party will recover; and the more confident be in your judgment, by how much more strong the *Fortunes* are dignified above the *Infortunes*; when you find ♂ Lord of the ascendant and posited in the sixt house, in ✶ or △ with ♀, nay, if he be in □ or ☍ of her, there's no great danger.

If the Lord of the sixt be Combust or Retrograde, in his Fall or Detriment, and in the eighth, in ☌, □ or ☍ of ♄ or ♂, you may doubt, and not unjustly, that the Disease will never leave the sick party till death; and if the ☽ have equall testimony to the former *Significators*, *viz.* if she also apply to the □ ☍ or ☌ of the Lord of the eight, your former judgment will be very certaine; If either the ☽ or Lord of the ascendant be in □ ☌ or ☍ to a benevolent Planet, Retrograde, the sick will recover, but not in haste, for it's an argument of the prolongation of the Disease, and relapsing out of one Disease into another: When you find the ☽ receded from ☍ of the ☉, to be swift in motion, and haftens to the □ or ☍ of ♂ it will come to passe, that the Disease which the *Querent* now undergoes, will be grievous and mortall; but if she salute at the same

time

all manner of Questions.

fame time the $*$ or $\triangle$ of ♃ or ♀, the sick shall recover. There's usually no danger if the ☽ at time of the Question be strong, and the Lord of the ascendant free from misfortune, and in no aspect to the Lord of the sixt, yet when the ☽ at time of the Question applies to ♄, or is impedited, it's an ill *Omen* and sign of a sicknesse at hand, and that the *Querent* mistrusts his owne health, is sick, but knowes not were to complaine, or in what part of the Body the infirmity is placed.

At the time of ones first lying down, if the ☽ be placed in the ascendant, in ☌ ☐ or ☍ of ♄ or ♂, or of any other unfortunate Planet, it's a sign of ill, & shews ill, unlesse the ☽ be in reception with the Planet or Planets so afflicting: It's very considerable to observe at the time of the Question, what Signe the ☽ is in; if in a fixed, expect a long fit of sicknesse; in a moveable Signe, quick dispatch; in a Common or Double bodied Signe, the Disease will not be very difficult to cure, but somewhat long in curing: and thus much more you must consider, that if there be translation of light (from that Planet who is Dispositor of the ☽, and he unfortunate) to the Lord of the ascendant, or Signe ascending, it gives great suspition that the *Querent* will have a sharp sicknesse, according to the nature of the Signes and Planets signifying the infirmity.

Testimonies that the Querent shall live and not dye of the infirmity now afflicting.

When it is demanded seriously, if you conceive the *Querent* shall escape the Sicknesse he now languishes under, or shall live, you must carefully have recourse to your Figure erected, and therein observe these rules following: That if the ☽ be separated from a malevolent, weak Planet (that is ill dignified) and is applying to a *Fortune* powerfully strong, the sick party will be restored to former health; where ♄ is Orientall of the ☉, and *Significator* of the Disease, it proceeding from Cold, (which is the true nature of ♄ without mixture) the Patient will recover; if you find in like case, that ♄ is Occidentall, and the generall *Significators* doe incline or manifest, that the Disease is more of Heat then Cold, the sick will also be recovered; yet you must ever understand, that ♄ is unlucky when he is Occidentall, &c. For the disposition of ♂, you shall find, that after his ☍ with the ☉, that is, when he is Occidentall, he is not so much to be feared (*viz.* his evill influence) as when he is Orientall; for the ☌ of the ☽ with ♂ is dangerous, and an argument of a strong sicknesse at hand, his ☍ and □ aspects doe lesse mischiefe; the ☽ doth more hurt in her encrease then in her decrease, so doth ♂ being Orientall, more then when Occidentall.

When you find there is any reception between the Lord of the ascendant and Lord of the eighth, and neither of them infortunated by the malignant Planets, after desperation, there will be recovery: the Lord of the ascendant in reception of the Lord of the eighth by House or Triplicity, the *Fortunes* assisting either with their △ or ✶ the degree ascending or of the sixt house, or the ☽ her selfe, there's no danger of death, but the sick will perfectly recover; so also, when the Lord of the ascendant shall happen to be a benevolent Planet, and plated in the first, tenth, eleventh, fift or third house, being no wayes endangered by the □ or ☍ configuration of the Malevolents, it prenotes sanity: so doth also the position of the *Fortunes* in the Mid-heaven or first house, at what time the sicknesse first assaulted the sicke person, nothing is a more sure argument of health, or that the party sick shall live, then when you find the ☉ ♃ ♀ or the ☽ in the ascendant of the Question, not any wayes damnified by the hatefull aspect of the Lord of the eighth or sixt; and this argument is more certaine, if the aforesaid *Significators* be in good Signes, that is, in either of ♃ his houses, or in ♋ or ♌, ♎ or ♉: when the *Moone* is in her owne house, or in the house of ♃ or ♀, and there in either of their aspect, free from any ill aspect of ♄ or ♂, she signifies health and life.

It's a good argument of recovery, when in your Question you find the *Moon* in ☌ with ♃, let ♃ be in what Signe he will it denotes good, but lesse in ♑ then in any other Signe, for neither the *Moon* or ♃ have any delight therein, that Signe being the Fall of ♃ and Detriment of the *Moon*; in very deed, no Planet delights to be in the Signe wherein he Fals, or is he

able

all manner of Queſtions. 255

able therein to expreſſe the ſtrength of his influence. When the *Moon* is applying to the Lord of the aſcendant by △ or ✶ aſpect, and ſhe be cleer of all misfortune, or not impedited by the Lord of the eighth, or ſixt eſpecially, health and life are promiſed: ſafety is alſo to be expected, when the *Moon* ſhall be well affected and poſited in a Succeeding houſe, provided, ſhe be encreaſing in light and motion, and not neer the bodies of ♄ or ♂, or infected with their Rayes: the *Moone* either in the firſt, tenth, eleventh, ninth, ſecond, third or fifth, in △ or ✶ with the Lord of the aſcendant, or with his Antiſcion, yea, if he be a malevolent Planet, ſo that neither the Lord of the aſcendant or the *Moon* have any other impediment, it doth argue life.

When at the firſt falling ſick of the infirme Body, the *Moon* is voyd of courſe, and at her next *Criſis* meets with a ✶ or △ of ♃ or ♀, in that very degree which makes a perfect *Cryſis*, the ſick ſhall recover, be he never ſo much pained or grieved at the time of demanding the Queſtion or acceſſe of the *Urine*: when in the firſt beginning or approach of a Diſeaſe, the *Sunne*, *Moon* and Lord of the aſcendant are free from the ill aſpects of the *Infortunes* or Lord of the eighth, there needs no feare or ſuſpition to be made of the death of the then ſick party, or when the Benevolent Planets are more potent then the Malevolent, they give aſſured hopes of life, and invite the infirme perſon to confide of his eſcape.

Arguments of Death.

When the aſcendant at time of firſt falling ſick, ſhall be the ſeventh houſe at the Birth, you may feare death, unleſſe the Profection of that yeer be the ſame Signe: what Profection is, you ſhall know in my Treatiſe of *Nativities*; thoſe Signes which are adverſe in a Nativity, are the Signs of the ſixt, ſeventh, eighth and twelfth.

When the five *Hylegiacall* places at the hour of Birth, at time of *Decumbiture* of the ſick, as alſo the Lord of the aſcendant, are oppreſſed, judge death immediatly to follow, unleſſe reception intervene betwixt the *Infortunes*, and the *Fortunes* interject
their

their comfortable aspects; for then, by a divine miracle as it were the party sick may escape.

He will be infinitely oppressed who in the houre of ♂ shall first get an hot Disease, and in the houre of ♄ a cold one.

The Lord of the ascendant and of the Figure Combust, doe undoubtedly declare death, unlesse there be some reception between the ☉ and them, such a chance happening, and the *Moon* proving fortunate, after all hopes of escape, a little hopes remaines.

The Lord of the ascendant and the *Moon* in ☌ with the Lord of the eighth, without the interposing aspects of the *Fortunes*, threatens death.

The Lord of the eighth in an Angle, the Lord of the ascendant in a Cadent, is alwayes mortall; the rather if he be an *Infortune*.

The application of the *Moon* to a Planet in the eighth, is alwayes dangerous: The application of the Lord of the ascendant unto the Lord of the eighth or unto malevolent Planets therein, the *Moone* being any manner of way corrupt, denoats death.

The *Moon* transferring the light and influence of the Lord of the ascendant to the Lord of the eighth, brings usually death: so also when the Lord of the eighth is in the ascendant, the Lord of the ascendant and the *Moon* being both afflicted: It also proves fatall when the Lord of the ascendant is infortunate in the eighth, the *Moon* being then corrupted or very weak, and in no essentiall Dignity: the Lord of the ascendant being Subterranean, and in any aspect to the Lord of the eighth in the eight, or if he be in the fourth, and the Lord of the eighth in the fourth, and they both in ☌, argue death: it's a very ill signe of life when the Lord of the ascendant is corporally joyned with the Lord of the fourth, sixt, seventh or twelfth, it seldome succeeds well with the sick person then.

Have speciall consideration to the *Luminary* of the time, for according to the well or ill affection thereof you may improve your Judgment. The Lord of the ascendant afflicted of an evill Planet in the eighth, without the benevolent aspect of the *Fortunes*, the *Moon* also then vitiated, shew great perill of death, and usually

all manner of Questions.

usually by reason of the ill government of the sick party, or some error in his ordering or course in Physick: it's a powerfull argument that the sick party will dye, when at time of his first Question to his Physitian, you find the Lord of the ascendant Combust in the ascendant.

The Lord of the ascendant and of the eighth unfortunate, prenote death.

The Lord of the eighth in the tenth house, and Lord of the ascendant in the fourth, sixt or seventh, afflicted of the malevolent Planets, argue death.

A Planet very strong, and placed in the ascendant, if he be Lord of the houre and of the eighth, portends death: if the Lord of the eighth be Retrograde, and in ☌ □ or ☍ of the ☽, it shewes death: The Lord of the eighth in the seventh, the *Moon* and Lord of the ascendant in cadent houses, infested with the ill aspects of *Infortunes*; and more certaine, if one of the malevolents be Lord of the eighth, or posited in the eighth; some say, if the *Moon* be in ☌ with ♄ or ♃, the sicknesse will have little good thereby, nor will he escape, unlesse ♄ be Retrograde and ♃ Direct.

When the Lord of the Ascendant is in ☌ with the Lord of the eighth, or in □ or ☍ of a Planet posited in that house, or in the Antiscion of the Lord of the eighth, without the benevolent ✶ or △ of ♃, and at the same time the ☽ be anyway afflicted, it's probable the sick will dye; but if the Lord of the ascendant be in reception with the Planet in the eighth, it's possible he may avoyd death; however, let him be assured a very long and grievous Disease he cannot: If the ☽ be with ♄ or ♂, without the assistance of some good aspect from ♃ and ♀; and if ♄ be slow in motion, or is going Retrograde, it's so much the worse, and it's one argument the sick will dye at that time; if other testimonies concurre, it's more certaine: The Lord of the ascendant in the seventh, in his Fall, or under the earth in the fourth or sixt or in other Cadent houses, afflicted by the malevolents, and the Lord of the eighth in the seventh, these are testimonies of death: A malevolent Planet neer to the degree ascending, or a violent fixed Star, *viz. Antares* in the fourth deg. of ♐, *Lans Australis* about the ninth of ♏, *Palilicium* in four of ♊, *Caput Me-*

K k *dusæ*

dufæ in twenty ♉, these prenote death. The Lord of the ascendant in ♌ or ♒, in any bad configuration of the Lord of the sixt or twelfth, shewes little hopes of recovery. Both the Lights afflicted of ♄ in Angles, give testimony of a tedious long sickness; so doe both the Lights, being ill dignified and under the earth, signifie the same: when as also the ☉ from the beginning of the Disease shall be corporally afflicted, or by the □ or ☍ of ♄ or ♂ impedited, or be in the perfect Antiscion of a malignant Planet, or shall apply and not separate, either death, or an extraordinary long sickness succeeds: The ☽ after the beginning of the Disease comming to ☍ of the Lord of the ascendant, and he Retrograde or Combust, argues death, or a sharp disease, not easily curable: ♄ in ☍ with the Lord of the eight, the ☽ in the fourth with ♂, or ☽ in the ascendant, and neer the degree ascending, are arguments of death: the ☽ besieged by the *Infortunes*, or between ☉ and ♂, or between ☉ and ♄, are ill *Omens* of health: who fals sick whilest the ☽ is under the ☉ Beames, *viz.* departing from Combustion, his Disease shall encrease till she hath passed the ☉ his ☍; but then if she prove ill affected, and come to an ill aspect of the Lord of the eighth, it threatens death, otherwise he or she will escape.

Any malevolent in the sixt, or any Planet peregrine and unfortunate in that house, shew great danger in the Disease; the Combustion of the ☽ in the eighth house, and in ♌, or in ♎, in □ or ☍ to ♄ or ☿, or in ☌ with the *Pleiades* in 24 ♉, or other violent fixed Starres, argues death: the ☽ being Lady of the sixt, or of the ascendant in Combustion, and the Lord of the eighth at the same time afflicted by ♂, or ill aspect of ♄ or ♂, shew death.

DARIOT *Abridged.*

In regard I have ever affected Dariot *his Method of judgment in sicknesses, I have with some abbreviation annexed it, in a farre more short way and method then heretofore published.*

If

all manner of Questions.

If the Party be sicke of whom the Question is Demanded.

THE *Significator* of the *Querent* in a Signe contrary to his *Dariot.* owne nature, as ♂ being Lord of the ascendant, and naturally hot and dry, if he be in ♋, which is cold and moyst; or if the Lord of the ascendant be in a Cadent house, chiefly in the sixt, he is sick.

A diurnall Planet being *Significator*, and he under the earth, ill affected, Combust, Retrograde, in his Fall or Detriment, weak, or in Termes of malevolents, or with violent fixed Stars, or besieged by the two *Infortunes*, these things happening, the party is sick. What was spoken of a diurnall Planet, must be understood of a nocturnall one (*consideratis considerandis.*)

When a Question was asked of me upon any *Urine*, or with- *Lilly.* out it, having erected my Figure, I observed this method, to know whether the *Querent* was ill or no.

If the ascendant were not afflicted, or the Lord thereof out of his essentiall Dignities, or in any evill aspect of ♄ or ♂, or Lord of the sixt.

Or if no Planet afflicted the sixt house by presence, or that the ☽ were not afflicted in the eighth or twelfth; or if I found ♃ or ♀ or ☋ in the ascendant, or the ☉ in the sixt, or the ☽ and Lord of the ascendant in any good aspect, or ♃ or ♀ casting a △ or ✶ to the cusp of the ascendant or sixt house, I would directly acquaint the party they were not sick, or that no sicknesse would succed upon this *Quere*, but that their mistrust of a sicknesse was grounded upon some sudden distemper of Body, which would presently be rectified.

Cause of the Disease inward or outward.

The inward cause and condition of the Disease we require *Dariot.* from the ill disposition of the *Significator*, in Signe, House and place of Heaven, his good or ill configuration with the malevolent Planets: where generally observe, any Planet may in

Kk 2   this

this case be malignant, if he be Lord of the eighth, twelfth or fixt, &c.

The outward cause is required from those *Infortunes* that doe afflict the Lord of the ascendant, or from the principall *Significators* in the Figure, or the ☽; for if you find the Lord of the ascendant sufficiently strong in essentiall Dignities, swift in motion, in a good house of Heaven, you may then judge the *Querent* is not naturally ill, but accidentally and outwardly afflicted, and if you find notwithstanding the strength of the Lord of the ascendant, that either ♄ or ♂ have some □ or ☍ aspect unto him, and neither of them be Lords of the sixt, or Dispositors of the ☽, you may judge some outward cause hath happened to the party, whereby it comes to passe he is not well, yet not perfectly sick; doe you then observe in what house that Planet is, or of what house he is Lord, and from the judgments belonging to that house, require satisfaction in *Art*; as for example:

If you find the Lord of the ascendant casually afflicted by *Saturne* or *Mars*, &c. and either of them are Lords of the second house, and there appeares no inward cause of a Disease, then doe you judge the *Querent* is in some want of money, (if the *Significators* apply,) or hath had lately damage, if the *Significators* are separated; the greatnesse or smalnesse of his losse judge according to the strength of the Planet afflicting, and quality of the aspect; where note, *Oppositions* herein are worse then □ aspects or *Conjunctions*: If it be the Lord of the fift, be the Planet good or ill, that afflicts, or hath evill aspect to the Lord of the ascendant, either by evill Dyet, Surfet, &c. or by losse at Dice, Tables or Sports (if the *Querent* be capable) or that the Father comes not off freely with his Pension; (this is when young people demand a Question, or are distempered) if it be the Lord of the seventh that oppresses the Lord of the ascendant, the party hath had lately some difference with his Wife (and so a Woman, on the contrary, with her Husband,) or some Law-suit, or wilfull Neighbour, contention, or Partner is the outward cause of his evill indisposition: in Youth, if the like configuration be upon the Question from the Lord of the seventh to the Lord of the ascendant, it's a Love-melancholly

all manner of Questions. 261

ty, his Friend, or the Maid he affects, or the man she longs after is unkind, and discontent for that occasion is the outward cause of this ill affectednesse in the Body, yet will no sicknesse follow it. *This is the Method which I ever observed, which I freely communicate to the world, and which, if well understood, will give knowledge sufficient to this way of judicature.*

Of the qualitie and nature of the Disease.

Although formerly I have briefly given directions herein, yet now I hold it fit to be more copious, and desire the Learner that he will contract what I write into such a Method as may best please his owne Phansie; and be inabled to make the best use of it for his owne advantage. When therefore you have erected your Figure, consider what Planet is significator of the Disease; and if you doe finde ♄ to be significator, he produceth continued and tedious Sicknesses, quartan Agues, Coughs, consumptions, &c. If he be in ♌ or in ♏ with ☋ or ☋, or Combust, or if ♄ be with violent fixed Starres, he afflicts the sicke party with pestilent and dangerous Feavers, and it may be doubted (where suspicion of Poyson is) that the Sicke hath been indeavoured to be Poysoned, or hath taken some potion equivolent to Poyson.

When ♄ is in Signes of the fiery Triplicity, as ♈ ♌ ♐, he usually signifies Hectick-Feavers; if he be in ♋ ♏ or ♓, the cause and matter of the Disease growes from some cold and moyst cause or matter, or distemper; and this more assuredly if ♀ or ☽, who are moyst Planets, have together with him any signification in the Disease, the matter then afflicting or cause of the disease is more grosse and vicious with long Paroxismes, with ebbing and flowing of the Disease; the sicke party is almost overwhelmed with horror, dread, and fearfull imaginations, with extreame chilnesse and coldnesse.

When ♄ is in fixed Signes, as in ♉ ♌ ♒, he afflicts the Patient with durable and long continued Agues and Feavers, pectorall rotennesses, or dry coughs, the joynt Gout, Leprosie, or generall Scabbinesse all over the Body, all manner of Gouts.

Kk 3 ♄ being

♄ being in moveable Signes, as ♈ ♎ ♋ ♑, prenotes generall Flux of humours all-over the Body, principally the Dropſie or Tympanicall humours. Being in common Signes, the Diſeaſe proceeds not from the diſaffection of one humour alone, but hath many changings, receding and reverting, and yet the Diſeaſe continues a long time.

♃ When he is author of the Sickneſſe, he demonſtrates ill affection of the Liver, and a corruption of the blood either by inflamation, or other cauſes of nature agreeable to the Signe wherein he is poſited, as if in ♋, or in a moyſt Sign the blood is wateriſh, or too thin, &c. if in ♈ ♌ or ♐, its overheated by ſome extravagant exceſſe of heat or choller, if in ♒ ♎ or ♊ the Blood over flowes, theres too much, breathing of a Veine is neceſſary or Sweating, if in ♉ ♑ or ♍, the blood is infected with Melancholly, too groſſe, and not fluent. ♃ in fiery Signs he cauſes Feavours proceeding from blood, yet without rottenneſſe or ſtore of putrifaction.

When ♂ is joyned with the ☉, it prenotes a diſtempered Feaver procreated, by putrifaction of the blood.

If ♂ be ſignificator of the Diſeaſe and in fiery Signes afflicting the Luminaries or the Aſcendant or Lord of the Aſcendant, he procreates hot burning Feavours, ſome mixture of Melancholly; if *Saturne* be mixed in the Judgement, that is, if he have any thing to do in the Signification of the Diſeaſe, or ♂ in any of his dignities.

When ♂ is in common Signes, the diſeaſe will not eaſily be diſcovered, it will come and goe, and be at no certainty, yet at what time it ſeemes to leave, if *Saturne* have any ſignification and be in aſpect with good Planets, the Diſeaſe will quite goe away, but if then *Saturne* be with the Lord of the eight or ſixt, the Sicke may expect death: Uſually when ♂ is in common Signes the Patient is vexed with many infirmities and they acute, returning when expectation is of amendment; the ſymptomes hereof are ſudden motions, and more quicke and ſpeedy Criticall dayes, either to good or ill, according to the nature of the Significator: ♂ under the beames of the ☉ in the ſixt or in the twelfth, in fiery Signes, brings ſcorching or burning inflaming Feavours, that is, Feavers exceeding, eſpecially in heat, and as it were boyling the Blood. ♂ be-

all manner of Questions. 263

♂ being the cause of a Feaver and in ♌, shewes ebolition or a boyling of the humours, continuall burning Feavers, whose originall cause springs from the great Veines neer the heart: When the ☉ at first lying downe of the Sicke party, is in ☌ □ or ☍ of ♄, or in *Saturne* his Antiscion, the Disease then afflicting is meerly Melancholly; if the ☉ be afflicted of or by ♂ with the aforesaid Aspects, the Disease Is from Choller: ♀ being Significatrix of the Disease, shewes it proceeds of intemperancy, too much Gluttony of some Surfeit, disaffection in the Belly, or in or neer the privy parts, or by some Womanish trick, &c. ♀ in fiery Signes, shewes a Feaver but of one dayes continuance, but if ♂ joyne in signification, it notes rotten Feavers arising from Fleagme.

When ☿ is unfortunate and is author of the Disease, the sick party hath his Brain disaffected, is disturbed with an unquiet Fancy or Minde, with a Frenzie, Falling-sicknesse, Cough, Ptissick, or the like. When the Lord of the ninth is in the sixt, the Disease is from some Poyson, Witchery, or Fascination, Charme, or by or from some occult cause; this is, when mistrust is of such like chances.

Whether the Disease be in the right or left side or part of the Body of him that demands the Question or is Sick.

When you finde the Lord of the sixt unfortunate or afflicted above the earth (that is in the 12, 11, 10, 9, 8, 7. houses) the Disease is in the right side of the Body, and in the upper part thereof; if the Lord of the sixt be under the earth, *viz.* in the 1, 2, 3, 4, 5, 6. houses, or vitiated in a diurnall Signe, the Disease is in the superiour and fore-part of the body, as in the fore-head, stomacke, &c. if in a nocturnall Signe, the infirmity is in the back part of the Body.

If the Significator of the Disease be in a Feminine Signe, and in Aspect to a Feminine Planet in a Feminine Signe or House, the Disease is in the left side of the Body. I ever finde this generall rule to hold true, *viz.* if the Lord of the sixt be a Masculine Planet and above the earth, the right side of the Sicke is pained; and if the Significator be in few degrees of the Signe,

the

the upper part of that Member is pained or grieved; if the Significator be in the middle of the Signe, the middle part of the Member is diſtreſſed, and ſo the lower part of the Member, when the ſignificator poſſeſſeth the lower degrees of the Sign.

Whether the Diſeaſe be in the Body, Minde or both.

You muſt underſtand in the firſt place, that the Signe aſcending the ☽ and the Lord of that houſe wherein the ☉ is, doe ſhew the Spirit of Man, and that the Lord of the Aſcendant, the Planet who is diſpoſitor of the ☽, doth denote both the externall and internall Members. Wherefore in giving judgement herein, you may conſider if the Aſcendant ☉ and ☽ be all vitiated or afflicted, the Diſeaſe is then through the whole Body, or no place is free: but if thoſe Planets who diſpoſe of the ☉ and ☽, or he that is Lord of the Aſcendant, or two of them at leaſt be afflicted, the Diſeaſe is in the Spirits together with ſome indiſpoſition of Minde; the reaſon hereof is, becauſe the Lord of the Aſcendant and Diſpoſitor of the ☽ are properly the Significators of the Animal faculties and infirmities in Man, or which may chance unto him; as deprivation of Sence, Madneſſe, Frenzie, Melancholly, &c.

If the Aſcendant, the ☽ and Lord of the Houſe of the ☉ are all or but two of them impedited, the infirmity reſts in the Minde but not in the Body.

If the Aſcendant and the ☽ be both unfortunate, and the Lord of the Aſcendant and Diſpoſitor of the ☽ free, the indiſpoſition is in the Minde and not in the Body. This generall rule many Aſtrologians obſerve, *viz.* that ♄ naturally foreſhewes or cauſeth Melancholly, all manner of diſtempers from Melancholly, and by conſequence the diſturbed Minde; wherefore whereſoever you finde ♄ Lord of the Aſcendant or of the Houre, or twelfth Houſe, or ſixt, or if the ☽ ſeparate from him, or if ♄ be in the ſixt houſe, or in the Aſcendant, or in ☌ ☐ or ☍ of the Lord of the Aſcendant, the ſick-party labours with ſome affliction of Minde, or with ſome vexatious care wherewith his minde is much troubled; now the contrary hereof ♃ effects, for he never oppreſſeth the Minde but the Body. if the

all manner of Questions. 265

the Lord of the Houſe of the ☽ and of the Aſcendant are unfortunate by the ☉, or Combuſt, or under his beames, the infirmity is Bodily.

If that Planet who rules the Signe wherein the Lord of the Aſcendant is in, and he who is Diſpoſitor of the *Moone* be infortunate in their fall, detriment or otherwayes very much afflicted, the Diſeaſe raignes more in the Minde then In the Body.

If a Planet in the Aſcendant, or the Aſcendant, or if the Lord of the Houſe of the *Moone* be oppreſſed in the twelfth by a ✶ ☐ or ☍ of ♂, the Diſeaſe is both in Body and Minde. A Planet being by nature malevolent, beholding the Aſcendant and not the *Moone*, and together with this, if the Lord of the Signe where the ☉ is be afflicted, the party is grieved in Minde, but not ſick in his Body. Alſo, if the degree aſcending and degree of that Signe wherein the ☽ is be more afflicted then the Lords of thoſe Signes, the Diſeaſe ranges more in the Minde then Body, and ſo the contrary when the Lords are more afflicted then the parts of the Signes before mentioned. If the Lord of the Aſcendant and the ☉ be in their exaltations, and the diſpoſitor of the ☽ in his detriment or fall, &c. the Diſeaſe raignes in the Body, not in the Minde. When the Lords of the places of the ☽ and of the ☉ be in their detriments, fals, or Peregrine, Retrograde, Combuſt, and the degree aſcending in ☐ of the ☽; and free from the ill aſpects of ♄ and ♂, then is the Patient vexed with a tormented Soule. Uſually when the ☉, the Lord of the Aſcendant, or houre, or of the twelfth houſe are ſignificators of the party inquiring, theſe ſhew a Minde vexed with haughtineſſe, vaine-glory, ſelfe-conceitedneſſe, Pride, &c.

Venus argues luxury, a laſcivious deſire to Women, wherwith both Body and Minde are diſturbed. ☿ ſhewes doating fancies, and fearfull imaginations, whereſoever you finde him a Significator and afflicted: as alſo, that he is ſtirred to miſtruſt upon vaine feares, his owne jealous fancies, or upon ſome flying reports. Over and above the many Directions formerly preſcribed, you muſt well conſider whether the degrees wherein the Lord of the Aſcendant, the ☉ or ☽ at time of the Birth (if you have the Patients Nativity) doe fall to be the degrees of

a Signe

a Signe wherein a present Eclipse is, at time of the sicknesse or neere it, or of some eminent great Conjunction; for I must tell you, these are all unfortunate.

The signe of the Eclips or of a great Conjunction threatning evill, or the Signe of the eighth House of the yeerly revolution of the World, falling in any of the Angles of the Nativity, especially in the ascendant, proves very dangerous.

When a Signe ascends upon the first falling sick, or demand of the Patient, wherein an *Infortune* was in the Nativity, it most fearfully torments the sick party, *viz.* it shewes he shall have a hard fit of Sicknesse: The ☌ of the ☽ with the ☉ is a very ill signe, when there's not above six degrees distance betwixt them, and the ☽ not yet passed by the ☉, that is, not having been yet in ☌ with him: however, upon the ☉ and ☽ their being in ☌ in ♈ or ♌, this misfortune is lessened; when the ☽ is twelve degrees from the ☉, she shewes little danger.

Of the Crysis, or dayes Criticall.

Sundry *Astrologians* have handled this part of *Medicinall Astrology* so learnedly, that I shall onely referre them to their excellent Works, which are publikely to be had; onely thus much I have ever observed, that to find the true *Crysis*, you must as neer as can be obtained, get the hour wherein the Patient first took his Bed; which if it cannot be had, then take the hour when first Judgment was required of the Physitian, and rectifie the *Moon* her motion to that very hour; if the Disease be not chronick, but acute, you shall find great alteration in the Disease and party infirmed, neer upon those times when the *Moon* comes to be distant from that her first place, 45. degrees; so also when she is 90. degrees from that place; and againe, when distant 135. for discovering whether the *Crysis* will be good or ill, you must note what Planet she is in aspect withall at those times, whether with a friendly Planet or an *Infortune*, if she be in a good aspect at those times with a benevolent Planet, it doth promise ease, and a better condition in the Disease; but if she then meet with an ill aspect of the Lord of the eighth or sixth, the Patient will be worse, his paine encrease,

all manner of Questions. 267

creafe, and the Medicine doe little good. I ufually obferve, and I doe not remember that I have failed, *viz.* that as oft as the *Moon* came to □ ☌ or ☍ of that Planet who did any wayes either afflict the afcendant, the Lord of the afcendant or the *Moon*, or when fhe came to the like afpect of the Lord of the fixt, or any Planet that was pofited in the fixt, I fay, then I did ever obferve the Patient to be much diftempered, the Difeafe high, and Medicines given about thofe times to work little or no good effect; when I obferved the *Moon* to come to a △ or ✶ of the Lord of the afcendant, or Lord of the eleventh, or Lord of the ninth or tenth, I ufe to pronounce to the Infirmed, comfort, and fome relaxation or an intervall of eafe; fo alfo, when the Lord of the afcendant came to any good afpect of the ☉ (if he had not power or dominion in the difeafe, I found the Patient's mind much enlightned.

When I find, that by God's bleffing the fick party fhall reco- *How long ere* ver, and it be demanded, When or about what time it is like to *the fick reco-* be? I ufually obferve, who is the Lord of the afcendant, and *ver.* which of the benevolent Planets he is in afpect with, and how many degrees there are diftant betwixt them, in what houfe they both are in, *viz.* whether in Angles, Succedant or Cadent, what Signes they poffeffe, whether Moveable, Fixed or Common, and according to difcretion and quality of the Difeafe, fo I frame my meafure of time; yet ordinarily if the afpect be in moveable Signes, I judge, in fo many dayes the party will amend, the more certainly, I determine, if the *Significators* be fwift in motion, angular. If the application be in common Signes, I neither judge moneths, weeks or dayes, but according as I can with difcretion frame my judgment, having firft obferved the nature of the Difeafe, and poffibility of determining in fuch or fuch a time, the *Ancients* did fay:

Moveable Signes fhew Dayes.
Common Signes, Weeks or Moneths.
Fixed Signes, Moneths or Yeers.
Angles are equivalent to moveable Signes.
Succedant to common Signes.
Cadent to fixed Signes.

Together with the principall *Significators*, confider the quick or flow motion of the ☽, the Signe fhe is in, and its quality, mix all together, and your judgment will be more rationall: I many times find, when the Lord of the afcendant moves out of the Signe he is in at the time of the Queftion, and hath effentiall Dignities in the Signe he is going into, the party recovers then, or fenfibly feels an alteration for good in himfelfe; and fo if the later degrees of a Signe are on the cufp of the fixt, *viz.* if I find 28. degrees, and the Signe common, I fay, the Difeafe will vary in leffe time then two weeks: I might give infinite rules, but in the judgment of a Figure or two fubfequent, I fhall better be underftood in the practicall part of it, and deliver the method I alwayes obferved; but becaufe, together with what I write, the *Reader* might have more variety of judgment; and becaufe nothing in this life is more irkfome then Sickneffe, or more delightfull then health, I have endeavoured to Englifh the *Jatromathematicks* of *Hermes*, much efteemed in all Ages, and here to infert them, as being neceffary to the Judgments of this Houfe.

Hermes Trismegistus *upon the firſt Decumbiture of the Sick.*

THE heavenly Rayes or Influences proceeding and emitted from the feven Planets are multiplied and difperfed into the feverall members of man, even whileft the conception in the Mothers Wombe, doth firſt begin to cleave together: neither verily doth it happen otherwayes when the Child firſt fees the light of this world, but even according to the pofition of the twelve Signes of Heaven, fo doe we affigne the Head to the Signe ♈.

all manner of Questions.

The *Sensitive* Parts or Instruments of Mans Body are thus attributed to the seven Planets.

The right Eye to the ☉, the left to the ☽.
The sense of Hearing and Eares to ♄.
The Braine to ♃, Blood to ♂.
Smelling and Tasting to ♀.
The Tongue, the Weesell-pipe of a mans Throat or Lung-pipe to ☿.

That member suffers a defect or imperfection, of which either at conception or birth an afflicted Planet had dominion, or did signifie the same.

There are also in Man foure more principall and generall parts; the *Head*, the *Breast*, the *Hands*, and *Feet*.

If the Planet who governeth any of those principall parts be unfortunate and ill affected, either at the time of Conception or Birth, the same Planet afflicteth or disfigureth all those parts so attributed unto himselfe, or some particular or principall part of those members.

As when the ☉ or *Moone* be ill disposed or viciated, either the one or both, the eyes receive prejudice; if ♄ the eares, teeth, or sence of hearing. When ☿ is oppressed, we finde a defect in the tongue, or stammering in speech. And in the same manner we may apprehend, whether any part in the Breast, Lungs, Liver, Spleen, Heart, or any of the intestine or inwards of the body be corrupted and infected, radically from the Birth or Conception.

In consideration of the Hands and Feet we shal observe, whether the Fingers, Nailes, or any of these are unperfect or viciated by the affinity of some predominating malignant Planet.

To such defects and imperfections as are within the compasse of cure, convenient Medicines are to be applyed, and we must resist the Diseases proceeding from influence of the Planets, by other Planets of contrary nature and power to the Planet afflicting.

To ♄ are assigned such Medicaments as doe coole or refrigerate, extenuate with drinesse and siccity.

To ☿ such as congeale, are flatuous and windy.

To ♂ such as are calefactive, warme and impletive, as unto a Planet being a very sharpe heater and procurator of blood.

To ♃ and ♀ things conglutinating, mollifying, and are effective to asswage and cure all Ulcers.

The *Moone* helps that Planet, or lends assistance to him, be he good or bad, to whom she applies.

To him therefore that would either cure the Sicke or heale the Lame, the position of Heaven ought to be well considered and knowne, set or erected for the houre of his first falling sick, or lying downe; the Planets and their respective disposition and mutuall habit to and amongst themselves, is carefully to be respected; for without the congresse and influence of these in humane and worldly affaires, nothing is either infirme or sound. No Patient can possibly be cured by the industry of his Physitian, be he never so learned, without the benevolent configuration of the Stars, and happy positure thereof; but he shal either perish, being destitute hereof, or recover and be preserved by their kinde influence.

If the certaine hour of the parties first falling sick cannnot exquisitely be knowne, then carefully take the position of Heaven at that time when judgment is required of the Physitian: therein observe from whom the ☽ is separated, to whom she applies, with what Planet she is in □ or ☍ unto, or with whom in ☌; if she be in configuration with the malevolents, she intimates the Disease will extend almost to death; but with the *Fortunes*, the sick will obtaine remedy more speedily: Observe if she be swift in motion, and encreasing in light, or whether both of them happen at once, or neither of them: for if after her ☌ with the ☉, when she begins to grow great, and as it were, to swell with the encrease of light and motion, she shall then be afflicted by the □ or ☍ of ♂, before she come to ☍ of ☉, and no intervening aspect of a benevolent Planet chance between, she signifies mortall and pernicious Diseases; but if conjoyned, or in good aspect of beneficiall Starres, the infirme Body shall recover, though he were absolutely perswaded he should not live or escape that Disease; but if the ☽ be decreasing in light and motion, and afflicted either by the □

or

or ☍ of ♄ (unlesse presently after ☍ with ♄ the vigor of the Disease remit) the Disease is not curable but mortall; but if she apply to benevolent Planets, the Disease will soone be cured: This is further to be considered, that during the encrease of the ☽ in number and light, the Disease encreaseth: when the ☽ growes slow in motion, the sicknesse diminisheth: this ought carefully to be regarded upon the first insult of every Disease.

Those who at the time of their first lying downe are oppressed by the malignant influence of ♄ or ☿, they are commonly heavy and drowsie, unwillingly moving their diseased Members, stupified or benummed with immoderate cold, or molested with unnaturall defluxions: the Disease by little and little stealeth upon the sick party, nor is he easily awaked though moved thereunto: He is silent in speech, fearfull, desirous of such Plaisters or fomentations as are very hot, and inforce heat; they delight to be without light, as to be in darknesse; he sighes continually, and gently drawes in his breath, or sucks it up, or is short winded; the Pulse is swift and painfull; warme things applyed gives them great comfort; they have feeble Pulses; the outside of their bodies are cold and dry whereby it comes to passe, that in curing such people, that the Physitian ought to apply such Medicines as are naturally hot, doe mollifie and constringe.

Who fall sicke upon any malevolent configuration of the ☉ or ♂, become disturbed in their Minds, perplexed in their Fancies, are troublesome and very rugged in their deportment; the superficiall parts of their bodies being inflamed with a fiery heat. They are prone to anger, make much clamor or noyse, looke peevishly, lye staring, alwayes thirsty by reason of the roughnesse of their parched tongues; desirous of Wine, cold Drinke, importuning the use of Bathes: no manner of Meat whets their appetite; they freely squander out their virulent language against every man; they have a short, depressed and inordinate Pulse; red rubicund faces, oppressed with fulnesse of body. For recovery of these Men, it conduces much to let Blood untill the fifth day, or prescribe such Medicines as evacuate and Purge the foulenesse of their bodies, and to administer

nister such other Remedies as the necessity of nature further requires. What Medicines are agreeable to the nature of ♂ are repugnant to ♄ as not calefactive, emollient, or mollifying and dissolving obstructions.

Medicaments which naturally are concurring with ♄, prove contrary to those of the nature of ♂; as those which are refrigerating or cooling, astringent or binding, and re-percussing.

All infirmities or passions, or tremblings of the heart, and such as proceed from the mouth of the Stomack, Diseases and paines in the Arteries, Veines and Joynts, have originall from the evill influence of ♂ and ☉.

Continued Feavers, Phrensies, Exulceration and inflamation of the Lungs and Lights, and such like Diseases, draw their originall from ♄ and ☿: against such Diseases, Medicines that refrigerate are most proper; of which sort are these:

Nightshade.	The stone Hematites.	Allum.
Coriander.	Purcel and	Flower of the Field-
Endive.	White of an Egge.	Vine.
Juyce of Poppy.	Flax-seed.	The Fruit of both
The Bark of the root	Reed.	Palm-Trees.
Alkakenge.	Leaves of Mallowes.	The Myrrh-Tree.
Knot-grasse.	Pomegranet.	Summach.
Singreen.	Hypocistis.	Fresh Roses.
Fleawort.	Cypresse-Tree.	Bull-rushes.
Lentils.	Blackbrery-Tree.	Ladanum.
Vine-leaves.	Acacia.	Saffron.
White Lead.	Quinces.	Patomagitum.
Silver-froth.	Pirapirastra.	

Such Medicines as are naturally calefactive or hot, are assigned to the dominion of *Mars* and the *Sunne*; whereof some are as followeth:

Oleum Cyprinum.	Unguentum Irinum.	White Daffodille
All things smelling	Cinamon.	Fenigreek.
sweet, and being fragrant.	Sweet Marjorum.	Spikenard
		Myrrh.

all manner of Questions. 273

Myrrh.	Cassia Odorata.	The fome of the Sea in-
Bdellium.	Frankinfence.	durate, or made hard.
Storax calamita.	Ammoniacum.	Helleborus.
The Root Sera.	Rue, or Hearbgrace.	Pyrethrum.
Ocymum.	Mirabolans.	Chryfocalla.
Cummin.	Dry Figges.	Onions.
Pix Liquida, & Solida.	The fome of Salt-peeter	Garlick.
Fat.	Granum Gnidium.	Leeks.
Marrow.	Staves-acre.	Radifh roots,
Galbanum.	The Stone Afius.	Chich Peafe.
Flower de Luce.	Galangal.	

To expulfe and recover thofe Difeafes which have their original rife and caufe from ♄ or ☿ (which afterwards you fhal have difcovered by the courfe of the ☽) fuch manner of Medicines as thefe muft be adminiftred, which do naturally heat and mollifie; but in repreffing Solar and Martiall Difeafes, the learned Phyfitian muft apply fuch Remedies, as by nature are refrigerative, cooling and repercuffive.

Of the fignes and conjectures of the Difeafe, and of life or death by the good or ill pofition of the ☽ at time of the Patients firft lying downe, or demanding the Queftion.

Whofoever fhall firft lye downe of their ficknefle, the ☽ decreafing in light and motion, in any of the twelve Signes, and afflicted by ♄ his □ ☍ or ☌, fhall in part or in all, be partaker of fuch Difeafes as follow, during the time of the continuance of their Difeafe.

Viz. With Head-ach, or heavineffe of the Head, or Rheume, falling downe into the Noftrils, finging in the Eares, ftuffing in the Head, wearineffe or dulneffe of the Eyes, diftillation of Rheumes and corrupt humours falling from the head into the Throat and Wind-pipe, weak Pulfes and inordinate, drowfineffe of mind, loathing of the Stomack, intemperate or unfeafonable Sweats, hot within, cold without, more afflicted by night then day ; if the ☽ be not favoured by the afpect of any good

☽ in ♈ in ☌
□ ☍ of ♄.

M m   Planet

The Resolution of

Planet, without doubt the sick party will dye, God sending no extraordinary remedy. To loosen the Belly represses the grief, to let blood is ill.

☽ in ♉ in ☌ ▫ ☍ of ♄.
Feavers proceeding from obstructions and distemper of the Ppæcordiacks and Arteries, *viz.* of the inward parts neer the Heart, Liver and Lungs, occasioned by too much Luxury, or from Surfets or inordinate Repletion; their Pulses are lofty and high, but immoderate, an inflation or puffing up of the Body, ulceration of the Lungs; if the ☽ be not supported with some gentle aspects of the *Fortunes*, the party will hardly live fourteen dayes; but if the ☽ be, as beforesaid, in any good aspect, beyond expectation the sick may recover. Those Medicines which purge or dissolve grosse Humours, and Phlebotomy are good.

☽ in ♊ in ☌ ▫ ☍ of ♄.
Who fall sick, the ☽ in ♊, afflicted of ♄, by ☌ ▫ or ☍, have the originall of their Disease occasioned by wearinesse of the mind, and over-burdening it with multiplicity of affaires, or some wearinesse in travell, or over-much exercise of body, feare of a small Feaver, the paine disperses it selfe all over the body, but principally in the Arteries or Joynts.

I ever find the Vitals much afflicted when ☽ is in ♊, at the time of any ones *Decumbiture,* and the sick inclinable to a Consumption; with such the Pulse is rare and little, afflicted with frequent sweatings, Simptomes of the Spleen, and the Disease more troublesome in the night then in the day; if ♂, together with ♄, at the same time afflict the ☽, most Authors hold, the sick will not live above ten dayes, unlesse the favourable aspect of ♃ or ♀ intervene, and then after a long time, the sick may recover.

☽ in ♋ in ☌ ▫ ☍ of ♄.
Who fals sick the ☽ afflicted of ♄ in ♋, is much afflicted in the Brest with tough melancholly Matter, or with slimy, thick Flegme, is vexed with Coughs, or abundance of Spittle and moysture, Catarres, Hoarcenesse, distillation of Rheumes, or descending of Humours into the Brest, their Pipes are narrow and obstructed, small Feavers, and many times feare of a Quotidian

all manner of Questions.

tidian Ague, but usually a Quartan Ague followes, holding a long time, Belly-ake, or some infirmnesse in the Reynes or Secrets. If the ☽ be decreasing and neer the Body of ♄, the sicknesse will continue a great space of time; and if together with her affliction, the Lord of the ascendant be impedited by the Lord of the eighth, there's small hopes of recovery.

Those who lye downe or first complaine, the ☽ being impedited of ♄ in ♌, the sicknesse shall proceed of ill melancholy Blood, the sick will be oppressed with unkindly heat in the Brest, intension of the Heart-strings, with violent Feavers, the Pulses are troubled, externall and internall Heats doe much annoy the sick, sometimes they are taken with a fit of the Stone, or faintnesse of Heart, or Swooning, and if the disease doe continue long, the sick is in danger of the Black-jaundies. ☽ *in* ♌ *in* ☌ ☐ ☍ *of* ♄.

Such things as gently moisten and heat, are good for the Diseased; when the ☽ comes to the ☍ of ♄, if the ✶ △ or ☌ of ♃ or ♀ assist not, many times the sick dyeth.

The ☽ in ♍ afflicted by ♄, the Sicknesse proceeds from Crudities and evill digestion in the Stomack, and from too much viscous Flegme obstructing the Bowels and Intrailes, pricking or shooting under the Ribs, inordinate Feavers, many times I find the sick afflicted when the ☽ is in ♍ in aspect of ♄ with the Wind-chollick, with extreame Melancholly, with the Gout or aches in the Thighes and Feet, &c. things which mollifie heat and dissolve, are most proper for the sick; when the cause of the Disease originally rises from this configuration of the ☽ in ♍, unfortunated of ♄, I seldome find by experience but that the Diseased continues sick a great while; for ♍ is an earthly Signe, and ♄ is slow. ☽ *in* ♍ *in* ☌ ☐ ☍ *of* ♄.

The ☽ in ♎ by ♄ afflicted, the Disease hath its originall from some Surfet of Wine, Gluttony, or Meat not fully digested, or too much Venery, the Brest is disaffected, so also the Head, no appetite to eat, a loathing in the Stomack, the Cough, Hoarcenesse, distillation of Rheums afflict him: I have found the sick party, upon this aspect of the ☽ to ♄, to have been troubled ☽ *in* ♎ *in* ☌ ☐ ☍ *of* ♄.

M m 2   with

with great paines in their Joynts, Knees and Thighes, and an itching in those parts, they fearing a Sciatica.

☽ in ♏ in ☌ □ ☍ of ♄.
♄ afflicting the *Moon* in ♏, the Disease is in *Ano* or *Anglice* [Arse-hole] usually an Ulcer there, or the Hemorroids or Piles, or some Exulceration or Bubo, [*Anglice*] a botch in the Privy-members.

I find by experience, if a man or woman enquire upon the *Moon* her affliction by ♄ in ♏, there's no retention of Urine, the party is vexed with the Stone in the Bladder, or with a swelling dropsical Humour, offending and swelling about their Knees and Legs; as also, sometimes they have a Flux, if a man then the Gonorrea; if a woman, too much aboundance of Menstrua's.

☽ in ♐ in ☌ □ ☍ of ♄.
♄ afflicting the *Moon*, the diseased party is sensibly oppressed with Deflux of subtill, thin, sharp Humours, griefes in the Arteries or Joynts, feare of a Feaver, extremities of heat and cold, many times a double accesse of a Feaver; what mitigates heat gently, and moystens, is good for such people as fall sick under this aspect.

I find by experience, that the *Moon* in ♐, afflicted by a ☌ of ♄, doth cause the Disease to proceed from Blood infected with choller and melancholly, and many times by too great painestaking, or violent exercise, and cold thereupon taken; upon the ☍ of the *Moon* and ♄, for the most part the sick hath a spice of the Gout, or some Tumour or Swelling in his Hands, or Thighes, or Feet, &c. If ♂ have any ill aspect to the *Moon* as well as ♄ at time of first falling sick, it proves a violent burning Feaver.

☽ in ♑ in ☌ □ ☍ of ♄.
The Disease proceeds from Cold or Melancholly, with subtill, thin Distillations, heavinesse of the Brest and Stomack, difficulty of breathing, dry Coughs, the Lungs oppressed intended Feavers, more pained in the night then in the day time: Medicines that heat and moysten moderately doe availe in this Disease.

I find the party still complaining of the Head-ach, or paine in

all manner of Questions.

in the left Eare, or of a Rumbling or Noyſe in his Head.

The Sickneſſe hath beginning, or is occaſioned from too much labour, weariſomneſſe or toyling the Body and Minde, want of ſleepe and due refreſhment of nature: the Malady ceaſeth on him unequally, with remiſſion and intenſion, untill the ☽ have paſt the oppoſition of her owne place, then if your fortunes have any good Aſpect to the *Moone*, the Sicke is recoverable. ☽ *in* ♒ *in* ♂
☐ ☍ *of* ♄ .

I finde the Sicke complaining or lying downe under the preceding malevolent Aſpect, to be grieved with winde or noyſe in the head, with faint fits or paſſions of the heart; or many times they have either a ſore throat, or are troubled with a riſing there, and in danger of ſuffocation.

The Malady its cauſe, is from cold diſtillations; the party is afflicted with continuall Feavers, oft and continuall ſighings, pricking or ſhootings under the Paps, extenſions of the precordiacks and hart-ſtrings. ☽ *in* ♓ *in* ♂
☐ ☍ *of* ♄ .

I finde the Sicke have ſurfeited by ſome extremity of cold, that their throat is oppreſſed with thicke fleagme, and their breſt is troubled with a rotten cough and aboundance of watery matter lodging there.

Thoſe Medicines that heat and gently caliſie are good in theſe caſes.

As we have treated of ſuch Diſeaſes as may afflict any one upon their firſt falling Sicke or Decumbiture, the ☽ *being in any of the* 12. *Signes and oppreſſed by* ♄ , *or indeed by* ☿ : *ſo now we will endeavour to ſhew the quality of the Diſeaſe from the* ☽ *her affliction from* ♂ *or the* ☉ *through the* 12. *Signes of the Zodiacke.*

Who fall ſick the ☽ in ☌ ☐ or ☍ of ♂ in ♈ , their diſeaſe ſhall proceed from a diſtempered affection of the Membranes or Pellices of the braine, continuall Feavers, no reſt or quietneſſe; an hot thirſty mouth, extreame thirſt, drineſſe of the tongue, hot Liver or inflamation thereof, much heat in the Breſt, high and ſublated Pulſes, keeping no order, a Phrenſie may be feared, or ☽ *in* ♈ *in* ♂
☐ ☍ *of* ♂

Mm 3 depriva-

deprivation of Sences: letting of Blood and such things as do coole and nourish are very helpfull.

If the ☽ next after her seperation from the Malevolent beames or aspect of ♂ doe also apply to ☌ or ☍ of ♄, and she decreasing in light and slow in motion, there's small hopes of life; let the sicke prepare for God. I finde, usually the ☽ being in ♈ afflicted of ♂ the party is almost ready to run mad, or hath some extreame paine or griefe in his Belly or smal guts occasioned by chollericke obstructions.

☽ in ♉ in ☌ □ ☍ of ♂.   The party falling sicke, hath too much abundance of ill Blood, continuall Feavers, the whole frame of the body obstructed, inflamation of the throat, neck and hinder-part therof, ach of the bones, ungentle slumbers, but no sleepe, a foolish longing after Wine and cold water. Blood letting and such things as moderately coole or allay heat are necessary.

I finde ☽ in ♉ afflicted by ♂, the Patient is afflicted with the strangury, or stone, or gravell in the Reines and Kidneys, with pestilent soare throats, or horcenesse, or some malignity there in that member.

☽ in ♊ in ☌ □ ☍ of ♂.   Who takes his or their Bed the *Moone* in ♊ afflicted by ♂, usually shall undergoe a violent and dangerous Feaver, obstructions; high and inordinate Pulses attend such; the blood is too hot, and a necessity there is of emission of blood, the whole body being neer corruption, by reason of the ranknesse of blood.

I finde those falling sicke the *Moone* in ♊ afflicted by ♂, to be pained all over the body, the Disease in no place setled, their Blood extreamly windy, corrupted, and what not, some lamenesse or griefe in their Armes or joynts, and afflicted with the stone or heat in the reines, and sometimes spitting of blood.

☽ in ♋ in ☌ □ ☍ of ♂.   The *Moone* afflicted by ♂ in ♋, the Sicke is sensible of great abundance of sweet fleagme in his stomacke, hath too much ingurgitated, or taken some surfeit, oft vomits or desires so to do, with eversion or turning of the ventricle.

I find

all manner of Questions. 279

I finde, ufually its a meer furfeit gotten by riot and exceffe, and moft that I have feen thus afflicted have been cured by Vomit; many times it turnes to a loofeneffe, or a rotten filthy cough, fometimes fpitting of blood.

In this cafe too much blood abounds and therby ftrong Feavers, very weake Pulfes, raving and ftrong raging fits, a difturbed Braine, depravation of appetite, heavineffe and drowfineffe all over the body, many diftempers of the heart; the body in danger of a Confumption; ufually they dye about the ninth day after the firft falling ficke, if other configurations of heavens accord. ☽ in ♌ in ♂ □ ☍ of ♂.

I finde the Blood over-heated, the party almoft ftarke raging mad, choller in exceffe abounding, the body over-dryed, a probability of the Plurifie; faintneffe and fwooning, or the heart very much afflicted; I evermore feare this dangerous ♂ or ☍ of ♂ and the *Moone* in this Signe, more then in any of the Zodiacke.

Ufually in alteration or flux in the Belly, or miferaicks followes this unluckie pofition, fmall Feavers, the originall choller and melancholly, the Pulfe remiffe, everfion of the ventricle loathing of food; death within thirty dayes, if the fortunes affift not. ☽ in ♍ in ♂ □ ☍ of ♂.

I have by experience found, the afflicted upon this afpect or afpects, to be tormented with the winde, chollicke, many times weakneffe in the legges or neere the ancles. Yet I did never finde any Difeafe eafily removeable, if the *Moone* at time of the decumbiture, or firft falling ill, was afflicted by ♂ in ♍.

The Patient is grieved with plenitude of Blood, and from that caufe hath intended Feavers, high Pulfes, abftaines from fleepe, hath no naturall reft; an inflamation all over the body. ☽ in ♎ in ♂ □ ☍ of ♂.

I obferve in this kinde, fick people upon this kinde are oppreffed with Blood over-heated, have taken fome furfeit by diforder in dyet; many times have the ftone or gravell in their kidneys, or great heat therein.   Glifter,

Glifter, and such things as gently coole, are best in this nature; many times the Disease is all over the Body, in every part; and most violent burning Feavers follow. Blood letting is good.

☽ in ♏ in ☌
☐ ☍ of ♂.

Its neither better or worse with the party inquiring, but that he or she hath some grievous infirmenesse in his or her privie parts. There's usually some exulceration, the Pox small or French (or Mesels, if children) the Hemerods or Pyles.

I observe the Sicke offended with snafling in the Head, or some grievous colds or rheumes in that member; if the party looke like a wanton, the French Pox or a Gonorrea or burnt Prick, without more words I doe judge: many times I find the party scabby and oppressed with breakings out, &c.

This is corruption of Blood, &c. such things as heat and comfort, are now necessary; the Disease usually is a scandalous one. Let a modest party propound the Question; there's cause to distrust foule play, &c. if a Man propound, the Wife may be faulty, &c, *in Contrario.*

☽ in ♐ in ☌
☐ ☍ of ♂.

Such an affliction of the *Moone* in ♐ intimates, the sick party is grieved with a very desperate Disease, occasioned from surfetting or gluttony, or too much repletion; he is tormented with high Feavours, with cholerick passions, with the Flux or Laske: the Pulses are few and faint, or beat slowly and weakly. If the Sicke escape the seventh day, or know properly that day when the *Moone* comes to a true ☐ of the place she was in at first lying downe; there's then hopes of recovery.

I daily find by experience, the sick party his Blood is overheated by some inordinate exercise, that he burnes extreamly, sometimes the malignancy of the pestilent Feaver is such, he is twice or thrice let Blood; they are besides many times offended with the Hand and Foot-gout, or Itches and breakings out, and sometimes with sore Throats, &c. at other times sharp Rheums offend their Eyes.

☽ in ♑ in ☌
☐ ☍ of ♂.

Here appears no perfect concoction, Choller abounds, the sick desires to vomit, there's inappetency of the Ventricle, a
swelling

swelling of puffing up the Sinews, a Flux of the Belly followes immediatly, continuall or oft returning Feavers, inflamation of the Breſt, ſome Exulceration offends the party, or a cholerick humour his Hands or Joynts of his Fingers. Obſtructive and conſtringent Medicines are uſefull, their Pulſes are remiſſe and flow.

I find the ſick Inclinable to the Yellow-jaundies, their Countenance meagre, and their Perſons exceeding leane, and that the Blood all over the Body is diſaffected, and the Diſeaſe is very hard to be cured by the moſt Learned; ſuch uſually have very little Blood, or their Blood is corrupted to purpoſe, or in the higheſt meaſure.

If the ☽ be ſlow in motion, and decreaſing in light, when a Diſeaſe firſt takes the party, and is afflicted of ♂, the Infirmity proceeds from moſt ſharp and violent affections, or vehement paſſions; any favourable Planet caſting his good aſpect unto the ☽, either at her firſt □ to her owne place, or when ſhe comes to ☍ of that degree of the *Zodiack* ſhe was in at the firſt lying downe, gives preſent remedy after twenty dayes.   ☽ *in* ♓ *in* ♂ □ ☍ *of* ♂.

Experience hath informed me, that upon the preceding aſpects, eſpecially upon the ☍, the ſick hath been pained at the Heart, troubled with ſwooning fits, had a moſt deſperate Feaver, the Blood ſwelling in all the Veines, high Pulſes; ſometimes they complaine of great paine in their Breſt, and draw their Wind with great difficulty.

When the ☽ is afflicted of ♂ in this Signe ♓, and is encreaſing in light, and ſwift in motion, the Body is full of groſſe Humours, the Diſeaſe proceeds from too much ingurgitation, ſwilling and drinking, the Diſeaſe is moſt prevalent in the night time, the party is vexed with a phrenetick Out-rage or *Delirium*, hath ſharp burning Feavers, vehement thirſt, and is deſirous of Wine.   ☽ *in* ♒ *in* ♂ □ ☍ *of* ♂.

Uſually I find, the party ſick or enquiring, when the ☽ is of ♂ in ♓ ſo afflicted, oppreſſed with a violent Looſneſſe, and grievouſly complaining of paine in their Bellies, or an extraordinary rotten Cough, and continuall defluxion of Rheume from the Head into the Throat, the party almost suffocated therewith, their Bellies swollen, and they in danger of a Dropsie.

Astrologicall APHORISMES beneficiall for PHYSICIANS.

IN *Questions concerning sick People, give the ascendant and his Lord and the Lord of the Figure for Significators of the sick party.*

2 *From the Signe of the sixt, the Lord of that House, Planets therein placed, and place of Heaven and Signe wherein the ☽ is, require the Disease or part afflicted, with relation to the ascendant.*

3 *The seventh house represents the Physician, the tenth his Medicine; if the Lord of the seventh be unfortunate, the Physician shall not cure; if the tenth house or Lord thereof, his Physick is improper.*

4 *The fourth house signifies the end of the sicknesse, and whether it will terminate quickly, or endure long: fixed Signes prolong, common Signes vary the Disease, moveable ones shew an end one way or other quickly.*

5 *That Physician who first visits his Patient in the houre of ♄, his Patient shall either be long sick, or long in curing, and suffers much torment in his cure; nor shall he be cured, untill almost both Physician and Patient despaired.*

6 *He that first enters upon a cure in the hour of ♂, shall find his Patient disaffected to him, and partly disdaine or reject his Medicines, his pains ill rewarded, and his person slighted.*

7 *He that first visits his Patient in the hour of ♃ or ♀, shall have good words of the sick, be well esteemed and paid for his paines; though he faile of the cure, yet shall he receive no prejudice thereby; I meane, in point of estimation.*

8 *When a Urine is brought, let the ascendant represent the sick Party, whether the Querent come with consent or no, for the Urine was sometimes of the essence of the sick.*

9 *If no Urine or consent of the sick party come to the Physician, then*

all manner of Questions.

the Ascendant presents the Querent; but the person and sicknesse must be required according to the relation the Querent hath to the sick party: A man for his servant, the sixt shall shew his person, not his Disease, that must be from the sixt to the sixt, which is the eleventh, & sic in aliis, where no consent is.

10 But in every Disease have care to the place of the ☽, for she is a generall Significatrix in all things.

11 The sick party is in great danger of death, when at the time of the Question asked, or when the sicknesse first invaded the sick party, both the ☉ and ☽ are under the Earth.

12 As no light is in this World without the presence of the ☉ or ☽, so no safety, or hopes of recovery in the sick, when they are obscured or subterranean at first lying downe of the sicke, and it's a greater argument of death, if either of them be then afflicted.

13 The □ or ☍ of the Fortunes, as it destroyeth not, so neither doth the benevolent aspect of the Infortunes profit, unlesse that aspect be with Reception.

14 If the ☉ and ☽, or Lord of the Figure, or Lord of the ascendant be free from affliction, and have no affinity with the Lord of the eighth, without doubt the sick party will recover; if two of these Significators be so affected, it will goe well with him, otherwise he dyes.

15 The Lord of the ascendant in his Fall, unfortunate or Combust, or else the Lord of the Figure, it's doubtfull the sick party will dye of that Infirmity.

16 When the Significator of the sick is feeble, and the Lord of the eighth strong and afflicting him, it's much feared the sick party will dye of his then infirmnesse, nature being weak, and the Disease prevalent.

17 If the Lord of the ascendant be placed in the eighth, and received of the Lord of the eighth by some essentiall Dignity, though the Lord of the ascendant receive not him againe, the sick party recovers beyond expectation.

18 The Physitian may justly feare his Patient, when the Lord of the ascendant and the ☽ do both apply by ill aspect to a Planet under the Earth; the contrary is to be expected, if they apply to a Planet above the Earth: the twelfth, eleventh, ninth, eighth seventh houses are above the Earth, the rest under.

19 The Lord of the eighth being on the cusp of the tenth, and the Lord of the ascendant under the Earth, there's great fear of recovery.

The Resolution of

20 If the ☽ be swift in course, and encreasing in light, and by a ✶ or △ apply to the Lord of the ascendant, though under the earth, it hastens the cure, the more easily if any Reception be ; the cure must needs be sooner if the application be above the Earth to the Lord of the ascendant.

21 If the Lord of the ascendant be in the sixt, or the Lord of the sixt in the ascendant, it protracts the Disease, and is an argument of much affliction therein ; so also doth the □ or ☍ of the Lord of the sixt to the Lord of the ascendant.

22 If the two benevolent Planets ♃ and ♀ be most powerfull in the Figure, judge well to the sick, or hope well ; if the Infortunes be most strong, judge the contrary.

23 The application of the Lord of the fourth, to the Conjunction of the Lord of the eighth, prolongs the Infirmity, and also signifieth Death, if the Lord of the fourth be an Infortune ; of a benevolent expect the contrary.

24 A Retrograde Planet Significator of the Disease, shewes the continuance of it, and argues the Bodies Consumption, Back-sliding and Relapses.

25 The Significator being stationary, shewes aptnesse and desire to vomit, and the oft change and variation of the Disease ; but if he be combust of the ☉, for the most part the sick dyes: and the reason is, a Planet stationary hath time to work mischiefe, because he moves not.

26 A Significator in his Fall or Detriment, shewes ill and much danger, and argues much distrust and fear in the sick party.

27 The ascendant and the ☽ being afflicted, and the Lord of the one and Dispositor of the other not so, the Disease is in the Body, not in the Spirits :

28 But the ascendant and ☽ free from misfortune, and their Lords unfortunate, the griefe lyes in the Spirits, not in the Body ; but if both be afflicted, both Body and mind are tormented : so also, if a malevolent Planet behold the ascendant and not the ☽, the Disease is in the Animals, not in the Body, and so on the contrary.

29 The Lord of the sixt in the ascendant, ninth, eleventh or tenth house, the Disease is manifest ; in the seventh or fourth, it lyes occult and not knowne, and so in the twelfth or eighth.

30 Moveable Signes easily cause the Disease to vary ; fixed Signes make it long and permanent, and not without much difficulty ; removeable, common, shew recidivation, or that it's now here, now there,

all manner of Questions.

there, or that the sick party *is* much better at one time then another.

31 In the beginning of Diseases, ever feare the ill positure and affliction of the ☽, mix the signification with the well or ill being of the Lord of the ascendant, and so judge of the good or ill attending the sick.

32 If the Nativity of the sick may be obtained, observe if the ☽ at the time of the first Decumbiture or Question asked, be then in a place where an Infortune was in the Radix, or in □ or ☍ thereof, the cure will goe on the more hardly, and be more difficult to overcome.

33 If in the beginning of a sicknesse the ☽ be in the sixt of the Nativity, fourth, seventh, eighth or twelfth, and both times there happens to be an Infortune, it doth manifest death, unlesse a Fortune at one of those times cast thither his benevolent Beames.

34 When the ascendant of the sicknesse is opposite to that of the Nativity, and is either the fourth, sixth, eighth, twelfth or seventh, the ascendant of the Revolution being not the same, it shews hardly any recovery.

35 When the Lord of the second doth infortunate the Lord of the ascendant the sick shall not be cured without much expence of his money; or if he dye, he spends most part or much upon his cure to no purpose.

36 The ☉ in the ascendant brings usually health immediatly; if in the sixt, the sicknesse presently changes; if the Lord of the eighth be combust, the sick shall recover and not dye at that time.

37 The ☉ is the candle or light of Heaven, and that Spirit which clarifies and beautifies those Signes he is in, destroying natures enemies.

38 Fear not the death of thy Patient if ♃ be in a good aspect to the ☉, although the Lord of the ascendant apply to the Lord of the eighth.

39 When a sicknesse takes one first, at what time the ☽ separates from combustion, the sicknesse will encrease untill the ☽ doth come to Opposition of the ☉.

40 The Lord of the ascendant being unfortunate in the eighth, the Patient will much encrease the Disease and retard the cure by his ill government and carelesnesse.

41 The Significator of the sick Occidentall, denotes chronick Diseases; but Orientall, new Sicknesse: consider the separation of the ☽, and as she separates or applyes, so will the Disease decrease or encrease, &c.

42 If ♄ be author of the Disease, it proceeds of Cold; if ♂ or the ☉,

it

it proceeds of Heat and Drinesse; and so doe in the signification of the rest of the Planets.

43 The ☽ *is more afflicted of* ♂ *when she is encreased in light, and more oppressed by* ♄ *in her wane: beware in the beginning of a sicknesse when the* ☽ *is thus unfortunated, and understand* ♂ *doth more mischiefe when he is in masculine Signes, Orientall and above the Earth: doe the contrary in the judgment of* ♄.

CHAP. XLV.
A sick Doctor, what was his Disease? If curable?

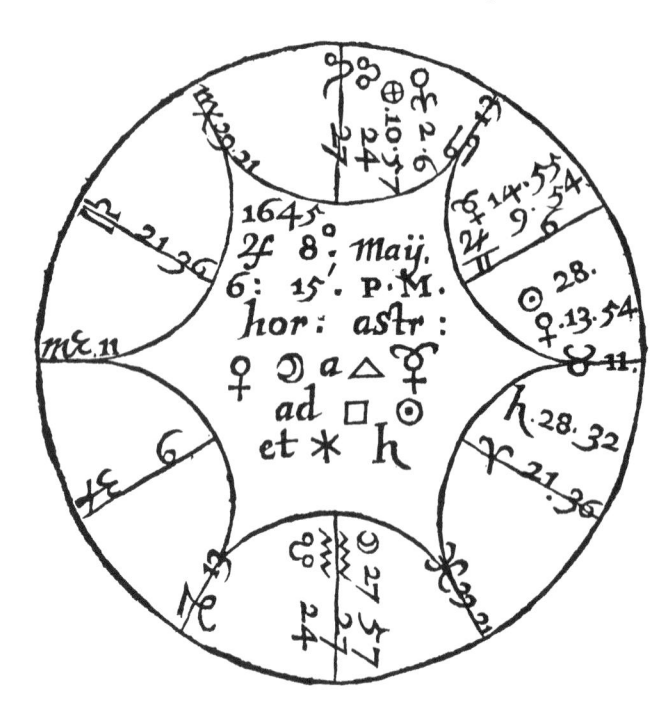

What part of the Body was afflicted.

THE Signe ascending in this Question is ♏, the *Chelæ* notable fixed Stars neer unto the ascendant, yet is it not affli-
&ed

all manner of Questions.

&ed by the evill pofition or prefence of any evill Planet; therefore I muſt next look to the fixt houſe, and ſee if it be afflicted, wherein I find ♄ in his Fall, who thereby afflicts that houſe, which naturally ſignifies Difeafes by his unlucky prefence, from whence I concluded, that from thence and from that houſe I muſt require the part or member of the Body afflicted or moſt grieved, as you may read *page* 244.

♈ repreſents the Head, as you may ſee *page* 245.
♄ in ♈ ſignifieth the Breſt, as *page* 113.
♂ Lord of the afcendant in ♌ doth ſignifie the Heart.

The Lord of the afcendant is ♂, and him you may find but lately ſeparated from a □ *dexter* of ♄, both of them in Cardinall Signes, ♂ at time of that □ in ♋, which prefents the Breſt and Stomack: from hence I poſitively concluded, as to the parts of Body grieved, they were the Head, Breſt, Heart and Stomack, and that there lodged in the Breſt or Stomack ſome melanchollick Obſtruction, the cauſe of all his difeafe and Miſery.

From what Cauſe the Sickneſſe was.

♄ Being principall *Significator* of the Infirmity, in his owne Termes, and the ☽ in his houſe applying unto him, did prenote Melancholly, and ſuch dry Difeafes as are occaſioned from melancholly diſtempers, and might abide in the Head and Breſt: what Infirmities ♄ naturally ſignifieth, ſee *page* 244. how to make a right mixture, your Phyſicians beſt know, and what Difeafes man may be ſubject unto in thoſe parts, and may proceed from ſuch cauſes as aboveſaid.

♂ Lord of the afcendant was alfo in the Termes of ♄, and the ☽ out of his Termes, applyed to a □ of ☉, and he in ♂ his Termes; ſo that Choller was a fecondary cauſe of this Doctor's ſickneſſe; and indeed when I came to ſpeak with him, he was afflicted with great paine and rumbling in his head, very ſilent, dull and melancholy, ſlept very little, had a very dry Cough, and complained of great weakneſſe and paine in his Breſt, and at the Heart; his Complexion was betwixt black and yellow, as if there was inclination to the Jaundies; he had beſides

sides these, a lingring Consumption and great wearinesse all over him, and in every joynt, for the ☽ is in an ayery Signe; and as ♏ doth ascend, which signifies the Secrets, Stone in the Bladder; so doth also the ☽ in ♒ signifie the Secrets and Diseases therein, &c. so had he difficulty in making Urine, voyded red gravell, and was greatly pained in those parts, &c. Having my selfe little judgment in Physick, I advised him to prescribe for himselfe such Physicall Medicines as were gently hot, moyst and cordiall, whereby he might for a while prolong his life; for the ☽ in the fourth in ✶ with ♄, argued sicknesse untill death: *He dyed the fourteenth of August following.*

Whether the Disease would be long or short?

♄ Being author of the Disease, shewed it would be permanent, or of some continuance, as *page* 248. for he is a ponderous, flow Planet: besides, the Angles of the Figure are all fixed, the ☽ and ☉ both in fixed Signes, and in ☐, out of Angles, both in the Termes of an *Infortune*; ♂ Lord of the ascendant and fixt in a fixed Signe; all these portended the longitude of the Disease: Besides, the Antiscion of ♂ fals neer the ☉, and thereby afflicteth him, being the *Luminary* of the time.

CHAP.

Chap. XLVI.
Whether the Sick would live or dye, and what his Disease was?

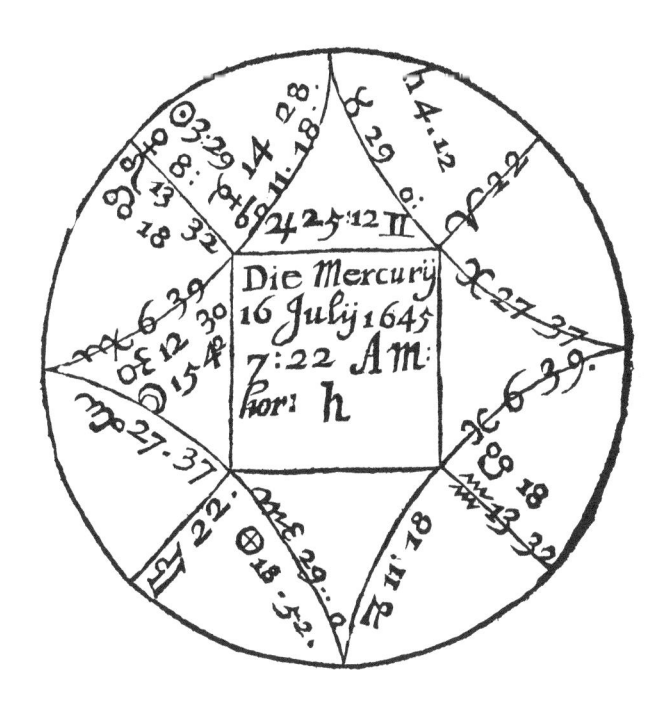

Judgment of the Figure aforesaid.

THe Signe ascending, *viz.* ♍, is in the Figure most afflicted by the corporall presence of ♂, who is partly Lord of the eighth house, therefore from that house and Signe must we require the Disease, cause, and member grieved : ♒ being the Signe of the sixt, is fixed, afflicted by ☋, and ♄ who is Lord of the sixt house is in ♉, a fixed Signe, earthly and melancholly, of the same nature and Triplicity that ♍, the Signe ascending, is of; the ☽ a generall *Significatrix* in all Diseases, being afflicted by her proximity to ♂ and posited in the
ascendant

ascendant, in an earthly, melancholly Signe, together with the other *Significators*, did portend the Patient to be wonderfully afflicted with the Spleen, with the Wind-chollick, and melancholly obstructions in the Bowels or small Guts, small Feavers, a remisse Pulse; and as the Signe ♍ is the Signe ascending, and ☽ and ♂ therein, it argued, the sick was perplexed with distempers in his Head, slept unquietly, &c. [*All which was true.*]

I perswaded the man to make his peace with God, and to settle his house in order, for I did not perceive by naturall causes, that he could live above ten or twelve dayes.

And my reasons were, because all the *Significators* did promise no lesse then death: for first, ☉ who was the temporall light at time of the *Quere*, and is *(fons vitalis potentiæ)* was in perfect □ of ♄ Lord of the sixt in Signes fixed.

Secondly, the ascendant was extreamly afflicted by the presence of ♂, he being naturally ill, and accidentally almost Lord of the whole eighth house.

Thirdly, the ☽ was neer *Cauda Leonis*, and afflicted by the crosse influence of ♂, in that house which signifies Life, *viz.* the ascendant.

Fourthly, the ☽ did separate from the ✶ of ♀, Lord of the ascendant, in Signes of long ascensions (which is more properly a □ aspect) and did transfer his vertue to ♃ Lord of the eighth.

The sick dyed the 28th of *July* following, ☿ comming to the degree of the ☉ in the Question, and therein to the □ of ♄ Lord of the sixt, the day preceding; and the ☽ to an ☍ of the ☉, the ☽ that day transiting the degree of the sixt house at time of the Question, *viz.* 14. of ♒, and ☉ the cusp of the twelfth.

Chap. XLVII.
Of the Crysis in Diseases.

CRysis is no other thing then a duell or contention betwixt nature and the infirmity; if nature at time of the
Cryst

all manner of Questions.   291

Cryſis overcome the malignity of the Diſeaſe, it's a good *Cryſis*; if the ſickneſſe prevaile, it's a pernicious and ill *Cryſis*. Or

CRYSIS is no more then this, *viz.* A ſudden alteration of man's body when he is ſick, tending either to health or further ſickneſſe; for when this *Cryſis* is, there's a ſharp fight, as it were, betwixt nature and the Diſeaſe, whether of them ſhall overcome.

Dayes *Criticall, Decretory* and *Chryſmall* are all one, and intend no more then a certaine and more ſure judgment of the infirmity afflicting, either more powerfully, or in a leſſe meaſure at thoſe times when the true *Chryſis* is.

The true *Cryſis* is beſt of all taken from that moment of time when firſt the ſickneſſe invaded the Infirme; which if it cannot be had, then it may be taken (but not ſo certainly) from the very hour when firſt the Water is brought to the Doctor to adviſe for recovery: but if no Urine come, then when the Doctor firſt ſpeaks with the ſick party, and is demanded by the *Infirmed* what he thinks of his ſickneſſe, and what courſe he would adviſe for cure thereof.

Every ſudden and vehement motion of the diſeaſe may be called a *Cryſis* as *Galen* ſaith; or it is, not a locall motion altogether, but an alteration of the Diſeaſe.

Or *Cryſis* imports judgment in the diſeaſe afflicting, and which way it will terminate, *viz.* for good or evill.

Hypocrates will have *Cryſis* to be an acute or ſwift reportation in diſeaſes, either to recovery or death: But, ſay ſome, *in regard there are more diſeaſes to terminate in health then in death* (except peſtilentiall diſeaſes) *where the matter and cauſe is ſo malignant and poyſonous, that nature many times doth not attend a fight or combate with the Diſeaſe, whereby it cannot properly be called a* Cryſis; *that definition of* Hypocrates *will not well hold, unleſſe it be in ſuch diſeaſes as doe determine in a recovery of the ſick party:* So ſome ſay.

Avicenna, in *Canticis*, agrees with *Galen*, and ſaith, *Cryſis* (*eſt velox motus morbi ad ſalutem vel ad mortem.*)

There are ſome that have contended, *That although in diſeaſes there is a* Cryſis, *yet is it not cauſed by influence of the Celeſtiall bodies, but from inferiour cauſes.*

Now if this were granted that *Decretory* or *Criticall-dayes* did

Oo 2   proceed

proceed from inferiour caufes, then according to divers ficknefses and variety of humours, the feverall *Criticall-dayes* were to be affumed, after a different way in tertians, quartans and continued Feavers: But this, as many learned fay, cannot be, therefore it is more generally received and concluded, That in regard of the great dominion and influence the ☽ hath upon our inferiour Bodies, whereby fhe doth excite and ftir up the humours, that fhe by her motion doth declare the true *Cryfis* of the difeafe, and that it is required from the time of the fick parties firft falling fick, and her recefse and accefse forward and backward to and from that place or degree of the Zodiack, wherein fhe was at the exact time of falling fick; or if that time cannot be procured, then as beforefaid, take her true place exactly rectified to the hour of the Patients firft asking advice. I have hereunto inferted a Table, wherewith if you enter with the place of the ☽ in Signe and degree, you fhall eafily difcover when fhe comes to an *Indicative* day, when to a *Semi-quadrate* or halfe *Cryfis*) when to a true □, when to an ☍ (which is called a full *Cryfis*, and fo to all the *Indicative* and *Criticall* dayes during the ficknefse, &c. As for example; let the place of the ☽ in the later Figure of the 16th of *July* 1645. be fuppofed the true period or beginning of a Difeafe, the place of the ☽ is 15. 42. ♍; becaufe 42. minutes doe almoft make one degree, I enter with 16. degr. under the Signe ♍ in the eighth column, fo that 16. degr. of ♍ is my *Radix*, or true place of the ☽; over againft 16. degr. to the right hand, I find 8. 30. over the head thereof ♎, fo that when the ☽ came to 8. degr. and 31. min. of ♎, it was the firft *Indicative* day, wherein the Phyfician might expect how the difeafe then would fhew it felfe; upon every *Cryfis* or *Indicative* day, have confideration with what Planet the ☽ is in configuration; if with a benevolent, expect fome remifnefse in the difeafe; if with a malevolent, a bad indication, &c.

Next on the right hand to 8. 30. ♎, you find 1. ♏, *viz.* when the ☽ came to the firft of ♏, fhe was then in *Semi-quadrate* to her firft place, and this is, as it were, halfe a *Cryfis*, at what time the difeafe might more or lefse manifeft it felfe according to that afpect the ☽ found at her being in that firft degree

all manner of Questions. 293

gree of ♏. In the next column on the right hand, you see 23. 30. over it ♏, it tels you, when the ☽ came to the 23. and 30. min. of ♏, it was a second *Indicative* day, whereby the Physician might further judge of the encrease or decrease of the disease: In the next column you find 16. over it ♐, when the ☽ came to the 16th of ♐ there was then a true *Crysis*, at what time the disease assuredly might be more fully discerned in one kind or other, and then, according to the aspects the ☽ in that degree had to the Planets, good or ill, so might the Patient or Physician expect a better or worse *Crysis* : and so In the same continued line or column, you run round the Heavens, ever observing the ☽ her comming to those places of the Zodiack, wherein she makes the *Indicative* or *Criticall* day, and what Planets she is then in aspect with, and whether in the Figure they promise good or ill : Besides this, you shall observe what dayes she transits the cusps of the sixt, seventh, and eighth houses, and how then she is aspected of the benevolent or ill Planets.

O o 3   *The*

The Resolution of

The Table followeth.

♈	♈	♉	♊	♋	♋	♌	♍	♎	♎	♏	♐	♑	♑	♒	♓
0 30	23	15 30	8	0 30	23	15 30	8	0 30	23	15 30	8	0 30	23	15 30	8
1 30	24	16 30	9	1 30	24	16 30	9	1 30	24	16 30	9	1 30	24	16 30	9
2 30	25	17 30	10	2 30	25	17 30	10	2 30	25	17 30	10	2 30	25	17 30	10
3 30	26	18 30	11	3 30	26	18 30	11	3 30	26	18 30	11	3 30	26	18 30	11
4 30	27	19 30	12	4 30	27	19 30	12	4 30	27	19 30	12	4 30	27	19 30	12
5 30	28	20 30	13	5 30	28	20 30	13	5 30	38	20 30	13	5 30	28	20 30	13
6 30	29	21 30	14	6 30	29	21 30	14	6 30	29	21 30	14	6 30	29	21 30	14
7 30	30	22 30	15	7 30	30	22 30	15	7 30	30	22 30	15	7 30	30	22 30	15
8 30	♉	23 30	16	8 30	♌	23 30	16	8 30	♏	23 30	16	8 30	♒	23 30	16
9 30	2	24 30	17	9 30	2	24 30	17	9 30	2	24 30	17	9 30	2	24 30	17
10 30	3	25 30	18	10 33	3	25 30	18	10 30	3	25 30	18	10 30	3	25 30	18
11 30	4	26 30	19	11 30	4	26 30	19	11 30	4	26 30	19	11 30	4	26 30	19
12 30	5	27 28	20	12 30	5	27 30	20	12 30	5	27 30	20	12 30	5	27 30	20
13 30	6	28 30	21	13 30	6	28 30	21	13 30	6	28 30	21	13 30	6	28 30	21
14 30	7	29 30	22	14 30	7	29 30	22	14 30	7	29 30	22	14 15	7	29 30	22
15 30	8	1 ♊ 30	23	15 30	8	1 ♍ 30	23	15 30	8	1 ♐ 30	23	15 30	8	1 ♓ 30	23
16 30	9	2 30	24	16 30	9	2 30	24	16 30	9	2 30	24	16 30	9	2 30	24
17 30	10	3 30	25	17 30	10	3 30	25	17 30	10	3 30	25	17 30	10	3 30	25
18 30	11	4 30	26	18 30	11	4 30	26	18 30	11	4 30	26	18 30	11	4 30	26
19 30	12	5 30	27	19 30	12	5 30	27	19 30	12	5 30	27	19 30	12	5 30	27
20 30	13	6 30	28	20 30	13	6 30	28	20 30	13	6 30	28	20 30	13	6 30	28
21 30	14	7 30	29	21 30	14	7 30	29	21 30	14	7 30	29	21 30	14	7 30	29
22 30	15	8 30	30	22 30	15	8 30	30	22 30	15	8 30	30	22 30	15	8 30	30
23 30	16	9 30	♋	23 30	16	9 30	♎	23 30	16	9 30	♑	23 30	16	9 30	♈
24 30	17	10 30	2	24 30	17	10 30	2	24 30	17	10 30	2	24 30	17	10 30	2
25 30	18	11 30	3	25 30	18	11 30	3	25 30	18	11 30	3	25 30	18	11 30	3
26 30	19	12 30	4	26 30	19	12 30	4	26 30	19	12 30	4	26 30	19	12 30	4
27 30	20	13 30	5	27 30	20	13 30	5	27 30	20	13 30	5	27 30	20	13 30	5
28 30	21	14 30	6	28 30	21	14 30	6	28 30	21	14 30	6	28 30	21	14 30	6
29 30	22	15 30	7	29 30	22	15 30	7	29 30	22	15 30	7	29 30	22	15 30	7

all manner of Questions.

You must observe, that upon any *Criticall* day (but especially upon the first Quartill) when ☽ meets with the body or aspect of a fortunate Planet, it's very probable (if the party be ordained for life) that nature will be fortified above the disease; and this her good aspect or application is a good indication of health, and that the Physician now imployed shall restore the sick party to former health by most easie Medicines; but if she meet at that time with the unluckey aspect of an *Infortune*, it gives the Physician little hopes at present; the *Crysis* is then ill, and the Physician must more warily proceed, &c. formerly men did repute the seventh, fourteenth and one and twentieth dayes for *Criticall* dayes; but in regard that the ☽ her motion is sometimes more slow, at other times more quick, the precise day cannot be had without compute or calculation of her true motion; which how to doe, I have given sufficient direction in my *Introduction*.

In giving Medicines, observe the motion of the ☽, for she being in
- ♈ ♌ ♐, the *Attractive* vertue is strengthned in the Plhegmatick.
- ♉ ♍ ♑, the *Retentive* is fortified in *Sanguine* people.
- ♊ ♎ ♒, the *Digestive* in the *Melanchollick*.
- ♋ ♏ ♓, the *Expulsive* in the *Cholerick*.

☽ in ♋ ♏ ♓, in ✶ or △ to
- ♃ Purge Melancholly.
- ♀ Purge Choller.
- ♂ ☉ Purge Phlegme.

The vertue retentive is stirred up from ♄, by reason of his frigidity.

Vegetative and Digestive		♃
Attractive and Irascible		♂
Vital and Natural potency	by	☉
Appetitive and Concupiscible		♀
Cogitative and Imaginative		☿
Expulsive		☽

Fiery Signes stir up red choller, viz.   ♈ ♌ ♐.
Earthly Signes, Black melancholly, or *Abram Melancholiam*,   ♉ ♍ ♑.
Ayëry Signes, Blood,   ♊ ♎ ♒.
Watry, Spittle and Flegme,   ♋ ♏ ♓.

I once intended a more large Discourse of Sicknesse, but

Master BOOKER having promised to undertake that labour I forbeare.

CHAP. XLVIII.
If a Servant shall get free from his Master?

THe first house, the Lord thereof, and the ☽, shall signifie the Servant; the tenth house and the Lord of that Signe shall denote his Master, let his condition be what it will be in this judgment; consider if the Lord of the ascendant be joyned to the Lord of the tenth house, and whether it be a perfect ☌, whether by body or aspect, whether with reception or not: if it be a ☌ by degree and minute, the Servant shall be freed easily, and in a short time; but if the Lord of the ascendant be separated from the Lord of the tenth some few minutes, it's an argument he is as good as freed already from his Master: if no such ☌ or aspect be betwixt the Lord of the ascendant, and Lord of the tenth, then have recourse to the ☽, and judge the same of her, as if she had been Lord of the ascendant, &c. I mean if she be so aspected as abovesaid.

But if neither the ☽ or Lord of the ascendant be separated from the Lord of the tenth, consider if either of them be separated from the ☉, or joyned with him, judge in the like nature of them as you would have done with the Lord of the ascendant and the Lord of the tenth, the same aspects considered: But if the Question be determinate and not absolute, *viz.* if he demand, *Shall I be freed from the service or slavery of this man my Master, in which I now live, or shall I ever be freed from his power?* then see if the Lord of the ascendant be cadent from an Angle, and have no aspect to the ascendant, or is in aspect with any Planet in an Angle, or with a Planet that doth behold the ascendant, or if he be in the third or ninth, or joyned to a Planet in them; then say, he shall be freed from his service, and shall depart from his Master: say the same if you find the like aspects, or have the same occasion, from the aspects of the ☽

But if the ☽ or Lord of the ascendant be in the ascendant, tenth,

tenth, seventh or fourth house, or if either of them be joyned to a Planet being in those angles, and that Planet be Direct, he shall not be delivered from his Master; but if the aforesaid Planet be Retrograde, it argues freedome, but with slownesse and difficulty: If the Lord of the ascendant be impedited in the ascendant, tenth, seventh or fourth, by corporall ☌ of any ill Planet, or by his □ or ☍, or if he is entring combustion, he shall not be freed from his service, &c.

Finis sexæ Domus.

The Significations of the seventh House.

It signifies Marriage, open Enemies, Law-suits, Controversies, Contracts, Warres, Bargaines, Fugitives, Thefts, &c.

Because the Demands which doe naturally appertain to the seventh house, require more consideration, and are more difficult to judge then of any other house, I have been enforced to be more large in delivering the opinions of the Ancients, as of some moderne Practisers; and have also published forty three significant Aphorismes; which, if well understood, will give great light, not only for better understanding what concernes this house, but the whole body of *Astrology*.

APHORISMES and Considerations for better judging any HORARY QUESTION.

1 SEE *the Question be radicall, or fit to be judged; which is, when the Lord of the ascendant and hour be of one nature or Triplicity.*

2 *Be not confident of the Judgment if either the first degrees or later of any Signe be ascending: if few degrees ascend, the matter is not yet ripe for judgment: if the later degrees arise, the matter of the Question is elapsed, and it's probable the Querent hath been tampering with others, or despaires of any successe: however, the Heavens advise you not to meddle with it at that time.*

3 *The position of* ♄ *or* ♂ *in the tenth, and they peregrine or unfortunate, or the* ☋ *in that house, the Artist hardly gets credit by that Question.*

4 *Judge not upon every light motion, or without premeditation of the Querent, nor upon slight and triviall Questions, or when the Querent hath not wit to know what he would demand.*

5 *Have speciall regard to the strength or debility of the* ☽*, and it's farre better the Lord of the ascendant be unfortunate then she, for she brings unto us the strength and vertue of all the other Planets, and of one Planet to another.*

6 *Behold the condition of* ♄ *in every Question, he is naturally ill by his excesse of cold;* ♂ *is of ill influence, because of his too much heat: in very truth, neither of them is cold or dry, but signifie so much in their vertue and operation, and therefore in all Questions they shew tardity and detriment in the Question, unlesse the* ☽ *and they receive each other in the signification.*

7 *See the condition of* ♃ *and* ♀ *be observed, who naturally are Fortunes and temperate, and never import any malice, unlesse by accident: where they are Significators without reception, they put forward the matter, but they best performe the matter in question when they apply by* △ *or* ✶*, and to purpose when in Essentiall Dignities.*

8 *In every Question where the Fortunes are Significators, hope well; but if the Infortunes, then fear the worst, and accordingly order your businesse.*

9 Gene-

all manner of Questions.

9. Generally consider the state of the ☽, for if she be void of course, there's no great hopes of the Question propounded, that it shall be effected; yet if she be in ♋ ♉ ♐ or ♓, your fear may be the lesse, for then she is not much impedited by being voyd of course.

10. See from what Planet the ☽ is separated, that Planet shewes what hath already been done: if from a Fortune good; if from a malevolent, ill; according to the nature of the house, &c.

11. The application of the ☽ shewes the present condition of the thing demanded, viz. her applying by a good aspect, and in a good house, to a good Planet, intimates the strong hopes of the thing intended.

12. The application of the ☽ to a Planet in his Fall, signifies anguish, trouble and delayes in the thing demanded.

13. A Retrograde Planet, or one in his first station, Significator in the Question, denotes ill in the Question, discord and much contradiction.

14. We ought warily to consider if evill Planets be Significators in any thing, for if they predict evill in the thing quesited, the vengeance is more heavy; if they foretell of any good, it's lesse then what is expected, it's imperfect, and nothing therein comes, without infinite solicitation and affliction, &c.

15. A Planet that is slow in motion, prolongs the thing quesited after, so that it's hardly performed; the nature of the Signe wherein the Planet is, doth herein much advantage the judgment.

16. When the Infortunes are Significators of any evill, doe you well consider if the Fortunes, viz. ♃ or ♀, cast not any aspect unto them, then the evill intended formerly is lessened; doe so when the Fortunes are Significators.

17. If the Fortunes signifie any thing, and are cadent, or ill placed in Dignities, or behold not the ascendant, or are Retrograde, then are they impedited, and shall performe little, if not received.

18. Notwithstanding Reception, if he be an Infortune, he performes but little; but if the same happen when the Fortunes are Significators, the thing is perfected.

19. A Planet Peregrine, viz. having no essentiall Dignities where he is, he is malicious beyond expression; if he be in essentiall Dignities, the lesse; for then he is like a noble soule that hath his enemy in his clutches, but scornes to hurt him.

20. And yet generally, if ♄ or ♂ be in House, Exaltation, Triplicity

and Angles, and then have signification in *a Question,* they performe the thing desired.

21 *Confide* not too much in the *assistance* a *Fortune* lends, unlesse he be in essentiall *Dignities;* for then he performes matters wholly, else but by halves.

22 *When* in a *Question* wherein both the *Fortunes* and *Infortunes* are either weak or equally ill placed, promise no *successe* upon that demand; deferre the Judgment untill the Heavens have a better Position.

23 *Beware* in all Judgments, when the *Significator* of the question is either Combust, or in Opposition to the ☉, he will then signifie nothing of the matter, no good, nor is he able to bring any thing to perfection.

24 *One Infortune* joyned to another, if good be signified by their aspect, yet will it have no effect, or come to any thing: If they signifie evill, it's probable that it may fall out with more malice then expected.

25 *The Lord* of the ascendant out of his essentiall *Dignities,* Cadant, &c. shewes the Querent is out of all hopes in his businesse.

26 *A Planet* within twelve degrees of the ☉, is said to be under his Beames, and then hath no fortitude, let it be in what Signe it will; when a Planet is within sixteen minutes of the ☉, he is said to be in Cazimi, or heat of the ☉, and then it's an addition of fortune, and he is wondrous strong.

27 *See* to what Planet the Significator commits his disposition, and if Orientall or Occidentall; if it be to ♄ ♃ or ♂, and they Orientall, the matter is sooner performed; later, if Occidentall, doe the contrary in ♀ and ☿.

28 *Observe* if the Planet that is Significator of the thing desired, be in a fixed Signe, moveable or common: fixed Signes shew stability, and that the thing shall continue, whether it be begun, or is to be begun: common Signes shew the oft probability of perfecting the thing, and yet not its conclusion: moveable Signes shew a sudden resolution or conclusion of the matter one way or other. From hence we begin *Foundations* of *Houses* and *Townes* when Significators are fixed; short *Journeys* when they are in moveable: but in things wherein we desire a mediocrity, we elect common Signes.

29 *The Lord* of the ascendant or the ☽ *with the Head* or *Taile of the Dragon*

all manner of Questions. 301

Dragon, brings damage to the *Question* propounded; see in what house they are in, and receive signification from thence.

30 Look whether the degree of the ascendant, or place of the *Signe* the *Significator* is in, be the then place of any *Eclipse* at hand; though the matter propounded be in a faire way to be concluded, yet shall it insensibly receive prejudice when least is expected, and hardly be concluded.

31 If you find the ☽ impedited in any *Question*, be it what it will, there will be the like stay, demur or hinderance in the thing quesited; and indeed there's seldome good end comes of a *Question* where the ☽ is impedited; if it be in going to *Warre*, you may feare the life of the *Querent*; if in a *Journey*, ill successe; if *Marriage*, an ill end of Wooing, &c.

32 If the Lord of the *Question* or the ☽ be in a *Signe* opposite to his owne house, as ♀ in ♐ or ♓, &c. the *Querent* hath no good hopes of his demands, he despaires, nor doth he delight in it, nor doth he care whether it be performed or not.

33 Consider diligently the Planet impediting the *Signifier* of the thing demanded, and what house he is either Lord of, or is posited in; from the nature or person of that house require the cause obstructing.

34 The neerer your *Significator* is to an *Angle*, the more good you may expect; lesse, if placed in a *Succedant* house; little, if in a *Cadent*.

35 In all *Questions*, know there's not so great an affliction to the ☽, as when she is in ☌ with the ☉; the ill aspects of the *Infortunes* doth much afflict her, but none so powerfull as her *Combustion*.

36 In any question, see if an *Infortune* aspect your *Significator*, and whether they be both *Peregrine*, *Retrograde*, *Cadent*, or in *Signes* contrary to their owne nature, it may then be doubted they inferre such a mischiefe in the question, as is inevitable, according to naturall causes.

37 Planets that are *Significators* in any thing, if they are in ☌, and in a *Signe* agreeing to their owne nature, then the thing quesited after is brought to perfection with much ease and facility, else not.

38 Have speciall regard to the *Significators*, and whether any frustration or prohibition be before the perfect aspect: the Planet frustrating describes the party or cause hindering the matter demanded.

39 Ever consider the ⊗, which if well dignified in any house, the querent gets by men, or things denoted by that house; and so, if ill dignified, damage from thence.

40 *In questions of Marriage, an unfortunate Planet in the seventh threatens ill agreement in Marriage, unlesse the same Planet be a Significator at the Birth.*

41 *If the Lord of the eighth be impedited or unfortunate in the eighth, the querent shall receive prejudice by the death of some woman, or concerning some debts due unto him from men deceased.*

42 *In what house you find ♃ and ♀ well dignified, you may expect benefit from such men and things as are signified by that house; as if in the third, from Kinred; in the fourth, from Father, or by Lands, &c. in the fifth by Play, &c. and so in other houses.*

43 *Beware of men and things appertaing to that house wherein ☊ is in; it seldome failes, but the querent shall receive damage, scandall or slander from men and matter signified by the house he is in.*

Chap. XLIX.
Of Marriage.

IF a Question be asked of *Marriage*, behold the ascendant and the Lord thereof, and the ☽, and the Planet from whom the ☽ is separated, and give those for the *Significators* of the *Querent*; and the seventh house, and the Lord thereof, and the Planet to whom the ☽ applieth, for the Signifiers of him or her concerning whom the Question is asked: and if it be a man that asketh the Question, joyne the ☉ and ☽ with his *Significators*, and make him partner in the signification; and if it be a woman, joyne ♀ and ☽, and make them partners: afterwards, behold what application the Lord of the ascendant or ☽ hath with the Lord of the seventh, and what application that Planet hath from whom the ☽ is separated, with the Planet to whom she doth apply, or ☉ with ♀; for if the Lord of the ascendant or the ☽ apply to the Lord of the seventh house, it doth signifie the *Querent* shall have his or her desire, yet with many petitions, solicitations and prayers: and if the application be by □ or ☍, and with reception, it signifieth that it shall be brought to passe with a kind of slownesse, labour and travell: but if the Lord of the seventh apply to the Lord of the ascendant

all manner of Questions.

aſcendant, or the Planet to whom the ☽ doth apply, unto the Planet from whom ſhe is ſeparate; or if the Lord of the ſeventh be in the aſcendant, the matter ſhall be brought eaſily to paſſe, with great good will of the man or woman queſited after; chiefly if there be an application by △ or ✶ aſpect.

Aphoriſmes of ALKINDUS *touching* MARRIAGE.

WHen the Lord of the aſcendant doth apply to the Lord of the 7th houſe, * it's an argument the Marriage ſhall be performed and done. alſo, if the ☽ doe apply unto ♀, and ſhe ſtrong, encreaſing in her motion, and in ſome of her owne Dignities, and the ☽ likewiſe, the Marriage ſhall be concluded: if ♀ doe behold the ☉, and the ☉ have any dignity in the aſcendant, and behold the Lord of his houſe, *viz.* of the Signe wherein he is, it doth ſignifie likewiſe the Marriage ſhall be concluded; but if the Planet applying, and he to whom he doth apply, be both cadent from the angles, and eſpecially if their Lords doe not behold them, it doth ſignifie there ſhall be good hopes at the firſt, but by dallying and tracting the time, there ſhall be trouble, and no Marriage at all performed: Alſo, if ☽ ☉ ♀ and Lord of the ſeventh, and Lord of the aſcendant be in angles, and they beholding one another, or if their Lords behold them, though with □ or ☍, yet it ſignifieth, the matter ſhall be firſt in deſpaire or ſuſpended, but afterwards it ſhall by the will of God, be brought to paſſe, and finiſhed by the conſent of all parties.

* *Or, if the Lord of the ſeventh apply to the Lord of the aſcendant.*

Of Marriage, whether it ſhall take effect or no?

Give unto the *Querent* the Lord of the aſcendant, the ☽ and the Planet from whom the ☽ is ſeparated; and unto the party enquired, the Lord of the ſeventh, and the Planet to whom the ☽ doth apply; and if the *Querent* be a man, then adde the ☉, but if a woman, adde ♀; and then behold what application there is between the Lord of the aſcendant and the Lord

of

of the seventh; for if the Lord of the seventh be in the ascendant, or apply to the Lord thereof, it will unwillingly be consented unto by the party desired; but if the Lord of the ascendant or the ☽ apply unto the Lord of the seventh, or be in the seventh, the Querent shall obtaine his purpose by his owne labour; but if none of these happen, yet if there be translation of light between them, then it shall be effected by the meanes of Friends or Acquaintance; also the ☽ in the tenth signifieth the same, also, the application of the ☽ with ♀ effecteth the matter, but by mediation of Friends: also, the application of the ☉ and ♀, especially when ☉ hath dignity in the seventh, *idem*: if the Lord of the ascendant be in the seventh, or with the Lord thereof, or behold him with a good aspect, or if the Lord of the seventh be in the ascendant, or with the Lord of the ascendant, or behold him with a good aspect, it doth give great encouragement for effecting the matter.

Of Marriage.

If a man aske, his *Significators* are, first, the Lord of the ascendant: secondly, the ☽; thirdly, the Planet the ☽ is separated from; fourthly, ☉, the naturall significator of men.

The *Significators* of the woman are, the Lord of the seventh, the Planet the ☽ applieth unto, the Planet in the seventh, ♀ the naturall significatrix of women: the like judge for the woman if she aske the Question, (*mutatis mutandis*) that is, the ascendant and other *Significators*, and ♀; the question asked by the woman, the seventh and his Lord, the Planet the ☽ applies unto; these are for the man, the ascendant and his Lord, the Planet the ☽ is separate from, the ☽ and ♀, so the *querent* hath three *Significators*, the party desired hath also three: It shall be, if the Lord of the ascendant or ☽ be in the seventh; secondly, if the Planet the ☽ separates from, applies to the Planet the ☽ applies to; thirdly, or the ☉ and ♀ apply to each other; fourthly, the Lord of the first in the seventh, or seventh in the first; fiftly, any translation of light from the *Significators*, or Reception of the *Significators*, or any collection by a More weighty Planet, the * *Signifiers* in interchangeable Dignities,

It shall be.
* Viz. one in the Termes, the other in the Triplicity of the Significator, or the like.

nities, the ☽ in the seventh giving vertue to the Lord of the ascendant, or Lord of the seventh.

The Lord of the seventh in the ascendant, the party desired *Which love* loveth best: The Lord of the ascendant in the seventh, the *most, or desire* Querent loveth best; and so of the other Significators, for those *it most.* that apply argue most love, &c. The Lord of the seventh in the seventh, especially in one of his owne houses, the party desired is free from love, hath little mind to Marriage, and her Portion is knowne, or the mans.

The Significators of the party desired, not beholding the Significators of the Querent, noteth the love of some other more then the Querent, or an averseneffe to the party now enquirng.

The applicatiō of the *Significators* frustrated, notes the Marriage to be broken off, by such a person or thing as that *Signifier* noteth, which you may know by the house he is in & Lord of, *viz.* if by the Lord of the 2d house, want of Riches; if Lord of the 3d by the Brother, &c. contrariwise, the Marriage being presaged by translation of light, or collection, it shall be furthered by such a one (as above mentioned) *viz.* if by the Lord of the second, by some friend promising Dowry; third, a Brother; tenth, a Mother; fifth or eleventh, a Friend; sixt, an Unckle, Aunt, or a Servant: Where note, that Marriages promised by ♂ □ or ☍, note performance with much adoe; △ or ✶, eafie; with Reception, best of all.

What shall be the occasion of hindring the Marriage.

Having carefully observed, that although there seem great probability of effecting the Marriage enquired of, yet you find just cause to judge, it shall not either really be acted, or much obstruction will be before it can be done; and you are desirous to know from whence the impediment shall come, the better to prevent it; consider what evill Planet it is who doth hinder the Reception of the disposition of the *Significators, viz.* of the man and woman, or who frustrates their aspect, or prohibits them, or interjects his Rayes betwixt the *Significators*; if he be the Lord of the second, they break off on the Querent's behalf,

Money or Fortune being wanting on that side, or poverty objected: if it be the Lord of the third, the Querent's Kinred, Brethren or Sisters, or some untoward Neighbour, or some Journey, &c. if the Lord of the fourth, the Parent will not agree, he will part with no Lands, no House, Houses or Tenements, will settle no Estate: if the Lord of the fifth Children may be the occasion, (if either party have any;) or if a Batchelour propounds, perhaps it's objected, he either is not capable of getting a Child, or that he hath had a Bastard, or is scandalized about such a thing, or that it's feared the party will be wanton, or given to luxury, too much to his pleasure and pastime, &c. vary your rule, and it serves if a woman propound, &c. If it be the Lord of the sixt, either some of his Fathers Kinred, *viz.* some Unckle or a Servant, or the like, or some infirmity or sicknesse in the *querent* may be the cause impediting.

If it be a Planet in the seventh, some other he or she Friend will impedite, or a publick Eenemy, or one he or she have formerly had variance with, or a Law-suit, &c.

If it be the Lord of the eighth, it may be feared Death will bereave the *querent* of Life ere the Marriage, or the *quesited* hath not a sufficient Portion, their Estate is disliked, it gives no content, it will not be accepted.

If the Lord of the ninth, one or other of the *quesited's* Kinred or difference in Religion, or some busie-headed Priest, or by reason of some long Journey to be undertaken by the *querent*, &c.

If the Lord of the tenth the Father of the *quesited*, or Mother of the *querent*, or some principall man, Officer or Magistrate.

If the Lord of the eleventh, the Friends of both parties dislike the Match, or such as at first brought on the matter, will now endeavour to dissolve the Match.

If the Lord of the twelfth, then there is some under-hand dealing and much jugling in the businesse, the matter shall be much retarded, and the *querent* shall never know by whom; the *querent* is much slandered, or some scandall privately insinuated doth much wrong, and will quite break the matter.

As you have notions whereby you may understand what may

all manner of Questions. 307

may be the obstacle in any Marriage, so by the same rules, rightly varied, you shall find who will assist or befriend the *querent* in his suit, or will endeavour to doe him good therein; I have herein dealt very candidly, and expressed the whole truth.

Whether a man shall Marry.

If the ☽ behold the ☉ or ♀ by a good aspect, or the Lord of the ascendant be in the seventh, or the Lord of the seventh in the ascendant, or either of them behold other with a good aspect, it signifieth Marriage to the Querent.

I observe, if the *Significators* be in Prolificall Signes, or Dignities of ♀, the party enquiring doth marry.

The time of Marriage.

The degree of the application of ☽ to ☉ or ♀, or Lord of the ascendant to the Lord of the seventh, or Lord of the seventh to the Lord of the ascendant; if it be in moveable Signs, Dayes; in common Signes, Moneths; in fixed Signes, Yeers; according to that time the Marriage shall be performed.

This must be understood when you find strong testimonies of Marriage, and that the *Significators* are swift.

How many Husbands a woman shall have.

Behold from the degree of the tenth house to the degree of ♂, and so many Planets as you shall find between them, so many Husbands shall she have; but if ♂ be in the eleventh house, then look from ♂ to ♃, and judge accordingly: some judge from ♂ to the Lord of the tenth; these rules are *Arabicall*: plurality of Husbands is best adjudged from the Lord of the seventh and ☉, ♂ being in common Signes, or many Planets in the seventh, or ☉ in ✶ or △ to many Planets in the seventh, argues plurality, or more then one.

Qq 2 *From*

From what part one shall Marry.

If the Lord of the seventh be in the ninth, he shall marry a Stranger, &c. if the Lord of the seventh and of the ascendant be in one quarter of Heaven, or in one house or Signe, usually the party marries one neer to the place of their own abode: consider the Signe of the seventh, the Signe and quarter of Heaven the Lord of the seventh is in, and judge by the major testimonies, from what part of Heaven the party shall live whom the *querent* shall marry; as if most concurre in South testimonies, the South; mix the quarter of Heaven and Signe, preferring the Sign before the quarter: but this will be best explained upon an example.

What manner of person he or she is.

For the man, note the Planet the ☽ is with; as if with ♀, say she is faire, slender and pleasant; and for the woman, judge by the Planet the ☉ beholdeth; ☉ in △ or ✶ of ♄, wise and painfull; ☉ aspecting ♃, honest; and so of the rest: the ☉ and ☽ in □ or ☍, note contention, separation and discords.

Whether man or woman be more noble.

If the Lord of the seventh be in an angle, and the Lord of the ascendant in a succedant house, the woman is best descended; and so if the Lord of the ascendant be in an angle, judge accordingly; in like manner one may judge of two Companions, or any one else: A more assured way is, by observing whether of the *Significators* is most superiour, and most potentiall in essentiall Dignities; if no such thing be, who is best placed in an angle, is most noble; and this will not faile.

Who shall be Master of the two.

Behold the Lord of the ascendant and the ☽; if the ☽ or the Lord of the ascendant be received in an angle, and he that is

the

all manner of Questions.

the receiver be an heavy or ponderous Planet, the *querent* shall be Master; and whether *Significators* shall be found weak, ill dignified, or in cadent houses, that party shall be subject.

Whether she be rich or not.

If the man aske, see the Lord of the eighth, or Planet in the eighth, for if they be strong, or ☾ applying to the Lord of the eighth by a good aspect, then she is wealthy (*& e contra*, poor;) if the woman ask of the man, and of her estate, judge after the same manner, for (*eadem est ratio.*)

Whether the MARRIAGE be Legitimate.

If the *Significators* of them, either of the man or woman be vitiated or joyned to ♄ or ♂, and they not *Significators* in the Question, or if they be with ☋, it sheweth unlawfull Marriage, *viz.* there hath been some wrangling or claime laid to the party by some former man or woman.

How they shall agree after Marriage.

If the Figure performe Marriage, note if the Lord of the ascendant and Lord of the seventh aspect each other with △ or ✶, they agree well : ☾ beholding her Dispositor, or Lord of the Exaltation of the house wherein she is, with good aspect, *idem* : The Lord of the seventh more weighty, and in an angle, she will be master, or strive for it : if neither the Lord of the ascendant, or of the seventh be in angles, then note the weightier, for that party signified by him, shall be master ; ☉ impedited, worst for the man ; if ♀ be impedited, worst for the woman ; if ☾ be impedited or unfortunate, is ill for them both.

Disagree.

The Lord of the ascendant and Lord of the seventh in □ or ☍, Lord of the ☾ impedited beholding the ascendant, or ♄,

♂ or a Retrograde or Combust Planet in the ascendant, doth note contention ever by the *querent*; *& e contra*, judge the like if the Lord of the seventh suffer the same afflictions, that then the *quesited* shall be the occasion of strife: the ☽ in her fall, or at □ or ☍ with ♄ or ♂, or any Retrograde Planet, if the ☽ then behold the ascendant, noteth brawling ever moved by the woman; ♄ ♂ or ☋ in the ascendant, *idem*, if the question be asked by the man.

Who shall be the cause of their Strife, or the authour of their Good.

If the Lord of the third be that Planet who doth afflict or impedite, and be in the ascendant or seventh house, it shall be by Brethren or Kinred; an *Infortune* in the tenth, notes brawling, and continuall chiding and wrangling: In the fourth, either a Divorcement or a willingnesse to it, or hinderance in Dowry; the ☽ infortunate beholding the ascendant, note brawling, separation and dishonest living: ill Planets in the tenth or fourth, ill persons make contention, or their Parents; no application between the Planet the ☽ separates from, and the Planet unto whom she doth apply, notes contention alwayes: if the ☽ doe aspect, or be in ☌ with ♄ or ♂, one of them shall dye quickly, or have some misfortune; if this ☌ be in the tenth or fourth, in a masculine Signe, the man shall suffer; if in a feminine Signe, the woman: The ☽ in △ or ✶ of good Planets, declares gifts from Friends; ☽ in □ of good Planets, by dead men; ☽ in ☌ of good Planets, promises good by their owne industry and labour; if the ☽ aspect ♄ or ♂, or be in the twelfth or eighth, or voyd of course, they shall have both troubles, griefes and sicknesse; in angles, notes a probability of separation or long disagreements.

That the Marriage shall be broken, and the cause thereof.

Behold the Planet who receiveth the light of the *Significator*; if he be a heavy Planet, and be hindered by □ or ☍ of an ill
Planet,

all manner of Questions.

Planet, or be Cadent, the intended Marriage shall be broken off againe, though at present it is very feasible.

Behold whether parties *Significator* is strongest, that party shall first marry after this dissolution.

If the ill Planet that hindereth the Marriage be Lord of the second or eighth house, it is for matter of Dowry; if Lord of the third, Brother; if Lord of the fourth or tenth, it is the Father or the Mother, or such like; and so judge of the rest.

If there be an ill Planet that carries the light between the *Significators*, it shall be by meanes of a Messenger; describe that Planet, and you may notifie the party.

That woman who doth depart from her Husband or become a Widdow, the ☽ being between the seventeenth degree of ♐, and the first minute of ♑, shall never returne or marry. *An Arabick Aphorisme, not overmuch to be credited without consent of other Significators*

Whoso is Espoused to a Wife the ☽ being in the twelve first degrees of ♑, shall lose her before marriage, or dye within six moneths, or live in discord with her.

Whether a Man or his Wife shall dye first, and the time when.

Behold the Lord of the ascendant and the Lord of the seventh, and see which of them goeth first to Combustion, and if the Lord of the ascendant, the *querent* shall dye first; if the Lord of the seventh, *e contra*: The Lord of the ascendant Retrograde or Combust, or in his Fall, or neer the Lord of the eighth, the Man, the Lord of the seventh in the like case, the Woman: ☉ unfortunate, the Man; ♀ unfortunate, the Woman.

Usually I observe, whose *Significator* is first Combust, and in what Signe; if he be combust in Tropick Signes, as ♈ ♋ ♎ ♑, it portends death in a short time; if in common Signes, *viz.* ♊ ♍ ♐ ♓, the time is longer: in Signes fixed, *viz.* ♉ ♌ ♏ ♒, it will be a longer time ere the party dye, &c.

Which of the two shall live longest

Behold the Lord of the ascendant, and of the seventh, which of of these two are in the best place of heaven, best dignified, and in good aspect with *Fortunes*, and more remote from the presence or ill aspect of the Lord of the eight house, that person shall live longest: Where you must observe, as to the Lord of the seventh, the Lord of the second in the Figure is his eighth house, and so Lord of, or *Significator* of death.

Whether she be a Maid, or Chaste, of whom the quere is.

Look if the Lord of the ascendant ♀ and the ☽ be found in fixed Signes, good Planets beholding them, then say, she is a Maid, and chaste: But if in place of the *Fortunes* there be *Infortunes*, say she is neither a Virgin, nor chaste; especially if ♂ be there, and he in the house of ♀ without Reception: Also, if ☽ and ☉ behold themselves and ♂, she is no Maid; but if the *Significators* be in moveable Signes, *Infortunes* beholding them, say then she desireth a man very much, and that she refraines and restraines her concupiscence very much, and casts off her Suitors; yet it is not to trust alwayes to this judgment, because the nature of women is changeable.

The *Significatrix* of the woman in her owne essentiall Dignities, or in △ to the ☉ or ♃ with any Reception, or the ☽ and the *Significatrix* in △ or ✶, in Reception, out of any mutuall Dignities, or ♀ in ♌ not afflicted, or the ☽ in ♒, free from □ ☌ ☍ of ♂, I judged honesty, and I found it ever true.

Whether a Damosell be a Maid or not.

Behold the ascendant and his Lord, and the ☽, and if thou findest them fixed and well disposed, it signifieth she is a Virgin; but if they be in common or movable Signes, or evil Planets be in fixed Signes beholding them, or aspect them any way, it is a doubt of *Legerdemain*; also ♏ ascending, argueth she is, or would be too familiar.

In many things I dissent from the *Ancients*, and so in this; for if ♂ be in ♌, and ♏ ascend, the *querent* is suspected and tempted, but yet is honest.

all manner of Questions.

Whether a Woman be honeſt to her Husband.

The Lord of the aſcendant, the ☽ or ♀ in fixed Signes, in aſpect of the *Fortunes*, ſhe is chaſte; theſe being in aſpect of the *Infortunes*, not chaſte, chiefly with ♂; ☉ or ☽ beholding ♂, ſhe is *meretrix*; ☉ and ☽ in no aſpect, nor ♂ with them, is ſuſpected a privy Harlot, or rather privately wanton; but not yet come to the act. *The Moon in ☍ to ♂, be in ♉, ſhe in ♏ or be in ♎ ſhe in ♈ · ill in this caſe.*

I muſt charge all ſonnes of Art to be ſparing in delivering judgment upon theſe queries, rather to be ſilent; for as men we may erre, and ſo by delivering an unluckie judgment, be authors of much miſchieſe.

Of a woman whether ſhe be corrupt, or hath a Lover beſides her Husband or Sweetheart.

Behold the aſcendant and his Lord, and the ☽, and ſee if they be both in angles or fixed Signes, then ſay the Maid is a Virgin, and they lye of her, or what is reported is falſe: if the Lord of the aſcendant and ☽ be in fixed Signs, and the angles be moveable Signes, ſhe was tempted, but gave no credit or admittance to the *Temptor*. If the ☽ be joyned to ♄ ♃ ♂ ☉ corporally by aſpect, ſo that there is between them but five degrees or leſſe, ſhe is tempted of ſome one who hath the effigies of that Planet to whom ſhe is joyned; but if the ☽ be joyned to ♀ or ☿, ſhe is tempted by ſome woman for a man, but ſhe makes not reckoning of the old or young Bawds words, but laughes her to ſcorne: If the angles be fixed Signes, and the Lord of the aſcendant or ☽ in movable or common, (for in this judgment the common are of leſſe importance) ſhe hath been attempted, and is ſtill tempted, but ſhe is honeſt; and hath been formerly deluded, if ſhe be with the ☊; but if then the ☽ be with ☋, ſhe hath formerly offended, and is ſtill guilty, nor will ſhe amend hereafter; the ſame may be ſaid of ♂, if he be in place of the ☋; yet ♂ impoſeth not ſo much malice on the woman as ☋: generally the ☽ in any Queſtion with ☋, imports miſ-reports of the woman, you may call them ſlanders.

The Resolution of

Whether a woman is honest.

This where suspition is of the quesited's honesty will hold true.

The ☽ in the last face of ♊, the woman seems to be corrupt, if the ascendant be a moveable Signe, or common, or if the Lord of the ascendant or ☽ be in moveable or common Signes she is no Virgin; the Lord of the ascendant combust in a moveable Signe, the woman hath been tempted and made a harlot by violence, or she was unwillingly drawn to lewdnesse; the Lord of the ascendant in a fixed Sign, and the ascendant fixed, though the ☽ be in a movable Signe, she is still a Virgin, and honest; the ☽ in the ascendant with ♄, the woman was abused by force, and not by her consent: if the ascendant be a fixed Signe, and the Lord of the ascendant in the fift, or the ☽ in the fift, or the Lord of the fift in the ascendant, or both of them corporally joyned in one Signe, it seems the woman hath newly conceived, or was lately tempted; but if they be separated asunder by three degrees, it seems the woman is delivered, or free from the party she was lately in fear of.

Whether a woman trades with any but her Husband.

These judgments must be carefully observed & well considered before judgment be propounded in the negative, viz. that she is not honest.

Behold the ascendant, his Lord, the ☽, and Planet from whom the ☽ is separated, these are *Signifiers* of the querent; the seventh house and his Lord, the Planet to whom the ☽ is joyned, are the *Signifiers* of the woman: see to whom the ☽ and Lord of the seventh is joyned, which if they be both joyned to the Lord of the ascendant, whether with Reception or ☌, say, the woman is not faulty, but honest: but if the Lord of the seventh, or the ☽ or either of them is joyned to the Lord of the Triplicity of the ascendant, viz. to him that is Lord of the Diurnall or Nocturnall Triplicity then ascending, or if any of them is joyned to the Lord of the seventh, and ☽ is separated from the Lord of the ascendant, it then seems she hath a Friend that she loves besides her Husband; the Lord of the seventh voyd of course, the woman hath no friend.

The Lord of the seventh, the ☽, or both, separate from any other Planet but the Lord of the ascendant, and he not separate

all manner of Questions.

parated above three degrees, the woman did love another, but she hath now left him: the Lord of the seventh with the ☊, the Woman is blamelesse, without he be in ☌ with some other Planet, then she is worthy to be blamed now, was also in times past, and in times to come will be; for if she be not faulty in act, she is in her desires and affections.

The Lord of the seventh or ☽ joyned with ♂, if the ☊ be there, it seems the woman hath a Sweetheart whom she loveth, and that useth her company: If ♂ be with ☋, and the Lord of the seveth be joyned as beforesaid, it minisheth the malice, and though the woman love some martial man, yet he cannot bring her under his Yoak, yet is she hard put to it, and much perswaded.

If ♂ be with the Lord of the seventh, or with ☽, or in one Signe in ☌, or with ☋, the woman hath a Sweetheart in contract, not farre from her house; and if they be in one degree, then he is in the house, and one of the familiars of the man that asks the Question, or of her owne Husband.

If the ☽ or Lord of the seventh separate from ♂, or ♂ from him, or that they be separated, perchance the woman had a Lover before she knew her Husband, but now they have one forsaken the other, or they have forgot each other.

♂ Lord of the seventh, or ☽ Lady of the seventh, in ♈ or ♏, and ♂ beholding any of them, *viz.* either of the Signes, or ☽, or in Reception with one or other, *viz.* ☽ and ♂, for if ♂ did receive the ☽, she did a long time love one, but she hath little to doe with him now: ☽ Lady of the seventh, in ☌ with ♂ or ♃ in any Signe whatsoever, the woman hath loved a certaine man, a *Noble man* or a *Bishop, viz.* a man of better quality then her selfe, &c. but if there be a mutuall Reception between them, they still love one another, or still some acts of kindnesse passe between them, and there wants nought but opportunity.

The Lord of the seventh or ☽ joyned to ☿, the woman seems to love a young Clerk, or a Merchant, or witty, nimble Fellow.

The Lord of the seventh joyned to ♀ with Reception, with or without any aspect, or else by a △ or ✶, or □ without

Rr 2 Re-

Reception, the Woman cares not for men, but hath friendship with women, or speaks wantonly, but is not naturally lewd or vitious.

The Lord of the seventh or ☽ in ♂ with ♄, the woman loveth an Old man, or a Religious man, or a Country-man, or a man of plaine sober carriage.

The Lord of the seventh joyned to the ☉, she loveth at present, and did love a certain great person, according to the quality of the *Demandant*; if it be with Reception, he hath or may have, if he please, to doe with her; but if it be without Reception, he cares not for her, but hath quite forsaken her: But if more Planets doe behold the ☉ as well as the Lord of the seventh, especially ♄ or ☿, more men have had to doe with her, nor is she yet amended, but somewhat tardy, &c.

If ones Lover or Wife hath a Sweetheart besides himself.

See if ♂ be in the seventh house, so that he be not in his owne house, then she hath one; if ♄ be there, she loveth one but lyeth not with him; if ♃ be there, she hath much adoe to be honest; if ♀, she is a merry wag, and is thought to be wanton, but is not: if ☿, she had a Friend but hath not now; if ☽ be in the seventh, she as yet hath none, but she will have, and will be common: if ☉ or ☊ be there, she is chaste and hath no Friend: After the same manner you may judge of Friends, or of the man, when the woman propounds the Question.

Hath she a Lover.

Any Planet in the seventh, (so he be not the Lord of the seventh) she hath one of his complexion, (if none be in the seventh, none;) thus doe for the man, but have relation to the eleventh house: The Lord of the seventh voyd of course, she hath none; or with ☊, *idem*: the Lord of the seventh or ☽ joyned to ♂, she hath a Sweetheart, or one whom she is familiar withall, that she doth much respect, but I say not in any dishonest way.

all manner of Questions.

If a Marriage shall be perfected or no.

Consider the Lord of the ascendant and the ☽, these are properly *Significators* of the *querent*; the seventh house and his Lord are for the *quesited*.

If the Lord of the ascendant or ☽ be joyned to the Lord of the seventh, in any of the dignities of the Lord of the seventh, and in the ascendant, eleventh or tenth, hardly in the seventh, the *querent* shall obtaine the party desired.

If both *Significators* behold each other with ✶ or △, out of the ascendant and eleventh, or ninth and seventh, or seventh and fifth houses, with or without Reception, no prohibition, frustration or abscission, or Retrogradation of the principall *Significators* intervening, the Match will be concluded if the *querent* please, (for we doe suppose a freedome of will in this nature) if a □ or ☍ be between the *Significators* (and no Reception) the matter will come to nothing.

A □ aspect with Reception of *Significators*, perfects the matter, but with a little difficulty; if no Reception be, there's onely hopes, no grounds whereby to judge the thing shall be effected really.

Contrary to all the rules of the *Ancients*, I have ever found, that when the Lord of the seventh hath been in the ascendant, the *querent* hath loved most, and when the Lord of the ascendant was in the seventh, the *quesited* loved best.

If the *Significators* aspect not one another, but some Planet transfers their influence one to another, and this with a benevolent aspect, then shall the matter be brought to passe by one signified by that Planet, whose description you may frame according to the Signe wherein he is, and his quality from the house he is Lord of: A masculine and diurnall Planet denotes a man, a feminine, nocturnall Planet, or a man of a feminine construction, *& sic e contrario*.

If a Planet transfers the *Significators* disposition, observe who that Planet is, and to whom he commits his disposition, and whether he be not Retrograde, Combust or unfortunate, or Cadent from his owne house, or in the figure, or in ☍ or □

aspect to an *Infortune*, without Reception; for then if no such thing be, the matter will be effected and continue, especially if he be a *Fortune*, and the Matrimony will take well, and the people love together.

Whether the Child conceived is the Sonne of him who is reputed his Father.

Behold the Lord of the ascendant and the ☽, who signifie the *Interrogant*; then observe the Signe of the eleventh and his Lord, these signifie the issue in Conception; if these *Significators* behold one another by △ or ✶, with Reception or not, the Conception is legitimate; if they behold one another with □ or ☍, with mutuall Reception, and perfect aspect, or the Lord of the ascendant or the ☽ in the fift, or if the Lord of the fift be in the ascendant, without the evill aspect of the *Infortunes*, or if the *Fortunes* one or both doe behold the fift house or his Lord, the Child conceived is legitimate and true begotten, &c. but if none of these things be, but that ♄ ♂ or ☿ behold the fift house, or Lord thereof, there may be just suspition the Child is conceived in adultery, and the Mother was stuprated.

Of a woman living from her Husband, whether she shall ever live with him againe or not, or be received into favour.

This Question will as well resolve the doubt concerning a Mistris, &c. or Sweetheart.

If the woman her selfe propound the Question, who is absent from her Husband or Friend, &c. *Whether she shall be received into favour or not againe?*

Consider herein the Lord of the seventh, which is the ascendant of the woman in this case, for the seventh is ever given to the banished or expulsed party; see if the Lord of the seventh behold the ascendant so partially, or with so true and good an aspect as himselfe doth, then without doubt she shal again return and come into favour; if the Lord of the seventh behold not the ascendant, but another Planet who is not impedited, yet beholds

all manner of Questions. 319

beholds the afcendant, the woman fhall be received againe by the mediation of fome perfon who fhall interpofe his friendfhip with the Husband or Friend, and reconcile them; if none of thefe things be, then have recourfe to the ☉, the naturall *Significator* of man, or the Husband, and of ♀, the naturall *Significatrix* of the woman; and if the ☉ be above the Earth, and ♀ behold the afcendant with a pleafant ✶ or △ the woman fhall return to her houfe or Sweetheart with eafe or without any great noyfe.

If the ☉ be under the earth, and ♀ above, and behold the afcendant with ✶ or △, the woman or wife fhall be received, but with fome importunity and delayes, with much adoe, and a great deale of labour, and all her Neighbours fhall take notice of it.

If the ☽ be encreafing in light, and in any good afpect to the afcendant, fhe fhall returne, but with much folicitation.

If the ☽ be decreafing in light, and in her fecond or laft quarter, and not neer the ☉ beames, but beholding the afcendant, shee will returne with much eafe and quickly.

Behold if ♀ be Occidentall, Retrograde and haftening to Combuftion, then of her owne accord the woman will returne to her Husband, fearing by her abfence fhe fhall offend him, and fhe is forry fhe ever departed from him; but if fhe be lately feparated from the ☉ beames, then it repents the man that he gave occafion to his Wife to abfent her felfe, or that he abufed her; but the woman will be angry and malapert, and feems fory that fhe fhall returne, nor will fhe much refpect her Husband after that time.

Chap. L.

Of Servants fled, Beafts ftrayed, and things loft.

THe *Signifier* of the thing loft is the ☽, wherefore if you find the ☽ applying to the Lord of the afcendant, or to the Lord of the twelfth from the afcendant, or to the Lord of the houfe of the ☽, the thing miffing fhall be found againe;

but

This principally concerns Cattle strayed but if the ☽ apply to none of these, nor abide in the ascendant nor in the second house, the thing lost or miscarried shall not be found: if the Lord of the house of the ☽ be in the third, or in a ✶ to the ascendant, there is some hope of finding the thing againe, during that aspect with the degree ascending: And againe, if he separate himselfe from the Lord of the twelfth, eighth, or sixt house, and apply unto the degree of the house of Substance, (what aspect soever it be) there is hope to find it again; or if the Lord of the house of the ☽ do behold ☽; but if you finde these Constellations contrary, judge the contrary; if the ☽ be fortunate by any of the two *Fortunes*, the thing that is lost chanced into the hands of some trusty body, which keepeth the same, and would faine restore it againe; or if that *Fortune* apply to the ascendant, or behold the same, or the ☽ behold the ascendant, that faithfull person will restore the same again to the owner.

The place where the thing is that is lost.

The *Signifier* of the place where the thing is at time of the Question, is the place of the *Moon* according to the nature of the Signe she is in, for if the Signe be Orientall, it is in the east part; if it be Occidentall, it is west, &c. Behold also the place of the *Moon* in the Figure, for if she be in the ascendant, it is in the east, &c. if the Lord of the house of the *Moon* be in humane Signes, It is in a place where men use to be, if in Signes of small Beasts, as ♈ and ♑ it is where such kind of Beasts be: Also, look to the ☽, and see if she be in a fiery Signe, it is where fire is; if in a watry Signe, where water is, &c. if the ☽ be with the Lord of the ascendant in one quarter, and there be not between them more then one Signe, the thing lost is in the house of him that lost it, or about it; but if there be between them more then thirty degrees, and lesse then seventy degrees, the thing is in the Town where the owner is, but if they be not in one quarter, it is then farre from the owner.

How

all manner of Questions.

How the things or Goods wer loft.

If you will know how and in what manner they were loft, behold from whom the Lord of the afcendant did laft feparate, and if he did feparate from ♄, the caufe of the loft thing was through forgetfulneffe of the owner, who knowes not where he laid it, or it is forgotten by reafon of fome cold or fickneffe which afflicted the lofer, efpecially if ♄ be Retrograde, if he be feparated from ♃, or in the houfe of ♃, then through faft or abftinency, or ordering of Lawes, or by his exceffe of care of governing of things, or managing the affaires of the houfe, or elfe by fome truft put upon him that carried it away or mif-laid it. *This was Frierly Aftrology and fuppofes fomewhat loft in an Abbey or Nunnery.*

If he be feparated from ♂, or in the houfe of ♂, it was loft through fear, or by fome fudden paffion, provoking the lofer to anger, fury, fire, or for emnity, or upon a quarrell. If from the ☉ or in his houfe, then by the meanes of the King, ftudy of hunting or paftime, or by meanes of the mafter of the Family, or a Gentleman. If from ♀ or in her houfe, then by drinking, Cards or Dice, or making merry in an Alehoufe or Taverne, or by paftime, or finging and dallying with women, &c. If from ☿ by reafon of writing, or fending, or dictating of Letters, or going on a Meffage: If from the ☽, or in the houfe of the ☽, it was loft by too frequent ufe, and fhewing the Commodity or thing loft, or the party made it too comon, or fome Meffenger, Widdow or Servant loft the fame. If the thing loft or miffing be a Beaft, and not a thing movable, the fignification in knowing the place, and the ftate thereof, is as the faid fignifications of things not having life, but that it is needfull to feek whether it fled away of it felfe, or fome other drove him away, whether it liveth or no ? and to find the caufe of the death of it, if it be dead.

Whether it be ftolen or no.

If you would know if the Beaft fled away by it felfe, or fome body took it, behold if you find the Lord of the houfe of the ☽ *This concerns Cattle.*

separating himselfe from any Planet, say then, that he fled away of his owne accord; but if the lord of the house of the ☽ be not separated from any Planet, but that another Planet is separating himselfe from him, say that some one or other took it and fled away; but if the lord of the house of the *Moon* be not in any of these two we speak of, behold what you see by the positure of the Lord of the second house, and judge by him as you judged by the Lord of the house of the *Moon*, and her separation; and if you find of these two no separation, say that the Beast is still in his place, or neer it, and that he fled not away.

Whether it be alive.

If you will know whether it be alive or not, behold the *Moon* and if you find her in application to the Lord of the eighth house from her, say it is dead; and if you find no such thing, behold her Lord, and if you find him applying to the Lord of the eighth house from the *Moon*, say likewise that it is dead, or it shall dye very shortly; but if in none of these you find application, take the signification from the Lord of the eighth house after the same manner.

Whether the thing missing be stolne, or fled of it selfe.

Stolen. If the *Significator* of the Theef be in the ascendant, or giveth his vertue to the ☽, or the ☽ to him, it is stolen, or the Lord of the ascendant to the *Significator* of the Thiefe, or the *Signifier* of the Theef apply to the Lord of the ascendant by □ or ☍, or the ☽ by ☌ □ or ☍, or the Lord of the house of the ☽, or of her Terme, or the Lord of the second house, or ⊗ or his Lord, or if any Planet be in the ascendant, and give his power to the *Signifier* of the Theef, or the *Signifier* to him by □ or ☍, if some of these constellations be not, it is not stolen, except there be an *Infortune* in the ascendant or second, or the Lord of the house of the ☽, or her Terme be Infortunate, or the ⊗ or his Lord, or the Lord of the ascendant, or the Lord of the second house be infortunate, these signifie losing.

Not stolne. Or if you find the Lord of the house of the ☽ separating from

all manner of Questions. 323

from any Planet, it is fled of its owne accord; if he separate not, but some other from him, it is driven away; the like in either by the Lord of the second, if he be in no such state or position, the thing abideth still, and is not stolen.

For Beasts strayed, or Fugitives, or any thing lost.

The *Significator* is ☽, wherefore the ☽ applying to the Lord *If found.* of the ascendant, or second house, or to her Dispositor, it shall be found, otherwise not; ☽ in the ascendant, or her Dispositor in a △ or ✶, gives hopes to find it; the Dispositor of the ☽ separating from the Lord of the fixt, eighth or twelfth, and applying to the Lord of the ascendant, or to the degree of the second house, good hopes also; ☽ in aspect to her Dispositor, good; ☽ infortunate of the Lord of the fixt, eighth, or twelfth house, it is in the hands of an ill person that will not depart from it, chiefly if the *Infortune* behold the ascendant or his Lord.

☽ Beholding ♃ or ♀, it is in the hands of an honest man *Restored.* that will restore it againe; if ♃ or ♀ have any aspect to the ascendant, or ☽ apply to the ascendant; ☽ in the ascendant, it is restored with trouble or paine; or the Lord of the twelfth *Fugitive in* in the twelfth house, the Lord of the seventh in the twelfth, *restraint.* the Fugitive is imprisoned.

The place: ☽ in the tenth, it is south; in the seventh, west; *The place.* in the fourth, north; in the ascendant, east, &c. the Dispositor of the ☽ in a humane Signe, it is in a place where men use; in ♋ ♏ or ♓, a place of Water or Wels; ☽ in the last face of ♑, it is amongst Ships; this must be when things are lost neer a Harbour.

☽ In ♈ ♌ ♐, in a place of fire; ☽ or her Dispositor being in movable Signes, it is in a place newly broken up.

☽ Within thirty degrees of the Lord of the ascendant the *Strayed.* thing is with the Loser, or neer him; ☽ more then thirty degrees from the Lord of the ascendant, it is farre off; the Dispositor of the ☽ separating from another Planet, it is strayed; another Planet separating from the Dispositor of the ☽, it is stolen.

Sf 2 ☽ Or

The Resolution of

☽ Or her Dispositor applying to the Lord of the eighth, or eighth house from the ☽, it is dead or will dye shortly.

☽ In the ascendant, or △ to the Lord of the ascendant; ☽ in △ to ☉, found.

The Lord of the second in the tenth or ninth, it is in the house of the *Querent*, or in the power of a familiar friend; ☉ in the ascendant (unlesse in ♎ or ♒) found; the Lord of the second in the eleventh or twelfth, farre off.

Of Beasts or Strayes.

If the Lord of the sixth be in the sixt, the Beasts be small: if the Lord of the twelfth be in the twelfth, the Beasts be great: if the Lord of the sixt be in the sixt or twelft, they be in a Pound; if the lord of the sixt be in fiery Signs, they shal be under fetters and locks; if the Lord of the ascendant and Lord of the hour be one Planet, then it is true they are in pound; if the *Moon* be in common Signes, they are in rushy grounds; if in an angle, they be in Closes or Grounds, if in a succedant, they be within the Closes, or about them, on the right hand of the owner; if the *Moon* be in a cadent house, they are in common Fields; if in ♋, where Dennes and water-beasts be, or some little Rivolet, if ♒ or ♓ in watry or fishing places, or neer Fish-ponds, in the last moity of ♑, in a place of Ships, or some Wood or Wood-yard.

This concerns Goods immovable.

Behold the Signe where the ☽ is, if in fiery Signes, in a place where fire is, or about a fire, or where fire hath formerly been made; the *Moon* in watry Signes, where water is, or about waters; the *Moon* in ayery Signes, in a place of many windowes, or open places, as Garrets, and such like; * the *Moon* in earthly Signes, in an earthly place, where houses are made of earth, or neer mud wals or clay; the *Moon*, or the Lord of the house where she is, be in a movable Signe, in a place new peopled, or a house new built, or where are hils, and in other places levell grounds; the *Moon* in a fixed Signe, in a plaine Country or champion; the *Moon* in a common Signe in a place of much water, according to the nature of the place where the thing was lost or missing.

* *This hath elation to beasts strayed*

Another

all manner of Questions.   325

Another Judgment.

Common Signs, as ♊ ♍ ♐ or ♓, do signifie within the house, if it be dead things, as rings, &c. but if it be quick or living things, or Catttle, it signifieth watry grounds, Ditches, Pits, Rushes, a Market-place; fixed Signes, the Goods are hid, or laid low by the earth, or neer it, in wals, or in hollow Trees; movable Signs, high places, Roofs, or Seeling of houses; watry Signes, in water, or under the earth, a Pavement, Foundations of houses, &c.

That the Beasts are lost.

The Lord of the fixt unfortunate by ♄ or ♂, the Beasts be lost, chiefly if the Lord of the fixt be cadent, or that the Cattle are drived away or stolen; if any Planet doe separate from the Lord of the house of the ☽, it is driven away or sold; if the Planet separate from the Lord of the second, *idem*; if you find none of these, the Beasts are not far off.

Dead or alive.

If the ☽ apply to the Lord of the eighth, it is dead, or to the eighth house; if the Lord of the house of the ☽ apply to eighth, *idem*; or if the *Significator* of the Beast be in the eighth, in □ to any infortune in the fourth.

In Pound or not.

If the Lord of the fixt or twelfth be in the ninth or tenth, then are the Beasts with some Justice or Officer, as Baily or Constable, or under Lock, or are commanded to be safe kept; for the most part Lord of the twelft or fixt in the twelft or fixt, they are kept close.

That the Cattle shall be found againe.

If the Lord of the fixt be fortunate by ♃ or ♀, and if they be found in the second, fift or eleventh houses, the Beasts will be had again; if the Lord of the Terme of the *Moon*, or the Lord of the Cusp of the fourth house be with the Lord of the ascendant, *idem*; or if the Lord of the fixt or twelft be in △ of ☉ out of angles.

Ss 3   How

How farre off a thing lost is from the owner.

The *Moon* in the same quarter with the Lord of the ascendant if there be but one Signe between them, the lost thing is in the house, or about his house that lost it; if there be more then thirty degrees unto seventy, the thing lost is in the Town, and in the same limits and bounds where the owner is; and if it be not within ninety degrees, the thing lost is farre distant from the owner; for usually when the *Significator* of the thing lost is in the same Quadrant, or the *Moon*, the goods are in the same Town or Hundred where the *querent* liveth.

Beasts stolen or strayed.

If the Lord of the house of the *Moon*, or Lord of the second doe separate from their owne houses, (if the goods be fixed) it is stolen; if moveable, fled of his owne accord.

In what place they are.

If the Lord of the sixt be in an angle, the Beasts be of small growth and in Pounds, Closes or houses; in cadent, in a Common, and are going way-ward; in succedant, in some Pasture neer hand.

Which way.

If the Lord of the sixt be in fiery Signes, east-ward in Woods or where Bushes, Brambles or Ferne have been burned; but in angles in fiery Signes, in Closes or Pound, or under lock.

The Lord of the sixt in earthly Signes, South on dry lands, or grounds, but if in an angle, in a Pound, or close Pound with a thing that earth is about it, *viz.* a mud wall; if a succedant, it is about Closes on the right hand of the *querent*.

The Lord of the sixt in an ayery Signe, they are most in plaine ground, if he be in an angle, they be in Pound or housed west from the place where they were lost; In succedant, on the right hand westward; in cadent, on the left and going away-

away-ward, *viz.* Straying further from their right Owner.

If the Lord of the fixt be in watry Signes, North, in a low place; if in an angle, in Close-ground, northward; in succedant, on the right hand of you northward; in cadent, in the Common on the left hand, where water is, or Medowes, going away-ward, or where people water their Cattle.

In what ground they be.

If the Lord of the fixt be in movable Signes, they are in hilly grounds.

If the Lord of the fixt be in fixed Signes, in plaine ground where is new building, or some grounds new plowed or turned up.

Common Signes, where water is, rushy grounds, ditches.

If the Lord of the Terme of the *Moon* be in a fixed Signe they are in a plain ground newly taken in, or nigh a new building.

In movable, in new land, or ground full of hils.

In common Signes, in a watry place, rushy or a marshy ground, nigh ditches and pits.

The Cattle shall to Pound

If the *Moon* be in the twelfth, they shall be had to Pound or be pounded, what signification soever, if the *Moon* be unfortunate, they shall toPound; if the Lord of the twelfth and principall *Significator* be unfortunate, they shall to pound, or be kept obscurely in some private or close place.

Long in Pound.

If ♄ be in the twelfth, or in the first (when the *querent* comes to know of you what is become of the Cattle) or the *Moon* in the twelfth, any of them unfortunate, then shall they be long in pound; if ♂ aspect ♄ or the *Moon* in the twelfth, with ♂ □ or ☍, they will be killed in Pound, or dye there, or be very neer starving.

From hence the movable, fixed or common Signes may easily

ly be knowne, when Sheep be stolen, whether and whertheye are killed or not? if ♄ be in the ascendant, fourth, eighth or twelfth, long in pound.

Escape the Pound.

If the Lord of the ascendant be in a movable Signe, in the third, ninth or tenth, they shall escape Pound; if the Lord of the ascendant be in the twelfth, though good, yet sick and ill in Pound.

If the Lord of the ascendant be in the eight, it's probable they dye in pound.

If the principall *Significator* of the ascendant be Retrograde they dye in Pound.

If the Lord of the sixt behold the Lord of the ascendant with ✶ or △, they will be had againe; if he behold him with □ or ☍, then they will be stopped: if he behold the *Moon* or the Lord of the house of the *Moon*, with ✶ or △, had againe; with □ or ☍, stopt or staid in some Village or Towne.

Whether the Fugitive shall be taken.

Give the ascendant and his Lord and the ☉ unto the *Querent*, and the seventh and his Lord unto the *Fugitive* or thing asked for, and behold what aspect is between them, and so judge; for if the Lord of the ascendant apply unto the Lord of the seventh with ☌ ✶ or △, or that the Lord of the ascendant be in the seventh, it betokeneth the *Querent* shall recover the things lost or Fugitive, gone away. Also, if the Lord of the seventh be in the ascendant, or apply to the Lord thereof, or there be any translation of light betwixt them, it sheweth the same with more facility.

Of the Moon.

For Fugitives, have respect to the *Moon*, being naturall *Significatrix* of them, by reason of her quick motion, for if she be in the ascendant, or apply to the lord thereof with a good aspect, or that the lord of the seventh or the *Moon* separate from the *Fortunes*, and be immediatly conjoyned to the *Infortunes*, all
these

all manner of Questions. 329

these shew, that the Fugitive shall returne and be recovered, or shall be so hindered, that he shall come againe.

The ☽ encreasing in light and number, he shall be long in search; decreasing, soon found, and with lesse labour: also, the ☽ separating from the Lord of the seventh, and joyned with the Lord of the ascendant, the *Fugitive* is sorry he went, and will send some to entreat for him; the Lord of the seventh Combust, signifies the *Fugitive* will be taken, will he, nill he; behold in what quarter the ☽ is, that way the *Fugitive* draweth, or intendeth to goe.

Whether he shall be taken.

The Lord of the seventh joyned to an *Infortune* in an angle, upon good search, the *Fugitive* will be taken; but if both be not in an angle, he shall be detained or staid by the way, but not imprisoned; if the Lord of the ascendant behold that *Infortune* who afflicts the *Fugitive*, the *querent* shall find the *Fugitive* detained by some one, to whom he ought to give money, or who wil demand mony before he do restore the *Fugitive* unto him: if the *Infortune* be in the ninth, he shall be staid in his jonrney and taken; the Lord of the seventh with a Planet stationary, in his first or second station, in an angle or succedant, he knoweth not which way to fly but shall be taken.

If a Fugitive shall be found, or come againe.

If the Lord of the seventh be in the ascendant, the *Fugitive* will returne of his owne accord; ☽ separating from the Lord of the ascendant, and joyned immediatly to the Lord of the seventh house, or to the seventh house, one will shortly bring newes of him; the Lord of the seventh combust, or entring combustion, the *Fugitive* shall be found (*volens, nolens;*) the ☽ separating from the Lord of the seventh, and joyned immediatly to the ascendant, or Lord thereof, the *Fugitive* repenteth his departure, and will send some to entreat for him; ☽ joyned to *Infortunes*, viz. ♄ ♂ or ☋, or to a Planet Retrograde, he shall be found or come againe, and hath endured much misery since his departure; the Lord of the seventh beholding an *In-*

T t *fortune*

The Resolution of

fortune from the seventh, the *querent* shall find him that is fled with some to whom he must give money before he can have him; ☽ separating from ♃ or ♀, he shall quickly come back againe, or, a thing lost shall suddenly be found; ☽ aspecting her owne house with ✶ or △, the *Fugitive* returneth within three dayes; for according to probability, the *querent* shall hear where he is within three dayes, if the distance be not too great.

Distance.

Behold the Lord of the seventh, and the Lord of the hour, and look how many degrees are between them, so many miles he is off from the place where he went from.

The former rule I doe conceive not so perfect as this which followes; see what distance there is betwixt the ☽ and *Significator*, viz. their aspect and what Signes they are in; give for every degree in a movable Signe seventeen houses or Furlongs, at discretion; in common Signes, give for every degree five Furlongs or distance of five houses; in fixed Signes, for every degree give one Furlong, or one house, &c. having relation to the thing lost, and whether it be in a Town, or in the Fields.

Of a Woman flying from her Husband.

The ☉ under the earth, ♀ Occidentall and Retrograde, she will returne of her owne will; ♀ Orientall, she cometh, but not willingly; Lord of the ascendant, the ☽, and Lord of the seventh in △, she returneth, with a ☐ or ☍ without Reception, never; ♂ in an angle, and giving the ☽ strength, and the ascendant movable, they shall be contented to be separated for ever.

Of a Thief and Theft.

Haly saith, you must know that the ascendant is the *Significator* of the *querent*, the Lord of the second is *Significator* of the thing that is stolen or taken away, and the seventh house is the *Significator* of the *Thiefe*, if there be no peregrine Planet in an angle or second house; the tenth house is the *Signifier* of the King,

all manner of Questions.

King, and the Signe of the fourth the *Signifier* of the place *This shall be* where the thing is, that is, or was taken away; whose proper *more copiously* significations you must know from the Lords of those houses, *handled in* whereby you may know the condition and state of what is mis- *some Chapter* sing, and if you find in the ascendant a Planet peregrine, put *following.* him as the *Significator* of the *Thiefe*, and especially if he be Lord *A most cer-* of the seventh house; but if no Planet be in the ascendant, look *tain rule.* if there be any in the other angles, and give him to be *Signi-fier* of the *Thief*.

Of the SIGNIFICATOR of the Thiefe.

The Lord of the seventh commonly signifies the *Thief*, but *A Planet is* especially if he be peregrine in the ascendant, or in any other *then peregrin* angle; but if he be not so, then behold if any othe Planet be pe- *when he is* regrine in any of the angles, call him the *Thief*; if none be pe- *neither in his* regrine in any of the angles, take the Lord of the hour, and call *House, Tripli-* him the *Thief*, and if it happen that the Lord of the hour be Lord *city, Terme,* of the seventh, then it is more radicall; if the Lord of the se- *Exaltation or* venth be in the ascendant, the *querent* is Thief; this will hold *Face.* where just suspition is made of the *querent's* fidelity, or most *I rather and* cause above all others, whose complexion and condition is ac- *more assured-* cording to the Planet, Lord of the seventh, and Signe thereof. *ly prefer the*
Lord of the
The SIGNIFICATOR of the thing stolen. *seventh, as*
more rational
and consenta-
* The *Significator* of the thing stolen is the Lord of the Term *nious to rea-* the ☽ is in; when thou hast found the *Significator* of the *son.* Thief, and understandest the nature of his disposition by the significant Planet and his aspects, know that the ascendant is * *This rule is* Signifier of the *question*, or *Demandant*, and if thou see the Lord *vulgar, and* of the ascendant draw towards the Lord of the seventh, or to *not of any cre-* the Lord of the houre, or be in the seventh, it signifieth that *dit.* the Thief shall be taken anon after, or it gives hopes of disco-very of the thing lost.

Of THEFTS.

The first house, which is the ascendant, is for the *querent*, and
Tt 2 his

This is a very good judgment, and may well be trusted. his Lord for him that hath lost the Goods, and signifieth the place from whence the Goods was taken; the seventh house and his Lord, and the peregrine Planet in an angle, and the Lord of the hour, signifieth the Thief, or party that took away the Goods.

The second house and the Lord of the second house and the ☽, shall signifie the Goods or thing that is lost, stolen or mist; the fourth house and his Lord shall signifie the place where it is laid, put or done, or conveyed unto, and is in at that instant of time.

The aspects of the ☉ and ☽, of the Lord of the ascendant, of the Lord of the second house, and of the Lord of the house of the ☽, to the lord of the ascendant, and their application and aspects one to another, shall tell and shew whether the Goods shall be found or had againe or not: If the lord of the second and the ☽ be in the seventh, in the Signe of the seventh, and the Lord of the seventh house behold them both by △ or ✶ aspect (though long out, *viz.* if the aspect be by many degrees distance) then is the Goods taken away by somebody, *viz.* they are not simply lost: if the ☽ be *Lady* of the second, and in the house of the lord of the hour, going to ☌ of the lord of the seventh house, then hath the party lost the thing or Goods in some place where he was, and hath forgot it, and it is neither lost nor stolen, but carelesly mislaid.

If the ☽ be Lady of the ascendant, and in the fourth, and the Lord of the second in the seventh, or in the sign of the eight house, in ☍ to the second house, at a ✶ or △ to the ☽, the thing is not stolen, but taken away in jest.

If the ☽ be Lady of the ascendant, and in the ascendant, not farre remote, and the ☉ Lord of the second in the tenth with the Lord of the seventh house, and the Lord of the seventh oppresse the ☽ with a □, then is the Goods stolen and taken away; if the ☽ be in the third, opprest with the Lord of the seventh house by his □ aspect, and Lord of the second also being Lord of the ascendant, and in the seventh, in the Signe of the seventh then it is stolen, but first it was taken in jest, and it will be hard to get it againe, except the ☉ and ☽ behold the ascendant.

If

all manner of Queſtions. 333

If ☽ be the ſeventh in the Signe of the Lord of the hour, the Lord of the hour being Lord of the ſeventh, then is the Goods not ſtolen or taken away, but overlooked and miſtaken. If ☽ be in the fift houſe and in ♑, and be Lady of the hour, and ♀ Lady of the ſecond in the tenth, in the Signe of the tenth, and ☽ in ☍ to the Lord of the ſeventh, then hath the party loſt the Goods as he went by the way, or was in ſome place where he left them: If the ☽ be Lady of the hour, in ♋, in the eight, and the Lord of the ſecond in the fift, and neither of them behold the Lord of the ſeventh, but the Lord of the ſeventh be in the ſeventh, then is the Goods taken away in jeſt by the Maſter of the houſe, and he will deny it: If the ☽ be lady of the hour in the fourth, in ☍ to the lord of the ſeventh, and the lord of the ſecond in the twelft, in a ✶ to the lord of the the ſeventh, then hath ſomebody taken the things away in jeſt: If ☽ be in the Signe of the lord of the ſeventh, and not beholding the lord of the ſeventh, but ☽ in the twelft, and lord of the ſecond in the ſixt, then is the Goods taken away in jeſt, if the lord of the ſecond did laſt ſeparate from the lord of the houſe of the ☽, then the Goods is ſtolen in jeſt, but will ſcant be had again. If the ☽ doe ſeparate from the lord of the ſecond by □, the Goods is taken away and ſtolen by ſomebody: ſometimes the ☽ is lady of the ſecond, and doth ſeparate from the lord of the houſe where in ſhe is, then it is ſtolen: If the lord of the aſcendant doe ſeparate from ♃ or from the lord of the ſecond houſe, then did the *Querent* lay it downe and forget it, and ſo it was loſt: but when the lord of the aſcendant and lord of the ſecond doe ſeparate from ♃, it is the ſurer: and ſometimes it fals out, that the ☽ is *Lady* of the aſcendant, and ſeparates from ♃, and doth apply unto the lord of the ſecond houſe, which did alſo laſt ſeparate from ♃, and ſometimes the lord of the aſcendant, as ☉ is alſo lord of the ſecond, and doth ſeparate from ♃, yet if it be ſo, it giveth all one judgment as aforeſaid: If the lord of the ſecond or ♃ doe ſeparate from the lord of the aſcendant, then did the party loſe the Goods by the way as he went, or in ſome place where he was, or elſe it tumbled out of his pocket privil into ſome ſecret place where it is not ſtolen or found: But if there be none of theſe ſeparations aforeſaid,

aforesaid, then see if the peregrine Planet or lord of the seventh or ☿, who is also for the Thief, doe apply to ♃, or the lord of the second; if they doe, then is the Goods absolutely stolen, and the Thief came with intent for to steale: If the lord of the second or ♃ doe apply unto the peregrine Planet, or to the lord of the seventh, or to ☿, who is for the Thief, then the Goods or the thing lost did offer it selfe to the Thiefe, or he came easily by them without trouble; for he that stole them, came not with intent for to have stolen it, but seeing the thing did lye so open, and so carelesly, he took it and carried it away. If ☽ be lady of the ascendant, and also lady of the second, and be in ♉, and apply by ♂ to the ☉, within one degree, and ☉ be lord of the third house, and ♂ be the peregrine Planet, and in the tenth, and ☿ apply to ♂, none of the abovesaid separations or applications impediting, or the lord of the seventh in the third, then the *Querent* did lose the thing by the way as he went, and it is not stolen from him.

Whether it be stolen or no.

For this, behold if the *Signifier* of the Thiefe be in the ascendant, or give his vertue to the ☽ or the ☽ to him, it is stolen; if the lord of the ascendant give his vertue to the *Signifier* of the Thiefe, it is stolen; if the *Signifier* behold the lord of the ascendant by □ or ☍, or the ☽ by ☌ □ ☍, or the lord of the house of the *Moon*, or the lord of the Terme of the *Moon*, or the lord of the second house, or the ⊗ or his lord, the thing is stolen.

And if any Planet be in the ascendant, and give his power to the *Signifier* of the Thiefe, or the *Significator* to him by □ or ☍, it is stolen: and if some of these constellations be not, the thing is not stolen, except there be an *Infortune* in the ascendant or second house, or the Lord of the house of the *Moon*, or of the Terme of the *Moon* is unfortunate, or the ⊗ or his lord be unfortunate, or the lord of the ascendant, or the lord of the second house be infortunate, all these signifie losse or losing.

That

all manner of Questions.

That the Goods are stolen.

If any Planet be in the ascendant peregrine, it is stolen; or the peregrine Planet give vertue to the ☽, or the ☽ to him, it is stolen; the Lord of ascendant peregrine, it is stolen; if the Thiefe be peregrine, that is, if he have no dignities where he is, it is stolen; if the *Significator* be with the Lord of the ascendant or in □ or ☍ to the Lord of the ascendant, it is stolen.

If any Planet doe separate from the Lord of the house of the ☽, it is stolen; if any Planet have respect to the Lord of the Terme of the ☽, with ☌ □ or ☍, it is stolen: if any Planet be separate from the Lord of the house of Substance, it is taken away: if the Thiefe have respect unto the Lord of the house of the ☽, with ☌ □ or ☍ it is taken away.

Not stolen.

If neither the Lord of the house of the *Moon* or lord of the second separate not themselves from one another, or any other Planet from them, then what you look for is in his owne place; if the *Moon* give vertue to ♄ or ♂, or to any Planet in cadent houses, or to the lord of the eighth, not stole, but missing, or else negligently throwne aside.

It will be (or is intended to be stolen.)

If the *Moon* be lady of the seventh, and give her vertue to a Planet in the second, or in the eleventh or fift, having her selfe neither ✶ or △ to the cusps of the houses, or if any Planet in the seventh give vertue to a Planet in the second, fift or eleventh, and have no ✶ or △ to the Planet in the seventh, it will be, or if the lord of the tenth be in ☌ □ or ☍ with the Thiefe, it will be stolen.

It is Lost or Stolen

If a Planet doe separate himselfe from the lord of the house of of the ☽, or from the Lord of the second, then it is taken away with hands and stolen: If the ☽ be Lady of the seventh, and give vertue to the Lord of the ascendant, it is stolen: if the Lord of the ascendant give vetue to the Moon in the seventh, it is stolen.

If any Planet in the ascendant give vertue to the *Signifier* of the Thief, it is stolen, or the Thief to the Lord of the ascendant, its stolen; but the Thief gives so much of the Goods to the owner againe, according to the vertne or light that the Thief giveth to the Lord of the ascendant; if any Planet in the ascendant be peregrine, it is stolen, and the Thief shall escape.

If the peregrine planet give vertue to the *Moon*, or the *Moon* to him, if the Thief aspect the *Moon* with ☌ ☐ or ☍, or aspect the Lord of the Terme of the *Moon*, it is stolen.

If the ☽ give vertue to ♄ or ♂, or if she give vertue to any Planet in a cadent house, or if the *Moon* give vertue to the Lord of the eighth, and he in a movable Signe, the things are stolen, but in fixed Signes, taken away.

If the Lord of the house of the *Moon* separate from any Planet, or the Lord of the second doe separate from any Planet, stolen.

If the Lord of the house of the *Moon* or second be in his owne house, and have vertue of ♄ or ♂, gone away by it selfe, and not stolen.

Of the age of the Thief.

The age is taken from the Planet that is *Significator* of the Thiefe, if he be Orientall, he is young; in the midst of his Orientality, then of middle age; if he be in the end of his Orientallity, he is old, faith *Haly*.

To judge by the distance of the Planets from the ☉, for by the ☉ the Planets are Orientall and Occidentall, by which the signification of age is taken, after *Haly*, and other Writers.

If together with this, you consider in what degrees of the Signe the *Significator* is in, you shall doe better, for a Planet Orientall and in few degrees, denotes youth, or younger; in more degrees, more age; frame the age according to an exact mixture.

If

all manner of Questions.

If ♄ ♃ or ♂ be significators, then behold the distance of them from the ☉; from their ☌ with the ☉ to the □ aspect, signifieth the age of 18. yeeres, and the neerer the ☉ the lesser in age, and from the □ to the ☍ signifieth the age of 36. from the ☍ to the next □ signifies the age of 45 from that last □ to the ☌ signifieth the age of 72. and so to the end of life.

Guido Bonatus saith, the ☉ being significator, and being between the ascendant and Mid-heaven or tenth house (which is all one) signifieth the thiefe to be young, and so increasing till he come to the angle of the earth.

And if ♀ or ☿ be significators, the age is taken by their distance or elongation from the ☉, from their ☌ with the ☉, being direct to the mid-way of their ☌ in their Retrogradation, signifies the age of the thiefe to be about 18. and the neerer the ☉ the younger, and from the mid way to their ☌ in their Retrogradation, signifieth the age of 36. or neer that age, the neerer to the ☌ the elder, and from the ☌ in the Retrogradation, to the mid-way of their ☌ in the direction, signifieth the age of 45. and from the mid-way to their ☌ in direction, signifieth the age of 72. and so to the end of life; and if the ☽ be signifier judge as by ♄ ♃ and ♂, as before is said.

The same *Guido* saith, ♀ signifieth the thiefe to be young, a woman or a Maid, ☿ of lesse age then ♀, ♂ signifieth full age, or in prime of his youth, ♃ more of yeers then ♂, and ♄ signifieth old age or decrepit, or well in yeers, the ☉ signieth as before is said; the ☽ being significatrix in the beginning of the Moneth to the first quarter, signifieth to be young; and if she be neer to the full ☽, it signifieth the middle age or perfect man; and if she be in the end of the Moneth, it signifieth the Thiefe to be aged, or of greater yeers.

The age of the Thiefe.

If the ☽ increase, he is young; if decrease he is old; if the significator be in the house of ♄, or aspected by him, or in the last degrees of a Signe, it signifies old age; ♄ signifies the same; ♂ ☉ ♀ ☿ from the Ascendant unto the tenth, signifie young yeers,

yeers, especially if they be in the beginning of Signes: from the tenth to the seventh, middle yeeres; if the significator be a superior Planet and direct, then he is of good yeers, if Retrograde elder or very old, and so judge of inferior Planets; for if they be Retrograde or joyned to Planets Retrograde, it augmenteth the age: thus if you mingle your signification, you may the better judge. The ☉ between the Ascendant and mid heaven argueth a childe, between the *Meridian* and *Occident*, accuseth a young Man, between the *Occident* and *Septentrionall angle*, a Man growne; and from the *Septentrionall* to the *Orientall*, accuseth a very old Man; Lord of the ascendant in the East quarter, or ☽ in the Ascendant, a young Man : ☿ alwayes signifies a Childe or a young Man, especially being in the *Ascendant* and *Orientall* : any Planet, except ♄, signifieth young Men; or if the signifier be joyned to ♀, ☽ increasing in light, or in the first, ten degrees or middle of the Signe, or the significator in the beginning of the *Orientall* quarter, signifies a Childe, or a young Man, or Woman, &c.

Whether the Thiefe be a Man or Woman.

Behold the Signe ascending and the Lord of the houre; if both be Masculine, the Thiefe is Masculine; and if the Lord of the houre and Ascendant be both Feminine, the Thiefe is Feminine; if the Signe Ascending be Masculine, and the Lord of the houre Feminine, it is both Masculine and Feminine, *viz.* there were two Theeves, both a Man and a Woman.

Also the Significator Masculine and ☽ in a Masculine Sign, signifieth a Man kinde, *& e contra*. If the Lord of the Ascendant and the Lord of the houre be both in the Ascendant in Masculine Signes, it is a Man; in Feminine Signes, a Woman.

If the Lord of the Ascendant and the Lord of the houre be the one in a Masculine, and the other in a Feminine Sign, both a Man and a Woman had a hand in the Theft.

The Angles of the Figure Masculine, a Man; Feminine, a Woman.

♀ Significatrix aspecting ♂ with □, notes impediment in hearing, principally in the left eare.

♀ ☿ ☽

all manner of Questions. 339

♀ ☿ ☽ noteth Women, ♄ ♃ ♂ and ☉ Men; respecting the Signe and quarter wherein they be.

If one Thiefe or more.

Behold the Signifier of the Thiefe; if he be in a fixed Signe, and of direct Ascensions, or a Signe of few Children, or of few shapes and likenesse; it signifies to be one and no more. If the Signe be of two bodies, *viz.* a common or bycorporeall Signe, it signifies more then one, and more likely if there be in the Signe many Planets peregrine: also when the ☉ and ☽ behold themselves by a □ in the Angles, it signifies more then one: Signes that signifie many Children are ♋ ♏ and ♓; few Children are ♈ ♉ ♎ ♐ ♑ and ♒. Divers shapes or formes, ♊ ♋ ♐ ♒: barren Signes are ♊ ♌ and ♍; Signes of direct Ascensions ♋ ♌ ♍ ♎ ♏ and ♐; Signes of oblique Ascensions are ♑ ♒ ♓ ♈ ♉ ♊. If the ☽ in the houre of the Question be in the Angle of the Earth, in a common Sign, there is more then one; if she be in any of the other Angles, in a fixed Sign, there is but one Thiefe. Looke how many Planets are with the Thieves significator, so many Theeves; the ☽ in a common Signe more then one. Lord of the Ascendant in a Male Signe, and Lord of the houre in a Female, Man and Woman (as aforesaid;) looke to which the ☽ doth agree, *viz.* to whom she applies, that person is the principall actor; the Angles moveable especially the first and seventh, or the Significator being in ♋ ♏ or ♓, more then one. The Sign wherin the significator of the Thiefe is in, if it be inmoveable, or a double bodied Sign, more then one. Both the Luminaries beholding one another from Angles, more then one; ☽ in the Ascendant, and it a double bodied Signe, doth demonstrate there were more Thieves then one.

Of the Cloathes of the Thiefe.

You must know the colour of the Cloathing by the Planets, Signs and degrees, and the House the Significator is in; and after the mixture the one with the other, accordingly judge the

colour

The Resolution of

colour of their Cloathes. If there be signification of many Theeves, judge them by the Lord of the triplicity the significators are in. The Significators of the Colours of the Planets after *Alcabitius* are these, ♄ Blacke, ♃ Green, Spotted, or Ashy, or such like; ♂ Red; ☉ Tawny or Saffron, I rather conceive an high Sandy colour. The Colors by mixing the Planets one with another are these; ♄ and ♃, a darke Greene, or deepe spotted with Blacke; ♄ and ♂ a darke Tawney, ♄ and ☉ a Black-yellow and shining, ♄ and ♀ a White gray, ♄ and ☿ a Black or Blewish, ♄ and ☽ a deepe Tawney, or deep Gray or Russet. ♃ and ♂ a Tawney, somewhat light spotted, ♃ and ☉ much after the mixture of the *Sunne* and *Mars* but more shining, ♃ and ♀ a Greenish Gray, ♃ and ☿ a Spotted Green, ♃ and ☽ somewhat a high Greene. ♂ and ☉ a deepe Red shining, ♂ and ♀ a light Red or Crimson, ♂ and ☿ a Red or a red Tawney, ♂ and the ☽ a Tawney or light Red.

They who are conversant in judging many Thefts, might much perfect this judgmet; I have known it hold true very many times; my greater imployments keeps me from further observations.

You must mix the colour of the Signifier with the colour of the House he is in, and thereafter judge the colour of their Cloathes; or judge the Colour by the Signes and the Degrees the Signifier is in; as if he be in the Signe, or House, or Terme of ♄, judge after ♄ as before; and if he be in the House of ♄ and Terme of ♃, judge after the mixture of ♄ and ♃, and so of all other as before.

For Names.

♃ ☉ and ♂ in Angles signifie short Names and of few Syllables, and being neer the Mid-heaven doe begin with *A* or *E*: ♄ or ♀ Significator, the Name is of more Syllables, as *Richard* or *William*; for the most part if the Querents Names be short, so is also the Quesited.

Names of Theeves or Men, as Astrologers write.

To know the Names by the Lord of the seventh House; or the Planet in the seventh House, or the Planet joyned with them, as followeth:

all manner of Questions. 341

Mens names.

☿	♂	Matthew.
☽	☿	Simon.
☉	♃	Laurence.
☿	☉	Clement.
☿	♄	Edmund.
♃	☉	John.
♄	♀	William.
♂	☉	Robert.
♂	☉	Peter.
♂		Anthony.
☉	☿	Benjamin.
♃	♄	Thomas.
☉		Roger.
☉		Phillip.
♄	☉	George.
☉	♄	Andrew.
☽	☉	Henry.
☽	♄	Nicholas.
♃	☉	Richard.
☉		James.
☉		Stephen.

The principall *Significator*. | The Planet joyned.

Womens Names

♂	☿	Katherine.
☿	♂	☉ Christian.
♄	☽	♀ Joane.
♀	♄	Isabel.
♄	☉	Elizabeth.
♄	☉	Julian.
☽	♂	☉ Mary.
☽	♀	Ellin.
♀	☿	Agnes.
☉	☿	Margaret.
☉	♀	Alice.
☉	☿	Edith.
☉	♀	Maud.
☉	♃	Lucy.
☉		Anne.
♃		Rachel.
☽		Nell, Ellenor.

The *Significator*. | The Planets conjoyned.

Some moderne Professors, have endeavoured to give aprobable conjecture what Christian name the Thief is of, or party enquired after, whether man or woman. first, they confider if the Planet who is principall *Significator* of the party enquired of, whether he be angular or no, and then whether he be in aspect (it matters not what aspect, good or ill) with any Planet or Planets; if he be in no aspect, then in whose Dignities he is, and from hence they make their mixture; for example; let us admit ☿ to be Lord of the seventh, and *Significa-*

Vv 3 *tor*

tor of a Maids Lover, and he in aspect, or in the dignities of ♂, I shall then have recourse to the Table before, and there I find in the first line over against ☿ and ♂ *Matthew*, I shall then say the man's name is *Matthew*, or of a name equivalent in length, or same number of letters: for my part I never use this way, nor yet have much credited it; yet I beleeve, were it well practised, we might find out very pretty conclusions, and goe neer to find the very name, or somewhat neer it.

Whether the Thief be of the house or not.

If both the Lights behold the ascendant, or be in their owne houses, the Thief is one of the Family, the Lord of the seventh in the ascendant, *idem*; the Lord of the sixt in the second, it is a Servant; if either of the *Luminaries* behold the ascendant, it is no stranger; ☉ opposite to the ascendant, it is an overthwart Neighbour; the Lord of the seventh beholding the ascendant with a friendly aspect, *idem*.

A Stranger or Familiar.

☉ and ☽ beholding the ascendant or the Lord of the ascendant in the first, or joyned to the Lord of the seventh, it is one of the house, or one that frequents the house; the *Luminaries* in their proper houses, or in the house of the Lord of the ascendant, the same; in the Triplicity of the Lord of the ascendant, a Neighbour; in the Terms of him, a Familiar; ☽ in the ninth in ☌ □ or ☍ to ♄ or ♂, brings back the Thief; without fail if they be Retrograde.

Another.

If ☉ and ☽ aspect the Lord of the ascendant, and not the ascendant, the Thief is knowne to the owner; the *Significator* of the Thiefe strong in the ascendant, noteth a Brother or Kinsman; *Zael*, Lord of the seventh in the ninth from his owne house, it is a Stranger; ☉ and ☽ beholding each other, a Kinsman; the Lord of the ascendant in the third or fourth, accuseth thine owne houshold-Servant; this I have oft proved true by experience.

all manner of Questions. 343

Rules by the Lord of the seventh house.

The Lord of the seventh in the ascendant or fourth, noteth one of the house, or of the houshold, or frequenting the house, and is in the City or Towne, and is one whom the *querent* least mistrusteth, and one which will hardly confesse the fact.

The Lord of the seventh in the second, noteth one of the houshold, or an acquaintance (if it be in a masculine Signe,) but if it be in a feminine Signe, it is his Wife, perhaps a Sweet-heart or Mayd of the house, and is within the power of the Loser, or some of his house, and may be recovered by money.

The Lord of the seventh in the third, one of the Kinred, Brotherr, Sisters, Cozens, or his onely Fellow by way of service, or some Neighbour often in his sight, or his Disciple, Messenger or Servant, &c.

The Lord of the seventh in the fourth, it is his Father, or some old Body, or of his Fathers Kin, or one dwelling in the Heritage or house of his Father, and the Thiefe hath given it to his Wife, or the woman to her Husband, or it is the good man or good Wife of the house, or else he is a Tiller or Labou- of the Land for the *querent*.

The Lord of the seventh in the fift, the Sonne or Daughter of him, or the Sonne or Daughter of his Cozen or Nephew, (if the Sign be a masculine) or of the hushold of his Father, or else his very Friend.

The Lord of the seventh in the sixt, a Servant, a Disciple or Labourer to the *querent*, or one conversant with some Churchman, a Brother or Sister of the Father, a sick body or unsteadfast, or grieved person.

The Lord of the seventh in the seventh, his Wife or Lady, or an Harlot, or a woman that useth to be suspected for such matters, or a Buyer or Seller in Markets; if it be a feminine Signe, the Taker is an utter enemy to the Loser, by some cause formerly happened between them, and dwels somewhat far from him, and the things are in his custody still, and hard to be recovered. *This must be warily understood.*

The Lord of the seventh in the eighth, a Stranger, yet seemeth

The Resolution of

eth to be one of the houshold, or one of his open enemies, or of his neer Kinswoman, for some cause of offence done, or some evill disposed person (and of the Livery of the Man) and he useth to come to his House, and either is kept by him, or else doth some servile acts, as a Butcher or Labourer doth, otherwhiles to kill Cattell, and it seemeth the thing lost will not be had againe but by either faire words, or dread of death, or by reason of some threats, or else the thing is lost by some Man absent, the which is not now had in minde at this time, but seem to be quite forgotten.

The Lord of the seventh in the ninth, an honest person, a Clarke, or a Church-man, and the Thiefe is out of the way or Country, a Disciple, or Governour to some Master of some priviledged Place, or a poore vagrant person, hard to be recovered but by some religious person as aforesaid.

I ever finde it to signifie one lodging in the House, when the thing was lost, or using the House.
    The Lord of the seventh in the tenth, A Lord, or Master, or Governour in the Kings house, or of his Houshold; or some Lady or Gentlewoman, if the Figure be Feminine, *& e contra*; or some crafts-Master; usually its some person that lives handsomely, and is not necessitated to this course of life.

The Lord of the seventh in the eleventh, a Friend or one knowne by some service done; or of the houshold of some man of the Church, or Neighbour, or servant in the place where the Querent hath some Lordship, and is put in trust. or is of the Houshold of the Querent his Mother, and by such a one or his meanes to be recovered againe.

The Lord of the seventh in the twelfth, a Stranger, envious a false person, and inthralled, incumbred or oppressed with poverty, and hath no riches; wherefore he hath visited many Regions, as some Enemy or Beggar doth, and he joyeth in it; judge his quality by the Signe and Place, and commix all these with the other testimonies of the Signes and Planets.

Whether the Thiefe be in the Towne or no.

Behold the Significator of the Thiefe, if thou finde him in the end of a Signe direct, or separating from Combustion, or applying to a Planet in the third or ninth House; say, he is gon

or

all manner of Questions.

or going out of the Town, for the removing of the *Significator* out of one Signe into another, denoteth change of Lodging or removing; if it be a superiour Planet, the rule is infallible.

If the Lord of the ascendant and the ☽ be not in one quarter but above ninety degrees asunder, it noteth departure, or a great distance betwixt the Goods and the Owner; but if they be in angles, and applying to Planets in angles, it noteth no farre distance, especially if the ☽ and the Lord of the ascendant be in one quarter.

Distance betwixt the Owner and the Thief.

If the Thief, *viz.* his *Significator*, be in a fixed Signe, account for every house betwixt the Lord of the ascendant and him, three miles; in common Signes, every house betwixt the ascendant and Thief, one mile; in movable Signes, for every house betwixt the ascendant and the Thiefe, account that so many houses on the earth are betwixt the Loser and the Thiefe. *These judgments best agree from the Country.*

If the Signe ascending be a fixed Signe, for every house give three miles; if a common Signe, then for every house give one mile; if a movable Signe, for every house reckon one halfe mile.

If his *Significator* be in an angle, he is still in the Towne; in a succedant, not far off, in a cadents he is far gone.

Where the Thief is.

☽ In an angle, at home; succedant, about home; if in cadent, far from home. *These are still for the Coun-*

The *Significator* of the Thief in an angle, in a house; ☽ in an *try.* angle, in his owne house; in a succedant, he is in Closes; ☽ in a succedant, in his owne Closes.

The *Significator* of the Thiefe in a cadent house, he is in a Common; ☽ in a cadent, in his owne Common, or that which belongs to the Towne he lives in.

If the *Signifier* of the Thief be within thirty degrees of the Lord of the ascendant, then is the Thiefe neer him that lost the

X x   Goods

The Resolution of

Goods; if within seventy degrees, within the Towne or Parish of him that lost the Goods, the more degrees betwixt them, the farther off they are from each other.

If the *Significator* be in a □ aspect to the Lord of the ascendant, he is out of the Towne; if the Lord of the seventh be strong, & in an angle, the Thief is not yet gone out of the Town or Parish where the Theft was acted; if he be found weak in an angle, he is gone, or departing.

Another.

It sometimes holds true, the Lord of the seventh in the ascendant, the Thiefe brings the Goods home willingly.

If the Lord of the seventh be in the ascendant, tell the *Querent* the Thiefe will be at home (before him) or before he get home *probatum est.*

If the Lord of the seventh be in the seventh, he is hid at home and dare not be seen.

If the Lord of the sixt be in the first or second with any of their Lords, the Thief is of the house of the *Querent*.

If the Lord of the ascendant and the *Significator* of the Theif be together, the Thief is with the *Querent, probatum est*; the very truth is, he cannot be far from him.

Toward what part the Thief is gone.

These things shal be more fully explicated in the succeding sheet.

If you would know to what part he is fled after he is gone out of Towne, behold the Planet that signifies his going out of Towne, and in what Sign he is; and if he be in a fiery Sign, say he is in the east part of the Towne or Country; if he be in a watry Signe, he is in the north; if in an Ayëry Signe, he is in the west; if in an earthly Signe, he in the south: Behold also in what quarter of Heaven he is in, and judge accordingly; if the *Signifier* be in the west, he is in the west; the east part is from the Mid heaven to the ascendant, &c. mix the signification of the Signe with the signification of the quarter, and thereafter judge, preferring the Signe before the quarter, onely making use of the quarter to ballance your judgment when other testimonies are equall.

Which

all manner of Questions.

Which way the Thief is gone.

Behold the significant Planet, in what Signe he is, and also the quarter, and accordingly judge; others judge by the place of the ☽; others behold the Lord of the seventh, and the Lord of the hour, what Signe and quarter they are in, and if they agree, then they judge thereafter; others regard the *Significator* to whom he doth apply, or render his power; others by the Lord of the fourth, I alwayes judge by the strongest, either of the *Significator* or the ☽.

If the *Significator* of the Thief be in a fiery Sign, he went east; earthly, south; ayëry, west; watry, north; see what angle ☽ is in, there is the Thief; in no angle, look for the Lord of the house of the ☽, to that part he went. *The peculiar quarter of heaven every Signe naturally signifie doth follow hereafter.*

See what Signe the Lord of the seventh is in; if in ♈, eastward; in ♉, in the South against the east; and so of the rest.

Of the house of the Thiefe, and the mark thereof.

If you will know the quality of the house the thing lost is in, and the signe and token thereof, and in what place the thing is, behold the Signe the *Significator* of the Thief is in, and in what part of heaven he is, and say in that part of the Towne the thing is; if it be in the ascendant, it is in the point of the east; in the seventh, just in the west; in the fourth, just in the north; in the tenth, it is south; and if it be between these angles, judge accordingly; as south-west or north-west; give the place of ☉ to be the house the Thief is in, and the place of the ☽ to be the door of the house; if the ☉ be in an Orientall Signe, the house is in the east part from the Master, or from him that lost the Goods.

The Door of the house.

To know in what part of the house the Door is, behold the place the ☽ is in, whether in the angles, succedants or cadents, and judge as it is said in the parts of the house, the which part

The Resolution of

is taken of or from the Signe the ☽ is in one way; if the ☽ be in a fixed Signe, say the house hath but one door; in a movable Signe, say the door is high above the earth, and it may be there is one other little one; and if ♄ have any aspect to that Signe, the door hath been broken and after mended againe, or else it is black or very old.

Or is well Bard with Iron.

If ♂ have any aspect thereunto, the gate or door shall have some token of burning or fire; and if ♄ and ♂ have a friendly aspect to the same Signe, the gate is Iron, or most part of it, or a good strong one; and if the ☽ be infortunate, the gate or door is broken or bruised; and if the ☽ have small light, the house hath no door opening to the high-way, but opens on the back part of the house.

Tokens of the Thiefs house.

If the ☽ be in □ ♂ or ☍ to ♂, the door is burned with iron, fire or candle, or hath been cut with some iron instrument; if the ☽ be in △ or ✶ to ♂, say the door of the Thiefs house is mended with iron; if the ☽ be but newly encreased in light, his gate or door is part under the earth, or under a Bank side, or they goe downe by a step, ☽ in a fixed or movable Signe, he hath but one door outwardly, in common Signs more then one.

Or men goe down by steps.

☽ In a fixed Signe, the gate is under the earth, viz. if in ♉, or the house standeth on the Bank-side, if in ♒; ☽ in movable Signs, the gate or door is above the earth, and a step to go up in to it (*probatum est,*) or one ascends somewhat in going into the house.

☽ Infortunate, the gate is broken, and note what part of heaven ☽ is in, that part of the house the door standeth in; if ♄ aspect the ☽ with ☌ □ or ☍, the door or gate is broken downe, old or black; if with ✶ or △, the door is mended againe.

Of the house where the Thiefe remaineth or dwelleth.

Behold the Signe wherein the *Signifier* is in, and in what part

all manner of Questions. 349

part of heaven he is, & say the Goods so taken are in that quarter of the Town, as if in the ascendant, east; the place of the ☽ sheweth in what part the gate is in; for if she be in an easterly quarter, the gate is on the east-side of the house; if in a westerly quarter, on the west; and if the ☽ be fixed, the house hath but one door, neer to the ground; if in a movable Signe the gate is up some steps; if ♄ behold the Signe, the gate is, or hath been broken, and is very ancient, or is black; if ♂ behold it, it doth encrease the signification, *viz.* that it is rent or crackt, or torne, or needs repaire; if at such an aspect the ☽ hath but then small light, say there is no great appearance of iron work.

Several men, several minds

Are the Goods in the Owners hands.

Lord of the Ascendant in an Angle, the Goods are in his hands; the Lord of the houre in an Angle the same: if the Lord of the House of the ☽ be with the Lord of the houre in an Angle, the Goods are in his hands, and are Goods moveable; if the Lord of the houre and the Lord of the terme of the ☽ and the Lord of the second be in an Angle with the Lord of the Ascendant, they are in his hands and fixt Goods; if any of these Lords be in an Angle, with □ △ or ✶ to the Lord of the Ascendant, the Owner shall have his Goods againe.

If the Lord of the Ascendant and Lord of the houre be in a succedant House, the Goods are about the Owner, ☽ or the Lord of the House of the ☽ in a moveable Signe, they are not farre from the Owner; if the Lord of the terme of the ☽, or the Lord of the second be in a succedent House, then the things are about the Owner, and not much elongated.

The Planets last before spoken of, or rehearsed, placed in cadent Houses, shew the Goods farre from the Owner.

Whether the Goods be in the custody of the Thiefe.

Behold the signifier of the Thiefe or Theeves; and if he or they give their power to another Planet, the things stolen are not in the keeping of the Thiefe or Theeves; if he or they give not their power to another, it remaineth in his own power, custody or possession.

Behold

Behold the Lord of the terme wherein the *Significator* of the Thiefe is, and by him judge the estate of the Thiefe; if an infortunate Planet be in a fortunate terme, he was of a vilde stocke, and now is in good state : If a fortune be in the terme of an infortune, say the contrary.

If he carried all with him.

Behold the Lord of the seventh and eight, if the Lord of the seventh be in an Angle, he was willing to have carried all away, but could not ; if in a succedent, and the Lord of the eight with him strong, he had all ; if both the Lord of the seventh and eight be in cadent Houses, he neither carried it away or had it.

The distance of the thing from the Owner.

These rules are much followed by those that practise in the Country.

Behold how many Degrees are between the *Significator* and the ☽ ; and whether the Signes be fixed, moveable or common; in fixed Signes account for every Degree a Mile ; in common Signes so many tenths of Miles ; in Moveable Signes so many Rods. How many Degrees betwixt the Lord of the seventh and the Lord of the houre, so many thousand Paces betwixt the Querent and the Fugitive.

Looke what distance is betwixt the Ascendant and his Lord, such is the distance betwixt the place where the thing was lost and the thing it selfe.

Looke how many Degrees the *Signifier* is in his Signe, and so many Miles are the Cattell from the place where they went, and in that quarter or coast where the Lord of the fourth is.

How farre the thing is from the Querent.

Behold the Lord of the Ascendant and the Ascendant, and see how many Signes and Degrees are betwixt the Lord of the Ascendant and the Ascendant ; and if the Lord of the Ascendant be in a fixed Signe, then give for every Signe (betwixt him and the Ascendant) foure Miles ; and if he be in a common Signe, give for every Signe a Mile and a halfe ; and if he be in

a mo-

all manner of Questions. 351

a moveable Signe, give for every Signe (betwixt them) halfe a Mile, and the overplus of the Degrees, according to the Signe the Lord of the Ascendant is in: *As for example*;

A Question was asked, and the seventh Degree of ♑ ascendded, and ♄ in ♏ foure Degrees; so there is between the Ascendant and ♄ three Signes, and ♄ in a fixed Signe; therefore I must give for every Signe foure Miles, three times foure is twelue, and there is three Degrees more to the which belong halfe a Mile; so the whole sum is twelve Miles and a halfe.

The Place where the Goods stolne are.

If you will know the place where the thing stolne is in; take Signification of the Place from the Signe the *Significator* of the Thiefe is in, and from the place of the Lord of the fourth House; if they be both in one Signification it is well; if not, behold then what place is *Signified* by the Lord of the fourth House, and judge by that Signe the nature of the place where the thing stolne is. If he be in a moveable Signe, it is in a place high from the ground; if in a fixed Signe, it is in the Earth; and if in a common Signe, it is under some Eaves of a House; and helpe your judgement in these by the Terme of the Signes, as if the *Significator* be in ♈, it is in a place where Beasts doe use that be small, as Sheep, or Hogs, &c. if he be in ♌, it is in a place of Beasts which bite as Dogs, &c. if he be in ♐, it is in a place of great Beasts that are ridden; as in a Stable of Horses, or such like: if in ♉ ♍ or ♑, it Signifieth a House or place of great Beasts, as Oxen, Kine, or such other Cattle: ♍ or ♑ Signifieth a place of Camels, Mules, Horses, Asses, and such like: ♍ hath the Signification of a Barn, and of such places as be under the Earth, or neer to the Earth, or Granaries, such as they put Corne in: ♑ Signifieth a place of Goats, Sheepe, Hogs, and such like. If he be in ♊ ♎ ♒, it is in the House; in ♊ it is in the Wall of the House; ♎ neer a little House or Closet; ♒ it is neer a Doore that is above a Doore or Gate, in some place on high. If ♋ ♏ or ♓, the thing is in Water, or neer Water, and these doe Signifie a Pit or Cistern: ♏ it is neer a place of uncleanWater, or where they use to cast

More certainly by the Lord of the fourth. This is where things are hid in grounds.

cast out filthy Water, as a Gutter: ♓ sheweth a place alwayes moyst.

The place where the thing lost or stolne is hidden.

Behold the place of the *Significator* of the Thiefe, and the Lord of the fourth, if they be both in one *Signification* and wel agreeing, if not, behold the Lord of the fourth; if he be in a moveable Signe, it is in an high place; if in a fixed Signe, it is on the Earth; if in a common Signe, in a covered place. Herein behold what Signe the ☽ is, or whether in the Ascendant or Mid-heaven, or about it, behold the forme or Signe that Ascends with her, and say the thing is in that place which the forme thereof representeth.

Where the Goods are.

Looke to the Lord of the second and his *Almuten*, (*viz.* he that hath most dignities there) there are the Goods: if the Lord thereof and the Lord of the fourth be both in one Signe, judge the things to be where they are, and the Thiefe and Theft both together; if they be not together, judge by the fourth, &c.

If the Lord of the fourth be found in a fixed Sign, the Goods are in the Earth, or in a House having no Chamber.

If the Lord of the fourth be in a moveable Signe, the Goods are in a Chamber above another, or in an upper Loft or Room.

If in a common Signe, in a Chamber within another Chamber. If the Goods be found in a fiery Signe, they are East; in an Earthy, South; in an Aery, West; in a Watery, North.

This is, when Goodsare certainly known to be out of the House.

If the Lord of the terme of the ☽ be in an angle, and in a moveable Signe, the Goods are in Closes where are both Corne and Grasse.

If in a succedent and fixed Signe, in Woods, Parkes, or in closed Grounds that lyeth from the High-way-side: if in a cadent and common Signes, in a Common of divers Mens, or Pasture or Meddow of divers Mens.

Haly faith, it was asked him one time when ♌ was Ascending

all manner of Questions. 353

ing and ♀ therein; and he faith, the thing was under a Bed neer a Robe or Covering; becauſe ♀ was in the Aſcendant, the which is *Signifecatrix* of a Bed, and after theſe conſiderations judge.

Loſt or ſtolen in what part of the houſe.

If the thing loſt or ſtolen be in the houſe, & you would know the place where it is, behold the Lord of the fourth, and the Planet which is therein; if it be ♄, it is hid in a dark place or part of the houſe, or in a deſolate or ſtinking place and deep, be it a ſiege-houſe or Jakes, where people ſeldome come.

If it be ♃, it ſignifies a place of Wood, Buſhes or Bryers.

If it be ♂, it is in ſome Kitchin, or in a place where fire is uſed, or in a Shop, &c.

If it be ☉, it ſignifieth the Cloyſter or Hall of the houſe, or the Place or Seat of the Maſter of the houſe.

If it be ♀, it ſignifieth the place of the Seat of a woman, or Bed, or Cloathes, or where women are moſt converſant.

If it be ☿, it is in a place of Pictures, Carving or Books, or a place of Corne, and chiefly in ♍.

If it be ☽, it is in a Pit, Ciſterne or Lavatory.

The true quality of the Planet and Signe doth ſignifie, I have exactly ſet forth from pag. 57. to pag 100.

The forme or likeneſſe of the entring of the houſe

Behold the place of the ☉, from him is knowne the forme and likeneſſe of the opening of the houſe; from ☽ is knowne the Sellar, and the place that holdeth the water, or a Pit; by ♀, the place of Mirth, Play, and women, &c. from the place of the ☊ is knowne the place of height, or higheſt Seat, Stool, Stairs or Ladder to climbe by; and from the place of the ☋ is knowne the place the Wood is in, or the houſe the Beaſts be in, or a Pillar in the houſe; and if ☿ be in a common Signe it is in a little Cell within another Chamber; if he be in a movable Signe, it is within a little Cell that hath another Chamber about it; if in a fixed Signe, it is in a houſe that hath no Sellar nor other Chamber, as many Country-houſes have not.

This hath relation as well to any other thing as to Thefts, and may be made good uſe of for ſeverall Diſcoveries.

Y y　　　　　　　　And

And if ♃ or ♀, or both of them be in the the tenth house, the door hath a faire opening; if ♄ be in the tenth, the opening of the door is neer some Ditch or Pit, or deep place; if ♂ be there, neer to the opening of the house is the place of making a fire, or killing of Beasts, or heading; if ☿ be in the tenth, say in the opening of the house, is a place where the Master of the house keeps his things in, *viz.* his instruments or Tools he uses about his Beasts; and if ☉ be in the tenth, in the opening is some Stoole or Seat to sit on, or a bed; if the ☽ be in the tenth house, say that in the entring of the house is a door under the ground, or some other neccessary thing that a man hath much occasion to use in his house, as a Furnace or Quern, or such like.

What is stolne by the Lord of the second or tenth House.

More properly by the Lord of the second.

♄ Lead, Iron, Azure, blacke or blew colour, Wooll, blacke Garments, Leather, heavy things, labouring tooles for the Earth: ♃ Oyle, Honey, Quinces, Silke, Silver: ♀ white Cloth, and white Wine, Green-colour.

♂ Pepper, Armour, Weapons, red Wine, red Cloathes, Brasse, Horses for Warre, hot things: ☿ Books, Pictures, implements: ☉ Gold, Oringes, Brasse, Carbuncles, yellow-Cloathes: ☽ ordinary and common Commodities.

The quality of the Goods stolne.

These Judgments are more proper for the Country then City.

Behold the Lord of the second; if he be ♄, it is Lead, Iron, or a Kettle, something with three feet; a Garment or some blacke thing, or a Hide or Beasts skin.

If ♃ be Lord of the second, some white thing; as Tyn, Silver, or mixed with vaines, as it were with yellow and white, or broad Cloath, &c.

☉ Signifies Gold and precious things, or things of good value. ♂ those which be fiery and belong to the fire, Swords, Knives. ♀ Such things as belong to Women, Rings, faire Garments, Smocks, Wastecoats, Peticoats.

☽ Beasts, as the Horse, Mules, Cowes, or Poultry in the Country

all manner of Questions.

try of all forts; ☿ Money, Books, Paper, Pictures, Garments of divers colours.

A signe of recovery.

The ☽ in the seventh Aspecting the Lord of the Ascendant with a △, ♀ or the Lord of the second in the Ascendant, ♃ in the second direct, ♀ Lady of the second in the Ascendant, ☽ in the tenth in △ to a Planet in the second: ☽ in the second, with a △ to the Lord of the second: ☽ in the second, to a □ of ☉ in the twelfth: the Lord of the Ascendant in the second, ☉ and ☽ aspecting each other with a △, ☉ and ☽ aspecting the cuspe of the second with a △: Lord of the second in the fourth, or in the House of the Querent, *viz.* in the Ascendant.

These are excellent and approved rules. This must be in Signes of short ascentions.

If it shall be recovered.

To know if it shall be recovered or not: For resolution hereof, behold the Lord of the terme of the ☽, the which is *Signifier* of the substance stolne to be recovered. If the Lord of the terme of the ☽, and the Lord of the house of the ☽ be increasing both in motion and number, and free from infortunes; it shews it shall be recovered whole and sound, and nothing diminished thereof.

Consider also the Lord of the houre, and take his testimony, as you did from the Lord of the terme of the ☽; behold also the application of the Lord of the Ascendant, unto the Lord of the terme of the ☽, or unto the Lord of the second House; or if that they apply unto him, for when he doth apply unto one of them, or to both, and the ☽ apply unto them both or to the Lord of her House, or if the ☉ doe apply unto the Lord of his House, and the ☽ be dimished in light; I meane if the Lord of his House, the Lord of the terme of the ☽, and the Lord of the House of the ☉, doe apply to the ☉; for the state of all these doe Signifie that the thing stole shall be found, and especially if the Planet *Signifier* be in an angle or succedant.

To encrease in motion is, whenas lately a Planet had moved slowly, and now encreases his motion, or moves more quick; to encrease in number is, when the day subsequent he is found to have moved more minutes then the day or the dayes preceding.

Also if the Lord of the terme of the ☽, or the Lord of the House of the ☽, or the Lord of the second house apply unto

Yy 2

The Resolution of

the Lord of the Ascendant, the Master of the thing lost shall recover the same. Also if the ☽ or Lord of the Ascendant apply unto the Ascendant, or one of them apply unto the Lord of the second House, or unto the Lord of the terme of the ☽, the thing stolne shall be had againe through inquisition and diligent search.

And if the Lord of the House of the ☽, and the Lord of the Terme of the ☽ be both diminished in their motion or number, say the more part is lost and shall not be recovered.

If the Lord of the terme of the ☽, and the Lord of the house of the ☽ be increasing in number and motion, and safe from ill fortunes, the thing shall be restored whole and nothing diminished; for if those *Signifiers* be not cadent from angles, it *Signifieth* the things shall be soon recovered; but if they be in angles, it *Signifieth* meanly, *viz.* neither very soone nor very late, *viz.* the recovery.

In what time it shall be recovered.

Behold the application of the two Planets that *Signifie* the recovery, and number the Degrees that are between them, or from the one to the other, and determine dayes, weekes, yeers, or houres, in this manner; Behold the place they are in, or the place of their application; for if they be in moveable Signes, the shorter time is required or it shal be in weeks, or in months; in fixed Signes it *Signifies* Moneths or Yeers; in commonSigns a meane betwixt both: helpe your selfe from these judgments: or if the *Significator* be quick in motion, they Signifie it shall be recovered quickly, or lightly: which *Significators*, if they be falling from angles, signifieth a time more short, wherein the Goods shall be recovered: These Judgements are made properly for this Chapter; you must not judge in other things by these, or by this Method.

Aphorismes concerning Recovery.

The Lord of the eight in the Ascendant, or with the Lord there-

all manner of Questions. 357

thereof, signifies the recovery of the theft. The Lord of the second in the eight, denieth recovery.

♄ also, or ♂, or ☋, signifieth dividing and losse of the thing, and that all shall not be recovered.

The Lord of the second in the Ascendant sheweth recovery.

The Lord of the Ascendant in the second, signifieth recovery after long search.

If the second House be hindered or the Lord thereof, it cannot be that all shall be found and recovered.

When the Lord of the Ascendant and the ☽, with the ☉, or the Lord of the tenth, or the Lord of the House of the ☽; or if the Lord of the seventh be with the Lord of the Ascendant, or have good aspect to him; or if the Lord of the seventh be in combustion; or at least the Lord of the tenth, and the Lord of the house of the ☽ agree well together, upon such a position it is probable the thing lost shall and may be recovered. When both the Luminaries are under the earth it cannot be recovered.

Whatsoever is lost, the ☉, together with the ☽, beholding the Ascendant cannot be lost but will, shortly be discovered.

Behold when the body of the ☽ and the body of the Lord of the Ascendant, *viz.* when one of them applyeth bodily to the Planet that signifieth recovery; the thing stole shall then be recovered; and if the application of the Significators be by Retrogradation, the recovery shall bee sudden, if the application be by direction, the recovery shall be before it be looked for.

Behold also the Lord of the term of the ☽, if he do apply to the same term, and the Lord of the house of the ☽ applies to the same house, or when the Lord of the second house applies to his own house: or when any of them apply to the Ascendant; all these do signify the time of recovery.

Look also if the ⊗ have any testimony with the Lord of the Ascendant, or with the ☽, because when any of them apply to each other, or the Lord of the house of the ☽ to the ☽, there is the time of the recovery in hope; and when the Lord of ⊗ applyes to the Lord of the Ascendant, or to the second house, or unto the place in which the ⊗ is, or to the ☽; all these

Y y 3   signify

358 *The Resolution of*

signify recovery: Behold also how many degrees is from the planet which signifyeth recovery, unto the angle he goeth first to, and the number of those degrees is the time of recovery.

When both the lights behold themselves in angles, it signifyeth recovery of the thing at length, but with labour and pain; and it signifies more then one thief; if the aspect be a △, it signifyeth the lighter recovery.

The ☽ in the Ascendant with any Fortune, it signifies recovery: If the ☽ be *sub radijs*, or combust, it signifieth the thing lost shall not be recovered, if it be, it shall be with much pain and labour; ☉ and ☽ in the tenth, sudden recovery.

If both ☉ and ☽ be nearer the Ascendant then any other angle, it signifyes recovery of the thing with much trouble, anxiety, strife, bloodshed, or quarrelling.

When ☉ is in the Ascendant, the thing stolen shall be recovered, except the Ascendant be ♎ or ♒; for therein the ☉ is weak. The ☽ in the Ascendant and ♃ with her, it shall be recovered.

Of the discovery of the thief, and recovery of the goods.

If ☽ be in the Ascendant, or in a △ aspect to the Lord thereof, thou findest the thief.

If there be a △ aspect between ☉ and ☽, it signifies recovery. If ☉ and ☽ be joyned to the Lord of the seventh, or beholding him by any aspect, he cannot hide himself.

If the Lord of the Ascendant apply to the second, or the Lord of the second to the Ascendant; if there be any application or translation of light between the Lord of the 8th, and the Lord of the second; or the Lord of the eighth be in the second, it signifyes recovery.

☽ in the second with one of the Fortunes, or applying with a good aspect to her own house, or the Lord of the sign wherein she is, sheweth recovery.

The chiefest signes of no recovery are if ♄ ♂ or ☋, be in the second, or the Lord of the second in the eighth, or combust, or when the Lord of the second applieth to the Lord of the eighth with any aspect, all or any of these are signes of no recovery. If the Lord of the second be in his exaltation, there is

a great

all manner of Questions.

a great hope of recovery, especially if there be any other testimony of the recovery.

Of Theft.

If the Lord of the seventh be in the ascendant, the theft shall be restored againe; if the Lord of the ascendant be in the seventh, it will be found after much enquiry; if ☽ be in the ascendant, or with the Lord of the ascendant, it will be found or may be found; if the ☽ be in the fift, with the Lord of the ascendant, it may be had; or if ☉ and ☽ be in the fift, and the Lord of the eighth be with the Lord of the ascendant in the ascendant, it will be found. *Thefts recoverable or no*

If the Lord of the second be in the eighth, it cannot be had; if ♄ or ♂ or ☋ be in the second, it will not be had; if the Lord of the second be in the ascendant, it will be had againe, and none shall know how; if the Lord of the ascendant be in the second, with great labour it may be had; if the Lord of the second be cadent, it will not be had; but if he be in his exaltation, it will be quickly restored; the sooner if ☽ apply unto him.

Other Judgments of Thefts.

Lord of the ascendant and Lord of the seventh joyned, it shall be got by searching of the *querent*.

Lord of the ascendant in the seventh, or the lord of the ascendant joined to the lord of the eighth, or Lord of the seventh in the ascendant, the Thief comes of his owne accord before he goes any farther; very many times I have found it so.

If ☽ be separated from the lord of the ascendant, and be joyned to the lord of the seventh, he shall be found, *viz.* the Thief.

The lord of the seventh joyned to an *Infortune* in an angle, he shall be taken: the Lord of the seventh joyned to a *Fortune*, he shall not be taken, unlesse that *Fortune* be under the ☉ beams, or impedited; if he goe to combustion, it signifies his death.

☽ joyned to an infortunate Planet, he shall be found; ☽ joyned to a retrograde Planet, he returnes of his owne accord. *I have oft found this true.*

The Resolution of

cord, if he went; if the same Planet be stationary, he shall not remove from his owne place untill he be taken.

Whether the Thief shall be knowne or not.

Most Planets in cadents, he shall be knowne: ☉ ☌ ☐ or ☍ to the *Significator* of the Thief, knowne; ☉ in ✶ to him, he is suspected, but not openly knowne.

Whether the Thief be suspected of the Owner or not.

If the Thief be in ☐ or ☍ to the lord of the ascendant he is suspected, a △ or ✶, not; if the Thieve's *Significator* be in ☌ with the ☽, the Owner suspecteth one with him, or using his owne company.

If the ☽ be in ☐ or ☍ to any Planet in the tenth or seventh, say he suspecteth one far from him, except the *Almuten* of the tenth or seventh house be in ☐ or ☍ to the ☽.

If ☽ have ☌ ☐ or ☍ to a Planet in the seventh, or to the *Almuten* thereof, the Owner suspecteth him; but if ☽ aspecteth another Planet, he suspecteth another, and not the Thief: if the ☽ be joyned to, or received of an evill Planet, the suspected is the Thiefe; look to the lord of the ascendant and the ☽, and take the strongest of them, who if he have received any vertue from evill Planets, *viz.* separated from them, he hath played the Thiefe; and so much the more being received of the Lord of the second: Lord of the ascendant in an angle, applying or separating to a Planet in a cadent house, truth is said of him; or ☽ conjoyned to a Planet in an angle, especially in the tenth, signifies the same.

Who did the Deed or Theft.

This where the querent is suspected a Knave.

Lord of the ascendant in the second, or seventh, it is the Owner himselfe; or lord of the second in the ascendant, the owner. If ☉ and ☽ be with the Lord of the 3^d, it's the Owners Kinsman; ☉ and ☽ in the fourth, Father or Mother, or a Friend; ☉ or ☽ in the fift, a Sonne or Daughter of the Owner; ☉ or ☽ in the sixt, a Servant; ☉ or ☽ in the seventh his Wife or a Woman.

☉ and

all manner of Questions. 361

☉ and ☽ together conjoyned, beholding the ascendant, the Owner's acquaintance; or if either of them behold the ascendant, *idem.*

☉ or ☽ in their proper houses, or in the ascendant, the Owner may be justly suspected.

If ☉ or ☽ be not together, but one of them behold the ascendant, it was one was borne, or formerly lived in the house where the robbery was done.

If ☉ or ☽ be in their owne Triplicity, the Thief retaines *A Familiar* him that lost the Goods; they having but a Face where they *of the house.* are, then he is not one of the house, but Kin unto him.

If ☉ or ☽ behold the ascendant, and not the Thief, the Thief entred not the house before he took it.

If the Thiefe have any great Dignities in the ascendant, the Thiefe is Kin to the *Querent*, or a very neer acquaintance.

♂ being *Significator* of the Thiefe, and placed in the tenth, the *querent* is the Thief, or very negligent.

The Lord of the seventh in the ascendant, he is suspected to be the Thiefe.

Whethes it be the first fact the Thief hath committed.

If ☉ and ☽ doe behold the Lord of the house where the ☽ is from an angle, he hath plaid the Thief more then once.

If ⊗ or Lord of the seventh be free from misfortunes, or ♃ *Significator* alone of the Thiefe, it is the first fact he hath committed.

♂ separating from the Lord of the seventh, or ♄ Orientall, *Viz. By vi-* it is not the first; ♂ *Significator*, he breaketh in*; ♀, under the *olence.* cloak of love; ☿, by subtilty and flattery.

Of Theft by Astrologie, or LILLIE *s best experienced Rules.*

Many Thieves, if peregrine Planets be in angles.   Number.

The *Sigtificator* in a Signe of Fruitfulnesse, *viz.* ♋ ♏ ♓; or in a Bycoporeall, *viz.* ♊ ♐ ♍ ♓; or beholding many peregrine Planets.

The angles fixed, or the ☽ or Significator in Signes of direct *One.* ascention, which are ♋ ♌ ♍ ♎ ♏ ♐; or in Signes not fruitfull. *viz.* ♈ ♉ ♊ ♌ ♎ ♐ ♑.

Zz   The

The Resolution of

The Sex.

Masculine, if the Lord of the hour, Lord of the seventh and his Dispositor be masculine, or if the Dispositor of the ☽ and the Planet to whom she applies be masculine; or if the *Significator* be in the masculine part of Heaven, *viz.* in the first, twelfth, eleventh, or seventh, fixt, fift, and Orientall.

Feminine, if the contrary to this happen.

Age.

Old, or in yeers, the *Significator* being ♄.
A man, if ♃ ♂ or ☉.
Not so old, if ☿ or ♀ oe *Significators*.

The ☽ for her age, *viz.* young, she in her first quarter; more man if in her second quarter; and so in her third quarter more aged; in her last quarter of greater yeers.

Where note, the ☽ or any Planet Orientall, denotes the Thief more young; Occidentall, more aged. Or thus; observe in what house the *Significator* is in, give for every house five yeers from the ascendant.

Or observe the degree descending in the seventh house, and give for every degree two yeers.

Or see the age of the Planet to whom the ☽ applyes, or the *Significator* of the Thief, or consider the day of the moneth the Question is asked, give for every day elapsed to the day of the Question two yeers.

The best way, and most sure is, to consider most of these wayes, and pitch upon the greatest number.

Forme and Stature.

Proportion great, if the *Significator* have much Orientality, and be in ♌ ♏ or ♐.

Proportion little, if his Occidentality be much, or the *Significator* in ♋ ♏ or ♓.

The upper part of his body is thick and strong, if the *Significator* be in ♈ ♉ ♌; his lower parts if in ♐ ♊ ♏.

Fat

Fat.

If the *significator* have much latitude from the *Ecliptick*, be Retrograde, or in his first station, or in the first part of ♈ ♉ ♌, or in the last part of ♊ ♏ ♐.

It's probable he inclines to talnesse, the ☽ in ♋ or ♓.

♎ ♍ or ♒ give fleshy bodies, and well proportioned.

Leane.

The *significator* having small latitude, or direct, or in his second station, or in the beginning of ♊ ♏ ♐, or in the summity of his Eccentricity.

☉ beholding the *Significator*, gives a handsome shape and fatnesse; the ☽ Beholding, gives temperature and moystnesse.

The Thiefs strength.

Significator in South latitude, the party is nimble; in North latitude, slow in motion.

A Planet in his first station gives strong bodies; going out of one Signe into another, weak and feeble.

Where the Knave is.

He flyes, or is running out of one place into another, or removing his Lodging, if the *significators* be going out of one Signe into another; or if his *significator* be leaving combustion, or the Rayes of the ☉; or if the Thiefs Dispositor seperate from the Lord of the first, and apply to a Planet in the sixt, eight or twelft.

He flies, or is farre distant if the *significator* of the Thiefe and thing sought after be not in one quarter of heaven, or apply to the Lord of the third or ninth, or if the *significators* be in the third or ninth.

He remaines,

If the Lord of the first be joyned to a Planet in a cadent house, and behold the ascendant.

The Resolution of
Who the Thiefe is.

A Familiar if ☉ and ☽ at one time behold the ascendant, or if the Lord of the first be joyned to the Lord of the seventh in the ascendant.

Or if ☉ and ☽ be in ♌ or ♋, or in the ascendant it selfe, or in the house of the Lord of the ascendant, and beholding him, or the Lord of the seventh house in the twelft or eight, the ☉ or ☽ in their exaltation, note one well knowne, but not of the Family.

The *Luminaries* in their Termes or Faces, the party is known to some of the houshold, but not of the Family; Lord of the seventh in the seventh he is of the Houshold.

A stranger

If the Lord of the seventh be in the third or ninth from his house.

Lord of the ascendant and lord of the seventh not of one Triplicity.

If you see the Thief is domesticall, then

☉ Signifies Father, or Master.
☽ The Mother, or Mistris.
♀ The Wife, or a Woman.
♄ A Servant, or a Stranger lying there by chance.
♂ A Son, or Brother, or Kinsman.
☿ A Youth, Familiar or Friend.

Whither is the Thief gone, or Fugitive.

Where you are principally to observe, that the ascendant, or a *significator* in the ascendant, signifieth the East; but this Table expresses the quarters of Heaven more fully.

First house East.
Second house Northest by East.
Third house North Northeast.
Fourth house North.
Fift housi Northwest by North.
Sixt house West, Northwest.

Seventh house West.
Eight house Southwest by South.
Ninth house South Southwest.
Tenth South.
Eleventh Southeast by South.
Twelft East, South-east.

The

all manner of Questions.

The Signes.

Aries *East.*	♈ *East.*	*This small dif-*
Taurus *South and by East.*	♌ *Northeast by East.*	*ference breeds*
Gemini *West and by South.*	♐ *East Southeast.*	*no error, let*
Cancer *is full North.*	♎ *West.*	*every one use*
Leo *East and by North.*	♊ *Southwest by West.*	*what he finds*
Virgo *South and by West.*	♒ *West, Northwest.*	*most true*
Libra *full West.*	♋ *North.*	
Scorpio *North and by East.*	♏ *North, Northeast.*	
Sagittarius *East and by South.*	♓ *Northwest by North*	
Capricornus *full South.*	♑ *South.*	
Aquarius *West and by North.*	♉ *Southeast by South*	
Pisces *North and by West.*	♍ *South, South-east.*	

The flight of the Thiefe.

It's swift, if his *Significator* be swift in motion, or joyned to Planets swift in motion, or being himselfe in Signes movable or of short ascentions.

His flight is uncertaine

If his or their *Significators* are in their second station, or joyned to stationary Planets in angles or succedants.

He makes slow haste

If his *Significator* is slow in motion, or joyned to Planets of slow motion, or in Signes fixed or of long ascentions.

He shall be taken.

If the Lord of the ascendant be in the seventh, or in ☌ to the Lord of the seventh; or the Lord of the seventh in the first, or joyned to the Lord of the first, or a Retrograde Planet; or if the ☽ separate from the lord of the seventh, to the ☌ of the lord of the first; or from the ☌ of the lord of the first to the lord of the seventh; or if ☉ and ☽ be in ☌ with the lord of the seventh, some say, if they behold him; or if the lord of the seventh be going to ☌, *viz.* Combustion; or if the lord of the ascendant be in ☌ in the ascendant, tenth or seventh, or an infortunate Planet in the seventh.

Not

Not taken.

If the lord of the seventh be in aspect with a *Fortune*, if in aspect to ♃ or ♀ in the eleventh, he escapes by friends; if in the third, by strangers.

The Goods restored.

If the lord of the first or second are in ☌ with the lord of the eight, or in any strong Reception:

Or if the lord of the second depart from Combustion; or *Sol* or ☽ in the ascendant or tenth house, it notes recuperation; the most part, if they are strong; lesse, if they be weak.

There's hopes of restitution when the Lights behold themselves with any aspect, chiefly in angles; or the lord of the seventh or eighth.

No Restitution.

If the lord of the second be Combust or the lord of the seventh in ☌ with the lord of the eight; or if the lord of the second behold not the first house, or his lord; or the *Sunne* and ☽ not aspecting themselves, or the ☋, or when both are under the earth.

Other Rules that the Thiefe shall be taken.

☽ In the seventh, applying to the lord of the eight.
Lord of the first in the ascendant.
☽ In the seventh, applying to a □ of ♂.
☽ separating from a □ of ♄ or ☿, applying to a □ of *Sol*.
☽ In the sixt, eight or twelfth.
☽ Separating from a ☌ of ♄, applying to a □ of ☿,
Lord of the seventh in the first.
☽ In the eight, in ☍ to ♂ in the second.

CHAP. LI.

Of Battle, Warre, or other Contentions.

IF one demand, whether he shall overcome his Adversary or not; give to the Querent the Lord of the ascendant the ☽, and the Planet from whom she is seperated; and unto the Defendant

all manner of Questions. 367

fendant the feventh and his Lord, and the Planet to whom th^e ☽ applyeth; and behold whofe *Significator* is in Angles and geft and with better Plenets, and fo judge.

If evill Planets be in the Afcendant, and Fortunes in the feventh, the Adverfary fhall overcome, *& e contra*. The Lord of the feventh in the Afcendant, betokens victory to the Querent, *& e contra*.

Whether one fhall returne fafe from Warre, or any dangerous Voyage.

Behold if the Lord of the Afcendant be ftrong, and with a good Planet, and well difpofed; it is a great teftimony of fecurity, *& e contra*. Behold alfo the feventh and the Lord thereof, and if they be Fortunate (although the firft be not fo) yet fhall the Party returne, though not without great croffes and lets, *& e contra*. Behold alfo the ☽ how fhe is difpofed; for her application with the good is Fortunate, *& e contra*. Evill Planets alfo in the eight, are no fmall Signification of feare, and terrour, or death. ♄ fignifies ruines or brufes, ♂ or the ☋ wounds by Weapons.

If one fhall returne fafe from Warre.

If the Lord of the Afcendant be with good or good himfelf, or a good Planet in the Afcendant, he fhall returne fafe. If the ☉ be with the Lord of the Afcendant in any part of the Queftion, he may not goe; becaufe the ☉ burnes him. If the Lord of the feventh be with a good Planet, and the Lord of the Afcendant with an evill, he fhall have fome impediment in his way, yet fhall not dye.

If an evill Planet be with the Lord of the firft, and a good one in the firft; if he then goe, he fhall fuffer great loffe, but not death; but queftionleffe he will be forely wounded.

If ♄ be in the firft, or with the Lord of the firft, let him not goe; becaufe loffe wil happen unto him by one whom he meeteth: If an ill Planet be with the Lord of the firft, and ♄ in the afcendant, or with his Lord, he fhall be wounded with Wood

or

368   *The Resolution of*

or Stone. If ♂ or the ☋ be in the Ascendant, or with the Lord thereof, or evill Planets in the first, or with the Lord thereof, he shall receive a wound, and go neer to dye thereof. Also if an evill Planet be in the eight, it is to be feared, death will ensue; if the ☉ be with the Lord of the seventh, or in the eight, it is ill to goe; and so of the tenth and seventh.

What will ensue of the Warre.

Behold the Lord of the seventh and first, and their Lords: the first House signifieth the Querent, the seventh his Adversary; if good Planets be in the first, and malevolent in the seventh, and the Lord of the Ascendant good, and Lord of the seventh ill; the Querent overcomes: but if an Infortune be with the Lord of the Ascendant, and an evill Planet in the Ascendant; and the Lord of the seventh good, and a good Planet there, the Querent shall be overcome, and shall be taken or slaine.

If both the Lord of the Ascendant and seventh be in the Ascendant, and on the behalfe of the Lord of the Ascendant, there be good Planets casting their benevolent aspects to the cuspe of the second; then the Querent will doe well in the Warre and obtaine money thereby; he shall have victory of his Adversary, or they will endevour to be reconciled.

Any Planet in the 10, 11, 12, 1, 2, 3. is conceived a friend to the Querent. So all Planets in the 9, 8, 7, 6, 5, 4. are reputed for the Quesited.

If both the Lords, *viz.* of the first and seventh, be in the Ascendant, and good Planets be on the part of the Ascendant, and evill on the part of the seventh; both Parties shall suffer losse; but the Querent shall have the better in the end. If the Lord of the seventh be in the Ascendant, of his Question, it shewes the Fortitude of the Actors; the contrary noteth the contrary.

If the Lord of the Ascendant be in the eight, or with the Lord of the eight, or the Lord of the eight in the Ascendant; it notes the death of the Querent.

If the Lord of the seventh be in the second, or with the Lord thereof; or the Lord of the second in the seventh, or with the Lord of the seventh; it notes the death of the Adversary.

Chap. LII.
Who shall doe best in a suit of Law.

IF the Lord of the Ascendant and seventh be in angles, neiher shall overcome: see which is joyned to an evil Planet in a cadent House, that Party shall be over-come: If both be joyned to Infortunes, both Parties will be undone by the Suit, or receive infinite prejudice. If the one be strong and the other weake, and he that is strong be not cadent, nor joyned to an Infortune; and he that is ill dignifyed, or in a weake quarter of Heaven or House, I say, if he be not in his owne House, or Exaltation, or with a good Planet; then the strongest in the Scheame overcomes. *This shall be more copiously handled, ere I conclude the judgements of this seventh House.*

He that is but meanly strong in the Figure, seems very fearfull; for sometimes he hopes to win, at othertimes to loose: and observe this in Questions, concerning Warres and Kingdomes, the Fortitude of a Planet is greater in his Exaltation then in his House, in all other Questions quite contrary.

Of Partnership, Society or Fellowship betwixt two, if it shall be, or not.

If good Planets be in the seventh and first, the Society shall be, and good will come of it: the continuance of it, whether for yeers, dayes, or moneths, is knowne by the Lord of the seventh. If you will know when it shall be, see if a good Planet be in the seventh, then the Society or Partnership shall be that yeere. If the Lord of the Ascendant and seventh agree in nature and quality, the Parties will agree; if not, they will disagree, and there will be perpetuall (or at least often) jangling.

Of two Partners, which shall gaine or doe best.

The Lord of the ascendant and seventh are to be considered, and in what state they be, and so judge; for if the *Significator* of the *querent* be in better dignities then the *quesited*, the *querent* prospers; *& e contra*. If evill shall come on the businesse, then

The Resolution of

then he whose *Significator* is in a cadent house, that party doth the worst; if any ones *Significator* be exalted, he gaineth.

See the second and his Lord, and the eight and his lord, and in which of these houses the best Planet, or the lord thereof in the best place, or joyned to the best Planet, he shall gaine most. The second house sheweth the *querents* substance, the eight the riches of the Companion or Partner; if both be good, both shall gaine. If both ill, both shall lose; if one good and the other ill, he that hath the good Planet shall gaine, the other shall lose.

Of familiarity betwixt Neighbour and Neighbour.

Whether Society or Friendship shall endure, behold if a good Planet be in the seventh, then he pretendeth thee or the *querent* good fellowship and meanes really, especially if the same Planet or the lord of the seventh behold the ascendant, or the lord thereof, with a △ or ✶ aspect; also it shall endure so many Months, Dayes or Yeers, as he hath Degrees to goe in the same House, or Signe, fixed, common, or moveable.

Of removing from place to place.

Behold the fourth and seventh houses, and their lords, and if they be good and strong, and well affected, and good Planets in the said houses, it is very good, *& e contra*.

Another.

The Lord of the ascendant stronger then the lord of the seventh, abide; if not, remove; if both be evill disposed, goe; both indifferent and better aspected of good then evill, stay; *& e contra*. ☽ separating from Infortunes, goe; from Fortunes, abide. Note, the ascendant is for the Journier (or the place he goeth from,) the seventh the Place whither he would goe Also if the Lord of the ascendant separate from Infortunes and apply to Fortunes, goe; if from Fortunes, and applieth to Infortunes, stay: and if the Lord of the ascendant and ☽ agree, the judgment is more certain.

Of

all manner of Questions.

Of removing from one place to another; or of two Businesses, which is best.

Consider the first and second houses, and their lords, and the lords of the places to which thou wouldest goe, and lord of the substance thou thinkest for to attaine there, see the seventh and eight houses and their lords, which of them is best and strongest, thither goe and remove. Or see the lord of the ascendant or ☽, whom if thou findest to be separated from evill Planets, and joyned to *Fortunes*, it is better to goe then stay, and doe any businesse thou intendest. If the Lord of the ascendant be separated from fortunes, and apply to infortunes, neither move or do the businesse thou intendest; see if the planet to whom the ☽ applyes be better then that she separated from, for then thou mayest remove, else not: &c.

If it be best to remove or stay in any place, whether Village, Territory, City or House.

See the lord of the ascendant fourth and seventh house; if the lord of the fourth be in the seventh, and be a good planet, and if the lord of the first and seventh be good, and with good planets, it is good to abide still: but if the lord of the seventh be with a good planet, and the lord of the fourth with an evill one, it is then not good to stay; for if he doe, he shall receive much dammage by abiding there.

Chap. LIII.
Of Hunting.

YOu shall know the lord of hunting by the ascendant, the ☽, and from the lord of the terme of the degree of the ☽ and from the lord of the hour; for the lord of the hour is of great force and strength, when he is in the ascendant, and the ascendant a signe of four footed beasts: in case of hunting see if the ascendant be a signe of four footed beasts, or an earthly signe, for these are good for hunting amongst mountaines, and hils; see the lord of the ascendant, and the lord of the hour, if they be fortunate or infortunate; and if either do behold other, or separate one from another, and if one be falling from ano- *Sith the Ancients have taken notice of such trifles, I must consent.*

ther,

ther, note this. Confider after if the feventh be a figne of four footed beafts, and if you do finde in the fame the lord thereof, or the lord of the hour; or the lord of the angle fortunate, judge that the beaft you feek for fhall be found and taken. But if the lord of the feventh be an Infortune, and the ☽ infortunate, the good planets falling from her, after much fearch fomething fhall be found, and little fhall be taken, and that with wearineffe of the body; which fhall be the truer, if the lord of the afcendant be ♄, and in the feventh houfe a figne of four footed beafts. If you finde ☽ in the feventh or in any of the angles, or the lord of the feventh, and fhe be fortunate, fay that he fhall fpeed in his *hunting*.

Of a Law-fuit or Controverfie betwixt two, who fhall fpeed beft, or whether they fhall compound, or have the matter taken up or not before they doe goe to Law.

Behold the afcendant, his lord and ☽, thefe fignifie the *querent*; the feventh houfe and his lord are for the *Adverfary*.

If the lord of the afcendant or the ☽ be joyned to the lord of the feventh, or be in ✶ or △ afpect with mutuall Reception, the parties will eafily of themfelves accord, and compofe all differences without mediation of any, or with a little entreaty.

But if one receive the other, and he that is received, receive not the other *Significator*, they fhall agree without Suit of law, but not without intermiffion of a third party or more; and thofe that intercede, for the moft part fhall be his Friends or Acquaintance that did receive the other Planet.

If they, *viz.* the lord of the feventh and afcendant are in a □ afpect, or in ☍, with mutuall Reception, or in a ✶ or △ without Reception, they will be reconciled, but firft they will have one little combate at law: and you muft obferve, that unity fhall proceed from that party whofe *Significator* is leffe ponderous, and commits his difpofition to the other; and this concord fhall be the more firme, if both *Significators* receive one another: If the lighter Planet be joyned to the more weighty, and receive him not, but the fuperiour Planet receive him, it argues, he that receives would accord whether his Adverfary will or not.   Having

all manner of Questions.

Having confidered the former *significators*, do you obferve the *significator* of the *Judge*, who is ever the lord of the tenth houfe, and whether he afpect either of the *significators*, viz. whether the lord of the afcendant or feventh, or be in ☌ with either of them; fee if the lord of the afcendant haftens to the ☌ of the lord of the feventh, or the lord of the feventh to him, and that the lord of the tenth houfe doth fruftrate their ☌, it's then an argument they fhall not agree before they have been at law, and herein the *Judge* or *Lawyer* feems faulty, who will not permit the parties to compofe their differences: fee if the ☽ transferre light between the lord of the afcendant and feventh; if fhe doe not, fee if any other Planet carry their influence or light to each other; for if it be fo, it's like fome or other interpofe their paines, and reconcile the parties though they be in law.

See after this, whether the lord of the afcendant or feventh be ftrongeft, for he whofe *significator* is moft powerfull, ought to have the victory; he is ftrongeft, who is in an angle, and in fome of his effentiall Dignities; the greater his ftrength is, how much greater the effentiall Dignity is wherein he is; and if he be alfo received by any other Planet, it's an argument that party is able, and that he hath the more Friends to affift him: if you doe find that they will compound, the firft mover thereunto, will be on the part of the lighter Planet, who commits his difpofition to the other; for if the lord of the afcendant be more light, and the lord of the feventh more ponderous, the firft motion of peace fhall come from the *querent*, and fo e contrario: A Planet in a cadent houfe is more weak, if not received or affifted by the afpect of fome other; if the lord of the feventh houfe be in the afcendant, then the *querent* without doubt overcomes, and the *Adverfary* will yeeld; the like happens to the querent, viz. that he fhall be overcome: and this happens not *When he is in* onely in law Suits, and for Moneys, but alfo in Fights, *the fame con-* Duels and Warre: fee further if the lord of the afcendant or fe- *dition.* venth be retrograde; for if the lord of the afcendant be retrograde, it argues the weakneffe of the *querent*, and that he will not ftand to it ftoutly, that he will deny the truth to his *Adverfary* nor will he beleeve that he hath any right to the thing in

The Resolution of

question; if the lord of the seventh be retrograde, it argues the same things on the *quesited's* part.

Behold the *significator* of the *Judge* who is to give sentence in the Cause, wch is the Lord of the tenth house, whether he be direct, and behold them, for then he will proceed according to order of law in the Cause, and will endeavour to shorten and determine it; but if he be Retrograde, it's an argument the *Judge* will not goe on or proceed according to order of law, nor will he care to end it; nay it's rather probable he will prolong it a longer time then he ought by law: judge the same if the Lord of the ascendant be separated from the Lord of the seventh, or the Lord of the seventh from the Lord of the ascendant.

See if the Lord of the ascendant be in aspect with the ☉ or ☽, or either of them joyned to him, so that no other Planet hinder their aspect, beware it be not a corporall ♂, for that signifies an impediment, unlesse the Planet were in the heart of the ☉, for then the Planet was fortified thereby; so is he in like nature, if the Planet be in either of the houses of the *Luminaries*, or if the ☉ and ☽ be in the ascendant, these argue the potency of the *querent*: if the Lord of the seventh be dignified or qualified as before I mentioned of the Lord of the ascendant, you must judge in like nature on the behalfe of the *quesited*: If the Lord of the ascendant be joyned to the Lord of the tenth, he that is the *querent* will acquaint the *Judge* himselfe, or make meanes to acquaint him with his Cause, and it may be he will endeavour to bribe the *Judge*, that so he may judge on his side: if the lord of the tenth receive the lord of the second, the *Judge* will have Money for his paines; but if the lord of the tenth receive the lord of the ascendant, the *Judge* hears the *querent's* importunities, otherwayes not.

If the lord of the tenth be more light then the lord of the ascendant, and joyned unto him, he will doe the *querent's* businesse, though he never speak unto him; if the lord of the second be joyned to the lord of the tenth, then the *Adversary* makes meanes to the *Judge*; and if the lord of the tenth receive the lord of the seventh, he will assist him; but if he receive the lord of the eight, he will take his Money.

If the lord of the tenth receive both *significators* the *Judge* will

all manner of Queſtions.

wіll compoſe the matter ere it doe come to a full Tryall.

If the Lord of the tenth be in the tenth, in his owne houſe, the *Judge* will then doe juſtice, and judge the cauſe for his honour, unleſſe that Planet be ♄: if the Lord of the tenth be only in his owne Termes or Triplicity, it's true the *Judge* will determine the Cauſe, but makes no matter which way it goes, if a Planet be in the tenth houſe that hath no dignity, or is not in Reception with the Lord of the tenth, it argues the parties will not be content, or ſtand to that Sentence, they both feare that *Judge*, and had rather have another *Judge* his Sentence, with which they would be content: if ♄ be *Judge*, he will not judge as he ought; if at that time ♃ ♀ ☉ ☿ or ☽ be in any aſpect to ♄ but ☍, the *Judge* will be ill reported of, but in a little time will be cleered, and the aſperſion taken off; but if any of thoſe be in ☍ to ♄, there will goe a hard report on the *Judge* for that his Sentence, and it will continue long; the *Judges* defamation will be great if ♂ be in ☍ to ♄, unleſſe ♂ be with ♄ in ♑, then the ſcandall will be the leſſe.

But to be ſhort, in theſe like Judgments obſerve this method; the *Querent* is ſignified by the Lord of the aſcendant, the *Adverſary* by the Lord of the ſeventh, the *Judge* by the Lord of the tenth, the end of the matter from the Lord of the fourth; conſider well the Lords of the houſes, their Fortitudes, and whether they be in Angles, Succedants or Cadents, Fortunate or not Fortunate; for the Planet that is moſt ſtrong, and beſt poſited, is the beſt man, and moſt likely to carry the victory, and hath the beſt Cauſe.

If more Planets be in the aſcendant and ſecond, the *Querent* ſhall have moſt Friends, *& ſic e contario*: if both *Significators* give their vertue to one Planet, there will be one who will intercede betwixt them: if the Signe aſcending and ſeventh be fixed, both *querent* and *queſited* are reſolutely bent to proceed in the Suit or Controverſie; if movable Signes be there, it's like they have no great ſtomack to the buſineſſe, but will end it very ſhortly; if common Signes be there, they will continue the Suit long, and have the Cauſe out of one Court into another; on whoſe part you find the *Infortunes*, that party ſhall receive moſt prejudice, ſorrow and trouble by the Contention.

You

You are to confider in this manner of Judgment the ☽ from whom fhe is feparated, and the Planet to whom fhe applyes are equally fignificant, as the afcendant and feventh houfe, &c.

Chap. LIV.
Of Buying and Selling Commodities.

The *Buyer* is fignified by the Lord of the afcendant and the ☽; the *Seller* by the Lord of the feventh ; fee if the ☽ be joyned with the Lord of the feventh, the *querent* may then buy the thing or Commodity he defires, and this quickly ; if the Lord of the afcendant be a more light Planet then the Lord of the feventh, the *querent* will occafion the fale of it, & *e contra*, if the Lord of the feventh be the lighter Planet : if the preceding *Significators* have no afpect to each other, behold if the ☽ or fome other Planet transferre not the light of the one to the other, a Friend fhall then appeare who will drive on the bargaine for them both, fo that the matter will be done : In this manner of Judicature, you muft diftinguifh what you are to buy ; as if a Servant or Sheep, Hogges, Coneys, &c. the fixt houfe and his Lord are then confiderable : if it concerne Horfes, Affes, Camels, Oxen or Cowes, Judgment muft be drawn from the twelft houfe and the afcendant : if a Houfe, Towne or Caftle, then the fourth houfe and his Lord, and fo confider in any other Commodity.

If the Lord of the feventh be in the afcendant, the *Seller* will importune the *querent* to buy ; the contrary if the Lord of the afcendant be in the feventh, for then the *querent* hath moft mind to buy : if either ♃ or ♀ be in the afcendant, the *Buyer* performes his work fuddenly without any labour ; fo if the ☉ be in the afcendant, and not corporally joyned to any other Planet ; if ☿ or the ☽ be in the afcendant, not infected with the evill afpect of an *Infortune*, they fortunate the *Buyer*, and he performes what he intended ; ♄ ♂ or ☋ in the afcendant, argue labour and difficulty, and that the matter will not be had without

all manner of Queſtions.

out much labour, & that the *Buyer* is a cunning companion, and means deceitfully, and will deceive the *Seller*, if poſſible: if the *Infortunes* be in the ſeventh, have a care of the *Seller*, he wil find out one trick or other to delude the *Buyer*; he is a crafty Fellow, &c. If the ☽ be voyd of courſe, unleſſe the *Significators* apply ſtongly, there's ſeldome any Bargaine concluded, or Commodity at that time bought, and yet both parties wrangle, and have ſome meetings to no purpoſe: If the Planet from whom the ☽ ſeparates enters Combuſtion, he that ſells his Land or Houſe at that time, ſhall never recover them againe: but if the Planet from whom the ☽ did laſt ſeparate, be free from miſfortune, and beholds the Lord of that Signe from whence the Judgment, or thing in queſtion is required; it's then poſſible the *Seller* may in time re-purchaſe the Lands or Commodities againe, or others of as good value.

Chap. LV.
Of Partnerſhip.

The Lord of the aſcendant is for the *querent*; Lord of the ſeventh for the *Partner* intended: but herein be carefull that you obſerve what Planet is in the ſeventh, and neer the cuſp of the ſeventh, and whether the party enquired of be more like to the deſcription of the Planet poſited in the ſeventh, or to the Lord of the ſeventh; take that Planet for his *Significator* who is neereſt to his deſcription, and conſider him as you would otherwayes the Lord of the ſeventh, and as you ought to doe of the Lord of the ſeventh, no other Planet being in the ſeventh.

Let the ☽ be partner in ſignification; the tenth houſe ſhall ſhew what credit there may come of the Partnerſhip: but whether the Partnerſhip will extend to good or ill, you muſt expect that from the fourth houſe and his Lord, and the Planet therein poſited, and the Planet to whom the ☽ applyes.

If the Lord of the aſcendant and the ☽ be in movable Signes without Reception by Houſe or Exaltation, or Triplicity or Terme, then there will happen Contention, and they will diſagree,

agree, but matters will againe be reconciled, and the Partnership will hold, but still they will be mistrustfull of one another, nor will much good come of it: but if the *Significators* be in fixed Signes, their society will continue long; but if no Reception be, little profit will from thence accrew to either party; if they buy any thing, the Commodities will lye long on their hands; if the *Significators* be in common Signes, it promises a gainfull Partnership, and that they will be faithfull to each other: If one *Significator* be in a movable Signe, and the other in a fixed, the disturbance arising will be lesse then at first may be feared: If ill Planets aspect both the *significators, viz.* Lord of the ascendant and Lord of the seventh, the Partnership will be ill for both, neither the one party or other will deal fairly; see where, and in what house or houses the evill Planets are posited, and from thence you may discerne the cause: I have oft acquainted you with the signification of the houses: an evil Planet in the ascendant, the *querent* is a false companion; judge the like if an evill Planet be in the seventh.

If the ☽ separate from one *Fortune* and apply to another, they will begin well and end well, though neither of them get any Wealth; but if she be separated from a good Planet, and apply to an ill, they begin well, but end in strife and hatred; and so the contrary: but if the ☽ be separated from an ill Planet and apply to another, they will begin Partnership with muttering and repining, continue it with feares and jealousies, end it with Law-suits.

A good Planet in the tenth, shewes they will obtaine reputation, and will rejoyce and delight in their mutuall Society.

A good Planet in the second, best for the *querent*; in the seventh for the *Partner*.

An ill Planet in the second, or ☋, the *querent* will get little, but be cheated, or entrust much, and get in few Debts.

If the Lord of the fourth apply to the Lord of the eleventh by ✶ or △; or if a good Planet be in the fourth, or if the Lord of the eleventh and fourth be in Reception, or if good Planets cast their ✶ or △ to the Lords of the ascendant and seventh, a good end may be expected by the Partnership intended: observe ⊗, how dignified, how aspected; if the Lord of the seventh

or

all manner of Questions.

or of the eight cast a □ or ☍ to it, the *querent* must expect no great good from his Partner, for it's like he will embeffell the Eftate, or their common Stock.

Chap. LVI.
Whether a City, Towne or Caftle, befieged, or to be befieged, fhall be taken or not.

THe afcendant and his Lord are for the *querent,* and thofe that doe or fhall befiege; the fourth houfe fhall fignifie the *Towne, City* or *Fort* befieged, or to be befieged, the Lord thereof the *Governour*; the fift houfe, Planets therein, and his Lord, the *Ammunition, Souldiery* and *Affiftants* the *Governour* and *Towne* may expect to relive or affift them * : If you find the Lord of the firft ftrong and fortunate, or joyned to the Lord of the fourth in the firft, or with the ☽ or Lord of the tenth, or in any houfe except the twelft, eight and fixt, conditionally, that the Lord of the firft receive the Lord of the fourth, or the ☽ receive the Lord of the fourth, though fhe be not received againe, it's an argument, the *Towne, Fort* or *Caftle* fhall be taken : or if the Lord of the fourth be in fuch houfes as behold not the fourth, (except the Lord of the feventh be in the fourth, then it will not be taken;) if the Lord of the fourth be with the ill *Fortunes,* and impedited, it's probable the City fhall be taken, and the Governour wounded, or if *Infortunes* be in the fourth without fome ftrong afpect of the *Fortunes,* It will be taken, or can it hold out long, or there may be treafon in Towne : If ☋ be in the fourth, it will be taken, and there will be fome goe about to betray or deliver it, or fome principall Work or Fort therein; the Signe fhewes which part of the Towne; nor doth the Governour think himfelf able to preferve it.

* in the Town and are in Garrifon.

If none of thefe Accidents or Configurations before rehearfed be, then have regard to the Lord of the fourth; if he be in in the fourth ftrong and fortunate, and not Retrograde or Combuft, or befieged of the *Infortunes,* or if the Lord of the feventh be there, free from all impediments, or if ♃ or ♀ or ☊

be therein, and no reception between the Lord of the ascendant and fourth, then the City, Fort or Towne at that time surrounded or besieged, shall not be taken or delivered to the Army now beliegieng it; nay, if there be both a *Fortune* and an *Infortune* in the fourth, the Towne shall not be taken, if the *Fortune* be neerest to the cusp of the house, or first of the two Planets which shall transit the degree of the fourth; and this you may averre with greater confidence, if the Lord of the ascendant be any thing weak, or a light Planet and unfortunate; but if the Lord of the ascendant be fortunate, and a *Fortune* therein, and he or the ☽ behold the fourth house, it notes surrendring or taking the City, Towne or Castle besieged: but if he be unfortunate and otherwayes impedited, and an *Infortune* in the second, or the Lord thereof Retrograde, or in □ or ☍ to the Lord of the ascendant, it signifies the *querent's* Souldiers will desert him, and will not continue the Siege, they have no mind to the work, or the *querent* wants fit instruments or materials for a Siege, or his Ammunition will not come opportunely, or the Souldiers will depart discontented for their pay, or their duties are too hard, so that he may expect no honour at this Siege.

CHAP. LVII.

Of COMMANDERS *in Armies, their abilities, fidelity, and whether by them Victory may be had yea or not, &c.*

AGain, consider well all the twelve houses and their proper *Significators*, and make the ascendant *Significator* of the querent, and his Lord; let the seventh & his Lord shew the opposite parties or *Adversaries* who may come to relieve the Besieged; let the eight be their Seconds or Friends, and the ninth their third house, and so all the other houses in order.

An *Infortune* in the ascendant, or beholding the house with □ or ☍, it notes, the *querent*, or that side he takes part with, will not manage their matters well, or prosecute the Warre discreetly: an *Infortune* in the ascendant, or being Lord of the ascen-

all manner of Questions. 381

ascendant, argues no great justice on the *querents* part, or that he hath no cause to begin the Warre or quarrell, but if either a good Planet be in the ascendant, or behold the ascendant with ✶ or △, it signifies a good ground or cause on the *querent's* behalfe; if an *Infortune* be in the second, and be not Lord of the second (or have Exaltation in the Signe,) if he, I say, behold the second with a □ or ☍, it's like there will be no Warre, but if any be, the *querent* shall have the worst; a *Fortune* in that house, or aspecting it, shewes the contrary, &c. If an *Infortune* be in the third, and ♂ be that Planet, and he strong, the *querent* is like to have good warlike Provisions; say the same if ♃ be there: but if ♂ be therein unfortunate, his Army is like to be composed of Thieves, Highway men, vagrant Fellowes, seditious, and such as will obey no commands.

If an *Infortune* be in the fourth, the place where the Warre is like to be, or where the Armies may engage, is like to be unfit for the *querent's* Army: if it be mountainous, the places are rough, inaccessible not habitable, full of Woods, no passage for Armies; if the place seem to be described moyst, it's miery, dirty, full of standing waters, Bogs, Rivers or Brooks, not fit to marshall an Army in, or wherein an Army can doe any service: If ♂ be in the fift, well dignified, or the good aspects of the *Fortunes* irradiate that house, or a *Fortune* be therein posited, then it's like the Army or Souldiers on the *querent's* part, will be good Souldiers, apt for fight, and obedient to their Officers; the *Infortunes* posited therein shew contrary qualities.

If either of the *Fortunes* or ☊ be in the sixt, the Carriage-Horse attending the Army, seem serviceable, high prized, and fit for the employment.

If ♂ be therein well dignified, the Horse entertained or employed will be fierce, impatient and hard to be governed.

But if ♄ be in the sixt without dignities, the Horse are old, rotten jades, unserviceable, tyred, over-spent, slow, not fit for this service, diseased, &c.

If a *Fortune* be in the seventh, the instruments of Warre and Fortification, the Canons and great Guns of the Army are faire, sound, well cast, and will performe their work: and this

Bbb 3   position

position of a *Fortune* in the seventh, denotes, the Enemy is no foole ; if an *Infortune* be there, or have the before-named evill aspects to the house, the enemy is weak, the *querent's* instruments are nought, will performe no service, the Enemy will rather fight by policy, craft and trechery, then man hood.

If a *Fortune* be in the eight, it's an argument no mortality or much destruction of men will follow, or wil there be many men wounded, or their wounds difficult to cure ; no great slaughters, fights, flights, or any set Battles will be betwixt the Armies on either part : but if ♄ be therein Retrograde, many prisoners will be taken, much ruine and destruction, much poverty and plundering will succeed.

If a *Fortune* be in the ninth, or have aspect to the house, the enemy is in a good posture, hopes to benefit himselfe by some false reports, or by some false allarums or sallies, and that he intends to act much by such like reports, and by witty inventions, for the Enemy is politick.

If a *Fortune* be in the tenth, or cast his ✶ or △ thither, it's an argument, the Commander in chiefe is a discreet man, understands what to doe in his place, and that the Officers of the Army are expert men, every one in his place being capable of what he undertakes : but if ♄ or ☋ be therein, or ♂, any wayes unfortunate, the Officers and Captaines are very asses and buzzards, have no judgment, simple Fellowes, the whole designe is like to be overthrowne by their knavery, and want of discretion and judgment ; I meane, the greater part of the Officers, &c. they are more fit for hanging, then to Command.

If a *Fortune* be in the eleventh, it shewes, the Conductors of the Army are men of good discretion and sound judgment, expert men in the art of Warre, know how to command and order their affaires, are valiant and carefull, and understand in every particular when to charge or retreat ; in a word, the Officers seem men of approved integrity and judgment.

If an *Infortune* be in the eleventh, the Conductor or Conductors may be men of fidelity, and assured Friends and Wel-willers to the cause they undertake, but they are unexpert, and not fit to undertake such a waighty imployment in hand, for

they

all manner of Questions. 383

they nothing underſtand the ſtratagems of Warre, whereby the whole cauſe is like to ſuffer.

If a *Fortune* be in the twelft houſe, thoſe againſt whom the Army is to go, are well provided, and reſolved to defend themſelves; they agree well, feare nothing, will ſtand it out to the laſt: but if an *Infortune* be there, they ſuſpect their owne abilities, are not capable of reſiſting, diſagree amongſt themſelves, feare ſurprizall every moment: It is, notwithſtanding, ever conſiderable, that if ♂ be in the twelft houſe, the *querent* may juſtly ſuſpect trechery, and indeed you have juſt cauſe to feare the ſame if ☋ be in the twelft. Now as you have conſidered the whole twelve houſes on the behalfe of the *querent*, ſo muſt you obſerve the ſame method and manner of judgment on the behalf of the *Adverſary*; onely conſidering what houſe for the *querent* is the aſcendant, the oppoſite houſe is the ſame for the *queſited*, and ſo every houſe in order: Which judgments rightly underſtood, will give great light to any manner of queſtion propounded in this nature by any prime *Officer* or *Commander*.

If the Armies ſhall fight.

Behold herein the aſcendant and his Lord, the ☽ and Lord of the ſeventh, ſee if they be corporally joyned in any angle, then it ſeems the Armies will fight: if there be no ☌ of the Lord of the aſcendant and ſeventh, ſee if they behold one another by □ or ☍, they will alſo then fight: if this happen not, ſee if any Planet transferre the light of one to the other by □ or ☍ aſpect, with or without Reception; if ſuch an aſpect be, there will be a fight betwixt them: but if the more ponderous of the two receive that Planet who transferres their light, no fight will be, but all things will be compoſed lightly.

Chap. LVIII.

If the Querent have open Enemies, or any Adverſaries, or many that doe envy him.

THis is a difficult Queſtion, and yet by *Aſtrologie* reſponſible, but you muſt juſtly conſider whether the *querent* doe de-
and

and thus much, viz. *Have I enemies or not?* Or, *Whether is such a man my adversary?* &c.

If any be nominated, require judgment from the seventh house and Lord thereof: if the Lord of the seventh aspect the Lord of the ascendant, with □ or ☍, or be in like aspect with the ☽, it's then very probable, the party enquired after doth envy the Querent, and wishes him no good: if the aspect be separated, they have lately been in some contest, or some difference hath been betwixt them; but if they are then applying to a □ or ☍, the enmity, difference or controversie is approaching, is not yet over, will grow to a greater height then now it is, and the party enquired after, doth what in him lyes to thwait and crosse the occasions of the *querent*. In like manner, consider if the Lord of the seventh be in the twelfth from the ascendant, or in the twelft signe from the place wherein the Lord of the ascendant is in, or from the place wherein the ☽ is, or if the Lord of the seventh be in ☌ with any Planet, or in any aspect with a Planet who is in ☍ or □ to the Lord of the ascendant or the ☽, without Reception, then the Quesited, or man or woman nominated, is averse, and an enemy to the Querent, but if it be not so, then he or she enquired after is no enemy.

But if the querent doubt his Brother, Father, or Servant; then take Signification from each particular House signifying them.

If the Question be absolute, (as thus) *Whether have I enemies yea or no?* you must require judgment herein from the twelfth house, and see if the Lord of that house be in □ or ☍ to the ☽ with or without Reception; if so, then he hath enemies that watch for an opportunity against him, but they doe all things clandestinely and cunningly, and desire to play their part when they can doe it without noyse or rumour of evill, that so they may still goe under the notion of Friends, when as in truth they are trecherous, false and deceitfull: Consider also where and in what house the Lord of the twelfth is, say confidently such people, men or women of such a quality or condition, are the Querent's adversaries: Many Planets in the seventh, denotes many enemies; * many Planets in the second, much want of money, if they are ill dignified, &c. and so doe in all the rest, observing how many Planets there are in the seventh, and of what houses they are Lords of, or from the houses whereof they

* Often and ever by me found true.

all manner of Questions.

they are Lords, from thence doe you require the quality of the people who are enemies, &c. remembring, that the □ aspect shewes envy and malice, yet posible to be reconciled, ☍ aspects without Reception, never, &c.

CHAP. LIX.

A LADY, *if marry the* GENTLEMAN *desired?*

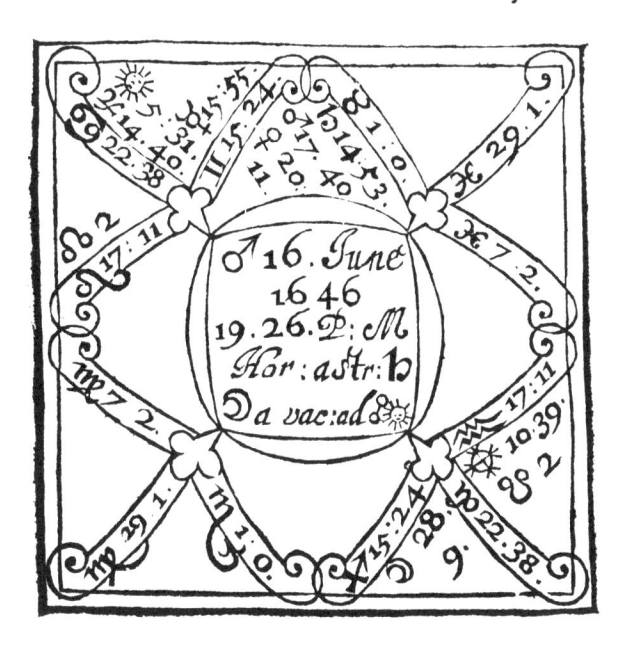

Judgment upon the Figure above-said.

THE true state of this *Ladies* cause stood thus: *A Gentleman had been a long time an earnest Suitor unto her for Marriage, but she could never master her affection so much as to incline to Marriage-thoughts with him, but slighted him continually; and at last, to the great discontent of the Gentleman, she gave him an absolute deniall: After which deniall so given, she became passionately affectionate of him, and did* sorely

sorely repent of her folly, and so churlish a carriage, wishing she might againe have former opportunities. This was her condition at what time she propounded the Question unto me.

The ascendant and ☉ are for the *querent*; ♄ Lord of the seventh, is for the man *quesited* after. The *querent* was moderately tall, of round visage, sanguine complexion, of a cheerfull, modest countenance, gray eyed, her haire a light browne, occasioned, as I conceive, by ☉ Lord of the ascendant, in the Termes of ♂, she was well spoken, and sufficiently comely.

Finding ♄ in the angle of the South, and in ☌ with ♂, and both in ♉, a fixed, earthly Signe, I judged the corporature of the quesited party to be but meane, and not tall, or very handsome, his visage long and incomposed, a wan, pale or meagre complexion, dark haire, or of a sad, chesnut colour, curling and crisp, his eyes fixt, ever downward, musing, stooping forward with his head, some impediment in his going, as treading awry, &c. [*this was confessed.*] Finding ♄ so, as abovesaid, elevated, and in ☌ with ♂, I judged the Gentleman to be sad, angry, much discontented, and scorning his former slights, (as ever all Saturnine people doe;) I judged him much incensed by a Kinsman or Gentleman of quality, signified by ♂, Lord of the third, in part, from the seventh, and of the fourth, being the tenth from the seventh; and that this Gentleman and he lived either in one house, or neer one another, because both *significators* are angular and fixed, [*and so it was.*] I said, the Gentleman had no inclination or disposition unto her, finding the ☽ separated from voyd of course, and applying to ☍ of ☉, Lord of the ascendant, it did argue there was small hopes of effecting her desire, because she her selfe, by her owne perversnesse, had done her selfe so grand a mischiefe. Whereupon she told me the truth of all, and not before, and implored my directions, which way, without scandall to her honour, it might be brought on againe, if possible: and indeed she was lamentably perplexed, and full of heavinesse. Hereupon, with much compassion, I began to consider what hopes we had in the Figure: I found ☉ applying to a ✶ of ♄; this argued the womans desire, and the strength of her affections towards the *quesited, fited*, becaufe fhe is fignified by the lighter Planet; but there was no Reception betwixt the *fignificators*, therefore that application gave little hopes: but finding Reception betwixt ♃ and the ☽, and betwixt ☉ and ☽, fhe in his Triplicity, ☉ in her Houfe; obferving alfo, that the ☽ did difpofe of ♄ in her Exaltation, and of ♃ in her Houfe, and that ♃ was very neer a ✶ *dexter* of ♄, ftill applying, and not feparated; as alfo, that ♃ was in his Exaltation, and a fortunate Planet ever affifting nature and the afflicted, and that he was able by his ftrength to qualifie and take off the malice of ♄: befides, the neernefſe of ♃ to the ✶ of ♄, made me confident that the *quefited* was intimately acquainted with a perfon of quality and worth, fuch as ♃ reprefented, whom I exactly defcribed, and the *Lady* very well knew: Unto him I directed to addreffe her Complaints, and acquaint him fully with her unhappy folly: I pofitively affirmed, in the Gentleman defcribed fhe fhould find all honour and fecrecy, and I doubted not but, by God's bleffing, he would againe revive the bufineffe (now defpaired of) and bring her to her hearts content: But finding that ♄ and ☉ came to ✶ afpect the 27th of the fame moneth, I advifed to haften all things before the afpect was over; and alfo gave direction, that the nineteenth of *June* neer upon noon, the Gentleman fhould firft move the *quefited* in the bufineffe: and my reafon was, becaufe that day ♄ and ♃ were in a perfect ✶ afpect.

My counfell was followed, and the iffue was thus: By the Gentlemans meanes and procurement the matter was brought on againe, the March effected, and all within twenty dayes following, to the content of the forrowfull (but as to me unthankfull) Lady, &c. In *Aftrologie*, the true reafon of this performance is no more then, firft, an application of the two *Significators* to a ✶, *viz.* the Lord of the feventh and firft: Next, the application of the ☽ to the Lord of the afcendant, though by ☍, yet with Reception, was another fmall argument; but the main occafion, without which in this Figure it could not have been, the application of ♃ to ✶ of ♄ Lord of the feventh, receiving his vertue which ♄ did render unto him, and he again transferred to the ☉ Lord of the afcendant, he, *viz.* ♃, meeting with no manner of prohibition, abfciffion or fruftration

untill

untill his perfect ♂ with the ☉, which was the 29th of *June*, so that no difficulty did afterwards intervene. I did acquaint this Lady, that very lately before the erection of this Figure, her Sweet-heart had been offered a Match, and that the Gentlewoman propounded, was such a one as is signified by ♀, one not onely of a good fortune, but excellently well descended: I bad her follow my directions, with hope and expectation of a good end, and told her she should not fear his marrying of ♀: Which judgment I gave, by reason ♂ was neerer ♀ then ♄, and so interposed his influence, or kept off ♄. I judged ♂ to be some Souldier, or Gentleman that had been in Armes: this I did the more to enlighten her fancy, which I found apprehensive enough. She well knew both the Gentlewoman and man, and confessed such matters were then in action.

Had the *Quere* been, *Who should have lived longest?* certainly I should have judged the woman, because ☉ is going to ♂ of ♃, and ♂ afflicts ♄ by his presence.

Had she demanded, *Whether the Quesited had been rich?* I must have considered ♃ Lord of his second house, whom I find in his Exaltation, Direct, Swift, &c. only under the Sun-beames; I should have adjudged his Estate good.

For Agreement, because ☉ and ♄ are applying to ✶, I should have conceived they would wel accord; yet doubtlesse ♄ wil look for much observancy, for as he is ill by nature, so is he vitiated by ♂, and made therby chollerick as well as melancholly, so will he be natually jealous without cause; yet the gentle ✶ of ♃ to both ♂ and ♄, seems by education, to represse that frowardnesse naturally he may be subject unto.

If it be demanded, *Will the querent be honest?* I answer, her *significatrix*, viz. ☉, is no way afflicted by ♂: her Signe ascending being ♌, and Reception betwixt ♃ and ☽, are arguments of a vertuous woman.

In this nature may you examine any Figure for discovery of what is necessary, &c.

CHAP.

all manner of Questions. 389

Chap. LX.
If she should marry the man desired?

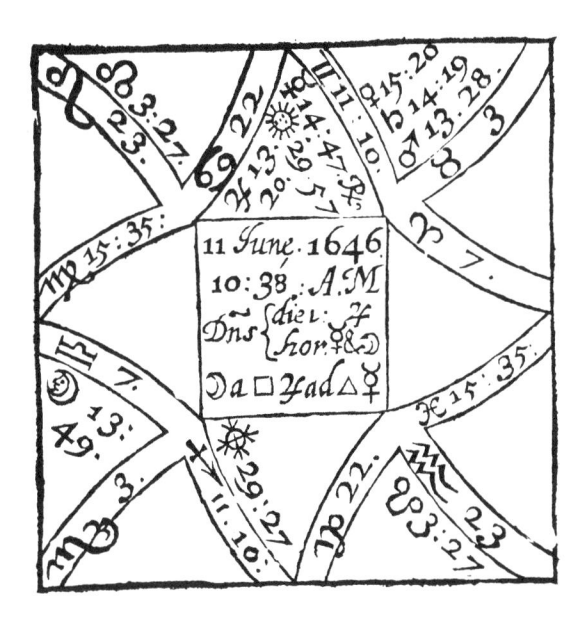

The Judgment.

THe *querent* was of tall stature, ruddy complexioned, sober, discreet and well spoken, &c. The *quesited* was very tall, slender, leane, and of a long visage, black haire: His talnesse I attribute to ♃, as being in the Termes of ♀, and the cusp of the seventh being also in his Termes: and indeed the being of a *significator* in the Termes of any Planet, doth a little vary the party from his naturall temper and constitution, so that he will retaine a small or great tincture from that Planet according as he is dignified: The sadnesse of his haire, I conceive to be from ♃ his aspect to ♄, and the ☽ her □ unto him, being her self subterranean.

♀ Is here *Significatrix* of the *querent*, Retrograde, under the

Ccc 3 Sun-

390 *The Resolution of*

Sun-beames, was in some distresse and feare that the *quesited* would not have her; and she might and had some reason for it, for ♃ was in his Exaltation, and neer the ✶ of ♀, an argument the man stood upon high termes, and had been tampering with another; yet were both *Significators* in a *Semisextile*, and in good houses, from which I gathered hopes, that there was some sparks of love betwixt them; but when I found the ☽ separating from a □ of ♃, and carrying his light by a △ aspect to ☿ the Lord of the ascendant, and he in an angle, receiving willingly, by his Retrograde motion, that her vertue which she brought from ♃. I was confident the Match would suddenly be brought to passe by such a one as ☽ was, or represented by her, who did much interpose in the businesse, and who at last, with a little difficulty, produced the Marriage to effect, to the content of both parties.

CHAP. LXI.
A Fugitive Servant, which way gone, when returne?

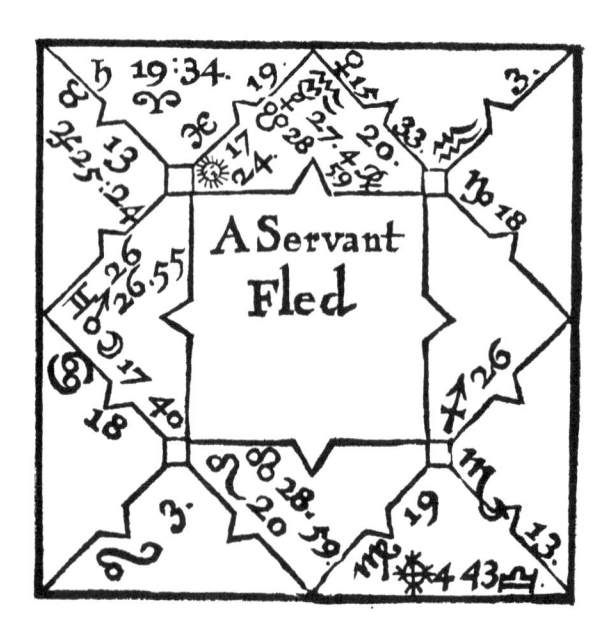

A Servant Fled

Judg-

The Resolution of Judgment upon the Figure beforegoing.

THe ascendant, and ☿ in ♒, together with ♂ posited in the ascendant, did signifie the *Master* of the *Servant*, who was short of stature, corpulent, of a good complexion, and ruddy, fresh countenance; his fatnesse I conceive from the north latitude of ☿, which was about one degree; as also, that the degrees ascending were in the Termes of ♂, in an ayery Signe, and in the Face or Decanate of ☉, now posited in a watry Signe, and in partill △ to ☽, both in moyst Signes, which argued a flegmatick, full body, &c.

The *Significator* of the Servant was ♂ peculiarly in this Figure, although many times ☿ shall signifie a *fugitive* Servant: The Servant was a young Fellow of about nineteen, a well set Fellow, short, big joynted, broad and full faced, dark browne haire, his teeth growing ilfavouredly, a Sun-burnt, obscure complexion, yet the skin of his body cleer.

I observed that he went away from his Master the Sunday preceding, at what time the ☽ was in ♊, a Westerne Signe, and that now ♂, the *Significator* of the Fellow was in the same Signe; as also, that ☿ the common *Significator* of Servants, was in ♒, a Westerne Signe, but South quarter of Heaven; it is true that ♊ hath some relation to the South quater, and ♒ to the North.

I judged from hence that the Servant went westward at his first departing, and that at the time of the Question, he was West from the *querent's* house; and this I judged because ♂ was angular, and every way as strong as the ☽, otherwayes I should have judged by the ☽: Forasmuch as ♂ the *Significator* of the Servant, and ☿ Lord of the ascendant, were suddenly hastening to a △ out of angles, I judged, that within a day or two he should have his Servant againe: I found the ☽ in the second, in her owne house; the Servant being a part of his Master's Estate, I judged from hence also, that the Master should not lose, but recover forthwith his lost Goods; and the rather, for that the ☽ was in the second, and in perfect △ of the ☉ *in* the eleventh, both of them in the Mediety ascending: the neernesse

392   *The Resolution of*

nesse of ♂ to the degree ascending, made me judge the Servant was not above three or four houses Westward from his Masters house.

The truth is, that upon Friday following betimes in the morning, he came home, and said he had been at *Kingston* upon *Thames*: which if true, then he was full West, or a little to the South, and neer a great Water, *viz.* the *Thames*, as ☽ in ♋ did or might signifie.

CHAP. LXII.
A Dogge missing, where?

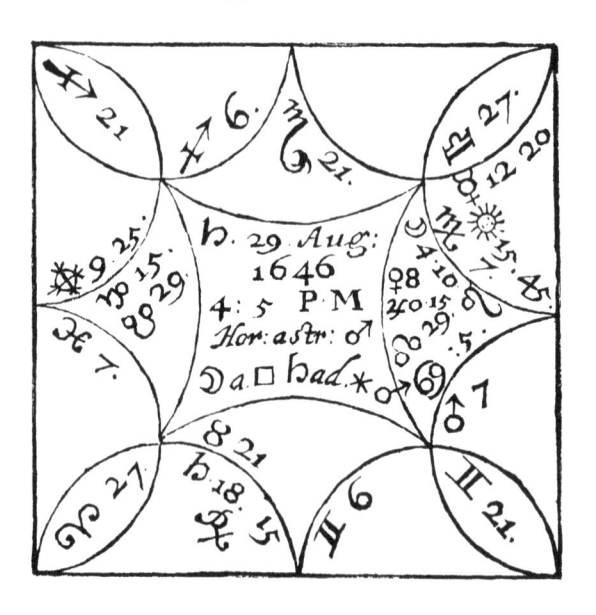

[Astrological figure: ♄ 29 Aug: 1646, 4:5 P M, Hor: astr: ♂]

Judgment upon this preceding Figure.

Living in *London* where we have few or no small Cattle, as Sheep, Hogs, or the like, as in the Countrey; I cannot give give example of such creatures, onely I once set the Figure preceding

all manner of Questions. 393

ceding concerning a Dogge (who is in the nature of small Beasts) which Dogge was fled and missing. The *Quere* unto me was, *What part of the City they should search, next if he should ever recover him.*

The *querent* was signified by the Signe ascending and the Lord thereof; and indeed in his person he was *Saturnine*, and vitiated according to *Cauda* in the ascendant, in his stature, mind or understanding; that is, was a little deformed in body, and extream covetous in disposition, &c.

The Signe of the sixt and his Lord signifies the Dogge; so must they have done if it had been a Sheep or Sheep, Hogs, Conies, &c. or any small Cattle.

The Signe of ♊ is West and by South, the quarter of heaven is West; ☿ the *significator* of the *Dog*, is in ♎ a Westerne Signe but Southerne quarter of heaven, tending to the West; the ☽ is in ♍, a South-west Signe, and verging to the Westerne angle: the strength of the testimonies examined, I found the plurality to signifie the West, and therefore I judged, that the *Dog* ought to be Westward from the place where the Owner lived, which was at *Temple-barre*, wherefore I judged that the *Dog* was about *Long-acre*, or upper part of *Drury-lane*: In regard that ☿ *Significator* of the Beast, was in a Signe of the same Triplicity that ♊ his ascendant is, which signifies *London*, and did apply to a △ of the Cusp of the sixt house, I judged the *Dog* was not out of the lines of Communication, but in the same quarter; of which I was more confirmed by ☉ and ♄ their △. The Signe wherein ☿ is in, is ♎, an ayery Signe, I judged the *Dog* was in some chamber or upper room, kept privately, or in great secrecy: because ☽ was under the Beames of the ☉, and ☿ ☽ and ☉ were in the eight house, but because the ☉ on Monday following did apply by △ *dexter* to ♄ Lord of the ascendant, and ☽ to ✶ of ♂, having exaltation in the ascendant; I intimated, that in my opinion he should have his *Dog* againe, or newes of his *Dog* or small Beast upon Monday following, or neer that time; which was true; for a Gentleman of the *querent's* acquaintance, sent home the Dog the very same day about ten in the morning, who by accident comming to see a Friend in *Long-acre*, found the *Dog* chained up under a table, and know-

D d d   ing

ing the Dog to be the *Querent's*, sent him home, as abovesaid, to my very great credit. Yet notwithstanding this, I cannot endure Questions of *Fugitives* or *Thefts*, nor ever would have done any thing, but with intention to benefit Posterity.

Usually I find, that all *Fugitives* goe by the ☽, and as she varies her Signe, so the *Fugitive* wavers and shifts in his flight, and declines more or lesse to East, West, North or South: but when the Question is demanded, then without doubt you must consider the strength both of the *Significator* and the ☽, and judge by the stronger, if both be equivalent in Fortitudes, judge either by the *Significator*, if he best personate the *Fugitive*, or by the ☽, if she most resemble him; with relation to either of them that comes neerest in aspect to the cusp of the house, from whence signification is taken.

Chap. LXIII.
Of Theft.

IT was the received opinion of Master *Allen* of *Oxford*, a man excellently versed in *Astrologie*, that the true *Significator* of a *Thiefe* is that Planet who is in an angle or second house, and beholds the seventh house: if no peregrine Planet be in an angle or the second house, then the Lord of the seventh shall be *Significator* of the *Thiefe*, if he behold the seventh house: otherwayes that Planet to whom the ☽ applyes, if he behold the seventh house; the rather, if the ☽ separate from the Lord of the ascendant. And he saith further, that a peregrine Planet in what angle soever, shall not be *Significator* of the *Thiefe*, unlesse he behold the seventh house, or have any dignity in the degree of the seventh: yet if one and the same Planet be Lord of the hour and of the ascendant, he shall signifie the *Querent*, though he behold not the ascendant: The truth is, I have ever found that if a peregrine Planet were in the ascendant, he was *Significator* of the *Thiefe*: next to the ascendant, I preferred the angle of the South, then the West angle, then the fourth house, last of all the second: many peregrine Planets in angles, many

are

all manner of Questions. 395

are or may be fufpected, juftly if they are in ☌ ✶ or △; not confenting, if in ☐ or ☍: ever prefer that peregrine Planet for your *Significator*, who is neereft to the cufpe of the angle he is in.

Money loft, who ftole it ? if recoverable ?

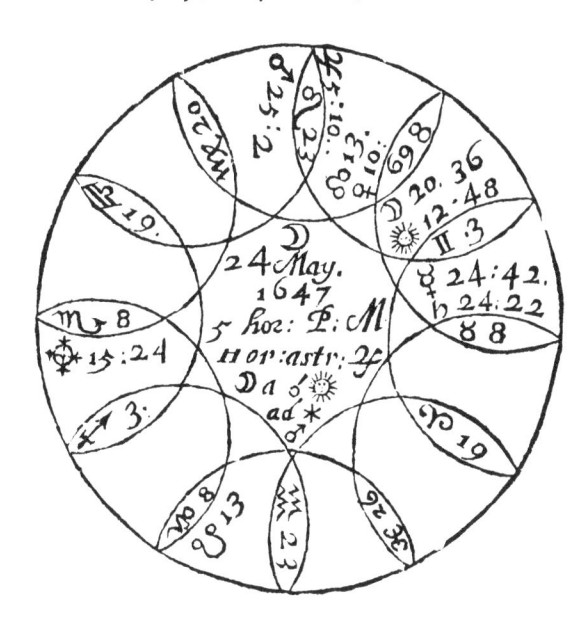

Judgment upon this Figure.

♏ Here afcends, and partly reprefents the *querent's* perfon, ♂ his mind and difpofition, who being in ☐ with ☿ and ♄ gave fufficient intimation unto me of the inclination of the *querent*, who was fufficiently ill conditioned, arrogant, proud, waftfull, &c.

♂ Is here in the 25. degr. and 2. min. of ♌, is angular, and but two minutes entred his own Termes, yet being in his Decanate, I refufed him for *Significator* of the *Thiefe*, and that juftly, nor indeed was he.

Ddd 2   In

In the next place, although ♄ was in the angle of the West, yet did I find him in his own Terms, and Decanate; I also passed by him.

In the next place, I found ☿ in 24. 42. ♉, lately separated or rather in □ of ♂, and now almost in partill ☌ with ♄; him I found truly peregrine, *viz.* having no essentiall Dignity where he is, therefore I adjudged ☿ to be *Significator* of the *Thief*.

But whether ☿ signified Male or Female, was the dispute, as also the corporature, quality, &c.

The angles are part Masculine, part Feminine, no certaine judgment could therfore arise from thence, the ☽ was in a Masculine Sign, applied to a masculine Planet in a masculine Sign, and ☿ usually is convertible in nature, according to the nature of the Planet he is in aspect with: he is now in aspect with ♂, and in ☌ with ♄; from hence I judged the Sex to be Male.

And said it was a young Youth of some fifteen or sixteen: young, because ☿ ever signifies Youth; but more young, because the ☽ was so neer the ☉, and scarce separated from him, I said he was of reasonable stature, thin visaged, hanging Eye-browes, a long Forehead, some blemish or scarres in his Face, because ♂ cast his □ dexter to ☿; bad Eye-sight because ☿ is with evill fixed Starres, of the nature of ♂ and ☽; a sad Haire, because of his neernesse to ♄; but of a scurvy countenance, one formerly a Thief or suspected for such knaveries: in regard ☿ the Youth his *Significator* was in ☌ with ♄ Lord of the third & 4th, I judged he was some Neighbours child; and as the ☽ was in ♊ and ☿ in ♉, I conceived he dwelt either opposite to the *querent* or a little Southwest; and because ☋ was in the ascendant, and disposed by ♂ Lord of the ascendant in the tenth, and the ☽ applyed to his ✶ aspect, and was within four degrees of the aspect: I judged he should not onely heare of, but have his Money within four dayes after the Question. He beleeved not one word I said, but would needs herswade me, that a Woman-servaut signified by ♂, was one Theef, and ♄ was another; but I stood firme to the true rules of Art, and would not consent unto it, because both those Planets were essentially dignified. The event proved directly true as I had manifested, both as to the person described, and to the day of the money returned, which was within three dayes after.

CHAP.

Chap. LIV.
Fish Stolen.

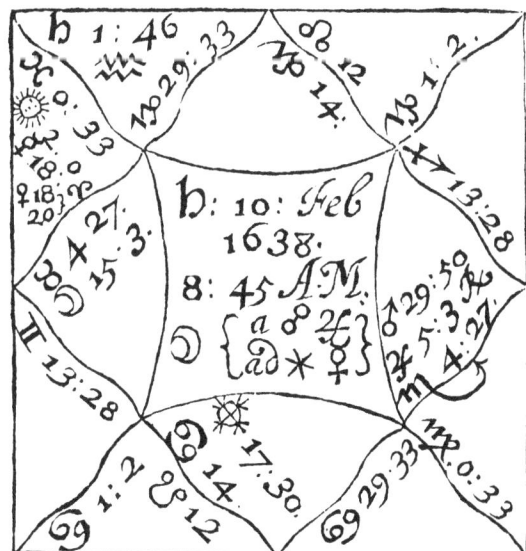

Living in the Country 1637. I had bought at *London* some Fish for my provision in Lent, it came down by the Barge at *Walton*, on Saturday the 10. of *Febr.* one of he Watermen, instead of bringing my Fish home, acquainted me, their warehouse was robbed last night, and my Fish stolen: I took the exact time when I first heard the report, and erected the Figure accordingly, endeavouring to give my selfe satisfaction what became of my goods, and, if possible, to recover part or all of them againe.

I first observed, there was no peregrine Planet in angle but ♃ whom I found upon the cusp of the seventh house, the thing I lost was Fish, therefore any Gentleman would scorne such a courfe Commodity: I considered the signification of ♃ in ♏, a moyst Signe, and the *Significator* of my Goods, *viz.* ☿ that he was in ♓, a moyst Signe, and that ⊗ was in ♋, a moyst Signe. Discretion, together with Art, assisted me to think he must be a man whose profession or calling was to live upon the Water, that had my Goods, and that they were in some moyst place, or in some low roome, because ⊗ was in ♋, and the ☽ in ♉ an earthly Sign.

Ddd 3

I was

I was confident I should heare of my Goods againe, becauſe ☿ Lord of my houſe of Subſtance, was applyed unto by a ✶ of ☽, who was Lady of my ⊗; and yet without hopes of recovering them, becauſe ☿ Lord of my ſecond, was in his fall and detriment, but as he was in his own Termes, and had a △ aſpect to ⊗, there was hopes of ſome of my Goods.

There being never a Waterman in that Town of *Walton* neer unto the deſcription of ♃ in ♏, I examined what Fiſherman there was of that complexion; and becauſe ♂ Lord of the 7ᵗʰ was departing the Sign ♏, *viz.* his owne, and entring another Signe, I examined if never a Fiſherman of ♂ and ♃ his nature had lately ſold any Land, or was leaving his proper houſe, and going to another habitation; ſuch a one I deſcovered, and that he was much ſuſpected of theevery, who was a good fellow, lived neer the *Thames* ſide, and was a meer Fiſherman, or man converſant in water; for all *Significators* in watry Signes, argued, he muſt needs live neer the water, or a watry place, that ſtole the Goods, or be much converſant in waters.

The man that was the Thiefe was a Fiſherman, of good ſtature, thick and full bodied, faire of complexion, a reddiſh-yellowiſh haire.

I procured a Warrant from a Juſtice of peace, and reſerved it privately untill Sunday the eighteenth of *February* following, and then with a Conſtable and the Barge-man, I ſearched only that one houſe of this Fiſherman ſuſpected; I found part of my Fiſh in water, part eaten, part not conſumed, all confeſſed. This jeſt happened in the ſearch; part of my Fiſh being in a bag, it happened the Thiefe ſtole the bag as well as the Fiſh; the Barge man, whoſe ſack it was, being in the ſame room where the bag was, and oft looking upon it (being clean waſhed) ſaid to the woman of the houſe, Woman, ſo I may have my ſack which I loſt that night, I care not: the woman anſwered; ſhe had never a ſack but that which her husband brought home the ſame night with the Fiſh. I am perſwaded the Barge-man looked upon the ſack twenty times before, and knew it not, for the woman had waſhed it cleane: I as heavily complained to the woman for ſeven *Portugall Onyons* which I loſt; ſhe not knowing what they were, made pottage with them, as ſhe ſaid.

The

all manner of Questions. 399

The remainder of my Fish I freely remitted, though the hireling Priest of *Walton* affirmed I had satisfaction for it, but he never hurt himselfe with a lye.

So that you see the peregrine Planet in an angle describes the Thiefe, and that either the ☉ or ☽ in the ascendant, and in essentiall Dignities, gives assured hopes of discovering who it was; the application of ☽ to the Lord of the second, argues recovery; a full recovery, if both the ☽ and the Lord of the second be essentially dignified; part, if accidentally fortified; a discovery, but no recovery, if they apply and be both peregrine.

CHAP LXV.

A Figure erected to know whether Sir WILLIAM WALLER *or Sir* RALPH HOPTON *should overcome, they being supposed to be engaged neer* Alsford, ♀ 29th *of* March, 1644.

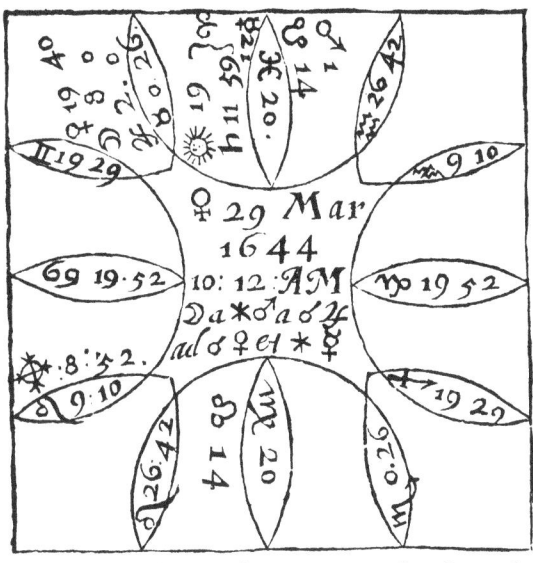

THe ascendant is for our Army, the ☽ ♃ & ♀ for our Generalls, viz. Sir *William* & Major Generall *Browne*, a valiant & prudent citizen of *London*, who may justly Challenge a large share of honor in that dayes service : Sir *Ralph Hopton* is signified by ♄ Lord of the seventh, his Army by ♑, in the descending

cending part of heaven, which is usually given to the Friends and Assistants of the Enemy; there is onely ♂ and ☊ in the ninth, so that by this it appeared Sir *Ralph* had no supplyes ready to attend that dayes successe, &c.

From the existence of the ☽ in her exaltation, and in the eleventh house with ♃, she being Lady of the ascendant, and having principall signification for us and our Army, engaged for the Parliament, I concluded all was, and would be well on our side, and the victory ours: by her separation from ♃, I said, I did verily conceive we had gained already from them some ammunition, or performed some service against them, which judgment was more strengthened by ☉, Lord of our assistants and substance, posited in the tenth house, in the very degree of his Exaltation; and though I did imagine, by reason of the proximity of ♄ to ☉, we should not gaine the whole, or have a perfect victory without diminution of some part of it, yet I was confident we should obtaine a considerable proportion of their Ammunition, and obtaine a compleat victory, the onely thing enquired after; for that the ☽ did apply to ♀, and then to a ✶ of ☿, he angular, I acquainted the *querent* that within eleven or twelve hours after the question we should have perfect newes, and it pleasing and good; for considering the fight was within fifty miles of *London*, I ordered my time according to discretion, not allowing dayes for the time, but hours; for you may see the ☽ is distant from ♀ eleven degrees, but withall is in her swift motion, and encreasing in light, all which were arguments of our successe, and the Enemies routing; as it did appeare the same Friday by a Letter that came from the Army, certifying, that our Generals took the Thursday before, one hundred and twenty Commanders and Gentlemen, five hundred and sixty common Souldiers, much Ammunition. That according to naturall causes in Art, the Enemy should be worsted, I had these reasons; first, because ♄ the Lord *Hopton's* Significator is *sub radiis*; next, he is in his Fall; thirdly, in no aspect of any Planet, but wholly peregrine and unfortunate, beholding the cusp of the seventh with a □ dexter, arguing losse to his Army, and dishonour to himself by the fight, &c.

CHAP.

all manner of Questions. 401

Chap. LXVI.

If his Excellency Robert *Earle of* Essex *should take Reading, having then surrounded it with his* Armie.

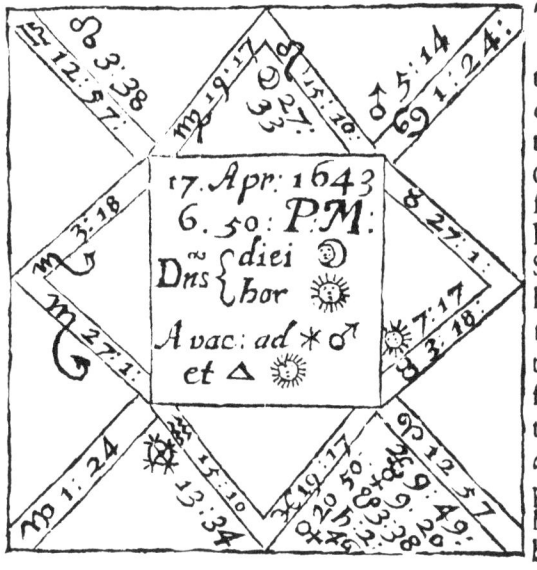

THe moſt honorable of the *Engliſh* nation *viz.* Essex the Kingdomes *Generall,* is here ſignified by ♂ Lord of ♏, the Sign aſcending: his Majeſty by the ☉ Lord of the tenth; the forces that were to relieve *Reading,* or to oppoſe and hinder his Excellency, by ♀ in ♓, and ☉ in ♉.

The Towne of *Reading* by ♒ the Signe of the fourth, the Governour Sir *Arthur Aſton,* reputed an able Souldier, by ♄ Lord of the fourth, their Ammunition and Proviſion in the Towne by ☿ Lord of the fift, and ♀ locally therein.

We have ♂ his Excellencies *Significator* excellently fortified, labouring under no one miſfortune (except being in his Fall) and of how great concernment it is in Warre, to have ♂ the generall *Significator* of Warre, friendly to the *querent,* this Figure well manifeſts; the ☽ ſeparated *(a vacuo)* and indeed there was little hope it would have been gained in that time it was; ſhe applyed to a ✶ of ♂, being in Signes of long aſcenſions, the aſpect is equivalent to a □; which argued, that his Excel-

Eee lency

lency would have much difficulty, and some fighting, ere he could get it: but because ♂ and the ☽ were in Reception, viz. ♂ in her house, the ☽ in his Termes and Face, and neer Cor ♌, placed also in the tenth, I judged his Excellency should obtaine and take *Reading*, and get glory and honour thereby.

Finding the ☉ his Majestie's *Significator* in the seventh, in a fixed Signe, I acquainted the *querent*, his Majesty would oppose what he could, and send Forces to relieve the Towne with all vigour and resolution, but I said he should not prevaile, for ♂ is better fortified then ☉.

I considered ♒ for the Town, and in regard I found not the Signe afflicted, I judged the Town strong, and capable of holding out; when I considered ♀ to be in the fift, I was confident they wanted not Ammunition. Having throughly considered all particulars, and well weighed that ♄ Lord of the fourth, signifying the Governour, was in his Fall with ☋, and that ☿ and ♃ were not farre from ☋, and that ♂ did with his □ aspect behold ♄, I said and sent somebody word, the most assured way, & which would certainly occasion the surrender of the Town, was, to set division amongst the principall Officers, and to incense them against their Officer in Chiefe, & that about eight dayes from the time of the Question, I beleeved his *Excellency* would be Master of the Towne, yet rather by composition then blood, because ☉ and ♂ were separated from their ✶ aspect, and ♂ was in like manner separated from the □ dexter of ♄ from Cardinal Signes; as also, because the application of the ☽ was so directly to the ✶ of the Lord of the ascendant, without any frustration or prohibition.

The Towne was delivered for the Parliaments use the 27th of *April*, 1644. three dayes after the time limited by me was expired: But it's observable, the very Monday before, being eight dayes after the Figure set, they began to treat.

The truth of this Siege was thus, that his Majesty in person did come, and was worsted and beaten back at *Causham-bridge*.

That Sir *Arthur Aston* the Governour, was hurt in the head, as ♄ in ♈ with ☋ well denotes: nor did they want ammunition, as ♀ in the fifth signifies.

It was delivered by Colonel *Fielding*, a very valiant Gentleman,

all manner of Questions. 403

man, a good Souldier, and of a noble Family, not without jealousie and mistrust of underhand dealing in the said Colonell by the King's party; for which he was brought to some trouble, but evaded: And I have since heard some of his Majesties Officers say thus, They did beleeve that *Fielding* acted nothing but what became a man of honour, and that it was the malice of his Enemies that procured him that trouble, &c.

A person of honour demanded this Question, and was well satisfied with what hath been spoken.

Had this very Question been of a Law suit, *Who should have overcome?* you must have considered the Lord of the ascendant for the *querent* or *Plaintiffe*, and the ascendant it selfe, together with the ☽: for the Enemy or *Defendant*, the seventh and his Lord, and Planets therein placed. In our Figure, in regard the ☽ applies to a ✶ of ♂, the *querent* therefore would have had the victory, by reason of the Verdict given by the *Jurors*, who ever are signified by the ☽; but because the ☉ is locally in the seventh, opposite to the ascendant, and is Lord of the tenth, *viz.* of the *Judge*, there's no doubt but the Judge would have been averse to the *Plaintiffe*, as his Majesty was to his Excellency and to the Parliament.

In this case I should have judged the *Defendant* a man of good estate, or able to spend well, because ♀ Lady of the eighth, *viz.* his second, is in Exaltation; and yet the ☉ and ♂ in ✶, might give strong testimonies that the Judge would labour to compound the matter betwixt both parties; the Dispositor of the ⊗ in his Fall, *viz.* ♄ in ♈ with the ☋, would have shewn great expence of the *querent's* or *Plaintiffs* estate and money in this Suit; and that such a man as ♄ would herein be a great enemy unto him, because ♄ and ♂ are in □. As ♄ is Lord of the third, he may shew an ill Neighbour, or a Brother or Kinsman; but as the third house is the ninth from the seventh, it may argue some pragmaticall Priest, or one of the *Defendant's* Sisters Husbands; wherefore the *Plaintiffe* must either take such a one off, or else compound his matter, or he must see whether his Enemies *Atturney* be not Saturnine, then shall he receive prejudice by his extreame rigid following the Cause: if ♄ signi-

Eee 2

fie his *Lawyer*, the damage is by him, or by some aged man, perhaps the *querent's* Father or Grandfather, or else some sturdy Clowne or ill Tenant, &c. for according to the nature of the Question, you must ever vary the nature of your rules; by exact knowledge whereof, you may attaine the perfection of the whole *Art*.

The eight HOUSE, and those QUESTIONS properly belonging unto it.

Of Death, Dowry, Substance of the Wife, &c.

CHAP. LXVII.
If the absent party be alive or dead?

THE true resolution of this Question depends much upon a right understanding, what relation the *querent* hath to the party enquired of, for you have oft read in the preceding judgments, that in every Question great care is to be taken, that the intentions of the *Demandant* and *quesited* party may be carefully apprehended, that thereby one *Significator* be not mistaken for another; wherefore for better satisfaction of this part of judgment we now are handling, you must enquire whether he, *viz.* the *querent*, enquire of the death of a Friend, or of his Wife, or a Father, or a Child, or of a Servant, &c. Give the first house and his Lord for the *significator* of the *querent*; but for the party *quesited*, give the Signe of that house he is signified by, the Lord thereof and the ☽ for his *Significators*: if you find the Lord of his ascendant in the fourth or eighth, either from his owne ascendant, or of the Figure, that configuration is one argument the man or woman enquired after, is deceased; (this must be judged where the party

ty

all manner of Questions.　　405

ty hath been long abfent, and in remote parts, and ftrong intelligence concurring therewith.)

Together with this, confider if the Lord of his afcendant or the ☽, be in the twelfth from his owne houfe, with any evill Planet, or if he be in the twelft, in afpect of any unfortunate Planet, either by □ or ☍, or if the ☉ be unfortunate or afflicted, or the ☽ in like manner, for then the abfent is dead : If the *Significator* of the abfent man or woman be in the fixt from his owne houfe, or fixt of the Queftion, or in any □ or ☍ or affliction of the Lord of the fixt, without Reception, or the benevolent afpect of a *Fortune*, the abfent is then fick : but if he be but going unto, and is not feparated from the afpect, he hath not been, but he will be fuddenly ill, or very fhortly : but if he be going from the ☌ of evill Planets, either by body or afpect, fo that he be furely feparated from them, or is departing from Combuftion, it argues the party enquired of hath lately efcaped a danger or ficknefle, or perill equivalent ; the greatnefle of the difafter or infirmity you fhall judge to be according to the quality of the Signes the *Significators* are in, and manner of afpect afflicting, having relation to the houfe from whence the afpects are.

It's confiderable, that you poyfe in your judgment, whether the *Significator* of the abfent party be in the fixt, and not joyned to the Lord of the fixt, or to any unfortunate Planet afflicting him, or whether he be in any amicable afpect with either of the *Fortunes*, or if he be ftrong in the Signe, you muft not then judge the man fick, but rather weary or drowfie, or perhaps he hath let blood of late, &c. or taken fome Phyfick for prevention of a difeafe which he feared.

I doe onely obferve, if the *Significator* of the abfent be ftrong, and feparated from a *Fortune*, and in a good houfe, the abfent lives ; if he be afflicted, or was lately in □ or ☍ of the *Infortunes*, he was perplexed, or fuffered much mifery, according to the nature of the houfe from whence afflicted ; but I judge him not dead, unlefle together with that mifchance, the Lord of the eighth doe unfortunate him.

　　　　　　　　Eee 3　　　　　　*Whether*

Whether one absent will returne or not, and when?

Consider by what house the absent party is signified, and what Planet is his *significator*; then see if his *significator* be in the first house (let his Journey be whither it will,) yet if it be a long Journey, and beyond Seas, then see if he be in the ninth, or if in the twelft, if a very long Journey was undertaken; or if he be in the fift, if a moderate Journey was intended, or in the third, if a short Journey: If he be in any of these houses, or do commit his disposition to any Planet in any of these houses, it signifies the absent will not dye in that Voyage, but returne: if he be in the seventh, he will returne, but not in hast; nay, he will tarry long; and he is at time of the Question in that country unto which he first went, nor hath he hitherto had any thoughts of returning; howsoever, now he hath: If he be in the fourth, he will stay and abide longer then if he were in the seventh: if his *Significator* be in the third or ninth, and in any aspect with any Planet in the ascendant, the absent is preparing to come home, and is fully resolved thereof; or if he be in the second, in aspect with a Planet in the 9th, he is endeavouring to provide moneys for his Voyage homewards, nor will it be long ere he be at home; but if he be in a Cadent house, and not behold his owne ascendant, he neither cares for his returne, or hath any thoughts thereof, nor can he come if so be he would: if he be cadent and also afflicted, and behold not the ascendant, but is otherwayes impedited, there's no hopes of his returne, nor will he ever come: but if either his *Significator* be Retrograde, or the ☽ joyned to a Retrograde Planet, and behold the ascendant, it imports his sudden return when not expected: if you find his *Significator* impedited, see what house he is Lord of that doth infortunate him; if it be the Lord of the fourth, the man is detained and cannot have liberty; if it be the Lord of the sixt, he is ill; if the Lord of the eight, he feares he shall dye by the way, or before he gets into his owne Country; if the Lord of the twelft, he is as a prisoner and cannot procure liberty: such configurations as these seem to impede his returne.

Having considered the *Significator* of the absent, now have recourse

all manner of Questions. 407

courſe to the ☽, the generall *Significatrix*, for if ſhe be in ☌ or good aſpect of the abſent's *Significator*, or commit her diſpoſition unto him, and he poſited in the aſcendant, it argues his returne; the neerer the aſpect is to the degree aſcending, the ſooner he returnes; the more remote, the longer it will be.

The *Significator* onely poſited in the eighth, without other Impediment, prolongs his returne, but at laſt he will come: but if unfortunated therein, he dyes and never returnes: ☽ ſeparating from the Lord of the fourth, ſeventh, ninth or third, or any Planet under the earth, and then joyned to the Lord of the aſcendant, or a Planet above the earth, the abſent will returne.

The time when he will returne.

You are herein with deſcretion to conſider, firſt, the length of the Journey; then the Lord of the aſcendant and *Significator* of the party abſent, and to obſerve, whether they are of the ſuperiour Planets or not, or whether the Journey was long or ſhort, or according unto diſcretion, in what ſpace of time a man might come and goe, or performe by water or land, ſuch or ſuch a Journey or Voyage; if you find both the *Significators* applying by ✶ or △ aſpect, obſerve in your *Ephemeris* when the day of the aſpect is, and then much about that day or neer unto that time, ſhall you heare ſome newes of the party, or have a letter fom him, or concerning him; this ſuppoſes the party ſo neer, that a poſſibility thereof may be, for if the diſtance be very farre, then you may judge within a fortnight or more of the day of the aſpect: But if you be asked, *When he will come home, or when the Querent ſhall ſee him?* then is it very probable, when both the *Significators* come to ☌, he will come home and the Querent ſhall be in his company; if the *Significator* of the abſent be in any Signe preceding one of his owne houſes, obſerve how many degr. he wants ere he gets out of that Signe and enters his owne houſe, and put them into dayes, weeks, moneths or yeers, according to diſcretion, and the nature of the Signe and place of heaven he is in; for movable Signes argue a ſhort ſtay in the place; common ones, more long; fixed doe prolong and ſhew long time,

Of

Of the death of the Querent, *or space of his owne life.*

If one is fearfull of death, or feels himselfe ill, or would be resolved, Whether, according to naturall causes, he may live a yeer, two, three or more, the better to dispose of some matters concerning his owne private affaires, and shall demand such a Question of you, give the ascendant, his Lord and the ☽ for his *Significators*, and see in what houses they are in, and how dignified essentially, unto whom they apply, or with what Planets associated: if the Lord of the first be joyned with any of the Fortunes, and commit his vertue unto him, and that Planet is well digfinied and commit his disposition to no Planet, then see if that Fortune be Lord of the eighth ; for if he be not, then assuredly the Querent out-lives the yeer, or two or three, or time by him propounded ; but if the Planet to whom the Lord of the ascendant is in ☌ with, or commits his disposition unto, be Lord of the eighth, then whether he be a good or an ill Planet, he kils (for every Planet must doe his office,) and signifies, that the Querent shall dye within the compasse of time demanded ; and this judgment you may averre with more constancy, if the ☽ be then impedited, unlesse some other Planet be joyned with the Lord of the ascendant, who receives either him or the ☽, for then he shall not dye in that space of time enquired of by him.

Consider if the Lord of the ascendant be joyned to an Infortune, who receives him not either by House or Exaltation, or by two of his lesser Dignities, and the ☽ also at that time unfortunate, it signifies the Querent's death.

If in like manner you find the Lord of the first joyned to the Lord of the eighth, unlesse the Lord of the eighth receive him, and so notwithstanding, as that the Lord of the first receive not the Lord of the eighth, though he receive the Lord of the first ; because if the Lord of the eighth receive the Lord of the first, and the Lord of the first the Lord of the eighth, whether Fortune or Infortune, you may justly feare the Querent's death ; but if the Lord of the eighth receive the Lord of the ascendant, so there be not mutuall Reception, it hinders not.

Having

all manner of Questions. 409

Having confidered judicioufly that the Querent fhall not dye, behold whe or in what time it wil be ere theLord of the afcendant is joyned to that Planet who receiveth him with a compleat ☌, untill that time and yeer or yeers fignified by that ☌, the Querent fhall be fecure, and fo may afcertaine himfelf, that at this time he fhall not dye.

But if you find upon juft grounds in Art the *querent* fhal dye, behold when and at what time the Lord of the firft is joyned to the Lord of the eighth, or to the abovefaid *Infortune*, who receives him not, but afflicts him, and is the interficient Planet; for when their perfect ☌ is, whether by body or afpect, at that time he is like to dye.

But if the Lord of the firft is fo difpofed or he in fuch a condition, as you conceive that by him alone, without other teftimonies, you cannot fufficiently judge of his death or life, then doe you confider the ☽, and judge by her pofition, as you did of the Lord of the firft: but as I related before, if the Lord of the eighth and the Lord of the firft be joyned together and each receive other, or at leaftwife, the Lord of the firft receive the Lord of the eight, it prenotes his death, as aforefaid: when the interficient Planet comes to the degree wherein the two *Significators* were in ☌, or if they were in □ or ☍ afpect, then when the malevolent *Interfector* comes to the degree of the Zodiack wherein the Lord of the afcendant was at time of the Queftion; or when the unfortunate *Anaretas* tranfits the degree afcending, and there meets with the malevolent afpect of the Lord of the fixt, or when an *Eclipfe*, or its oppofite place fals to be either the degree afcending or the degree of the Signe wherin the Lord of the afcendant was, or of the ☽, if you judged by her, and not by the Lord of the afcendant.

When, or about what time the Querent *may dye?*

When the Queftion is abfolute, and without limitation, and the *querent* fhall propound unto you, bring an *Aftrologian*, his Queftion in this manner of way, viz. *When fhall I dye, or how long may I live?* In this demand, you are to behold the Lord of the
F f f afcendant

ascendant, the ascendant it self, and the ☽, the Lord of the 8th or infortunate Planet in the eighth, and that Planet unto whom either the Lord of the first or the ☽ is joyned by body or malevolent aspect, and you shall determine the death of the *Querent* according to the number or distance of degrees which are betwixt the Lord of the first and the Lord of the eighth, or of that Planet to whom either the Lord of the ascendant or ☾ is joyned, for those number of degrees shall shew either moneths or yeers: If the Lord of the first be in ☌ with the Lord of the eighth in an angle, it notes so many yeers; for in these judgments, angles do not accelerate death, but shew that life and nature are strong, and a possibility of overcoming the malignity of the humour afflicting: if the abovesaid ☌ be in a succedant house, it notes so many moneths; but note, if the Signe be fixed, it gives halfe yeers, halfe moneths: if in a cadent house, so many weeks: you must understand this Question with mature judgment, and well consider whether the *Significators* are extreamly afflicted, or have sufficieutly manifested that according to naturall causes, the *Querent* cannot long live, or that death is not farre from the *Querent*.

If the *Significators* doe not presage death at present, then acquaint him, it's possible, he may live so many yeers as there are degrees betwixt the ☌ of the Lord of the ascendant and the Lord of the eighth, or of that Planet at time of the Question afflicting him. The *Ancients* have ever observed, that the Lord of the ascendant is more in this judgment to be considered then the ☽, and therefore his affliction or ☌ with the Lord of the eighth, or Combustion with the ☉ is especially worth consideration, and most to be feared; for naturally the Lord of the first doth signifie the life and body of the *querent*, and not by accident.

If the Lord of the ascendant be separated from the Lord of the eighth, or the Lord of the eighth from him, or from that Planet who did afflict him, it's not then probable the *querent* shall dye, in so many yeers as there are degrees betwixt them, *viz.* from that their separation: where observe, the ☌ of the ☽ with the Lord of the eighth, doth not much hurt, unlesse the Lord of the first be also joyned with him; for let the ☽ be

afflicted

all manner of Queſtions. 411

afflicted, yet if the Lord of the aſcendant be ſtrong, it's no great matter; but if the ☽ be well Fortified, and the Lord of the aſcendant be weak and afflicted, the ſtrength of the ☽ aſſiſts nothing for the evaſion of the *querent*; for although in the *querent's* affaires ſhe hath much to do, yet in this manner of judgment little, where life or death are in queſtion.

Whether the Man or Wife ſhall dye firſt.

This doth more neerly depend upon the Nativity of either party, then upon an horary Queſtion, and therefore I would adviſe in the reſolution of this Queſtion, that firſt the *Artiſt* doe demand of the *querent*, his or her age, or if they have it, the time of their Birth, and that he erect the Figure thereof, and ſee what poſſibility there was in the *Radix*, of the length or ſhortneſſe of the *querent's* life if time give you leave, ſee if the ☉ or ☽ in the *Radix*, or the aſcendant of the Nativity, doe neer the time of the Queſtion, come to any malignant direction, or whether the *querent* be not in or neer a Climactericall yeer or yeers, which are the ſeventh, fourteenth, one and twentieth, 28. five and thirtieth, two & fortieth, &c. or whether you find not maleficall tranſits of the infortunate Planets either by their neer ☌ to the degree of the ☉ ☽ or aſcendant in the *Radix*, or whether they caſt not their □ or ☍ aſpects to the degrees of the ☉ ☽ or aſcendant of the *Radix*, now at this inſtant time of the Queſtion; this I would have well conſidered: and then erect your Figure according to the time of the day given, and behold who asks the queſtion, and let the Lord of the aſcendant be for him or her, the Lord of the ſeventh for the queſited party; ſee which of them is weakeſt, or moſt afflicted in the Figure, and whether the aſcendant or ſeventh houſe hath any malevolent Planet poſited therein, or whether there ariſe with the aſcendant, or deſcend with the cuſp of the ſeventh, any maleficall fixed Starres; for in this manner of judgment they ſhew much: Behold whether the Lord of the ſeventh, or of the aſcendant goe to combuſtion firſt, or to the affliction of any malignant Planet, or to the Lord of the eighth; for it is an aſſured rule, that if the Lord of the

Fff 2 aſcendant

The Resolution of

ascendant be most afflicted, or first goe to combustion, and the first house it selfe be unfortunated by the presence of an *Infortune*, that then the *querent* dyeth first: and so judge for the *quesited*, if the same misfortunes befall to the seventh house, and his Lord, &c.

What manner of death the Queret shall dye.

In this manner of judgment observe the Lord of the eighth, if he be therein posited, or what Planet is neerest to the cusp of the house, and hath Dignities therein; for you must take signification of the quality of death from either of these, or from that Planet who afflicts the Lord of the ascendant, and have Dignities in the eighth: If the Planet signifying death is either ♀ or ♃, you may assure the *querent*, he or she shall dye a fair death: and observe what Diseases they or either of them in the Signe they are in doe signifie, and what part of mans body they represent in that Signe, and you may certifie the *querent*, that the disease or infirmity he or she shall dye of, will be of the nature of the Planet, and in that part of the body they signifie in that Signe. Usually, good Planets in the eighth, a fair, gentle death; malevolent ones, either strong Feavers, or long continued Sicknesses, and much afflicting.

CHAP. LXVIII.
Whether the Portion of the Wife will be great, or easily obtained, or whether is the Woman enquired after rich or not.

Herein vary your ascendant, and then the Question as well resolves the demand concerning the estate of a man as of a woman. The *querent* is still signified by the Lord of the ascendant and first house, his substance and Estate by the second house, Lord thereof, Planet or Planets posited in the house, and the Lord of ⊗ and place of heaven, and Sign wherein it is found.

That which is the occasion of this Question, is, if a man propound the Question, Whether the Woman he enquires after

all manner of Questions.

ter be rich, &c. Behold in this judgement the Signe of the eight house, the Lord thereof, the Planet posited therein.

The cusp of the eight in the termes of ♃ or ♀ give good hopes of Wealth, or ♃ or ♀ posited in that house; plenty of Wealth if they are essentially dignified, direct, and free from Combustion; not so much, if they or either of them be Retrograde, Combust, or slow in motion: for though in essentiall dignities and so qualified, they expresse a sufficient and large proportion, yet with some kinde of trouble it will come to the *querent*.

The Lord of the eight in the eight no wayes impedited, gives good hopes of some Inheritance or Land to fall to the wife or woman, or by some Legacy, some Estate; the more certaine, if either the Lord of the fourth in the figure, or the Lord of the tenth and the Lord of the eight be in any benevolent aspect out of Angles or succedant houses, or out of the eleventh and eight. ☉ in the eight and in ♒ or ♌, or any of the houses of ♃ or ♀, they casting their △ or ✶ aspect to ⊗ : you need not feare but the estate of the quesited party is sufficient, and if the dispositor of ⊗ doe but cast his ✶ or △ to it, or else is in a good aspect of ♃ or ♀ : these argue the Woman inquired after to be a good Fortune, and you are not to make doubt of his or her Estate.

♄ or ♂ Peregrine in the eight, either poore or little of what is promised will be obtained, or extreame contention about it.

The Lord of the eight Combust, slow performance, scarce ability in the Parents to performe what is promised.

☋ in the eight, no fortunate Planet being there, there's cheating intended, or more will be promised then performed.

Lord of the eight in the second, or in △ or ✶ to the Lord of the second, the *querent* shall have what is promised, in □ with difficulty, in ☍ never, without much wrangling; if no reception hardly at all. Its impossible to give such generall Rules as will hold ever certaine, therefore I advise every Practiser to well weigh the *querent* his Condition, and the possibility the Figure promises, and so frame his conjecture.

Chap. LXIX.
If one be afraid of a thing, Whether he shall be in danger of the same or not.

Behold the afcendant and his Lord, and the ☽; if you finde the ☽ infortunate, or if the Lord of the afcendant be infortunate, and falling from an angle; or efpecially in the twelfth and ☽ with him; it fignifies the fame Fear is true, and certaine that there is caufe for it, or that great labour and griefe fhall moleft him, and that many things fhall be demanded of him, or he charged with many matters not appertaining to him, or of which he is guilty. If the Lord of the afcendant doth afcend from the twelfth into the eleventh or tenth, or fhall be joyned to Fortunes; it fignifies the thing feared fhall not appertaine to him, or he be molefted thereby, or that he need not be afraid, nor fhall the matter doe him ill, but he fhall efcape that feare. When the Lord of the afcendant fhall be in one degree with Fortunes, no ill is towards the *Querent* (if the Fortunes unto which the Lord of the afcendant doth apply, or which apply unto him be in the mid heaven, and the ☽ apply unto thofe Fortunes, and fhe be in an angle or elevated above him, it fignifies he that is afraid fhall eafily be delivered from feare; nor hath he any grounds for it.

Subftance. The fignifier of the queftion applying to infortunes, it is true; to a fortune, and not received of an infortune, it is falfe. Many have judged, that if the ☽ be in the eight, fixt or twelfth, and apply to any Planet in a Cadent houfe, the Sufpition is not true, or the report will hold long, but that it will be fmothered and vanifh to nothing: the ☽ in △ to ☉ difcovers all fuddenly.